The Neuroscience of Suicidal Beha

M000277927

Nearly one million people take their own lives each year worldwide – however, contrary to popular belief, suicide can be prevented. While suicide is commonly thought to be an understandable reaction to severe stress, it is actually an abnormal reaction to regular situations. Something more than unbearable stress is needed to explain suicide, and neuroscience shows what this is, how it is caused, and how it can be treated. Professor Kees van Heeringen describes findings from neuroscientific research on suicide, using various approaches from population genetics to brain imaging. Compelling evidence is reviewed that shows how and why genetic characteristics or early traumatic experiences may lead to a specific predisposition that makes people vulnerable to triggering life events. Neuroscientific studies are yielding results that provide insight into how the risk of suicide may develop; ultimately demonstrating how suicide can be prevented.

Kees van Heeringen is Professor of Psychiatry, Chair of the Department of Psychiatry and Medical Psychology, and Director of the Unit for Suicide Research at Ghent University, Belgium. He is also the cofounder of the Flemish Expertise Centre for Suicide Prevention. Professor van Heeringen's research has been awarded the Stengel Award by the International Association for Suicide Prevention.

Cambridge Fundamentals of Neuroscience in Psychology

Developed in response to a growing need to make neuroscience accessible to students and other non-specialist readers, the *Cambridge Fundamentals of Neuroscience in Psychology* series provides brief introductions to key areas of neuroscience research across major domains of psychology. Written by experts in cognitive, social, affective, developmental, clinical, and applied neuroscience, these books will serve as ideal primers for students and other readers seeking an entry point to the challenging world of neuroscience.

Books in the Series

The Neuroscience of Expertise by Merim Bilalić
The Neuroscience of Intelligence by Richard J. Haier
Cognitive Neuroscience of Memory by Scott D. Slotnick
The Neuroscience of Adolescence by Adriana Galván
The Neuroscience of Suicidal Behavior by Kees van Heeringen

The Neuroscience of Suicidal Behavior

Kees van Heeringen

Ghent University

CAMBRIDGE
UNIVERSITY PRESS

University Printing House, Cambridge CB2 8BS, United Kingdom

One Liberty Plaza, 20th Floor, New York, NY 10006, USA

477 Williamstown Road, Port Melbourne, VIC 3207, Australia

314–321, 3rd Floor, Plot 3, Splendor Forum, Jasola District Centre,
New Delhi – 110025, India

79 Anson Road, #06–04/06, Singapore 079906

Cambridge University Press is part of the University of Cambridge.

It furthers the University's mission by disseminating knowledge in the pursuit of
education, learning, and research at the highest international levels of excellence.

www.cambridge.org
Information on this title: www.cambridge.org/9781107148949
DOI: 10.1017/9781316563205

First published 2018

Printed in the United States of America by Sheridan Books, Inc.

A catalogue record for this publication is available from the British Library.

ISBN 978-1-107-14894-9 Hardback
ISBN 978-1-316-60290-4 Paperback

To all Valeries

To the one and only Myriam

Contents

List of Figures   *page* viii
List of Tables   ix
Preface   xi

1 What Is Suicidal Behavior, and Can It Be Prevented?   1

2 Stress, Vulnerability, and Suicide: The Stress–Diathesis Model   23

3 The Dark Side of the Brain: Neuroscience Approaches to
   Suicidal Behavior   40

4 Lethal Signals: The Molecular Neuroscience of Suicidal Behavior   63

5 I Think, Therefore I Do Not Want to Be: The Cognitive
   Neuroscience of Suicidal Behavior   85

6 Images of the Suicidal Brain: Systems Neuroscience and Suicide   102

7 "In my end is my beginning": A Neurodevelopmental
   Perspective on Suicidal Behavior   125

8 I Predict, Therefore I Cannot Be: A Predictive Coding Account
   of Suicidal Behavior   146

9 Predicting the Unpredictable: Neuroscience Contributions to
   Suicide Prediction   165

10 The Treatment of Suicide Risk: Neuroscience Aspects   182

Glossary   206
References   211
Index   269

The color plate section can be found between pp. 114 and 115.

Figures

1.1 Suicide rates in the world   *page* 5
1.2 Leading causes of death, United States, 2015   9
1.3 The suicidal process   10
2.1 The IPT model of suicidal behavior   32
2.2 The IMV model of suicidal behavior   33
2.3 A neurocognitive model of suicidal behavior   37
3.1 Gene expression: from DNA to proteins   48
3.2 Single nucleotide polymorphism (SNP)   48
3.3 Proposed model of epigenetic factors   51
3.4 Gray and white matter in the brain   58
4.1 The hypothalamo–pituitary–adrenal (HPA) axis   65
4.2 Hippocampal glucocorticoid receptor expression   69
4.3 Neurotransmission system   72
4.4 Serotonin neurotransmission system   73
4.5 Serotonin neurotransmission   73
5.1 The Stroop test   88
5.2 The Wisconsin Card Sorting Test: screenshot from
    computerized version   91
5.3 Example problem-solving vignette from
    the MEPS   92
5.4 The Iowa Gambling Task: screenshot from a
    computerized version   95
6.1 Periventricular white matter hyperintensities   104
6.2 Frontothalamic circuitry and suicidal behavior:
    findings from structural imaging studies   106
7.1 The effects of childhood maltreatment on brain
    structures and connectivity   139
8.1 Schema to illustrate cortical and thalamic
    pathways   151
9.1 Sensitivity-specificity diagram   167
9.2 ROC curves   167
9.3 Model of connections between biomarkers
    associated with suicidal behavior   169
10.1 Black-box warning   185
10.2 Antidepressants and expectancies: brain
     mediators   187

Tables

1.1 Nonsuicidal reasons for self-harm   *page* 3
1.2 Risk factors for suicidal behavior   11
9.1 Neurobiological factors studied in meta-analysis   171
10.1 Possible mechanisms involved in an increased risk
      of suicidal behavior with antidepressant treatment   186

Preface

As a young psychiatrist, I was asked to see a patient at the physical rehabilitation department of the university hospital. I went to see this patient, who turned out to be a bright young girl named Valerie. She stayed at the rehabilitation department of the university hospital because she lost both her legs after having jumped from a bridge a few weeks earlier.

It was a hot summer, and later that day I was sitting on a nice terrace in the beautiful center of Ghent, enjoying a glass of beer with a couple of friends. We enjoyed ourselves, watching and discussing the girls strolling along. But, in my mind, I was trying to find an answer to this question: Why on earth had the intelligent young girl whom I met earlier that day done such a horrible thing, with such terrible and irreversible damage to her body? I could not know at that time that meeting Valerie would have such an impact on my professional life. A few years later I founded the Unit for Suicide Research at Ghent University.

Valerie told me that she had made a date with her boyfriend on the day of her suicide attempt. She wanted to talk to him because she did not feel well. So, she agreed to meet him even though she was supposed to be in school that morning. While she was talking to her boyfriend she noticed an uncle passing by. This uncle knew that she had to be at school instead of spending time with her boyfriend, and he looked very angry at her. Seeing so much anger on his face somehow urged her to take her bicycle, go to a nearby highway bridge, and jump in front of the oncoming cars. Subsequent conversations with Valerie made clear that her "not feeling well" was a manifestation of a depressive episode. She wanted to meet her boyfriend and tell him about her dark mood and the negative thoughts and painful feelings about herself and the future, which frightened her so much. Later she also told me that her father took his own life when she was 5 or 6 years old.

Crucial aspects of the story of Valerie will be discussed in this book. We will learn from intriguing brain imaging studies how reactions to angry faces may constitute a vulnerability to suicidal behavior. We will learn from genetic studies that suicide indeed may run in families and that we are now beginning to understand how our genes may make us vulnerable to suicidal behavior. We will see that depression and suicidal behavior are common, also among young people. The sad reality is that epidemiological data continue to show unacceptably high and still increasing rates of suicidal behavior among young people in many areas across the world, including the United States.

The harsh reality in the case of Valerie was that she suffered from a depressive episode that was not recognized by herself, her family, school-teachers, or her primary care physician, and which thus was not treated. In addition, there was a family history of suicide, which should have prompted any person in her environment or any caregiver to consider a strongly increased risk of suicidal behavior in this girl. Depression and familial loading are the two major ingredients of the lethal cocktail that kills so many people every day anywhere in the world.

This book addresses the neuroscientific foundations of a model that explains suicidal behavior as the tragic outcome of an interaction between a vulnerable individual and the world in which she or he lives. Chapters 1 and 2 address the occurrence of suicidal behaviors and their risk factors, and provide a model of the interactions between these risk factors by describing the specific vulnerability to suicidal behavior and elucidating how specific stressors interact with this vulnerability to lead to self-destructive behaviors. Chapter 3 describes the neuroscience approaches to the study of these vulnerability and stress-related factors. The following chapters elaborate on these approaches in much more detail by focusing on findings from molecular (Chapter 4), cognitive (Chapter 5), and systems (Chapter 6) neuroscientific studies of suicidal behavior. Chapter 7 takes a developmental perspective, and focuses on the devastating neurobiological consequences of traumatic events during childhood, such as sexual and physical abuse. A novel under-standing of brain functioning in the form of the predictive coding model is explored in relation to suicidal behavior in Chapter 8, showing that a surprisingly large proportion of neurobiological findings described in the previous chapters can be integrated in a fascinating computational model of suicidal behavior. Our limited capacity to predict suicidal behavior and treat suicide risk is a major problem in suicide prevention. Chapter 9 focuses on the implications of a neuroscientific approach for the predic-tion of suicidal behavior, while Chapter 10 focuses on the problems and opportunities in treating suicidal behavior from a neuroscientific point of view.

Exploring the neuroscience of suicidal behavior is an intriguing jour-ney into the dark side of the brain. This book will show that individuals may become suicidal because of deficiencies in neurobiological mechan-isms that normally provide protection to painful consequences of life. It is commonly believed that suicide is a normal response to an abnormal situation. Scientists know that the opposite is true: Suicide is an abnormal reaction to a normal situation. Suicidal behavior is commonly triggered by, for example, the breakup of a romantic relationship, the loss of a job, being bullied at school, a depression, or experiencing financial difficulties. Such terrible situations are, however, very common and lead to suicidal behavior in only a minority of exposed individuals. This book will describe why and how people may become so vulnerable that exposure to difficult circumstances may lead them to take their own life. But this book will also show that the study of these mechanisms makes it possible to prevent suicide.

What Is Suicidal Behavior, and Can It Be Prevented?

Learning Objectives

- What are suicidal and nonsuicidal self-injury behaviors?
- How common are suicidal behaviors?
- Why are common myths about suicide wrong?
- What is the stress–diathesis model of suicidal behavior?
- How do mental disorders such as depression relate to suicide?
- What are the three main approaches to suicide prevention?

Introduction

Every 40 seconds someone in the world takes his or her own life, and each day more than 120 Americans kill themselves (WHO, 2014; MMWR, 2017). Sadly, the number of American suicides is increasing each year. Many more individuals attempt to take their own lives, and the number of suicide attempts increase, particularly among young people. Nonsuicidal, self-injurious behaviors are even far more common than suicide attempts.

Many myths regarding suicide continue to exist, as we will see later. One of the most persistent myths is the idea that suicide cannot be prevented or that suicide risk cannot be treated. This view contributes to the continuing high number of people who kill themselves, or who try to do so. The costs of suicide are huge from an economical point of view. For example, the total cost of suicidal behavior in the United States is estimated at $93.5 billion. But also at individual levels the costs of suicide are huge. Every suicide is the tragic outcome of profound personal suffering and mental pain. But every suicide also affects the people who stay behind – with feelings of shame, guilt, and pain – and who consequently may become suicidal themselves. The lifetime prevalence of exposure to suicide is nearly 22%, indicating that more than one in five individuals will experience a suicide in their close surroundings (Andriessen et al., 2017). Stopping mental pain is commonly cited as the major motivation for suicide, but the sad reality is that suicide does not stop mental pain: suicide only transfers the pain to those left behind.

Suicide is preventable. It is estimated that every $1 spent on preventive interventions saves $2.5 in the cost of suicide (Shepard et al., 2016). Suicidal behavior never has one single cause, but the many causal factors are now well known, and insights in to the mechanisms leading to suicidal behavior have increased substantially. These insights make it possible to develop preventative strategies at various levels.

1.1 Behavioral Aspects of Suicidal Behaviors

The neologism "suicide" most probably first appeared in the seventeenth century, coming from the words *sui* (of oneself) and *caedere* (to kill). The World Health Organization defines suicide as "the act of killing oneself deliberately, initiated and performed by the person concerned in the full knowledge or expectation of its fatal outcome." Suicide attempt is defined as "any non-fatal suicidal behavior, referring to intentional self-inflicted poisoning, injury or self-harm, which may or may not have fatal intent or outcome" (WHO, 2014).

Until the end of the 1960s, suicide attempts were considered failed suicides. Since then, several terms have been introduced that reflect the operationalization of nonfatal suicidal behavior as separate behaviors. These terms include "parasuicide," "pseudosuicide," "deliberate self-harm," "self-harm," and "nonsuicidal self-injury" (NSSI), reflecting the increasing insight that suicidal behavior is not a homogeneous phenomenon but a spectrum of self-destructive behaviors that may differ from each other in terms of lethality, planning, and intent. However, even these terms are difficult to operationalize: "lethality" may refer to medical or somatic damage due to the suicide attempt or to the methods used to attempt suicide, while there are no objective measures of "planning" or "intent." There have been numerous approaches to classifying nonfatal suicidal, self-injurious behaviors based on theoretical, behavioral, clinical, or epidemiological characteristics, but disagreement persists (Silverman, 2016). A distinction between NSSI and attempted suicide, mainly based on suicidal intent, is now commonly made in research and in clinical guidelines, particularly in the United States. *The Diagnostic and Statistical Manual of Mental Disorders*, fifth edition (DSM-5), the manual of psychiatric diseases, includes suicidal behavioral disorder and NSSI as clinical situations that require a more in-depth investigation to determine if a formal diagnosis as a mental disorder should be considered along with a proposed set of diagnostic criteria. Under suicidal behavior, specifiers are included relating to the violence of the method used, the medical consequences, and the degree of planning involved.

Table 1.1 Nonsuicidal reasons for self-harm (Edmondson et al., 2016)

Responding to distress
- Managing distress (affect regulation) – managing painful unpleasant emotional states, including making emotional pain physical, blocking bad memories
  - Interpersonal influence – changing or responding to how others think or feel; help-seeking
  - Punishment – usually of self, occasionally of or by others
  - Managing dissociation – either switching off or bringing on feelings of numbness and unreality
  - Averting suicide – nonfatal self-harm to ward off suicidal acts or thoughts

Self-harm as positive experience
  - Gratification – self-harm as comforting or enjoyable
  - Sensation seeking – through a sense of nonsexual excitement or arousal
  - Experimenting – trying something new
  - Protection – of self or others
  - Developing a sense of personal mastery

Defining the self
  - Defining boundaries – self-injury as a means of defining or exploring personal boundaries
  - Responding to sexuality – through self-harm as creating quasi-sexual feelings or expressing sexuality in a symbolic way
  - Validation – demonstrating to self and occasionally to others one's strength or the degree of one's suffering
  - Self as belonging or fitting in – to a group or subculture
  - Having a personal language – including one for remembrance: a means of conjuring up or acknowledging good past feelings or memories

The report of many nonsuicidal reasons by self-harming individuals supports a categorical distinction between suicide attempts and NSSI (Edmondson et al., 2016). Most common themes in studies of nonsuicidal reasons for self-harm behavior include managing distress and exerting interpersonal influence, followed by punishment and managing dissociation (see Table 1.1).

Less frequently described but nonetheless repeatedly endorsed are reasons to do with averting suicide, sensation seeking, defining personal boundaries, and coping with sexuality. There also appear to be motives for the act that are perceived as positive or adaptive, at least by the self-report of respondents, in terms of self-affirmation or validation.

Criticism regarding the use of the term NSSI is due to the fact that much of the literature on NSSI focuses on young people, and indeed few studies have been carried out in adults. Furthermore, there are obvious difficulties in labeling behaviors as definitively nonsuicidal when they greatly increase the risk of future self-inflicted death as is shown in longitudinal studies (see later discussion). Underestimation of suicide risk associated with NSSI implicates the danger that those with NSSI will be given lower priority and receive poorer treatment than others (Kapur et al., 2013). An additional problem is that suicidal intent may be difficult to assess reliably, given that individuals engaging in self-harming behaviors often report ambivalence (i.e., not caring whether they live or die) and multiple motivations. A study in adults even found that one-third endorsed experiencing suicidal thoughts while engaging in NSSI (Klonsky, 2011). Retrospective evidence suggests that the strongest risk for engaging in NSSI is a history of suicidal behavior and ideation (Brunner et al., 2007), while other studies show that NSSI frequently precedes suicidal thoughts and behaviors, suggesting that NSSI may act as a "gateway" to suicidal behavior, whether or not via the enabling of the capability for suicide (Whitlock et al., 2013; Grandclerc et al., 2016). An alternative view is to regard NSSI and suicide attempts as dimensional variants of self-injurious behavior, with the presence or absence of suicidal intent not representing a categorical distinction (Orlando et al., 2015). Such an interpretation is supported by the apparent similarity of neurobiological underpinnings for NSSI and suicidal thoughts (Maciejewski et al., 2014). Such an underlying and possibly common neurobiological vulnerability, i.e., a shared so-called diathesis, is the major topic of this book.

1.2 Epidemiological Aspects

1.2.1 Occurrence of Suicidal Behaviors

Suicide rates vary greatly according to regions and countries, as shown in Figure 1.1 (WHO, 2017).

According to the most recent global estimations, 804,000 suicide deaths occurred worldwide in 2012, representing an annual global age-standardized suicide rate of 11.4 per 100,000 individuals in the population (WHO, 2014). This means that in 2012, every 40 seconds someone in the world took their own life. In the same year, suicide accounted for 1.4% of all deaths worldwide, making it the fifteenth leading cause of death. Globally, suicides account for 56% of all violent deaths: More

Age-standardized suicide rates (per 100 000 population), both sexes, 2015

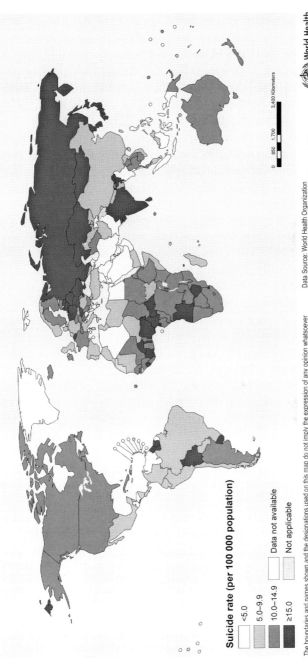

Suicide rate (per 100 000 population)

- <5.0
- 5.0–9.9
- 10.0–14.9
- ≥15.0
- Data not available
- Not applicable

Data Source: World Health Organization
Map Production: Information Evidence and Research (IER)
World Health Organization

0 850 1,700   3,400 Kilometers

World Health Organization

Figure 1.1 Suicide rates in the world. See color plate 1. Age-standardized suicide rates (per 100 000 population), both sexes, 2015

http://gamapserver.who.int/mapLibrary/app/searchResults.aspx

people die from suicide than from crimes and war combined. In general, Asian and Eastern European countries have the highest rates, Central and South American and eastern Mediterranean countries have the lowest rates, and rates in the United States, Western Europe, and Africa are somewhere in between. But the situation is changing rapidly, with, for instance, strong increases in the United States in recent years, as we will see later. Although differences in rates between countries and regions may to a certain extent reflect differences in case ascertainment and in the availability and recency of reported data (Windfuhr et al., 2016), they more probably are genuine, and influenced by differences in the prevalence of specific risk and protective factors (see later discussion) and broader societal factors (such as social deprivation and political change).

Despite an increase in the global population, the absolute number of suicides has fallen by about 9%, from 883,000 to 804,000 between 2000 and 2012. The global suicide rate has fallen 26% (23% in men and 32% in women) during the 12-year period from 2000 to 2012, which is faster than the 18% decrease in overall mortality. Unfortunately, increases in suicide rates (these are the number of death by suicide per 100,000) have been reported in many countries. For example, suicide rates have increased in the United States in recent decades more than 30%, from 10.5 in 1999 to 13.0 in 2014, and thus are now higher than the global average (Curtin et al., 2016).

Self-injury mortality (SIM), a combination of known suicides by any method and estimated deaths from drug self-intoxication that have been classified by medical examiners and coroners as accident or undetermined, also increased substantially in the United States. There were an estimated 40,289 self-injury deaths in 1999 and 76,227 in 2014. The estimated crude rate for SIM thus increased 65% between 1999 and 2014. The SIM rate thereby continuously exceeded the kidney disease mortality rate and surpassed the influenza and pneumonia mortality rate by 2006. By 2014, the SIM rate converged with the diabetes mortality rate. Also by 2014, SIM accounted for 32 and 37 years of life lost for male and female decedents, respectively (Rockett et al., 2016).

Increases in rates of suicide and self-injury mortality have been related to many factors, ranging from adverse economic changes to reductions in the availability of psychiatric beds (Bastiampillai et al., 2016). Concerning economic factors, a study of 63 countries estimated that an excess of 5,000 suicide deaths worldwide in 2009 were related to the global financial crisis, with the effect of unemployment on suicide rates being stronger in countries with lower pre-crisis unemployment rates

(Nordt et al., 2015). In the United States, economic downturns such as the 2007/2008 recession were associated with an increase of 1.22 deaths per 100,000 population among those with lower educational levels, compared with an increase of 0.17 per 100,000 in those with more than 12 years of education (Harper et al., 2015). Careful analysis of epidemiological data suggests that recession may hurt but that austerity kills, particularly via increased suicide rates (Stuckler & Basu, 2013). An increase in unemployment rates, however, may not explain the effect of financial crises on suicide rates, and the causal relationship between the increase in unemployment and increase in suicide has indeed been questioned for both the United States and Europe (Fountoulakis, 2016). When unemployment rates are low, the suicide rate among unemployed persons is high, but when unemployment increases and the composition of unemployed persons shifts to include more mentally healthy persons, the suicide rate of unemployed persons decreases. In addition, it appears that the number of suicides increases several months before unemployment increases. The most likely explanation is that mental health care deteriorates during periods of economic crisis and austerity. Also, patients constitute a specifically vulnerable group, which is hit harder by a crisis in a selective and accumulated way. This accumulation of stressors might be the cause behind the increase in suicide rates (Fountoulakis, 2016).

There are few regional or national data on the occurrence of nonfatal suicidal behavior or NSSI in the general population. Most data regarding suicide attempts come from studies of visits to general hospitals following self-injurious behavior, a few providing data that enable the calculation of national rates. Between 2006 and 2013 approximately 3.5 million visits to US emergency departments for attempted suicide and self-harm were reported, suggesting an annual population-based rate of approximately 170 per 100,000 (Canner et al., 2016). In Europe, Ireland has a national registry of such visits to general hospitals countrywide, based on which the rate of self-harm (with varying levels of intent and various underlying motives) was estimated at 204 per 100,000 in 2015 (NSRF, 2016). Nationwide individual-level register data on the entire population living in Denmark from 1994 to 2011 revealed an average incidence rate of self-harm of 131 and 87 per 100,000 among females and males, respectively. Among women in the 15–24 age group, an almost 3-fold increase in rates was observed during the study period (Morthorst et al., 2016). Based on data from the WHO World Mental Health (WMH) Survey Initiative, involving 17 countries from different parts of the world, the estimated lifetime prevalence of suicide attempts in the overall cross-national adult general population sample is 2.7% (Nock et al., 2008). A systematic review of studies of the prevalence of NSSI and deliberate self-harm (DSH) in adolescent samples across the globe shows a mean lifetime prevalence of 18% and 16%, respectively (Muehlenkamp et al., 2013). The number of emergency department visits for self-inflicted injury among adolescents has increased substantially from 2009 to 2012 in the United States (Cutler et al., 2015). Noteworthy is the increasing use over the last decade of potentially more lethal methods such as hanging and jumping from heights as a method of self-harm (Vancayseele et al., 2016). Research clearly shows that the use of more lethal methods increases the risk of future fatal suicidal behavior.

1.2.2 Demographic Influences

Three times as many men die of suicide as women (though in low- and middle-income countries the male-to-female ratio is much lower, at 1.5 men to each woman). Globally, suicide rates are 15.0 for males and 8.0 for females, and suicides account for 50% of all violent deaths in men and 71% in women (WHO, 2014). Rates of attempted suicide are generally higher among females than among males. For example, the Irish national registry report shows that rates in 2015 were 186 and 222 for males and females, respectively (NSRF, 2016).

The proportion of all deaths due to suicide and the rank of suicide as a cause of death vary greatly by age. In high-income countries suicide is most common among middle-aged and elderly men, but rates among young people are increasing. Globally, among young adults 15–29 years of age, suicide accounts for 8.5% of all deaths and is ranked as the second leading cause of death (after traffic accidents). Among adults aged 30–49 years, suicide accounts for 4.1% of all deaths and is ranked the fifth leading cause of death. Rates of nonsuicidal self-harm are highest in young age groups. In the United Kingdom, for example, two-thirds are younger than 35 years (Geulayov et al., 2016). Figure 1.2 clearly shows that suicide is a leading cause of death in young people, particularly those aged between 10 and 35 years.

Seasonal variation in suicide rates has also been reported, with peak incidences in spring and summertime, and suicide rates appear to correlate with latitude and exposure to sunshine (Christodoulou et al., 2012). In the next chapter, neurobiological effects on the geographic distribution of suicidal behaviors will be discussed, ranging from genetic factors to lithium concentrations in drinking water.

Rank	10–14	15–24	25–34	35–44	45–54	55–64	65+
1	Unintentional Injury 763	Unintentional Injury 12,514	Unintentional Injury 19,795	Unintentional Injury 17,818	Malignant Neoplasms 43,054	Malignant Neoplasms 43,054	Heart Disease 507,138
2	Malignant Neoplasms 428	Suicide 5,491	Suicide 6,947	Malignant Neoplasms 10,909	Heart Disease 34,248	Heart Disease 76,872	Malignant Neoplasms 419,389
3	Suicide 409	Homicide 4,733	Homicide 4,863	Heart Disease 10,387	Unintentional Injury 21,499	Unintentional Injury 19,488	Respiratory disease 131,804
4	Homicide 158	Malignant Neoplasms 1,469	Malignant Neoplasms 3,704	Suicide 6,936	Liver Disease 8,874	Respiratory disease 17,457	Cerebro-vascular 120,156
5	Congenital Anomalies 156	Heart Disease 997	Heart Disease 3,522	Homicide 2,895	Suicide 8,751	Diabetes Mellitus 14,166	Alzheimer's Disease 109,495
6	Heart Disease 125	Congenital Anomalies 386	Liver Disease 844	Liver Disease 2,861	Diabetes Mellitus 6,212	Liver Disease 13,728	Diabetes Mellitus 56,142
7	Respiratory disease 93	Respiratory disease 202	Diabetes Mellitus 798	Diabetes Mellitus 1,986	Cerebro-vascular 5,307	Cerebro-vascular 12,116	Unintentional Injury 51,395
8	Cerebro-vascular 42	Diabetes Mellitus 196	Cerebro-vascular 567	Cerebro-vascular 1,788	Respiratory disease 4,345	Suicide 7,739	Influenza & Pneumonia 48,774
9	Influenza & Pneumonia 39	Influenza & Pneumonia 184	HIV 529	HIV 1,055	Septicemia 2,542	Septicemia 5,774	Nephritis 41,258
10	Benign Neo, or Septicemia 33	Cerebro-vascular 186	Congenital Anomalies 443	Septicemia 829	Nephritis 2,124	Nephritis 5,452	Septicemia 30,817

Figure 1.2 Ten leading causes of death, United States, 2015. See color plate 2.

1.2.3 The Suicidal Process

Self-injurious thoughts and behaviors are risk factors for future suicide attempts and for death by suicide (Ribeiro et al., 2016). The strongest risk factor for suicide is a previous suicide attempt, and there might be a 70-fold increase in the likelihood of a subsequent attempt and close to a 40-fold increase in the likelihood of death following a suicide attempt (Harris & Barraclough, 1997). Characteristics of prior attempts – including number, recency, intent, and lethality – thereby appear to be important indicators of risk of subsequent suicide.

Early research focused heavily on distinguishing NSSI from suicidal outcomes, but more recent findings indicate that the longitudinal effects of NSSI on suicidal behavior may be much stronger than originally anticipated (Asarnow et al., 2011; Wilkinson et al., 2011). Individuals engaging in DSH have a substantially increased risk of suicide (Beckman et al., 2016). For example, based on a median 5-year follow-up of a large cohort, the suicide rate was estimated at 278 per 100,000 in self-poisoning patients versus 7 per 100,000 in controls. The median time from hospital discharge following self-poisoning to suicide was nearly 600 days (Finkelstein et al., 2015).

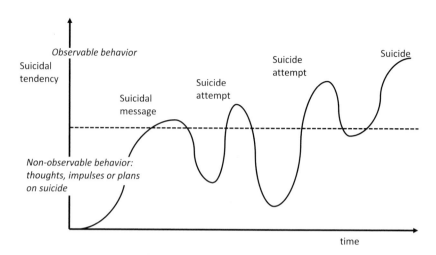

Figure 1.3 The suicidal process
(adapted from Retterstøl, 1993).

Findings from longitudinal epidemiological studies thus suggest a relationship between suicidal thoughts, nonfatal suicidal behaviors including NSSI, and suicide. Such findings support the concept of the suicidal process, which is also apparent from psychological autopsy studies of individuals who died due to suicide. The suicidal process is defined as the development and progression of suicidal thoughts and behaviors as a process within an individual and in interaction with their surroundings. The process may evolve through thoughts about taking one's own life, which may grow through often repeated nonfatal suicidal behaviors with increasing lethality and suicide intent, and end with death by suicide (van Heeringen, 2001).

Figure 1.3 shows an example of such a suicidal process that may start with fleeting thoughts about suicide or with a wish for a temporary oblivion or escape from emotional pain, which may precipitate suicidal behaviors. Stressors such as adverse life events and major depressive episodes may thus precipitate suicidal behaviors in the course of the process (Oquendo et al., 2014a; see also Chapter 2). Only small parts of the process – above the dotted line – may become known to those closest to the person (Retterstøl, 1993). The general population National Comorbidity Survey in the United States shows cumulative probabilities of 34% for the transition from suicidal thoughts to a plan, 72% from a plan to a suicide attempt, and 26% from thoughts to an unplanned attempt. About 90% of unplanned and 60% of planned first suicide attempts occur within 1 year of the onset of suicidal thoughts (Kessler et al., 1999). A recent study in the United States in Rochester, MN, documented that, first, approximately 60% of individuals succumbing to suicide died on their index attempts. While men were more likely than women to use firearms, females using guns were just as likely as their male counterparts to die on an index suicide attempt. Second, more than 80% of subsequent suicides occurred within a year of initial attempt. One in 19 (males 1 in 9, females 1 in 49) suicide attempters died during a follow-up of 3–25 years. Of dead index attempters, 72.9% used guns, yielding an odds ratio for gunshot death, compared with all other methods, of 140 (Bostwick et al., 2016).

Epidemiological data, including studies in twins, provide support for an interaction between life events and a common vulnerability, or shared diathesis, in suicidal ideation and nonfatal and fatal suicidal behaviors (see, e.g., Maciejewski et al., 2014). Stress–diathesis interaction models of suicidal behavior will be described in more detail in Chapter 2.

1.3 Risk Factors for Suicidal Behaviors

Further support for a stress–diathesis interaction model of suicidal behavior is found in studies of risk factors in suicidal behavior, showing that such factors may be proximal or distal (see Table 1.2).

Table 1.2 Risk factors for suicidal behavior (Hawton & van Heeringen, 2009)

Distal
- Genetic loading
- Early traumatic life events
- Restricted fetal growth and perinatal circumstances
    - → Personality characteristics (such as impulsivity, aggression)
    - → Neurobiological disturbances (such as dysfunction of the serotonin and stress-response systems)

Proximal
- Psychiatric disorder
- Physical disorder
- Psychosocial crisis
- Availability of means
- Exposure to models

The next sections will address known proximal and distal risk factors. It should be noted that the term "risk factor" in quoted studies commonly is an umbrella term. A distinction should be made between "correlates" (characteristics associated with suicidal behavior), "risk factors" (a correlate that precedes suicidal behavior and can be used to divide the population into high- and low-risk groups), and "causal risk factors" (a risk factor that is identified when its manipulation of a risk factor systematically changes the probability of suicidal behavior). The discussion of the prediction and treatment of suicide risk in Chapter 9 will make clear that the distinction between these three terms is crucial: Causal risk factors are predictors and valuable treatment targets; non-causal risk factors are predictors, but less effective treatment targets; and correlates may be poor predictors and ineffective treatment targets.

1.3.1 Distal Risk Factors

Distal or predisposing factors that may increase the risk of suicidal behaviors include genetic influences and early-life adversity, which will be discussed in detail in Chapters 4 and 7. Twin and adoption studies show that the heritability of suicidal behaviors (the extent to which genetic individual differences contribute to individual differences in suicidal behavior) is between 30% and 50%. When the heritability of psychiatric conditions is considered, the specific heritability of suicide attempts is estimated as 17% (Turecki & Brent, 2016). The identification of specific genes remains elusive, despite a wealth of candidate gene and genome-wide association studies, as we will see in the next chapters. Early-life adversity involving childhood abuse and parental neglect may exert its risk-increasing effect via the neurocognitive deficits (involving, e.g., decision making and problem solving) that are associated with suicidal behaviors, whether or not via changes in the reactivity of the stress-response system and detrimental effects on brain structures (see Chapter 7).

Impulsivity appears to play a role in a substantial proportion of self-harming behaviors including NSSI (Lockwood et al., 2017). For example, the goal of relief from a terrible state of mind may drive impulsive behavior for short-term gain over long-term objectives. Hence, impulsivity may increase the vulnerability to engage in a readily accessible though maladaptive behavior, such as self-harm, to moderate affect. Successful implementation of this strategy in alleviating distress may lead to negative reinforcement of self-harming behavior. However, while this line of reasoning intuitively appears to be correct, study findings are difficult to interpret because of large variances in the conception and measurement of impulsivity and the precision with which self-harm behaviors are specified. For example, the effects of cognitive impulsivity (relating to difficulties maintaining focus or acting without forethought) may differ from those of behavioral impulsivity. The impulsivity of self-harming behaviors does not appear to correlate well with the impulsivity as a personality trait. Elevated trait impulsivity may also lead to the experience of more painful and provocative experiences over time. Through habituation, individuals may have a dampened response to the aversive nature of self-harm, which contributes to the maintenance of the behavior. Taken together, and despite methodological issues, the findings suggest that distinct impulsivity facets confer unique risks across the life-course of self-harm (Lockwood et al., 2017).

A combination of increased levels of impulsivity and aggression is common in suicide attempters, but the contribution of both trait characteristics to suicide risk appears to differ. For example, aggression is a better predictor of suicidal behavior than impulsivity among depressed individuals (Keilp et al., 2006). A history of impulsive-aggressive behaviors is indeed commonly found in suicides, and particularly among young suicides (Turecki, 2005). In fact, part of the familial liability to suicide may be transmitted through impulsive-aggressive behaviors. These behaviors aggregate in families, and first-degree relatives of suicides and attempted suicides are more likely to exhibit aggression than relatives of controls (Turecki, 2005). Impulsive-aggressive behaviors may thus play a role in mediating familial transmission of suicidal behavior and, as such, may be considered as a behavioral endophenotype in genetic studies of suicide, as will be discussed in Chapter 4. Impulsive-aggressive behaviors are linked to both suicidal behaviors and reduced activity of brain neurotransmitters such as serotonin, which may act as a common distal neurobiological risk factor.

The association between changes in brain neurotransmission and the occurrence of suicidal behaviors is among the most replicated findings in biological psychiatry. Many studies link suicidal behaviors to alterations in the serotonin neurotransmission system, most probably as a distal risk factor that may become manifest via personality characteristics (such as impulsivity and harm avoidance) or neurocognitive deficits. Other neurotransmitters implicated in suicidal behaviors are glutamate and GABA (see Chapter 4).

Blunted cortisol reactivity to stress may well be a trait marker of suicide risk. First-degree relatives of individuals who took their own lives show a blunted cortisol response to an acute laboratory stressor (McGirr et al., 2010). In addition, suicide attempters with and without a family history of suicide show a lower cortisol response to stress in the laboratory when compared with individuals with suicidal thoughts and controls, but the lowest cortisol reactivity to stress is observed in suicide attempters with a family history (O'Connor et al., 2017). Findings like these suggest that blunted cortisol reactivity to stress as a trait may be a heritable marker of suicide risk. The reality, however, is more complicated, as we will see in Chapter 4.

Interestingly, increasing evidence points at infection with the brain-tropic parasite *Toxoplasma gondii* as a distal neurobiological risk factor for suicidal behaviors. Seropositivity is associated with increased risks of suicide attempts and suicide, possibly via immunologically induced changes in neurotransmitter activity (Pedersen et al., 2012; Flegr, 2013). In addition, there appears to be an additive effect of IgM (but not IgG) class antibodies to *T. gondii* and *Cytomegalovirus* on the odds of a suicide attempt (Dickerson et al., 2017). The association between infections and suicide was confirmed in a nationwide, population-based, prospective cohort study in which more than 7 million individuals were observed during a 32-year follow-up period. An increased risk of death by suicide was found among individuals hospitalized with infection in prospective and dose–response relationships, and the population-attributable risk (the reduction in incidence that would be observed if the population were entirely unexposed to infection, compared with its actual exposure pattern) associated with hospitalization with infection accounted for 10% of suicides. The strongest associations with suicide occurred in patients with human immunodeficiency virus and viral hepatitis (Lund-Sørensen et al., 2016). The findings indicate that infections may have a relevant role in the pathophysiological mechanisms of suicidal behavior, although the nature of the mechanisms remains unknown. For example, it remains to be demonstrated to what extent infections and their antibiotic treatment may lead to altered brain function and suicidal behavior via changes in the gut microbiome. Immunological aspects of suicidal behavior will be discussed in more detail in Chapter 4.

1.3.2 Proximal Risk Factors

Proximal risk factors act as precipitants of suicidal behaviors, and include adverse life events (discussed in Chapter 2) and psychopathology. Depressed mood, mental pain, and hopelessness are crucial ingredients of the suicidal state of mind, and nearly all suicidal behaviors occur in the context of psychopathology, irrespective of whether structured criteria for specific psychiatric disorders are met. Psychological autopsy studies consistently show the presence of psychiatric disorders in approximately 90% of individuals who took their own lives in the Western world. Nearly all psychiatric disorders show an increased risk of suicide, but some psychiatric illnesses are more strongly linked with suicidal behavior than others (Harris & Barraclough, 1997). Risks are particularly increased in major depressive disorder, bipolar disorder, schizophrenia, alcohol- and drug-related disorders, eating disorders, and personality disorders. Younger age at suicide is associated with cluster B personality disorders and substance abuse, while in older age groups there is a stronger association with psychopathology such as major depressive disorder.

Depressive episodes in the context of major depressive or bipolar disorder account for at least half of all suicides. Long-term cohort studies show standardized mortality ratios for suicide of approximately 20-fold for individuals with index diagnoses of major depressive disorder and 15-fold for those with bipolar disorder (Rihmer & Döme, 2016). Concerning the latter, suicidal behavior appears to be more common in bipolar II than in bipolar I disorder (Shaffer et al., 2015). Suicidal behaviors in individuals suffering from mood disorders occur almost exclusively during a severe episode.

Several issues are noteworthy in this context. First, the risk of suicidal behavior during a depressive episode does not only depend on the severity of depressive symptoms including suicidal thoughts. Some clinical characteristics indeed have a stronger predictive value for suicidal behavior than severity of depressive symptoms, and these characteristics include levels of hopelessness and mental pain. In view of their strong association with suicidal behaviors, the combination of these two cognitive emotional factors appears to be a particularly "lethal cocktail" in depressed individuals. Mental pain that is perceived to be without end is the common motivation for suicide in depressed individuals.

Mental pain (psychological pain, emotional pain, or "psychache") is an emotional and motivational characteristic of substantial importance for our understanding of suicidal behavior (Troister & Holden, 2010). Intense negative emotions, such as guilt and shame, may be due to the frustration of psychological needs such as closeness, appreciation, and independence. These emotions may become a generalized experience of unbearable mental pain. Consequently, suicide commonly is an escape from mental pain. Several theories, measurements, clinical risk assessments, and studies have been developed over the past decade to describe, assess, and confirm mental pain as a central key in suicide (Verrocchio et al., 2016). However, everybody knows mental pain due, for example, to the loss of a loved one, and the clear majority of people suffering from mental pain will never contemplate suicide. There thus must be some additional features that make mental pain unbearable to such an extent that relief via suicide is sought. There appear to be at least two of such additional relevant issues, namely, the severity of the mental pain and levels of hopelessness (van Heeringen et al., 2010).

Hopelessness, or the lack of a foreseeable change for the better in the future, contributes substantially to the suffering from mental pain. Hopelessness is more than simple pessimism, and it reflects the inability to generate positive events that may occur in the future. Long-term longitudinal studies have shown that increased levels of hopelessness (i.e., a score of 9 or higher on Beck's hopelessness scale) predict suicidal thoughts, (multiple) suicide attempts, and death due to suicide (Brown et al., 2000; Kuo et al., 2004).

Second, mixed depressive episodes, which are present in up to 60% of mood-disordered individuals and which are characterized by depressive symptoms plus co-occurring hypomanic symptoms, substantially increase the risk of fatal and nonfatal suicidal behaviors.

Third, as the clear majority of individuals with mood disorders will not take their own lives and up to 50% will never attempt suicide, other factors play a significant contributory role. These factors may include familial and personality-related characteristics and a history of adverse early life events as distal risk factors, which again points at the crucial role of the specific vulnerability or diathesis to suicidal behavior in determining suicide risk. The prediction and treatment of suicide risk in mood-disordered individuals thus is critically dependent on the identification of this diathesis, as will be discussed in Chapter 9.

In addition to psychiatric disorders as proximal suicide risk factors, there are important environmental risk factors. The availability of methods such as firearms, pesticides, or medication may lower the threshold for suicidal behavior. In 2014, about 21,000 suicides in the United States involved a firearm. Gun ownership predicts state-wide overall suicide rates, with the full model accounting for more than 92% of the variance in state-wide suicide rates. The correlation between firearm suicide rates and the overall suicide rate is significantly stronger than the correlation between non-firearm suicide rates and the overall suicide rate. These findings support the notion that access to and familiarity with firearms serves as a robust risk factor for suicide (Anestis & Houtsma, 2017). Studies in several countries have shown that legislation reducing firearm ownership lowers firearm suicide rates. Restrictive firearm legislation is associated with reduced suicide rates (Resnick et al., 2017). As greater firearm availability is associated with higher firearm and overall suicide rates, reducing availability and access to firearms can be expected to contribute substantially to suicide prevention (Mann & Michel, 2016). Broadly reducing availability and access to firearms, however, does not appear feasible in the United States, so that other targeted initiatives need to be studied urgently. Further issues concerning restriction of access to methods of suicide will be discussed later.

Proximal precipitating factors may also include exposure to models of suicidal behavior. Suicide is sometimes called "contagious," as the risk of suicide may increase among vulnerable individuals when they are exposed to examples in the close environment or in the media. Suicides in the close environment, such as a fellow student or a close family member, may lower the threshold for suicidal behavior among vulnerable individuals. A related phenomenon is the clustering of suicides that occur closer together in space and time than would normally be expected (Robinson et al., 2016). Media reporting of suicide affects suicide rates, particularly among adolescents and young adults, when details of a method are provided and when the suicide is romanticized rather than depicted as associated with mental illness and deficient coping. There is substantial evidence of a negative impact of the Internet on the occurrence and on the methods used in suicide and self-harming behaviors (Pirkis et al., 2016). However, given additional evidence for positive impacts, the Internet is increasingly used as a powerful approach to suicide prevention.

1.4 Prevention

Textbox 1.1 shows some of the most common myths concerning suicide that hamper its prevention.

Many of these myths interfere with the prevention of suicide. Each manifestation of the suicidal process should be taken seriously, and the existence of suicidal thoughts should always be explored. Talking about suicide does not cause suicidal behavior. Many people, including health care staff, are afraid to talk about possible suicidal thoughts and feelings because they think that that may lower the threshold for self-destructive behavior. No study has ever proven that, as we will discuss in more detail in Chapter 10. On the contrary, talking about suicide provides an opportunity to stop the social isolation that is typical for so many suicidal

Textbox 1.1 Myths about Suicide[*]

Myth: You must be mentally ill to think about suicide.

Fact: Most people have thoughts of suicide from time to time and not all people who die by suicide have mental health problems at the time of death. However, many people who take their own lives do suffer from ill mental health.

Myth: People who talk about suicide aren't serious and won't go through with it.

Fact: People who kill themselves have often told someone that they do not feel life is worth living or that they have no future. Some may have actually said they want to die. While it's possible that someone might talk about suicide as a way of getting the attention they need, it's vitally important to take anybody who talks about feeling suicidal seriously. Most people who feel suicidal do not actually want to die; they do not want to live the life they have.

Myth: Once a person has made a serious suicide attempt, that person is unlikely to make another.

Fact: People who have tried to end their lives before are significantly more likely to eventually die by suicide than the rest of the population.

Myth: If a person is serious about killing themself, then there is nothing you can do.

Fact: Often, feeling actively suicidal is temporary, even if someone has been feeling low, anxious, or struggling to cope for a long period of time. This is why getting the right kind of support at the right time is so important.

Myth: Talking about suicide is a bad idea, as it may give someone the idea to try it.

Fact: Suicide can be a taboo topic in society. Often, people feeling suicidal don't want to worry or burden anyone with how they feel and so they don't discuss it. By asking directly about suicide you give them permission to tell you how they feel. People who have felt suicidal will often say what a huge relief it is to be able to talk about what they are experiencing. Once someone starts talking, they've got a better chance of discovering other options to suicide.

Myth: People who threaten suicide are just attention seeking and shouldn't be taken seriously.

Fact: People who threaten suicide should always be taken seriously. It may well be that they want attention in the sense of calling out for help, and giving them this attention may save their life.

Myth: People who are suicidal want to die.

Fact: Most people who feel suicidal do not actually want to die; they do not want to live the life they have. The distinction may seem small but is in fact very important and is why talking through other options at the right time is so vital.

* Reprinted from Samaritans website, www.samaritans.org.

individuals. What studies have shown is that suicide prevention is possible. Suicide prevention practices can be implemented at three different levels, which are called the universal, selective, and indicated prevention levels (Nordentoft, 2011).

1.4.1 Universal Strategies

Universal prevention programs are designed to influence everyone, reducing suicide risk by removing barriers to care, enhancing knowledge of what to do and say to help suicidal individuals, increasing access to help, and strengthening protective processes like social support and coping skills. Universal interventions include programs such as public education campaigns, school-based "suicide awareness" programs, education programs for the media on reporting practices related to suicide, and school-based crisis response plans and teams.

Means restriction is another example of successful universal suicide prevention. As the ease of access to a method is related to the rate of suicide by that method, restriction of the access to that method can be expected to contribute to suicide prevention. Such a preventive effect has indeed been demonstrated for, among others, a reduction of the pack size of analgesics, limited access to pesticides by means of lockboxes, and making hotspots safer, e.g., by means of barriers on bridges. Studies in several countries have shown that legislation reducing firearm ownership lowers firearm suicide rates, with incomplete substitution by other methods. If such a reduction is not feasible, other preventive interventions aiming at a reduction of gun suicides should be studied urgently.

These may include smart gun technology and gun safety education campaigns, potentially reducing access to already purchased firearms by suicidal individuals (Mann & Michel, 2016). As it is well established that media attention regarding suicide can influence suicide rates, influencing media coverage of suicidal events is a component of many national suicide prevention programs. For example, awards for sober mentioning of suicide in the media have been launched in quite a few countries as means to improve and encourage media coverage in accordance with the WHO guidelines.

The availability of carbon monoxide and its relation to suicide rates have been investigated in studies of detoxification of coal gas and in the introduction of mandatory catalytic converters. The detoxification of domestic gas in United Kingdom is associated with a marked decline in carbon monoxide suicides in both genders concomitantly with reduced availability of toxic domestic gas. The effects of mandatory catalytic converters in all gasoline-powered cars sold since 1993 include decreases in the number of suicides, without substitution of other methods, in many countries including the United States (Nordentoft, 2011).

1.4.2 Selective Interventions

Selective strategies address subsets of the total population, focusing on at-risk groups that have a greater probability of becoming suicidal, i.e., individuals who may show a vulnerability to suicidal behavior. Selective prevention strategies thus aim to prevent the onset of suicidal behaviors among specific subpopulations, the most important being the mentally ill, alcohol and drug abusers, those with a newly diagnosed severe somatic disease, prisoners, and homeless persons (Nordentoft, 2011).

This level of prevention includes screening programs; gatekeeper training for "frontline" adult caregivers, including general practitioners and peer "natural helpers"; support and skill-building groups for at-risk groups in the population; and enhanced accessible crisis services and referral sources. Increasing access to mental health care is an example of a powerful selective prevention approach. A range of studies demonstrates that a recent diagnosis of severe somatic illness is associated with an increased risk of suicide. This evidence is most clear from studies of neurological diseases and cancer, and forms the basis for recommendation of careful crisis management in these patients and evaluation of suicide risk (Nordentoft, 2011).

Given the topic of this book, neurobiological approaches in the context of selective suicide prevention among vulnerable individuals merit some additional attention. Observational studies indicate that long-term pharmacotherapy by means of antidepressants and/or mood stabilizers reduces the risk of fatal and nonfatal suicidal behavior among depressed patients by up to 90%, and suicide rates have decreased progressively and significantly through the eras of pre-treatment, electroconvulsive treatment (ECT), and antidepressants (Rihmer & Döme, 2016). The marked decline in suicide rates in countries where antidepressant use has increased in the past two decades further suggests that the adequate treatment of mood disorders may contribute substantially to the prevention of suicidal behaviors. An increase in antidepressant usage, however, may well reflect greater access of vulnerable individuals to improved mental health care. The finding that the introduction of the black-box warning has led to a marked decline in the use of antidepressants in children and adolescents but also to a sharp increase in suicide mortality in the same age groups suggests that changes in mental health care affect suicide rates (Rihmer & Döme, 2016).

Lithium probably is the strongest antisuicidal medication available for major depressive and bipolar disorder (see also Chapter 10). Meta-analyses demonstrate the effect of long-term lithium therapy for affective disorders and conclude that lithium is effective in the prevention of suicide, but also in the prevention of nonfatal suicidal behavior and death from all causes in patients with mood disorders. The finding of a negative correlation between lithium levels in drinking water and suicide rates in quite a few areas around the globe, from Japan to Texas, is remarkable (Rihmer & Döme, 2016). The mechanisms by means of which lithium may exert its antisuicidal effect are not yet clear, but will be discussed in detail in Chapter 10.

1.4.3 Indicated Prevention

Indicated strategies address specific high-risk individuals within the population, i.e., those evidencing early signs of suicide potential. At this level, programs include skill-building support groups in high schools and colleges, parent support training programs, case management for individual high-risk youth at school, and referral sources for crisis intervention and treatment (Nordentoft, 2011).

Indicated prevention strategies thus target individuals in whom the suicidal process has already become manifest by means of, e.g., suicide attempts. Continuity of care of suicide attempters who were admitted to crisis services is an important indicated prevention target. Continuity of care thereby aims at getting people in treatment for the underlying vulnerability to suicidal behavior after successful crisis intervention. As will be discussed in Chapter 10, evidence-based treatments targeting the vulnerability to suicidal behavior are now available.

Chapter 1 Summary

- Fatal and nonfatal suicidal behaviors and nonsuicidal self-injury behaviors can be regarded as separate categories of behaviors, which appear to share a common vulnerability.
- Suicidal behavior is the consequence of an interaction between stressors and such a vulnerability (or diathesis).
- Suicide prevention is possible through combinations of interventions at individual and societal levels.
- The prevention of suicide at the individual level, however, is hampered by difficulties in its prediction and treatment.
- A neuroscience approach to suicidal behavior may contribute to suicide prevention by defining biomarkers for the prediction of suicide risk and by determining a neurobiological substrate for the treatment of suicide risk.

Review Questions

1. Is depression a sufficient condition for suicidal behavior?
2. Suicide runs in families. Is this due to genetic factors or to imitation effects?
3. Neurobiological interventions are important at the level of indicated suicide prevention, but how might they also be relevant for selective suicide prevention actions?
4. How are economic turmoil and suicide linked?
5. The relationship between the Internet and suicide prevention is complicated. What are the issues at stake?

Further Reading

Hawton, K. & van Heeringen, K. (2009). Suicide. *Lancet, 373,* 1372–1381.
Jamison, K. R. (2000). *Night falls fast: Understanding suicide.* New York, NY: Random House.
O'Connor, R. & Pirkis, J. (2016). *The international handbook of suicide prevention* (2nd ed.). Chichester: Wiley Blackwell.
Williams, J. M. G. (2014). *Cry of pain: Understanding suicide and the suicidal mind.* London: Piatkus.

CHAPTER TWO

Stress, Vulnerability, and Suicide

The Stress–Diathesis Model

Learning Objectives

- Understand why suicide is not a normal reaction to an abnormal situation, but rather an abnormal reaction to a normal situation.
- Learn about the crucial importance of a diathesis for understanding and preventing suicide.
- Are mental health problems a sufficient and/or necessary condition for suicidal behavior?
- What are the known causes of the diathesis to suicidal behavior?
- Describe the three diathesis components of the cognitive psychological "cry of pain" model of suicidal behavior.
- How are disturbances of the stress-response system involved?
- Describe common myths about suicide and how they may interfere with its prevention.

Introduction

Can anyone take his or her own life if exposed to sufficiently severe stressors? Or, as in the case of Valerie, is it possible that people (try to) kill themselves after a seemingly ordinary event? Sometimes suicide may seem an understandable reaction to severe and enduring problems, such as losing the battle against recurrent episodes of depression. People who have experienced depression and cancer say that the psychological pain they felt when depressed is much worse than the physical pain from their cancer. Fortunately, a clear majority of depressed individuals will not take their own lives. Stress models of suicidal behavior cannot explain the observations that even extreme stress does not lead to suicidal behavior in all exposed individuals. Suicide is not a normal reaction to an abnormal situation. On the contrary, suicidal behavior is an abnormal reaction to a normal situation, with which a clear majority of people will cope without becoming suicidal. Such observations have led to the recognition that the development of suicide risk involves a vulnerability or diathesis, which may predispose individuals to such behavior when stress is encountered. Any explanatory model of suicidal behavior thus considers proximal risk factors and distal vulnerability factors, and their interaction. This chapter will show how scientists have developed intriguing models of this interaction based on findings from neurocognitive and neurobiological studies.

2.1 Stress–Diathesis Models: General Issues

Suicide and attempted suicide are complex behaviors, and many proximal and distal risk factors have been identified. (See the previous chapter.) As seen in the previous chapter, proximal risk factors are the factors in the causal chain that precipitate suicidal behavior, while distal risk factors reflect characteristics of a specific vulnerability or diathesis. To promote full understanding the effects of these risk factors on the occurrence of suicidal behavior, explanatory models have been developed. Such models aim at helping to understand suicidal individuals, facilitating the assessment of suicide risk, and defining targets for treatment and prevention. Stress has been identified as a key determinant of mental problems, so that a variety of models to explain such problems have featured stress as a primary determinant. Such models suggest that negative events, if sufficiently severe, can precipitate disorders even without reference to individual biological or psychological characteristics.

Vulnerable or diathetic individuals respond with abnormal or pathological reactions to physiological stimuli or the ordinary conditions of life that are borne by most individuals without injury (Zuckerman, 1999). The self-destructive reaction following exposure to an angry face, as described in the story of Valerie in the Preface to this book and as seen in suicide attempters in neuroimaging studies (see Chapter 6), is a good example of an abnormal reaction to a normal situation. The occurrence of such an abnormal reaction reflects the existence of a vulnerability or diathesis. As intuitively straightforward as the diathesis concept is and despite intensive discussion in the literature, few precise definitions are available. A diathesis is commonly conceptualized as a predisposition factor, or set of factors, that make possible a disordered state. It reflects a constitutional vulnerability to develop a disorder (Ingram & Luxton, 2005).

The diathesis concept has a long history in medical terminology. The word "diathesis" stems from the Greek idea of predisposition, which is related to the humoral theory of temperament and disease (Zuckerman, 1999). The term has been used in a psychiatric context since the 1800s.

Theories of schizophrenia brought the stress and diathesis concepts together, and the terminology of diathesis–stress interactions was developed by Meehl, Bleuler, and Rosenthal in the 1960s (Ingram & Luxton, 2005).

In the modern sense, the biological traits produced by the (genetic) disposition are the diathesis. The term has been broadened, however, to include cognitive and social predispositions that may make a person vulnerable to a disorder such as depression. In this broader sense, the diathesis is the necessary antecedent condition for the development of a disorder or problem, whether biological or psychological. The "cry of pain" model of suicidal behavior, as described in detail further in this chapter, is a clear example of such a psychological approach to the study of the diathesis to suicidal behavior. In most models, whether biological or psychological, the diathesis alone is not sufficient to produce the disorder but requires other potentiating or releasing factors to become pathogenic. The diathesis, in this case, includes the vulnerability to stress (Zuckerman, 1999).

Most stress–diathesis models presume that all people have some level of diathesis for any given psychiatric disorder (Monroe & Hadjiyannakis, 2002). However, individuals may differ regarding the point at which they develop a disorder depending on the degree to which predisposition risk factors exist and on the degree of experienced stress. Thus, relatively minor stressors may lead to a disorder in persons who are highly vulnerable. This approach presupposes additivity, or the idea that diathesis and stress add together to produce the disorder. So-called ipsative models more specifically posit an inverse relationship between components such that the greater the presence of one component, the less of the other component is needed to bring about the disorder. Thus, for example, minimal stress is needed for depression to occur in individuals with strongly "depressogenic" thinking patterns (Ingram & Luxton, 2005). Such models assume a dichotomous diathesis, i.e., either one has it (a gene, a unique combination of genes, a psychological characteristic, or a brain pathology) or one does not have it (Zuckerman, 1999). If the diathesis is absent, there is no effect of stress so that even severe stress will not lead to the development of the disorder. When the diathesis is present, the expression of the disorder will be conditional on the degree of stress: As stress increases, so does the risk for the disorder in persons who possess the diathesis (Ingram & Luxton, 2005). However, most disorders in the psychiatric domain probably have a polygenic basis that allows for varying degrees of the diathesis, including variations in neurotransmitter activity levels. In this case, the probability of a disorder would increase as a function of both levels of stress and the strength of the diathesis.

The conceptualization of a diathesis as dynamic implies that such a diathesis is continuous rather than dichotomous. For example, schema models, which explain depression as a consequence of maladaptive patterns of thoughts and beliefs, were commonly regarded as dichotomous models: If an individual possesses a "depressogenic" schema, he or she is at risk of depression when events occur that activate this schema. More recent discussions of the schema model, however, have pointed at the possibility of a continuous character by describing the depressogenic nature of schemata as ranging from weak or mild to strong.

In line with the possibility of a continuous diathesis, it should be noted that the interaction between stress and a diathesis might not be static and may change dynamically over time. The diathesis may increase or decrease so that the amount of stress needed for the development of pathology may need to decrease or increase, respectively. The "kindling" phenomenon (Post, 1992) provides an example of the dynamic character of the interaction between stress and vulnerability: Repeated occurrences of a disorder may cause neuronal changes that result in more sensitivity to stress. The kindling theory thus proposes that diatheses may change so that more or less stress becomes necessary to activate vulnerability factors (Ingram & Luxton, 2005). Later in this chapter the potential role of sensitization will be highlighted. It is not clear, however, whether the diathesis changes under the influence of negative circumstances or whether residua and scarring add to the diathesis and thus increase vulnerability. The potential to change the diathesis has huge implications for suicide prevention, as such a potential implicates the possibility that the diathesis is amenable to treatment. We will see in Chapter 10 that adequate treatment of suicide risk not only focuses on proximal risk factors such as depression, but also targets underlying vulnerabilities, for which neurobiological and psychological treatments exist.

Finally, a diathesis may theoretically consist of one single factor or be constituted by multiple components. Polygenic disorders or interpersonal cognitive disturbances provide examples of mental health problems related to diatheses that are composed by multiple factors.

2.2 Stress–Diathesis Models of Suicidal Behavior

Early descriptions of the roles of stress and a diathesis in the development of suicidal behavior were grounded in sociobiology (De Catanzaro,

1980). Further studies focused on cognitive psychological characteristics. For instance, studying a college population, Schotte and Clum (1982) described a stress/problem-solving model of suicidal behavior in which poor problem-solvers under high life stress are considered to be at risk for depression, feelings of hopelessness, and suicidal behavior. Rubinstein (1986) developed a stress–diathesis theory of suicide in which the effects of specific situational stressors and the categories or predisposing factors of vulnerable individuals in a given culture were integrated in a biocultural model of suicidal behavior. Mann and Arango (1992) then proposed a stress–diathesis model based on the integration of neurobiology and psychopathology, which still forms the basis for much of the current research in suicidology. Changes in the serotonin system were emphasized in this model, particularly regarding their role as a constitutional risk factor as opposed to a state-dependent risk factor for suicidal behavior.

The next sections will focus on the stress component and the diathesis component of stress–diathesis models of suicidal behavior, followed by a description of a number of such models.

2.2.1 The Stress Component

Psychosocial crises and acute episodes of psychiatric disorders may constitute the stress component of stress–diathesis models of suicidal behavior (Mann et al., 1999). Poverty, unemployment, and social isolation have all been implicated in suicide. These factors are clearly not independent from each other or from psychiatric illness. Psychiatric disorders can lead to job loss, to breakup of marriages or relationships, or to the failure to form such relationships. It is difficult to separate the impact of psychosocial adversity from that of psychiatric illness, and they can combine to increase stress on the person (Mann, 2003).

Population-based studies shed further light on the association between traumatic or stressful life events and nonfatal or fatal suicidal behaviors. Data from 21 countries across the world using the WHO World Mental Health Surveys show that a range of traumatic events is associated with nonfatal suicidal behaviors, with sexual and interpersonal violence consistently showing the strongest effects (Stein et al., 2010). There is a dose–response relationship between the number of traumatic events experienced and the subsequent risk of suicidal behavior, but the effects are subadditive with a decay in the strength of the association with more events. The general pattern of findings holds true across high-, middle-, and low-income countries, regardless of the presence of post-traumatic stress disorder (PTSD), and are not mediated by the presence of psychiatric disorders. The results of this study suggest that completely eliminating traumatic events would lead to a 22% reduction in suicide attempts.

Nationwide data from Danish registers on more than 7,000 suicides and 142,000 controls show that individuals who die by suicide have an odds ratio of 9 of having been exposed to imprisonment when compared with controls (Fjeldsted et al., 2016). People who die by suicide have a 1.5-fold higher risk of having experienced a divorce. Stressful life events, such as divorce and imprisonment, are more frequent in temporal proximity to the date of death among the suicide cases than for end of exposure for controls. Stressful life events are thus strongly associated with subsequent suicide.

2.2.2 The Diathesis Component

It has become clear that the diathesis to suicidal behavior may be due to childhood adversity and (epi-)genetic effects (Mann & Haghgighi, 2010). Childhood trauma is common. General population surveys show that up to one in three males and one in five females report a history of childhood physical abuse, while childhood sexual abuse is reported by 13% of females and 4% of males (Roy, 2012). General population studies such as the Epidemiologic Catchment Area (ECA) Study and the US National Comorbidity Survey consistently show that exposure to childhood trauma is an independent risk factor for suicidal behavior. Recent data from the US National Comorbidity Survey Replication indicate that exposure to childhood physical or sexual abuse or witnessing domestic violence accounts for 16% and 50% of suicidal ideation and attempts, respectively, among women and 21% and 33% of ideation and attempts among men (Afifi et al., 2008). In addition, clinical studies have indeed shown that childhood adversity, such as deprivation and physical or sexual abuse, is a risk factor for psychopathological phenomena in later childhood and adulthood, including depression and suicide. However, not all individuals will develop psychopathology following exposure to childhood adversity, indicating the existence of a diathesis in some but not all individuals. Neuroanatomical, physiological, and genomic alterations may contribute to the long-lasting detrimental effects of exposure to childhood adversity on the risk of psychopathology (Miller et al., 2009).

The involvement of serotonin and other neurotransmitters, the (epi-)genetics of suicidal behavior, and the role of gene–environment interactions are discussed in detail elsewhere in this book. Postmortem and neuroimaging studies have clearly demonstrated structural and functional changes in the brains of individuals with a history of suicidal behavior, which may correlate with components of the diathesis. (See Chapter 6 and van Heeringen et al., 2011). Postmortem findings include fewer cortical serotonin neurons in key brain regions such as the dorsal and ventral prefrontal cortex, which also appear to correlate with components of the diathesis (Mann, 2003). These components may include aggression and/or impulsivity, pessimism and hopelessness, and problem-solving or cognitive rigidity. Some of these characteristics are discussed as intermediate phenotypes of suicidal behavior elsewhere in this book. Recent studies have used neuropsychological approaches to the study of the diathesis, and have focused particularly on decision-making processes (Jollant et al., 2007; Dombrovski et al., 2010; see Chapter 5).

Currently available evidence as reviewed in this chapter suggests that the diathesis to suicidal behavior is continuous. It can be hypothesized that the diathesis becomes more pronounced during the course of the suicidal process that commonly precedes completed suicide (van Heeringen, 2001). Suicide is indeed commonly preceded by nonfatal suicide attempts, which are commonly repeated with an increasing degree of medical severity, suicidal intent, or lethality of the method used. Several studies have provided support for a kindling effect on the occurrence of suicide attempts. Findings from clinical studies point at the possibility that each time such a suicidal mode becomes activated, it becomes increasingly accessible in memory and requires less triggering stimuli to become activated the next time. This phenomenon can be used to explain findings from epidemiological studies in suicide attempters, showing that each succeeding suicide attempt is associated with a greater probability of a subsequent suicide attempt (Leon et al., 1990; van Heeringen, 2001; Oquendo et al., 2004).

The concept of a continuous diathesis may explain differences in suicidal reactivity between individuals, e.g., why individuals differ in their suicidal reaction to similar life events, varying from deliberate self-harm with no or minor physical consequences to completed suicide. Repeated exposure to stressors may thus gradually diminish the resilience toward stress, due to which stressors of decreasing severity may lead to suicidal behaviors with increasing suicidal intent. Increasing evidence points at a role of increasing neuropsychological deficits in the medial temporal cortex–hippocampal system, perhaps due to the detrimental effects of stress hormones on serotonergic neurons.

As discussed in more detail elsewhere in this book, studies of levels of the serotonin metabolite 5-HIAA in the cerebrospinal fluid of suicide attempters have shown that (1) depressed suicide attempters have lower levels than depressed nonattempters; (2) repeating attempters have lower levels than so-called first-evers; (3) the use of violent methods is associated with lower levels than the use of nonviolent methods; and (4) attempted suicide patients with lower levels show a poorer survival in terms of death from suicide. (For a review, see van Heeringen, 2001.) Such findings point at a possible increase of the vulnerability to suicidal behavior during the suicidal process, which is paralleled by a decrease in serotonergic functioning.

2.3 Examples of Stress–Diathesis Models of Suicidal Behavior

2.3.1 Cognitive Models of Suicidal Behavior

Mark Williams has described a diathesis for suicidal behavior in cognitive psychological terms in his highly influential "cry of pain" model (Williams & Pollock, 2001). Textbox 2.1 shows the three cognitive psychological components of the diathesis to suicide.

The identification of the neuropsychological correlates of the three cognitive components reflects an interesting and important characteristic of the "cry of pain" model, in addition to its clinical relevance, and suggests the potential of more in-depth neurobiological studies of this model. Further cognitive studies of this psychological stress–diathesis model have focused on the differential activation of suicide risk in the context of recurrent mood disorders, and thus provide an example of how the diathesis to suicidal behavior may change over time (Williams et al., 2008). Long-term follow-up studies have shown that recovered depressed patients are at high risk for recurrences and that later episodes of depression require less activation from negative life events than earlier episodes – in other words, sensitization may occur. From a cognitive perspective, it has been suggested that sensitization (and increased risk of relapse and recurrence) is brought about by increased cognitive reactivity to small changes in depressed mood. Cognitive reactivity has thereby been defined as the relative ease with which maladaptive cognitions or cognitive styles are triggered by mild (non-pathological) mood fluctuations. Such reactivity is assumed to be the observable result of an underlying differential activation process that has occurred over the learning history of the individual. Thus, an association is formed between depressed mood and hopeless and suicidal cognitions,

---

Textbox 2.1 The Cry of Pain Model

The three components of the diathesis to suicidal behavior according to Mark Williams's "cry of pain" model:

1. *Sensitivity to signals of defeat*: Using the "emotional Stroop task" (see Chapter 5), Williams and colleagues clearly demonstrated attentional biases (or so-called perceptual pop-outs) in association with suicidal behavior: An involuntary hypersensitivity to stimuli signaling "loser" status increases the risk that the defeat response will be triggered.
2. *Perceived "no escape"*: Limited problem-solving abilities may indicate to persons with them that there is no escape from problems or life events. Further study has revealed that such limited abilities correlate with decreases in the specificity of autobiographical memories. To generate potential solutions to problems, a person apparently needs to have access to the past in some detail. Overgeneral memories prevent the use of strategies, which are sufficiently detailed to solve problems.
3. *Perceived "no rescue"*: The occurrence of suicidal behavior is associated with a limited fluency in coming up with positive events that might happen in the future. This limited fluency is reflected not only by the perception that there is no escape from an aversive situation, but also by the judgement that no rescue is possible in the future. It is thereby interesting to note that the fluency of generating positive future events correlates negatively with levels of hopelessness, a core clinical predictor of suicidal behavior. This suggests that hopelessness does not consist of the anticipation of an excess of negative events, but indicates that hopelessness reflects the failure to generate sufficient rescue factors.

---

establishing a response pattern that may easily be reinstated when mood deteriorates at later times, thus increasing risk for further suicidal crises. Risk of further suicidal ideation and behavior, therefore, is determined by the ease with which these reverberatory patterns of processing become reestablished, following recovery, in the face of mild negative affect.

These findings may help us to understand the apparent divergence between treatments' proven efficacy in addressing important continuous variables (hopelessness, depression, and problem solving) and their relatively weak effects on suicidal behavior itself. It suggests that the critical risk factor is not the resting level of these variables assessed after treatment and during follow-up or when patients are in remission, but

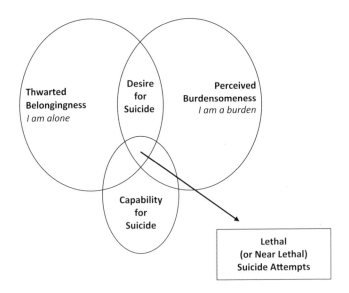

Figure 2.1 The IPT model of suicidal behavior (Van Orden et al., 2010).

rather how easily activated these variables are in response to mood challenges. Before considering treatments to be successful, a reactivity procedure should be included toward the end of therapy to investigate which patterns of thinking and impulses come to mind under such "activated" conditions (Brown et al., 2005). Hopelessness and suicidality may disappear altogether when patients are euthymic, but remain ready to be reactivated when depression returns. It is this vulnerability toward which therapeutic efforts should be focused (Williams et al., 2008).

Joiner's "interpersonal-psychological theory of suicidal behavior" (IPT) is a second example of a psychological model of suicidal behavior in which stress–diathesis interactions may play a role (Hagan et al., 2016). Four main predictions that can be derived from the IPT are supported by rapidly increasing empirical evidence (see Figure 2.1). First, two interpersonal states – thwarted belongingness and perceived burdensomeness – act as proximal risk factors for developing a passive desire for suicide. Second, the likelihood of developing an active desire for death by suicide is highest when both states are experienced concurrently and as hopeless.

Third, suicidal intent is most likely when suicidal desire and a reduced fear of death co-occur. Fourth, serious suicidal behavior will occur in the presence of all constructs: co-occurring thwarted belongingness,

perceived burdensomeness (and hopelessness regarding both), fearlessness about death, and elevated pain tolerance (known as the capability
for suicide). Although each factor is necessary, none alone is sufficient to
result in death by suicide. With regard to the capability for suicide, and
as described in Chapter 1, epidemiological data suggest that nonsuicidal
self-injury may facilitate the development of suicidal behavior via its
effect on the capability for suicide. Preliminary evidence indicates that
the capability for suicide is, at least in part, based on a genetic predisposition. In studies of twins, variations in acquired capability and pain
tolerance are best explained by a combination of genetic and environmental factors, with genetics accounting for up to 55% of differences in
pain tolerance (Hagan et al., 2016). Neural substrates underlying the
gender differences in the rate of fatal suicidal behavior were recently
studied using MRI (Deshpande et al., 2016). Male-specific networks
appeared to be more widespread and diverse than the female-specific
ones. While the male-specific networks involved motor regions, such as
the premotor cortex and cerebellum, limbic regions dominated the
female-specific network. The findings suggest that suicidal desire generally leads to fatal/decisive action in males, while in females, it may
manifest as depression, ideation, and generally nonfatal actions.

The Integrated Motivational–Volitional Model of suicidal behavior
(O'Connor, 2011) builds on predominant factors from existing theoretical models, and conceptualizes suicide as a behavior (rather than a by-
product of mental disorders) that develops through premotivational,
motivational, and volitional phases (see Figure 2.2). The premotivational

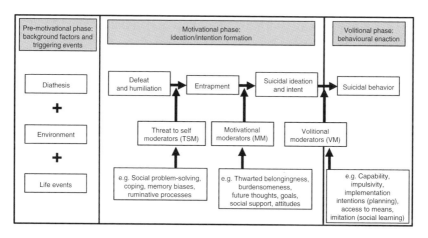

Figure 2.2 The IMV model of suicidal behavior (O'Connor & Nock, 2014).

phase describes the stress–diathesis interaction. The motivational phase describes the factors that govern the development of suicidal ideation and intent, whereas the volitional phase outlines the factors that determine whether an individual attempts suicide.

Extending the "arrested flight" model (see next chapter), the theory posits that suicidal thoughts derive from feelings of entrapment where suicidal behavior is considered the salient solution to life circumstances, and entrapment is triggered by perceived defeat or humiliation. Feelings of entrapment are exacerbated by specific state moderators (factors that facilitate/obstruct movement between stages), such as brooding (ruminative cognitions that repetitively compare one's present situation with another unachieved benchmark), poor problem solving, and attribution biases. In the presence of motivational moderators such as interpersonal states (perceived burdensomeness and thwarted belongingness), impaired subjective goals, and disrupted future positive thinking, such appraisals lead to suicidal ideation. The translation from suicidal thoughts to actions is determined by behavioral enaction factors (volitional moderators) that include access to the means of suicide, acquired capability (fearlessness about death and pain insensitivity), exposure to the suicidal behavior of others, and impulsivity. Although relatively new, different aspects of the Integrated Motivational–Volitional Model have already been tested empirically. For example, the Integrated Motivational–Volitional Model of suicidal behavior explains a considerable amount of variance in suicide attempts, suicidal ideation, defeat, and entrapment (Dhingra et al., 2016).

2.3.2 Clinical Stress–Diathesis Models of Suicidal Behavior

Mann and colleagues (1999) have proposed a stress–diathesis model based on findings from a clinical study of a large sample of patients admitted to a university psychiatric hospital. When compared with patients without a history of suicide attempts, patients who had attempted suicide show higher scores on subjective depression and suicidal ideation, and reported fewer reasons for living. In addition, suicide attempters show higher rates of lifetime aggression and impulsivity, comorbid borderline personality disorder, substance use disorder or alcoholism, family history of suicidal acts, head injury, smoking, and childhood abuse history. The risk for suicidal acts thus is determined not only by a psychiatric illness (the stressor), but also by a diathesis as reflected by tendencies to experience more suicidal ideation and to be more impulsive and, therefore, more likely to act on suicidal feelings. Mann and colleagues describe a predisposition to suicidal acts that appears to be part of a more fundamental predisposition to both externally and self-directed aggression. Aggression, impulsivity, and borderline personality disorder are key characteristics, which may be the result of genetic factors or early life experiences, including a history of physical or sexual abuse. A common underlying genetic or familial factor may therefore explain the association between suicidal behavior with the aggression/impulsivity factor and/or borderline personality disorder, independent of transmission of major depression or psychosis. Suicide risk was also associated with past head injury, and the authors hypothesize that aggressive-impulsive children and adults are more likely to sustain a head injury, which may lead to disinhibition and aggressive behavior. The serotonin neurotransmission system may also play a role. Given the evidence linking low serotonergic activity to suicidal behavior, it is conceivable that such low activity may mediate genetic and developmental effects on suicide, aggression, and alcoholism (Mann et al., 1999).

Based on a review of studies of clinical predictors of suicide, McGirr and Turecki (2007) provide a second example of a clinical stress–diathesis model. The model is based on the clinical observation that psychopathology, for the most part, appears to be a necessary but not sufficient factor for suicide. Therefore, a promising avenue for improved clinical detection is the elucidation of stable risk factors predating the onset of psychopathology, through which suicidal behavior is precipated. The authors describe personality characteristics as stable risk factors, which can be regarded as reflecting preexisting endophenotypes and which interact with the onset of psychiatric disorders (the stressor) to result in suicide. While the authors acknowledge the potential role of personality characteristics, such as neuroticism and introversion in relation to suicide, they focus their review on impulsivity and aggression, which were discussed in Chapter 1 as potential distal risk factors. Impulsivity in this context is regarded more as a behavioral dimension than as the explosive or instantaneous actions relating to an inability to resist impulses. The behavioral dimension describes behaviors that appear to occur without reflection or consideration of consequences, are often risky or inappropriate to the situation, and are accompanied by undesirable outcomes. They do not necessarily include aggressive behaviors, but high levels of impulsivity correlate with high levels of aggression. A correlation between aggression, impulsivity, and hostility has been confirmed in suicides using psychological autopsies (see the next chapter for an explanation of this study approach). Studies of fatal and nonfatal suicidal behavior have indeed pointed at a role of this behavioral dimension. Impulsivity thus appears to be involved not only in self-harming behaviors without suicidal intent, but also in high-lethality and fatal suicidal behaviors.

With respect to aggression, more extensive histories of aggression have been associated with suicide attempts in clinical samples and those meeting criteria for major depression and bipolar disorder, and with adolescent suicide completion. In addition, depressed suicides and borderline suicides exhibit higher levels of aggressive behaviors than diseased controls. Levels of impulsivity tend to correlate with those of aggression and hostility.

The involvement of impulsivity and aggression in the diathesis of suicidal behavior has been a matter of debate for many years, as discussed in Chapter 1. The controversy is fueled by, among others, epidemiological observations that many attempted and completed suicides do not appear to be aggressive or impulsive and by theoretical discussions about the multifaceted nature of the aggression and impulsivity concepts.

2.3.3 A Neurocognitive Model of Suicidal Behavior

In 2008, Jollant and co-workers published a pivotal study in the neurobiological domain (Jollant et al., 2008). Using functional MRI techniques (see Chapter 3 for technical issues), they investigated the reactivity to facial emotional expressions in a group of currently euthymic young males with a history of depression. Findings in young males with a history of attempted suicide were compared with those in young males without such a history. Relative to affective comparison subjects, suicide attempters showed greater activity in the right ventrolateral cortex and decreased activity in the right superior frontal gyrus in response to prototypical angry versus neutral faces, greater activity in the right anterior cingulate gyrus to mild happy versus neutral faces, and greater activity in the right cerebellum to mild angry versus neutral faces. Thus, suicide attempters were distinguished from nonsuicidal patients by responses to angry and happy faces, which may suggest increased sensitivity to others' disapproval, higher propensity to act on negative emotions, and reduced attention to mildly positive stimuli. The authors conclude that these patterns of neural activity and cognitive processes may represent vulnerability markers of suicidal behavior in men with a history of depression.

A few years later, Jollant and colleagues (2011) proposed a stress–diathesis model of suicidal behavior based on a review of

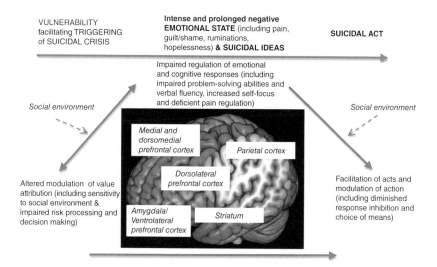

Figure 2.3 A neurocognitive model of suicidal behavior (Adapted by F. Jollant in 2017 from Jollant et al. 2011). See color plate 3.

neuropsychological and neuroimaging studies (findings from these studies will be thoroughly reviewed in Chapters 5 and 6). More in particular, they proposed that a series of neurocognitive dysfunctions, some with trait-like characteristics, may facilitate the development of a suicidal crisis during stressful circumstances: (1) an altered modulation of value attribution, (2) an inadequate regulation of emotional and cognitive responses, and (3) a facilitation of acts in an emotional context (see Figure 2.3).

The findings from the 2008 study cited earlier, showing a significantly greater response to angry (but not happy) faces in the brains of suicide attempters, is a striking example of the first neurocognitive alteration in association with suicidal behavior. This alteration reflects an inability of suicide attempters to accurately assign value to external events to which they thus may become particularly sensitive. The inability to learn to assign adequate value to long-term risk, therefore, appears to be a key cause of disadvantageous decision making in suicide attempters. Interestingly, disadvantageous decision making has been shown to correlate with the occurrence of greater problems in affective relationships. In other words, and as frequently observed in clinical practice, suboptimal decisions taken by vulnerable patients lead to more stressful problems that may trigger a suicidal crisis. A second neurocognitive alteration may involve a deficient regulation of the emotional state once it has been triggered. According to current diagnostic classifications, this acute and more prolonged emotional state corresponds to a depressive state with particular cognitive, emotional, and neuroanatomical characteristics. From an emotional point of view, these characteristics include mental pain and hopelessness, as discussed in the previous chapter. Suicidal thoughts may progress to suicidal behaviors via the third neurocognitive alteration, i.e., the facilitation of acts in this particular emotional context. The authors suggest a particular role of disturbed response inhibition and cognitive reappraisal of emotional stimuli in order to reduce negative affect in this third facet of the diathesis to suicidal behavior.

Chapter 2 Summary

- There are many pathways to suicide. Studies in the domains of neuropsychology, cognitive psychology, neurobiology, and clinical psychiatry have provided increasing evidence in support of a stress–diathesis model of suicidal behavior.
- While depression is the common final pathway to suicidal behavior, the vast majority of depressed individuals neither attempt nor complete suicide. It appears that a diathesis to suicidal behavior differentiates depressed individuals who will kill themselves from other depressed individuals.
- The diathesis may be due to (epi-)genetic effects and childhood adversity, and is reflected by a distinct neurobiological, psychological, or clinical profile.
- Vulnerability traits are open to modification early in life, and interventions during sensitive periods of development may have durable effects on personality and thereby affect vulnerability to suicide.
- The diathesis can be demonstrated and treated beyond depressive episodes, as will be discussed in much more detail in Chapter 10. For example, reducing the diathesis for suicidal behavior might be possible as evidenced by the clinical effects of lithium, clozapine, or cognitive behavioral therapy (Mann, 2003).
- An important issue is the potential interdependence of the stress and diathesis components, as the diathesis may increase the probability of exposure to stressors. Such an interdependence of stress and diathesis components would mean that interventions targeting the diathesis may also decrease exposure to stressors and suggests that relief of stress effects would enhance the efficacy of therapeutic interventions.

Review Questions

1. Why is depression not a sufficient factor for suicidal behavior?
2. How do stress factors and a specific diathesis interact in the development of suicide risk?
3. What are the neuropsychological correlates of the three diathesis components of Mark Williams's "cry of pain" model?
4. Describe the neurocognitive three-step suicidal process model of suicidal behavior.

Further Reading

Jollant, F., Lawrence, N.L., Olié, E., Guillaume, S. & Courtet, P. (2011). The suicidal mind and brain: A review of neuropsychological and neuroimaging studies. *The World Journal of Biological Psychiatry, 12,* 319–39.

O'Connor, R. C. & Nock, M. (2014). The psychology of suicidal behaviour. *Lancet Psychiatry, 1,* 73–85.

Williams, J. M. G. (2014). *Cry of pain: Understanding suicide and the suicidal mind.* London: Piatkus.

Van Orden, K. A., Witte, T. K., Cukrowicz, K. C., Braithwaite, S. R., Selby, E. A. & Joiner, T. E. (2010). The interpersonal theory of suicide. *Psychological Review, 117,* 575–600.

CHAPTER THREE

The Dark Side of the Brain

Neuroscience Approaches to Suicidal Behavior

Learning Objectives

- Do animals show suicidal behavior?
- What is a psychological autopsy?
- Is our genetic make-up a stable characteristic, or can it change?
- How could our diet influence the occurrence of suicide?
- Is suicide more common during the winter months?
- How can we visualize functions of the brain that may make people suicidal?

Introduction

The essence of the neurobiology of suicidal behavior is summarized in Textbox 3.1.

Neuroscience approaches to the study and understanding of suicidal behavior may differ somewhat from those targeting other behaviors. As suicide appears to be a uniquely human behavior, there is a lack of animal models: Despite anecdotal reports in the literature and in movies, animals do not kill themselves, although they do show self-injurious behaviors. Much information is available from postmortem studies of brain tissue, in which brain characteristics of suicides are compared with those of individuals who died from other causes. Physical autopsies as postmortem studies are sometimes accompanied by psychological autopsies, which are standardized interviews with individuals who were in close contact with the deceased, covering a wide range of health- and personality-related issues. More recently, a wealth of information has become available from neuroimaging and genetic studies showing how individuals may become vulnerable to adverse environmental influences, which thus may induce suicidal thoughts and wishes.

3.1 Animal Models of Suicidal Behavior and Its Risk Factors

Animal models are used in neurobiological research to investigate the etiology, the course, and the potential treatment of an illness or

---

Textbox 3.1 The Essence of the Neurobiology of Suicidal behavior

1. A specific vulnerability to suicidal behavior is mediated by an underlying predisposition or diathesis.
2. This underlying predisposition or diathesis interacts with environmental stressors throughout the lifespan.
3. This interaction then modifies the structure and/or function of neural circuitry.
4. This results in rendering an individual more likely to engage in a suicidal act.

---

behavior. However, despite the intensive study of thousands of animal species, suicide as such has not been identified in nonhuman species (Preti, 2011). Components of stress–diathesis models, such as impulsivity and aggression (see Chapter 2), and neurobiological risk factors for suicidal behavior, such as disturbed stress-response or serotonergic neurotransmission systems (see Chapter 4), can be modeled and studied in animals. The reproduction of the role of motivational and volitional issues in suicidal behavior in animal models, however, is a huge challenge. Concerning motivation, three mechanisms have been suggested for research, with relevance for the study of suicidal behavior: unfavorable spreading due to demographic pressures or human intrusion, altruistic sacrifice to protect the group, and grief over loss of a beloved owner (Bourgeois, 1987). But the extent to which animals may be capable of willing and planning their own death to stop unbearable suffering is another issue.

As early as 1897, the French sociologist Emile Durkheim argued that contemporary knowledge of the animal mind does not really attribute to them an understanding anticipatory of their death or of the means to accomplish it. He noted that instances where animals seemingly kill themselves may be quite differently explained. For example, if the irritated scorpion pierces itself with its stinger (which is not at all certain), it is probably from an automatic, unreflecting reaction. The motive energy caused by his irritation is discharged by chance and at random; the creature happens to become its victim, though it cannot be said to have had a preconception of the result of its action (Durkheim, 1897). Similarly, Durkheim stated that if dogs starved to death after the loss of their masters, "it is because the sadness into which they are thrown has automatically caused lack of hunger; death has resulted, but without having been foreseen." Since neither the scorpion nor the dog used self-injury or fasting "as a means to a known effect," he concluded, "the special characteristics of suicide are lacking."

Self-destructive, self-endangering, and self-harming behaviors do exist in animals (Preti, 2011). Animals subject to sudden confinement and pets experiencing separation from their owners may show self-destructive behaviors. Stressful situations such as crowding, isolation, separation, and confinement – especially when perceived as uncontrollable – can result in self-endangering behaviors in animals. Monkeys reared in isolation showed a higher risk of self-endangering behavior in adulthood, a finding that parallels the impact of childhood abuse or neglect on the risk of suicide in humans. But it remains doubtful whether self-endangering behaviors in animals really resemble self-harming behavior in humans, or whether they are extreme attempts to escape from confinement only.

The impairing effects caused by internal parasites are thought to stimulate self-endangering behavior in some species of insects – such as butterfly species – and mammals – such as the fatal "suicidal" attraction to the feline shown by rodents parasitized by *Toxoplasma gondii*. (See also Chapter 1.) There is no evidence, however, that parasite-induced behaviors are in any way comparable to the psychopathology leading to suicide in humans (Preti, 2011). Thus, animal models of suicide do not exist, but many correlates of suicidal behavior as described in the previous chapter have been identified in animals. These include early life adversity (ELA), impulsive aggression, hopelessness, and the cry of pain.

Maternal separation in rodents, as an analog of human disrupted parenting, acutely increases stress hormones in the blood, the typical markers of stress. However, maternal deprivation also produces long-lasting effects: Converging evidence shows that the activity of the main inhibitory neurotransmitters in the brain is diminished in rats exposed to maternal deprivation (Preti, 2011). Monkeys separated from the mother during development exhibited depressive-like symptoms in later separation. Maternally deprived monkeys reared with inanimate surrogates of the mother showed less pronounced symptoms in later separation. Increased self-administration of alcohol and self-endangering behavior were reported in maternally deprived monkeys, providing evidence of face and predictive validity of this model with respect to known correlates of major depression, i.e., increased comorbidity with alcohol abuse and increased risk of self-harming behavior (Preti, 2011).

In nonhuman primates, a low-cholesterol diet results in increased impulsive-aggressive behavior. In humans, clinical and epidemiological studies report a modest but consistent link between low cholesterol levels and suicidal behavior (see Chapter 4). It is still unresolved whether low cholesterol in humans is a mere marker of affective disorders, resulting from poor diet, or whether it has an independent role in suicidal behavior. Cholesterol is necessary to form new synapses in the brain; thus a deficient supply of cholesterol may result in impaired synaptic plasticity, with long-term cognitive and behavioral consequences (Preti, 2011).

As described in the previous chapters, hopelessness is a crucial ingredient of the lethal cocktail of depressive symptoms that may lead to suicidal behavior. As hopelessness cannot be formally operationalized in animals, current animal models of hopelessness leading to suicide rest on the learned helplessness paradigm (Seligman, 1972). In the development of helplessness, electrified foot shock is used as an aversive stimulus. After a series of inescapable shock trials, a subgroup of animals ceases any attempt to escape: when retested after some delay, some of them try to escape again; others indefinitely display a despair-like behavior, failing to escape. The latter animals are considered to have learned helplessness as a permanent response to the aversive shock. Helplessness in this context is the acquisition of the belief that there is no relation between a given behavior and the outcome of that behavior: Essentially, animals would have learned that they have no control of the situation. Learned helplessness is considered an analog of hopelessness in humans (Krishnan & Nestler, 2008). Even though the learned helplessness paradigm has good face validity (the extent to which it is subjectively viewed as covering the hopelessness it purports to measure), its ecological validity (the correspondence with real hopelessness in humans) is poor. Moreover, the model is an approximation of stress-related depression, but generally animals that have developed learned helplessness do not show any inclination to harm themselves. Therefore, this model cannot be used to infer correlates of human suicidal behavior (Preti, 2011). However, the validity of learned helplessness may increase when combined with other characteristics, such as in the "arrested flight model."

Mark Williams's "cry of pain" model was presented in Chapter 2 as a cognitive psychological example of stress–diathesis models of suicidal behavior. Perceived defeat, no rescue, and no escape are its three main components (Williams, 2005). Williams has clearly described that the origins of his "cry of pain" model can be found in animal models of entrapment developed by Gilbert (Gilbert & Allan, 1998). In this entrapment model, the combination of defeat (a stressful event) and entrapment (no escape from the situation) can lead to severe "helplessness" in animals. In this model, defeat is conceived as a sense of failed social struggle and loss, resulting in reduced social rank. Defeat can be related to interpersonal conflict and to the perception of failure in attaining social and material resources. Entrapment refers to the awareness that all escape routes are blocked, leading to the perceived inability to escape from the current situation. In Williams's view, suicidal behavior is reactive to stressful situations when the perception of defeat is associated with the awareness of no escape and no rescue. This model mimics the role of helplessness ("no rescue") and hopelessness ("no escape") in human suicidal behavior, with an important role for stress. However, this stress induced by social defeat does not lead to self-inflicted death in animals.

3.2 Psychological Autopsy Approaches

The psychological autopsy is a commonly used method to study the causes and circumstances of suicides. The procedure involves investigating a person's death by reconstructing what the person thought, felt, and did before death, based on information gathered from personal documents, police reports, medical and coroner's records, and face-to-face interviews with families, friends, and others who had contact with the person before death (Hawton et al., 1998). Standardized instruments that can generate psychiatric diagnoses and identify developmental or environmental risk and protective factors that may have been associated with the suicide are frequently added, particularly in research.

Information is usually obtained from multiple sources, including those closest to the deceased (Chachamovich et al., 2013). For personal and developmental history, a parent or a partner is usually the most appropriate informant, when available. In the case of young suicides, a sibling or a close friend may also be important to provide information about aspects of the individual's life that parents may have been unaware of, such as drug use or interpersonal problems. Obtaining information from health service providers can offer details about medical treatments, use of medications, and other mental and physical problems that may not be adequately remembered by other informants. Interviewing more than one informant independently is recommended. Similarly, interviewing informants who are related to the individual in different ways may allow access to complementary information. The timing of the interview is also important; the informant should not be approached too soon after the death (to avoid triggering an intense emotional reaction), but not too late either (to avoid recall bias). The interviews used in psychological autopsies are usually semi-structured, combining open-ended questions with standardized instruments. Open-ended questions are helpful to collect information about the trajectory of life events, childhood development, and parent–child relationships. Standardized instruments can gather information about impulsive aggression and other personality traits. The selection of instruments for psychological autopsy interviews is dependent on the objectives of each study, but assessments of psychiatric disorders and personality disorders/traits are commonly included.

It is usually desirable to include controls, and selection of the most appropriate control group must be determined by the hypotheses of the study. If social influences on suicide are the main study focus, it may be necessary to match the control group for the presence of psychiatric disorder. Sometimes a study will have more than one focus of attention and this may necessitate the use of two control groups. For example, a study that aims, first, at identifying the extent to which suicide is associated with psychiatric disorder and, second, at identifying social and other risk factors in depressed individuals may require both an unselected control group and one matched with a subgroup of the suicides for presence of depressive disorder (Hawton et al., 1998). Another important consideration is whether living or dead controls should be used. For example, investigation of risk factors associated with suicide within a specific diagnostic group will require use of living controls, whereas dead controls will be necessary for a study of the needs of relatives bereaved by suicide. It should be noted that using informants for controls may have negative consequences for families, particularly when interviews may highlight current problems (Hawton et al., 1998).

The psychological autopsy method was originally developed by Erwin Shneidman (1981) as a tool to determine the cause of a suspicious death (i.e., to differentiate suicides from killings) in forensic examinations. Soon after its introduction, it was used in scientific investigations by researchers interested in the causes and circumstances of suicide. Dozens of psychological autopsy studies have been conducted since then. For example, more than 30 psychological autopsies have been carried out in Asian countries (Khan et al., 2016). In addition, psychological autopsy studies have shed light on the causes and circumstances of suicide in special populations such as doctors and nurses (Hawton et al., 2002, 2004), the Inuit (Chachamovich et al., 2013) and rural Chinese youngsters (Zhang et al., 2010). Systematic reviews and meta-analyses are available (Cavanagh et al., 2003; Arsenault-Lapierre et al., 2004,

Yoshimasu et al., 2008). In the United States, psychological autopsies have been accepted into evidence in legal proceedings and can play a critical role in the outcome of both civil and criminal litigation.

Nevertheless, the use of psychological autopsy approaches to the study of suicide may present considerable methodological problems (Hawton et al., 1998; Pouliot & De Leo, 2006). Such problems may include research design, identification of subjects, sources of information and issues concerned with approaching relatives and other informants, choice and recruitment of controls, the difficulties of conducting psychological autopsy interviews with relatives, problems for interviewers, the selection of appropriate measures to obtain information, and achieving valid and reasonably reliable conclusions from diverse information sources.

Several studies have investigated the reliability and validity of psychological autopsy findings. Kelly and Mann (1996) provided evidence of the reliability of the psychological autopsy as a method of determining psychiatric diagnosis by comparing psychological autopsy-generated diagnoses in suicides and nonsuicides with chart diagnoses generated by clinicians who had treated the subjects prior to death. Comparison of research diagnoses with clinician antemortem diagnoses indicates good reliability. There appears to be very good agreement between proxy-based data and data from individuals themselves regarding suicide attempts and life events (Conner et al., 2001). Schneider and colleagues (2004) showed very good reliability of diagnoses based on information from living controls and informants. Nevertheless, there is a great need for standardization of the psychological autopsy approach to the study of suicide (Pouliot & De Leo, 2006; Snider et al., 2006).

3.3 Physical Autopsy

Postmortem brain samples obtained from suicides and controls offer enormous opportunities to study molecular mechanisms and genomic processes associated with suicide (Pandey & Dwivedi, 2010; Almeida & Turecki, 2016). Early studies of molecular mechanisms used cells, such as platelets and lymphocytes, or spinal cord fluid (see later discussion) and always raised the question of whether such abnormalities reflect similar changes in the brain or have any relevance to the neurobiology of suicide. The availability of appropriate brain samples from well-established brain collection programs not only has addressed these issues, but also has resulted in many neurobiological studies related to suicide and established the significance of these abnormalities in the brain.

However, quite a few methodological issues are at stake in postmortem brain studies. To obtain useful information from such studies, it is important that the quality of the postmortem brain samples conform to certain standards. For example, one of the main problems in studies of postmortem brain samples is the prolonged postmortem interval. Recent postmortem brain collection programs have minimized this limitation, and postmortem tissue, in most cases, is obtained at relatively shorter intervals, not exceeding 24 hours. An important requisite for postmortem brain studies is careful neuropathological examination for abnormalities. It is important to obtain good toxicological screening of postmortem samples by determining medications either in the postmortem samples themselves or in the blood of the subjects. Finally, the quality of postmortem brain samples should be adequate for determining levels of protein and gene expression (via messenger RNA [mRNA]). The quality of tissue is commonly examined by determining the pH of the samples and the RNA integrity number.

Quite a few studies have combined physical and psychological autopsy approaches to study associations between behavioral and neurobiological characteristics. For example, Sequeira and colleagues (2009) looked at the expression of genes in 17 cortical and subcortical brain regions from suicides with and without major depression and controls diagnosed by means of psychological autopsies.

Postmortem studies are essential for the direct investigation of molecular and (epi-)genetic brain correlates of suicide (Almeida & Turecki, 2016).

3.4 Genetics

Given the substantial heritability of suicidal behaviors, apparently independent of associated psychopathology, many genetic studies have been performed in the past decades, using different methodologies.

Genes contain the recipes for proteins. When a gene is actively signaling a cell to make a certain protein, that gene is said to be expressed. There are three major milestones in gene expression: transcription of DNA to another molecule called RNA, translation to an amino acid chain, and protein folding with modification.

Proteins are the end-products of gene expression, and their roles include helping regulate transcription, translation, and protein folding by acting as enzymes. For simplicity, gene expression can be viewed as a

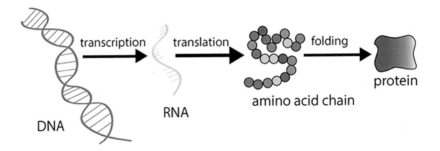

Figure 3.1 Gene expression: from DNA to proteins (Carmichael, 2014). See color plate 4.

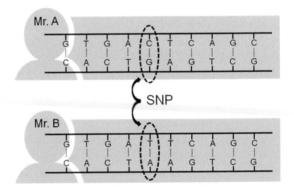

Figure 3.2 Single nucleotide polymorphism (SNP).
© 2011 Hashiyada M. Published in DNA Biometrix under CC BY-NC-SA 3.0 license. Available from: http://dx.doi.org/10.5772/18139.

linear process that begins with DNA and ends with protein. (See Figure 3.1.) However, gene expression is part of an enormous and incredibly complex system of feedback loops: Gene expression produces proteins, which in turn regulate gene expression.

Genetic association studies look at a correlation between suicidal behavior and genetic variation to identify candidate genes or genome regions that contribute to its occurrence. A higher frequency of a single-nucleotide polymorphism (SNP, pronounced "snip"; see Figure 3.2) allele or genotype in a series of individuals with a history of suicidal behavior can be interpreted as meaning that the studied variant increases the risk.

SNPs are a single nucleotide change in an area of an organism's DNA that is different in more than 1% of the population. SNPs occur in the DNA in 1 out of every 300 nucleotides. In the human genome, this means that there are at least 1 million SNPs in the human's 3-million-nucleotide genome. SNPs are the most widely tested markers in association studies (and this term will be used throughout), but microsatellite markers, insertion/deletions, variable-number tandem repeats (VNTRs), and copy-number variants (CNVs) are also used.

Genetic association studies include (1) case–control studies, (2) family-based association studies, and (3) genome-wide association studies (GWAS). Genetic association studies have investigated approximately 50 candidate genes. Results of these association studies will be discussed in Chapter 4, but in general have been rather disappointing. Possible reasons include heterogeneous definitions of studied suicidal behaviors, difficulties in controlling for confounding factors (such as psychiatric diseases), technological limits, and interactions between genes and between genes and environmental characteristics (Brezo et al., 2008; Mirkovic et al., 2016).

Given the likelihood of the involvement of a multitude of genes (the so-called polygenic mode of inheritance), more recent studies employ functional genomic methodologies such as microarray technologies for looking at expression of thousands of genes simultaneously, and genome-wide arrays for hundreds of thousands of SNPs. DNA microarrays are also known as DNA chips, and they are used to measure the expression of large numbers of genes simultaneously or to genotype multiple regions of a genome. The method used by Affymetrix has been the most commonly used technology in expression studies of suicidal behavior. Currently available Affymetrix chips for expression analysis allow for monitoring of more than 45,000 transcripts, which represent most of the human genome. In microarray studies, total RNA is isolated from selected postmortem brain tissue using standard RNA extraction methods and then purified. Published human postmortem studies have primarily used frozen tissue. RNA quality control is an essential part of microarray expression studies in general, but in the context of postmortem brain studies, this is a particularly important step: A number of variables may influence RNA quality and increase between-sample variability, including demographic factors, cause and circumstances of death, and post-autopsy tissue handling. If performed well, microarray studies give a snapshot of brain gene activity prior to death. Notable advantages include the non-hypothesis-directed nature of the design, the high-throughput capabilities of the approach, and the more direct connection to neurobiological changes than pure genetic approaches. Microarray studies may also be useful in elucidating relevant gene–gene interactions.

Linkage studies are based on the finding that alleles (variant forms of genes) that are closer together on a chromosome tend to be inherited together. The first linkage efforts used families ascertained through psychiatric diseases with comorbid suicidal behaviors, and resulted in the identification of loci for suicide risk, none of which contained known candidate genes. Similar to the case–control approach in candidate gene studies, samples used in linkage studies are commonly heterogeneous. Disentangling susceptibility genes for suicide risk from those for other psychiatric manifestations is challenging and raises quite a few crucially important questions: Are there suicide-specific vulnerability genes, and are vulnerability genes or alleles different across comorbid psychiatric disorders? Results of genetic studies of suicidal behavior will be discussed in detail in Chapter 4.

The term "epigenetics" refers to the study of the epigenome, the chemical and physical modifications of the DNA molecule that functionally regulate the genes of an organism. They do so by altering the capacity of a gene to be activated and produce the messenger RNA (mRNA) it encodes (Turecki, 2014a). mRNA is a large family of molecules that convey genetic information from the DNA to the ribosome. The ribosome is a complex molecular machine that serves as the site of protein production: It links amino acids together in the order specified by mRNA.

Epigenetic regulation of gene function allows for the adaptation of the genome to the needs of the organism ("genomic plasticity"). It has long been clear that epigenetic processes occur as a result of physical and chemical environmental signals. However, only recently has it been revealed that the social environment also triggers epigenetic responses. The epigenome thus is an interface through which the environment can influence genetic processes and, as a result, regulate behavior at least partially in response to environmental needs (Turecki, 2014a).

Figure 3.3 summarizes the nature and effects of epigenetic molecular changes, which will be discussed in detail in Chapter 4, and indicates how they relate a distal risk factor such as early life adversity (ELA) with suicidal behavior many years later. Stable epigenetic factors are likely to act distally, influencing the diathesis, whereas dynamic epigenetic factors and proteomic changes are likely to underlie psychopathological states that act more proximally, precipitating suicidal behavior. To date, however, most of the research investigating epigenetic factors in suicidal behaviors has focused on presumably stable epigenetic marks (e.g., DNA methylation) that are thought to act distally (Turecki, 2014b). Epigenetic marks associate with genomic responses to environmental stimuli, and because suicidal behaviors are strongly associated with histories of ELA (such as childhood physical or sexual abuse or parental

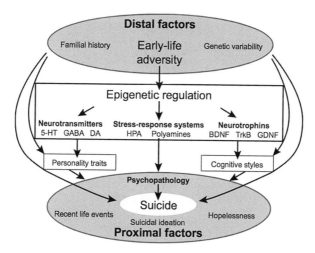

Figure 3.3 Proposed model of epigenetic factors (Reprinted from *American Journal of Preventive Medicine*, 47(3), Turecki G., Epigenetics and suicidal behavior research pathways, S144–151, copyright (2014), with permission from Elsevier).

neglect), most of the initial investigations of epigenetic factors associated with suicidal behaviors have focused on individuals with histories of ELA. Epigenetic effects on the major molecular mechanisms involved in the occurrence of suicidal behaviors will be discussed in detail in Chapter 4.

The involvement of genetic risk factors in suicidal behaviors is supported by studies in the domain of genetic epidemiology, including family, twin, and adoption studies.

3.5 Epidemiology

3.5.1 Genetic Epidemiology

Family-based studies clearly indicate a two to ten times increased risk for suicidal behaviors as compared with controls, independent of psychiatric history. Familial predisposition to suicidal behaviors was also shown in a large-scale, population-based Swedish study focusing on individuals hospitalized for suicide attempts between 1968 and 1980. Investigators reported that suicide attempts or suicides in parents and suicide attempts in siblings increased the risk for proband suicide attempts between two and three times (Mittendorfer-Rutz et al., 2007). Overall, family studies have indicated that heritability may be lowest for suicidal ideation, somewhat higher for suicide attempts, and highest for fatal suicidal behavior (Brezo et al., 2008). Surname studies of suicide provide additional evidence for genetic contributions to suicide risk. Surnames carry information about genetic relatedness or distance and, in patrilineal surname systems, are a close substitute for Y-chromosome markers and haplotypes (groups of genes that are inherited together from a single parent), since surname transmission is similar to the transmission of the non-recombining part of the Y chromosome. In Austria it was shown that surname region accounted for a highly significant and substantial (38%) portion of the variance in district-level suicide rates (Voracek & Sonneck, 2007).

Unlike family-based designs, twin studies allow for a better control of the influences of the shared environment. Pooling published twin studies more than 10 years ago demonstrated a 175 times higher relative risk among monozygotic twins (MZTs) than dizygotic twins (DZTs) (Baldessarini & Hennen, 2004). However, the authors urged caution in interpreting these results, given the low prevalence of suicidal behaviors in twins and lack of control of postnatal environmental influences. Specifically regarding suicidal ideation, another twin study found only a statistical trend for its concordance in MZTs when compared with DZTs (Cho et al., 2006). The results of co-twin studies rule out exclusively psychosocially based explanations of this pattern. A meta-analysis of all register-based studies and all case reports aggregated shows, however, that concordance for completed suicide is significantly more frequent among monozygotic than dizygotic twin pairs (Voracek & Loible, 2007).

Adoption studies suggest a 7 to 13 times higher risk for suicidality among biological relatives of adoptees than among adopted relatives, and stronger heritability for suicides than attempts (Wender et al., 1986). These estimates must be considered in the light of several limitations, including the low number of adoption studies, poor control of psychiatric confounders, lack of more recent adoption data, and shortage of data from other countries.

Population-based epidemiological studies demonstrate a significant contribution of additive genetic factors (heritability estimates: 30%–55%) to the broader manifestation of suicidal behavior (suicide thoughts, plans, and attempts) that largely overlaps for different types of suicidal behavior and is largely independent of the inheritance of psychiatric disorders. Non-shared environmental effects (personal experiences) also contribute substantially to the risk of suicidal behavior, whereas effects of shared environment (family) do not (Voracek & Loible, 2007).

On a map of Europe, the countries with relatively higher suicide rates form a so-called J-curve, which starts in Finland and extends down to

Slovenia. This maps onto the second principal component identified for European gene distribution, representing the ancestral adaptation to cold climates and the Uralic language dispersion. It has been suggested that people living within the J-curve share genes which may not tolerate excessive amounts of alcohol, the combination of which is more likely to end in suicidal behavior (Marusic, 2005).

3.5.2 Environmental Influences

Potential geographical and seasonal effects on neurobiological underpinnings of suicide have been reported in epidemiological studies using divergent approaches. These include, e.g., dietary characteristics, altitude, and meteorological and chemical factors. Findings will be discussed here in some detail because of their relevance for our understanding of the neurobiology of suicidal behavior.

Concerning dietary characteristics, recent epidemiological studies suggest an association between the depletion of fatty acids and suicide. A systematic review shows that mood-disordered individuals may have a depletion of omega-3 PUFAs compared with control groups that contribute to suicidal thoughts and behavior in some cases. However, depletion of omega-3 PUFAs appears not to be detectable in all patients who engage in suicidal behavior. A limited contribution to suicide prevention can therefore be expected from increasing PUFA intake (Pompili et al., 2016). A large population study in Japan using dietary questionnaires did not find a link between n-3 PUFA intake and fish consumption, on the one hand, and suicide, on the other hand (Poudel-Tandukar et al., 2011). Similarly, a large cohort study in the United States did not find a suicide risk–lowering effect of the intake of n-3 PUFAs or fish (Tsai et al., 2014). A substantial amount of data from divergent areas in the world, from Texas to Japan, consistently shows that higher levels of lithium in drinking water are associated with a reduced risk of suicide in the general population. It is suggested that low but long-lasting lithium exposure can contribute to suicide prevention via enhancing neurotrophic mechanisms, neuroprotective factors, and/or neurogenesis. (For an overview of epidemiological findings and their interpretations, see Vita et al., 2015.) Implications for suicide prevention will be discussed in detail in Chapter 10.

There is a positive correlation between altitude and suicide rates. For example, among 2,584 US counties, those at higher altitude have higher rates than those at lower altitude, after controlling for age, gender, race, household income, and population density (Brenner et al., 2011).

Decreased oxygen saturation has been suggested as the link between altitude and suicide (Haws et al., 2009). Lithium levels in water may also provide a link, but study results are not equivocal. In Austria, lithium effects on suicide mortality are moderated by altitude, with lower levels of lithium in drinking water and higher suicide rates at higher altitudes (Helbich et al., 2013). However, in the United States, lithium levels in groundwater appear to increase with altitude (Huber et al., 2014).

Seasonal variation in suicide rates is reported in many studies, indicating that suicide rates peak in the spring and early summer and dip during the winter months in both the Northern and Southern Hemispheres. Various climate factors appear to be related to seasonal variations, including temperature, hours of sunshine, solar radiation, and precipitation. A recent Austrian study demonstrated that the number of suicides correlates positively with hours of daily sunshine for the day of suicide and up to 10 days prior to suicide, and negatively with daily hours of sunshine for the 14 to 60 days prior to suicide, independent of season (Vyssoki et al., 2014). It has been suggested that the increase in temperature might be particularly relevant to explain such findings (Tsai, 2015). In addition, it appears that the association between sunshine and suicide is enhanced among individuals taking serotonergic antidepressants, indicating the involvement of the serotonergic neurotransmission system (Makris et al., 2016).

Solar radiation has been proposed to be a more powerful factor, as compared with other climate variables, affecting the suicide rate. This may be important because light plays a major role in the regulation of circadian rhythms, which are closely related to the aggravation of mood disorders. The influence of solar radiation on the seasonality of the suicide rate might be explained by many factors (Jee et al., 2017). Exposure to sunlight is assumed to trigger suicide risk via several hormones related to emotional regulation, including serotonin, melatonin, cortisol, and L-tryptophan. The acute and rapid change in serotonergic function caused by exposure to sunlight might explain the seasonality of suicide based on effects similar to those observed with antidepressants. Biochemical studies have indicated that there are higher concentrations of serotonin during the spring and summer than during the fall and winter. Moreover, several neuroimaging studies have reported seasonal fluctuations in cerebral serotonin transporter (5-HTT) binding, lowest in the summer and highest in winter in healthy subjects and patients with mood disorders.

Second, changes in the internal circadian rhythm needed to adapt to variations in sunlight exposure due to seasonal changes might also trigger suicide risk in subjects with circadian rhythm vulnerability, such as those with mood disorders. Other studies have reported that affective disorders and female suicide have significant seasonal variations, suggesting effects of increased luminance and stimulation of the pineal gland. Light is a central and powerful modulator of circadian rhythms and its effects. When subjects with circadian rhythm vulnerability are exposed to sunlight, especially during the seasonal transition period, they might easily succumb to emotionally unstable states, which may then lead to suicide attempts (Jee et al., 2017).

Other studies suggest a role of chemical factors, e.g., air pollution. Acute air pollution exposure (particularly nitrogen dioxide and fine particulate matter) in Utah is associated with an increased suicide risk (Baklan et al., 2015). Findings in Taiwan predict a classical seasonal pattern of an increased number of suicides in early summer by increased air particulates and decreased barometric pressure, in which the latter is in accordance with higher temperatures. Gaseous air pollutants such as ozone increase the risk of suicide at longer time scales (Yang et al., 2011). Ambient air pollution is also associated with increased suicide risk in Asian countries such as China and Japan (Lin et al., 2016; Sheng et al., 2016). Weather may mediate the effects of air pollution on suicide rates, not only via temperature but also via rainfall. Suicide rates may decrease, but nonfatal suicidal behavior appears to be more common on rainy days (Barker et al., 1994).

3.6 Peripheral Biomarkers

A wide range of body fluids can be studied in the quest for peripheral biomarkers, which are objectively measured characteristics outside the brain as indicators of suicide risk. Biomarkers may serve as neurobiological substrates for the prediction and treatment of suicide risk, as we will see in Chapter 10. These fluids include blood (serum, lymphocytes, platelets, red blood cells), cerebrospinal fluid (cerebrospinal fluid), saliva, and urine.

3.6.1 Blood

The usefulness of lymphocyte white blood cells to explore the neurobiology of suicide is evident concerning (1) the role they play in immune response (cytokine production) alterations and (2) their role in HPA axis dysfunction and neuroendocrine regulation (Pandey &

Dwivedi, 2012). Lymphocytes may also be important in studying gene expression, as many of the genes that are potentially involved in suicidal behaviors are also expressed in lymphocytes, and several of these genes have similar characteristics in both brain and lymphocytes. Platelets have been used for studies of neurotransmitter functions, including monoamine oxidase, adrenergic receptors, 5-HT2A receptors, and brain-derived neurotrophic factor (BDNF). Although these studies provide important information, the significance of these studies and of the use of platelets as models of brain function is less clear. Blood platelets exhibit various components that are similar to those in the brain neurotransmitter system – for example, intracellular levels for biogenic amines, metabolizing enzymes such as monoamine oxidase, and several other membrane receptors. However, the organization of neurotransmission systems is much more complex in the brain including their mutual modulation. One of the most compelling similarities between the receptors, especially the 5-HT receptors, and 5-HT uptake is the observation that the proteins for the human platelet serotonin uptake site and the brain serotonin transporter are identical in structure and are encoded by the same single-copy gene. Platelets have the potential to be very useful for the study of suicidal behaviors and may possibly result in diagnostic and prognostic biomarkers.

Neuroendocrine studies, often called "the window to the brain," provide another useful method for studying central serotonergic function using peripheral sources. The procedure involves the administration of serotonergic probes, such as serotonin (5-HT) precursors like 5-hydroxytryptophan, or 5-HT agonists/antagonists. A 5-HT agonist/antagonist, such as mCPP, buspirone, or ipsapirone, stimulates 5-HT receptor subtypes. Certain hormones such as prolactin, adrenocorticotropic hormone (ACTH), or cortisol that are released as a result of 5-HT acting on the serotonergic system can then be measured (Pandey & Dwivedi, 2012). The dexamethasone-suppression test (DST) is used to assess adrenal gland function by measuring how cortisol levels change in response to the intake of dexamethasone. A normal result is a decrease in cortisol levels on administration of dexamethasone. The DST was historically used for the diagnosis of depression, but specificity and sensitivity are limited to such an extent that the test is no longer used in a clinical context. However, the test is still used in neurobiological studies as a measure of the sensitivity of the stress-response system (the HPA axis), which is often dysregulated in suicidal individuals (see Chapter 4).

3.6.2 Cerebrospinal Fluid

Studies of the 5-HT metabolite 5-HIAA in the spinal cord or cerebro-spinal fluid (CSF) were the first to demonstrate the association between deficiencies in the 5-HT system and suicidal behaviors (Åsberg et al., 1976). Since then, numerous studies have investigated CSF correlates of suicidal behaviors including, among others, amines, hormones, inflammatory markers, and stress-related markers. Relevant findings will be discussed in Chapter 4. When interpreting findings, it should be taken into account that the relationship of levels 5-HIAA in CSF and in the brain is not completely clear, and that such levels can be influenced by many factors including gender, age, treatment, and dietary characteristics. For example, long-term use of antidepressants tends to increase CSF 5-HIAA (Oquendo et al., 2014b).

3.6.3 Saliva and Buccal Swabs

Saliva samples are commonly used in neurobiological studies of suicidal behavior, e.g., in genetic and neuroendocrine investigations. A buccal swab, also known as buccal smear, is a way to collect DNA from the cells on the inside of a person's cheek. Buccal swabs are a relatively non-invasive way to collect DNA samples for genetic studies.

3.7 Brain Imaging

Neuroimaging provides a great opportunity to study in vivo the links between genetic, environmental, neurobiological, and neuropsychological findings regarding suicidal behaviors. Several brain imaging techniques are available to study (1) structural characteristics, (2) functional characteristics, and (3) levels of biochemical compounds in the brain.

3.7.1 Structural Brain Imaging

Structural brain imaging studies focus on gray matter, which consists of neuronal cell bodies, neuropil (dendrites and axons), and glial cells (astroglia and oligodendrocytes). These glial cells provide nutrients and energy to neurons. They help transport glucose into the brain, clean the brain of excess chemicals, and may even affect the intensity of the neurons' communications. Because these cells are not surrounded by white myelin, they take on the natural grayish color of the neurons and glial cells (see Figure 3.4).

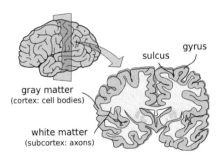

Figure 3.4 Gray and white matter in the brain (Reprinted by permission from Macmillan Publishers Ltd: *Science Reports*, art nr 5644, Budday et al., A mechanical model predicts morphological abnormalities in the developing human brain, copyright 2014). See color plate 5.

White matter is a second target of structural brain imaging. It is found in the deeper part of the brain below the cortex and contains nerve fibers (axons), which are extensions of nerve cells (neurons). Many nerve fibers are surrounded by a type of sheath or covering, called myelin. Myelin gives the white matter its color. It also protects the nerve fibers from injury and improves the speed and transmission of electrical nerve signals.

Structural changes in the brain are studied using magnetic resonance imaging (MRI) and diffusion tensor imaging (DTI). MRI can be used to create detailed images of the brain. The MRI technique uses a very powerful magnet to align the nuclei of atoms inside the brain, and a variable magnetic field causes the atoms to resonate, a phenomenon called nuclear magnetic resonance. The nuclei produce their own rotating magnetic fields that a scanner detects and uses to create an image. DTI is an MRI-based neuroimaging technique, which makes it possible to visualize the location, orientation, and anisotropy of the brain's white matter tracts. DTI measures mean diffusivity (MD), fractional anisotropy (FA), radial diffusivity (Dr), and axial diffusivity (Da). In particular, FA is highly sensitive to microstructural changes by reflecting the directional coherence of diffusion within white matter bundles, their architecture, or structural integrity, but not very specific to the type of changes (e.g., radial or axial). To maximize the specificity, studies commonly use multiple diffusion tensor measures (e.g., MD and FA, or Da and Dr) to better characterize the tissue microstructure. Thus, white matter pathology (due to ischemia, myelination problems, axonal damage, inflammation, or edema) can be visualized.

Magnetic transfer imaging (MTI) is a relatively new and highly sensitive technique to visualize changes in macromolecular structural integrity of brain tissue in association with suicidal behavior, even when conventional MRI is negative (Chen et al., 2015). MTI creates a contrast between tissues by exploiting the phenomenon of magnetization exchange between the spins of free water and water bound to macromolecules. The efficiency of these exchange phenomena is measured by the magnetization transfer ratio (MTR), which depends on both the amount and states of macromolecules. Lower MTR in gray matter is believed to be associated with abnormalities of cell membrane proteins and phospholipids. Furthermore, Wallerian degeneration triggered by distant axonal damage and microscopic lesions has also been implicated as a mechanism underlying cortical MTR reductions. MTI can thus demonstrate subtle biophysical alterations with macromolecular concentration changes (Chen et al., 2015).

3.7.2 Functional Brain Imaging

Functional brain imaging techniques include functional MRI (fMRI), single photon emission computed tomography (SPECT), and positron emission tomography (PET). fMRI is a technique for measuring brain activity by detecting the changes in blood flow in the brain in response to neural activity, which creates what is referred to as a blood-oxygen-level dependent (BOLD) signal that can be measured using fMRI. When a brain area is more active, it consumes more oxygen, and to meet this increased demand, blood flow increases to the active area. fMRI can thus be used to produce activation maps showing which parts of the brain are involved in a psychological process. In contrast, resting state fMRI (rsfMRI) can be used to evaluate regional interactions that occur when a subject is not performing an explicit task. Because brain activity is present even in the absence of an externally prompted task, any brain region will have spontaneous fluctuations in BOLD signal. The resting state approach is useful to explore the brain's functional organization and to examine if it is altered in association with (risk factors for) suicidal behavior.

SPECT is an imaging technique using gamma rays that is based on conventional nuclear medicine imaging and tomographic reconstruction methods. The images reflect functional information about the spatial concentration of radiopharmaceuticals. The technique requires injection of a gamma-emitting radioisotope into the bloodstream of the study participant. The marker radioisotope is attached to a specific ligand to create a radioligand, whose properties bind it to certain types of tissues. When the radioligand binds to, e.g., specific receptors in the brain, the ligand concentration can be measured by a gamma camera. SPECT studies have been used successfully to study brain correlates of clinical and neuropsychological correlates of suicidal behavior, as will be discussed in Chapter 6.

Similarly, a PET scanner detects radioactive material that is injected to create an image. Commonly used radioactively labeled material includes oxygen, fluorine, carbon, and nitrogen. When this material gets into the bloodstream, it goes to areas of the brain that use it. So, oxygen and glucose accumulate in brain areas that are metabolically active. When the radioactive material breaks down, it gives off a neutron and a positron. When a positron hits an electron, both are destroyed and two gamma rays are released. Gamma ray detectors record the brain area where the gamma rays are emitted. This method provides scientists with an image of the function of the brain. Regarding suicidal behavior, PET scans have been instrumental in visualizing disturbances in the serotonergic neurotransmission system (see Chapter 6). Moreover, PET has been used to study the effects of specific treatments such as ketamine on brain correlates of suicidal thoughts, as will be discussed in Chapter 9.

3.7.3 Biochemical Brain Imaging

Magnetic resonance spectroscopic imaging (MRSI), or spectroscopy, is a noninvasive imaging method that provides spectroscopic information about cellular or metabolic activity in addition to the image that is generated by MRI alone. Spectroscopy analyzes molecules such as hydrogen ions or, more commonly, protons. Several products of metabolism can be measured, including amino acids, lipid, lactate, alanine, N-acetyl aspartate, choline, creatine, and myoinositol. The frequency of these metabolites is measured in units called parts per million (ppm). Results of the spectroscopy studies of suicidal behavior will be discussed in Chapter 6.

Chapter 3 Summary

- A wide variety of approaches to the neurobiological study of suicidal behavior is available, ranging from the study of drinking water to the use of sophisticated brain scans.
- There is an intriguing convergence of findings from divergent study approaches. For example, lithium is the strongest currently available antisuicidal drug, which might be due to structural brain changes that are associated with its use and that may protect against the development of suicide risk.

- Nevertheless, many challenges remain. While the association between serotonergic neurotransmission systems and suicidal behavior probably is the most replicated finding in biological psychiatry, it is unclear how this association can be explained.
- While epidemiological studies indicate that the heritability of suicidal behavior is considerable, the results of genetic studies, in general, are disappointing.
- Overall, suicidal behaviors appear to be complex manifestations of an interaction between multiple contributing genetic and environmental factors. Key environmental contributors, including distal risk factors such as childhood adversity and proximal risk factors such as psychosocial stress, therefore need to be included in the design of genetic studies. For example, evidence is indeed emerging that childhood trauma mediates the relationship between genetic variation and functioning of the neurobiological stress response system, which may predispose to suicidal behavior.
- It is thus becoming clear that the use of one particular neurobiological study approach will not lead to a breakthrough in our knowledge of suicide risk. It appears that we will need the full range of approaches as described in this chapter to obtain a thorough understanding of underlying mechanisms involved in the development of suicide risk, which may lead to adequate prediction and treatment.

Review Questions

1. What are the major limitations of animal models in the study of suicidal behavior?
2. What are epigenetic effects, and why are they important in explaining suicide?
3. What can we learn from genetic epidemiology about the causes of suicide?
4. What are major environmental influences on the occurrence of suicidal behavior?
5. Which neurobiological pathways may be involved in explaining these influences?

Further Reading

Gilbert, P. & Allan, S. (1998). The role of defeat and entrapment (arrested flight) in depression: An exploration of an evolutionary view. *Psychological Medicine*, 28, 585–98.

Preti, A. (2011). Animal models and neurobiology of suicide. *Progress in Neuro-Psychopharmacology and Biological Psychiatry*, *35*, 818–30.

Turecki, G. (2014). Epigenetics and suicidal behavior research pathways. *American Journal of Preventive Medicine*, *47*, S144–S151.

van Heeringen, K. & Mann, J. J. (2014). The neurobiology of suicide. *Lancet Psychiatry*, *1*, 63–72.

CHAPTER FOUR

Lethal Signals

The Molecular Neuroscience of Suicidal Behavior

Learning Objectives

- What are molecules and how can they be involved in suicidal behavior?
- How does the stress response system go wrong in suicidal individuals?
- What is the role of disturbed neurotransmission in suicidal behavior?
- Why are epigenetic mechanisms so important for our understanding of suicide?
- What is brain plasticity and how is it related to suicidal behavior?
- How is toxoplasma infection related to suicide?

Introduction

Proteins are the machinery of life, but when things go wrong they contribute to premature death, including suicide. Without proteins, cells cannot function. Proteins are large molecules, group of atoms bonded together, representing the smallest unit of a chemical compound that can take part in a chemical reaction. Molecules vary greatly in size from, for example, two atoms of the same element in O_2 (or oxygen) to hundreds or even thousands of molecules that join together in chains to form proteins of considerable lengths. In our brain and body approximately 20,000 different proteins are involved in metabolism, growth, and regeneration.

Signaling is a major role of molecules, and molecular neuroscience addresses the neurobiology of the brain by studying the mechanisms by which neurons express and respond to molecular signals. Many different kinds of molecules transmit information, and some molecules carry signals over long distances, while others act locally to convey information between neighboring cells. In addition, signaling molecules differ in their mode of action on their target cells. Some signaling molecules can cross the plasma membrane, enter a cell, and bind to intracellular receptors in the cytoplasm or nucleus, whereas most bind to receptors on the target cell surface. A receptor is a protein molecule that receives a signal by binding to a molecule (its "ligand").

Molecular neuroscience uses tools from molecular biology and genetics to understand how (epi-)genetics may affect neurobiological functions and how neurons communicate. By reviewing the major molecular studies of suicidal behavior this chapter will make clear how changes in molecular characteristics of, for example, cholesterol, sex hormones, and serotonin may increase the risk of suicide. For each category of molecular findings, changes in association with suicidal behavior and, as far as known, the roles of neurobiological mechanisms such as (epi-)genetics will be described.

4.1 Stress-Response Systems

As seen in Chapter 2, the stress–diathesis model posits that stressful events can precipitate suicidal behavior in individuals with a diathesis or vulnerability to suicidal behavior. The stress–response system thus potentially is a key candidate in the search for neurobiological correlates of suicidal behavior. Appropriate responses to biological and psychological stressor systems are crucial for survival, and there are different interrelated stress-response systems. Functional molecular problems in these systems exist, and indeed interfere with survival as they may increase the risk of premature death due to suicide. Involved in suicidal behavior are the hypothalamus–pituitary–adrenal (HPA) axis system, the noradrenaline (or norepinephrine) neurotransmission system, and the polyamine system.

4.1.1 The HPA Stress System

Stress activates the HPA system, which is shown in Figure 4.1, via the release of a hormone (corticotropin-releasing hormone, CRH) from the hypothalamus into the circulation. CRH in turn activates the CRH receptor 1 (CRHR1) in the pituitary, leading to pituitary release of, among others, adrenocorticotropic hormone (ACTH). Once in the main circulation, ACTH triggers cortisol release from the adrenal cortex, which mobilizes energy, potentiates the actions of certain neurotransmitters, dampens inflammatory responses, and activates glucocorticoid receptors (GRs), which bind cortisol when levels are high (Oquendo et al., 2014b). GR stimulation increases glucose levels and the breakdown of lipids, mobilizing energy resources and enhancing memory storage and consolidation, thus preparing the organism for similar events in the future. Mineralocorticoid receptors (MRs) are higher affinity receptors (affinity is a measure of the strength of attraction between a

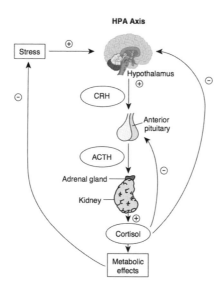

Figure 4.1 The hypothalamo–pituitary–adrenal (HPA) axis. See color plate 6.

receptor and its ligand) that are occupied under basal conditions, thereby maintaining the HPA axis tone. When bound to corticosteroids, MRs and GRs regulate gene transcription, mediating later effects of stressors. Negative feedback commences when corticosteroids bind to MRs and GRs, and thus stop the stress-induced activation of the HPA axis (Oquendo et al., 2014b).

Cortisol and suicide are related. A large study investigating nearly 400,000 primary care patients shows that the danger of fatal and nonfatal suicidal behaviors is nearly seven times greater among patients who are treated with oral glucocorticoids than in those with the same underlying medical condition who are not treated with glucocorticoids (Fardet et al., 2012). However, studies looking at the relationship between HPA axis activity and suicidal behaviors report inconsistent results. Findings include both lower and higher levels of salivary, urinary, and plasma cortisol and loss of diurnal variation, due to less decline in afternoon cortisol levels and higher HPA activity in the morning (Lindqvist et al., 2008; Keilp et al., 2016; Mann & Currier, 2016; Reichl et al., 2016). Lower plasma cortisol levels are found in relatives of suicide completers and predict suicide (Jokinen et al., 2010; McGirr et al., 2011). A recent meta-analysis of 27 studies found no significant effect of a history of suicide attempts on cortisol. However, significant associations between cortisol and suicide attempts were observed as a function of age. In studies where the mean age of the sample was below 40 years, the association was positive (meaning that higher cortisol is associated with suicide attempts), and where the mean age was 40 or above, the association was negative (indicating that lower cortisol is associated with suicide attempts). Changes in HPA axis activity, as indicated by age-dependent variations in cortisol levels, thus appear to be associated with suicidal behavior (O'Connor et al., 2016).

Perhaps more important than the measurement of such baseline activities is the question whether the reactivity of the stress system to (whether or not particular) stressors is changed in relation to suicidal behavior. Remember the story of Valerie in the Preface: Her suicidal behavior was triggered by the confrontation with her angry uncle. Functional studies using laboratory stress induction or pharmacological challenges of the HPA axis suggest disturbances in association with suicidal behavior. There is a more than a four-fold risk of dying by suicide in depressed individuals who do not suppress cortisol after administration of dexamethasone (Mann et al., 2006; see Chapter 3 for a description of the dexamethasone suppression test). Attenuated cortisol responses to laboratory social stress (such as the Trier Social Stress Test or the Maastricht Acute Stress Test) are found in self-harmers, suicide attempters, adolescents engaging in nonsuicidal self-injury, in relatives of individuals who died by suicide, and in offspring suicide attempters (with intent to die) of patients with mood disorders (McGirr et al., 2010; Kaess et al., 2012; Melhem et al., 2016; O'Connor et al., 2017; Plener et al., 2017). In response to challenge with the drug fenfluramine, a potent serotonin releaser and reuptake inhibitor that stimulates prolactin and cortisol release, depressed individuals who went on to make future suicide attempts show a blunted cortisol response to the drug consistent with a potential serotonin deficit in stimulating ACTH or CRH release (Keilp et al., 2010). The results of a study using the Cyberball paradigm (which we will discuss in detail in Chapter 6) and a public speaking stress test are intriguing, and very relevant for our understanding of suicidal behavior given the role of social exclusion as a trigger. This study shows that cortisol output during public speaking stress is particularly reduced in women after exposure to ostracism (exclusion) during the Cyberball game (Weik et al., 2017).

Relatively few studies have looked at candidate genes involved in the HPA stress-response system. A promising candidate gene is the CRH receptor 1 (CRHR1) gene that is associated with cortisol response to dexamethasone challenge. Another factor is the GR and its chaperone proteins FKBP and SKA2, which are involved in the translocation of GR to the nucleus (Mann & Currier, 2016). Molecular chaperones are proteins that are primarily involved in the folding of proteins that gives them their particular shape, which is crucial for their function by, for example, binding to receptors. A nonresponsive GR feedback mechanism leading to dysregulated stress responses serves as the epicenter of a stress-related phenotype such as suicidal behavior (Roy & Dwivedi, 2017). Early-life experiences play a crucial role in the shaping of the HPA-stress-response system. Other types of chaperones are involved in transport across membranes ("translocation").

Molecular understanding of this maladaptive HPA axis response in adult suicide victims indeed suggests an important link between adverse early-life experiences and dysregulated GR activity in the hippocampus. The observations from studies in rats suggesting that maternal behavior regulates the tone of the HPA axis via methylation were recently translated to humans through studies investigating hippocampal tissue from individuals who died by suicide with and without a history of childhood adversity, as well as normal controls (Turecki, 2014b). And this is where epigenetics come into play, and disturbances in folding and translocation are involved that may provide the missing link between the heritability of suicidal behavior and the interaction with the environment.

Epigenetic studies investigate how genetic expression may be influenced by external factors, and a variety of epigenetic mechanisms have been described, as shown in Textboxes 4.1 and 4.2.

External factors may thus alter how genes are expressed without altering the underlying DNA sequence, and include adverse environmental influences. For example, we will see in Chapter 7 how epigenetic effects explain the increased risk of suicide following exposure to early life adversity (ELA), such as childhood physical or sexual abuse. In this

---

Textbox 4.1 Epigenetic Mechanisms

Methylation: the most studied epigenetic modification where attachment of a methyl group to cytosine residues by the DNA methyltransferase enzyme renders a substantial change in information processing during gene expression

Histone modification: a posttranslational modification (PTM) to histone proteins, which act to package DNA into chromosomes. The PTMs made to histones can impact gene expression.

Textbox 4.2 DNA Methylation

DNA methylation refers to the addition of a methyl group to a cytosine residue, in particular when a cytosine is followed by a guanine (CpG dinucleotide). Around 70%–80% of CpGs are methylated in the genome. This epigenetic mark globally associates with decreased transcriptional activity, although there are documented exceptions. Most work on DNA methylation has focused on CpG islands, which are defined as short CpG-rich regions that are present in roughly half of the genes in vertebrate genomes. CpG islands are overrepresented in promoter regions, where methylation levels are very low, leaving surrounding DNA and transcription start sites unwrapped and accessible for transcription. Most studies correlate DNA methylation states with gene expression levels, potentially implicating several mechanisms. The methylation of certain CpG dinucleotides, notably in gene promoter regions, impairs the ability of regulatory proteins (such as transcription factors) to bind the DNA and to promote gene expression. DNA methylation is a dynamic mechanism, particularly in the brain, that can rapidly respond to environmental factors, in physiological as well as pathological processes. From an evolutionary point of view, one might speculate that the brain, being the specialized organ for sensing internal and environmental stimuli, has evolved so as to be particularly prone to epigenetic plasticity.

case, methylation levels in the GR gene are significantly higher in abused individuals who die by suicide than among nonabused individuals who die by suicide and healthy controls (McGowan et al., 2009). See Figure 4.2.

Subsequent studies suggest that the resulting decrease in GR expression in depressed individuals who die by suicide may be mediated by different molecular pathways, depending on the presence or absence of ELA. A genome-wide methylation study of promoter DNA methylation in hippocampi of suicides with a history of early life trauma showed a bidirectional pattern of hypomethylation and hypermethylation status of gene promoters (Labonté et al., 2012a). Acquired methylation changes due to traumatic early life experiences thus can be perpetuated in later life with an increasing risk of suicide in the individuals who were abused during childhood (Labonté et al., 2012b; Haghighi et al., 2014).

Abnormal functional response of GRs as part of a dysregulated HPA axis is not only moderated by their impaired cellular transcription but also affected by their compromised availability in the nuclear

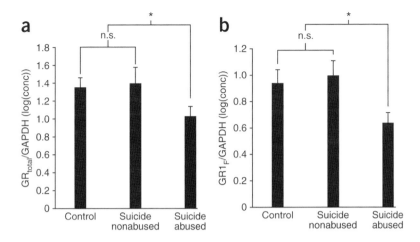

Figure 4.2 Hippocampal glucocorticoid receptor expression. (a, b) Mean $\pm$ s.e.m. expression levels of total glucocorticoid receptor (GR) mRNA (a) and glucocorticoid receptor 1_F (GR1_F) in 12 suicide victims with a history of childhood abuse, 12 nonabused suicides, and 12 control subjects (b). Outliers excluded from analysis included $n = 2$ control subjects, $n = 1$ suicides with a history of childhood abuse for glucocorticoid receptor 1_F and an additional $n = 1$ suicide with a history of childhood abuse, and $n = 3$ nonabused suicides for overall levels of glucocorticoid receptor. * indicates $P < 0.05$; n.s. indicates not statistically significant. (Reprinted by permission from Macmillan Publishers Ltd: *Nature Neuroscience*, 12(3), 342–348, McGowan et al., Epigenetic regulation of the glucocorticoid receptor in human brain associates with childhood abuse, copyright 2009).

compartment as transcription factors. This implicates chaperone proteins such as FKBP and SKA2, which act as molecular escorts to help translocate GR to the nucleus where GR acts as a transcription factor (Roy & Dwivedi, 2017). FKBP5 inhibits GR signal transduction, and FKBP5 sequence variants are associated with an increased risk of suicidal behavior, especially in people with ELAs (Turecki & Brent, 2016). Genetic variations within FKBP5 interact with ELA in determining suicide risk following exposure to stress (Mandelli & Serretti, 2016). Regarding SKA2, suicides show an exclusive DNA methylation signature with functional implications in altering GR responsiveness predominantly in their prefrontal cortex. Moreover, observations from peripheral blood tissue of living cohorts align with the brain findings replicating a similar functional impact of SKA2 epigenetic mark on its own expression in relation to suicidal ideation (Guintivano et al., 2014). The relevance of the chaperone protein findings for the prediction of suicidal behavior will be discussed in Chapter 9.

4.1.2 The Norepinephrine Stress System

Stress activates the norepinephrine (NE) stress response system in parallel with the HPA system. Activation leads to NE release from a dense network of neurons originating in the locus coeruleus (LC) and projecting widely to the forebrain, leading to enhanced arousal, vigilance, and anxiety (Oquendo et al., 2014b). NE receptors are distributed throughout the cortex, thalamus, hypothalamus, hippocampus, amygdala, and basal ganglia. NE neurotransmission is terminated via reuptake by NE transporters or via catabolism by monoamine oxidase (MAO) or catechol O-methyltransferase (COMT). The involvement of the NE stress system in suicidal behavior is suggested mainly via postmortem studies, but findings are not equivocal. The results of CSF studies of the NE metabolite MHPG are equally inconclusive.

Postmortem findings in suicides include fewer NE neurons in the LC, and greater prefrontal cortical beta-adrenergic receptor binding and lower alpha$_2$ adrenergic binding. However, suicides who use violent methods apparently have fewer beta-adrenergic receptors than those using nonviolent methods (Oquendo et al., 2014b). In addition, there is lower NE transporter binding in the LC but not the hypothalamus in association with suicide. Taking into account the lack of consistency, these findings may, in general, reflect cortical noradrenergic overactivity, possibly due to excessive NE release in response to the stress leading to suicide, and resulting in a depletion of NE due to the smaller amount of NE neurons found in suicides (Mann & Currier, 2016).

A monoamine oxidase A (MAO-A) gene polymorphism leading to high activity is more prevalent in male but not female suicides with mood disorders compared with nonpsychiatric comparison subjects, although MAO-A and MAO-B activity does not seem altered in association with suicide. The Val/Val genotype of COMT, which renders COMT more efficient at catabolizing norepinephrine, appears to be more prevalent in healthy live male but not female comparison subjects than in suicides. The Met/Met genotype appears to have an opposite, protective effect in males. Thus, genetic studies suggest lower norepinephrine function in suicide, which could be secondary to down-regulation in response to chronic stress (Oquendo et al., 2014b).

4.1.3 The Polyamine Stress System

Polyamines are small molecules containing two or more amine groups that have a multitude of functions, including regulation of gene transcription and posttranscriptional modifications, as well as modulation of protein activities (Turecki, 2014b). Representative polyamines comprise putrescine, spermidine, spermine, and agmatine. They are released following stressful stimuli, and present a unique pattern of response known as the polyamine stress response (PSR). The PSR can be induced by direct neuronal stimuli or in response to hormonal signals, such as glucocorticoids, and manipulated pharmacologically with anti-anxiety drugs and lithium. The magnitude of the PSR is related to the intensity of the stressor. Spermidine/spermine N1-acetyltransferase 1 (SAT 1) is a rate-limiting enzyme in the catabolism of polyamines.

Several studies report alterations in the mRNA and protein levels of components of the polyamine system in cortical and subcortical brain regions of individuals who died by suicide and in peripheral samples from suicide attempters (Turecki, 2014b). Postmortem studies particularly and consistently indicate a down-regulation of SAT1 expression, and direct quantification of spermidine and putrescine indicates increased concentrations in cortical brain tissue. A whole-gene sequencing effort of SAT1, however, identifies no variant or assessed region of SAT1 with a significant association with attempted suicide, nor evidence for replication of previously reported associations (Monson et al., 2016). As will be discussed in more detail in Chapter 9, longitudinal investigation of SAT1 blood levels suggests that changes in expression levels of the SAT1 gene predict suicide risk.

Key polyamine genes in the brain are regulated by epigenetic mechanisms, and evidence of differential epigenetic regulation of some of these genes in suicide is accumulating (Fiori & Turecki, 2011). There is strong evidence for a relationship between the HPA and polyamine systems (Turecki, 2014b). In the context of the growing evidence of epigenetic regulation of HPA activity by early life events as described earlier, it is of interest to note that polyamine metabolism influences such epigenetic modifications. In addition, there is growing evidence that epigenetic processes also regulate gene coding for components of the polyamine system.

4.2 Neurotransmission

Neurotransmitters are chemical messengers that allow the transmission of signals from one neuron to another via synapses, as shown in Figure 4.3.

More than 150 neurotransmitters have been identified in the brain. Neurotransmitters with relevance for our understanding of suicidal

Generic Neurotransmitter System

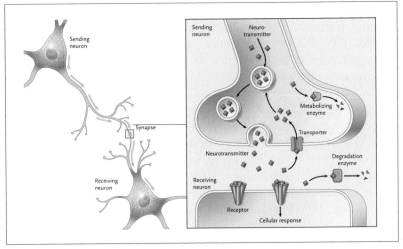

Figure 4.3 Neurotransmission system.
Source: NIDA (NIH) public domain, via Wikimedia Commons. See color plate 7.

behavior include serotonin, dopamine, norepinephrine (see earlier discussion), gamma-amino-butyric acid (GABA), and glutamate. In general, neurotransmitters are divided into two basic types: inhibitory neurotransmitters that calm the brain (such as serotonin and GABA) and excitatory neurotransmitters that stimulate the brain (such as dopamine and glutamate).

4.2.1 Serotonin (5-HT)

Serotonin (or 5-hydroxytryptamine [5-HT]) is an evolutionarily very old neurotransmitter, and omnipresent in plants and animals including humans. Changes in the serotonin system in relation to suicidal behavior are among the most replicated findings in biological psychiatry. The mechanisms by means of which such an old and omnipresent molecule contributes to a comparatively recent and uniquely human phenomenon as suicide are enigmatic. Of note, Chapter 8 will present a hypothetical explanation for this remarkable relationship.

As shown in Figure 4.4, cell bodies in the dorsal and median raphe nuclei provide extensive serotonergic innervation throughout the brain.

There are seven 5-HT receptor families, many with several subtypes. As shown in Figure 4.5, the presynaptic 5-HT transporter (5-HTT or

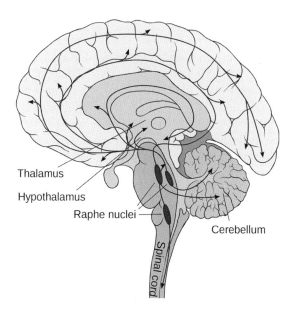

Figure 4.4 Serotonin neurotransmission system (Lynch, 2010). See color plate 8.

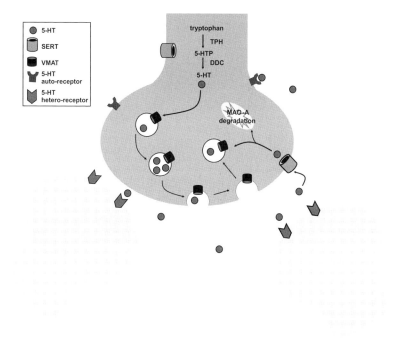

Figure 4.5 Serotonin neurotransmission (Reprinted from *Trends in Neurosciences*, 33(9), Daubert EA & Caudron BG, Serotonin: a regulator of neuronal morphology and circuitry, 424–434, copyright 2010). See color plate 9.

SERT) removes serotonin from the synaptic cleft to interrupt neuro-transmission. Tryptophan hydroxylase (TPH) is the rate-limiting enzyme in 5-HT synthesis, and two isoforms are present in humans. TPH1, found primarily outside the brain after birth, is implicated in intrauterine neurodevelopment, while TPH2 is specific to the brain. 5-HT breakdown involves oxidation of 5-HT by MAO-A and aldehyde dehydrogenase to produce the metabolite 5-hydroxyindoleacetic acid (5-HIAA).

Altered serotonergic function in association with suicidal behaviors has been shown in a multitude of studies of cerebrospinal fluid (CSF), peripheral tissues, postmortem brain tissue, in vivo neuroimaging (see Chapter 6), and molecular brain characteristics (see Chapter 3 for technical issues). CSF studies show decreased levels of 5-HIAA in suicide attempters, particularly in those using violent methods or making attempts of higher lethality (Mann & Currier, 2016). Moreover, a meta-analysis of prospective studies shows that individuals suffering from major depression who have below-median levels of CSF 5-HIAA are 4.5 times more likely to die by suicide than those in the above-median group (Mann et al., 2006). Studies of postmortem brain tissues reveal localized decreased 5-HT transporter binding in the ventromedial prefrontal cortex and anterior cingulate. More 5-HT neurons, greater TPH2 gene expression and protein in 5-HT neurons, and lower 5-HT transporter expression and protein favor enhancement of 5-HT transmission. This potentially occurs in response to lower levels of 5-HT release, which is reflected in a low 5-HIAA/5-HT ratio in the brainstems of individuals who die by suicide and the lower 5-HIAA concentration in the CSF of serious suicide attempters (Mann & Currier, 2016). The interpretation of findings is a matter of debate, but this reduction in 5-HT release is possibly due to an increase in 5-HT_{1A} receptors in the dorsal nuclei as demonstrated in association with nonfatal and fatal suicidal behaviors (Sullivan et al., 2015; Mann & Currier, 2016). In line with a proposed central role of the 5-HT_{1A} receptor in the regulation of brain serotonergic activity (Popova & Naumenko, 2013), it has recently been suggested that the up-regulation of 5-HT_{1A} autoreceptors, as demonstrated in postmortem and neuroimaging studies, is crucial in explaining changes in the serotonin system in association with suicidal behavior (Menon & Kattimani, 2015). The up-regulation of these receptors may well be associated with homeostatic up-regulation of mechanisms aimed at increasing central serotonin bioavailability, thus explaining compensatory increases in serotonergic activity as reflected by, e.g., more serotonergic neurons and decreased transporter binding (Menon & Kattimani, 2015). Support for this hypothesis was found recently in a prospective study showing an association between greater index 5-HT$_{1A}$ receptor binding in the raphe nucleus, more subsequent suicidal ideation, and greater lethality of subsequent suicidal behavior during a 2-year follow-up of depressed individuals (Oquendo et al., 2016). The potential central role of the up-regulation of 5-HT$_{1A}$ autoreceptors in the development of suicide risk will be elaborated in the context of a computational neuroscience approach to suicidal behavior in Chapter 8.

With regard to candidate genes, some but not all studies report associations between TPH1 and TPH2 genes and suicidal behaviors (Mann & Currier, 2016). Receptor genes appear not to be linked to suicidal behavior. One of the most studied polymorphisms concerns the 5-HTT or SERT gene upstream regulatory region. The serotonin transporter plays an important role as a regulator of serotonergic signaling at synapses. The gene of the serotonin transporter (SLC6A4) is situated on chromosome 17 (17q11.2); it has a common functional promoter polymorphism (5-HTTLPR, rs4795541), which consists of a short (S) and a long (L) allele. The L allele of this marker has been found to transcribe the gene two to three times more efficiently than the S allele does. Many, though not all, studies document an association between the low expressing S allele and suicidal behavior (Mirkovic et al., 2016).

As genes can only partially explain suicide risk, studies have incorporated environmental factors in a vulnerability model, investigating whether polymorphic variations in the 5-HTT, 5-HTR$_{1A}$ and 5-HTR$_{2A}$, and TPH genes can interact with stressful life events to increase the risk of suicidal behavior (Antypa et al., 2013; Mandelli & Serretti, 2016). The interaction between stress and the 5-HTT gene and its effect on the occurrence of suicidal behavior has received great attention since the publication of the pioneering and pivotal study by Caspi and colleagues. These authors demonstrated that stressors increase risk of suicide attempts, but only in those with a low-expressing 5-HTT S allele (Caspi et al., 2003). Most, though not all, subsequent studies confirmed this finding of an increased suicide risk after exposure to two or more stressful life events in 5-HTT short-allele carriers. (See Mandelli & Serretti, 2016, for an overview.) In particular, significant effects are observed in those exposed to childhood maltreatment, childhood trauma, child abuse, and severe stressful life events, and in school-aged children exposed to maltreatment. Despite inconsistencies in results, with even one study finding the opposite (an increased suicide risk in the long-long genotype), the clear majority of studies indicate that the 5-HTT genotype moderates the effect of stress on the occurrence of suicidal behavior. It appears, however, that the interactive effect on suicide risk is specific in the context of preexisting psychiatric problems (Mandelli & Serretti, 2016). Gene x environment studies of a modulating effect of polymorphisms of the 5-HTR_{1A} and 5-HTR_{2A} genes and the TPH1 and TPH2 genes on suicide risk following exposure to stressful life events yield inconsistent results. However, the number of studies is low, and further studies are clearly needed.

4.2.2 Glutamate/GABA

Gamma-amino butyric acid (GABA) and glutamate are the major inhibitory and excitatory neurotransmitters in the brain, respectively. Given the putative antisuicidal properties of ketamine, a glutamate antagonist via N-methyl-D-aspartate (NMDA) receptor binding (see Chapter 10), interest in the involvement of glutamate in the development of suicide risk has increased substantially in the past decade. Studies of glutamate receptor binding in the brains of suicides have yielded inconsistent findings (Oquendo et al., 2014b). Genetic studies of the involvement of glutamate/GABA systems in suicidal behavior yield inconsistent results, although evidence of genes encoding glutamate receptors and the GABA A receptor is increasing (Gray et al., 2015; Yin et al., 2016). In keeping with an early finding of no changes in the concentration of GABA in the forebrain of suicides (Korpi et al., 1988), a recent spectroscopy study (see Chapter 3 for technical issues) found no differences in levels of glutamate and GABA in the prefrontal cortex in association with suicidal behavior (Jollant et al., 2017).

The few available gene x environment studies, investigating variants within genes pertaining to glutamate and GABA systems in combination with exposure to ELA, report no significant results (Mandelli & Serretti, 2016).

4.2.3 Dopamine

Dopamine is synthesized from L-dopa in the ventral tegmental area and substantia nigra. Dopamine binds to five receptor subtypes and is metabolized via MAO and COMT to homovanillic acid (HVA). In noradrenergic and adrenergic neurons dopamine is metabolized to norepinephrine. Dopamine is implicated in mood, motivation, aggression, reward, working memory and attention, making it a prime candidate for the molecular study of suicidal behavior (Oquendo et al., 2014b).

However, only few suicide studies find associations with changes in dopaminergic functioning looking at receptors and metabolites. One study of striatal dopamine binding combining psychological and physical autopsies suggests imbalances in the expression of dopamine receptor and transporter genes independent of ELA (Fitzgerald et al., 2017). The paucity and inconsistency of results preclude identifying dopaminergic function as a marker of suicide risk (Oquendo et al., 2014b).

4.3 Neuroinflammation

Rates of nonfatal and fatal suicidal behavior are increased in inflammatory and autoimmune diseases such as asthma, allergies, lupus, and multiple sclerosis. It has been suggested that the spring peak of suicides (see Chapter 1) is due to increased seasonal aero-allergens leading to inflammation (Brundin et al., 2015). The risk of death by suicide is increased among individuals hospitalized with infection in prospective and dose–response relationships, suggesting a causal relationship (Lund-Sorensen et al., 2016). There are neurotrophic disease-producing agents (so-called pathogens, such as viruses, bacteria, or parasites) of low virulence, which reside relatively quietly within the central nervous system of immunocompetent hosts (who are thus able to produce a normal immune response) after infection. Such pathogens include the parasite *Toxoplasma gondii*, and accumulating research now shows that such chronic, low-grade infections may exert effects on the host brain to a much larger extent than previously thought. As already discussed in Chapter 1, repeated studies now confirm that there is a significantly increased risk for suicidal behavior in individuals who are positive for *T. gondii* infection (Brundin et al., 2015). Seropositivity for this parasite is associated with a nearly two-fold increased relative risk of nonfatal and fatal suicidal behavior (Pedersen et al., 2012). As approximately 10% of suicides could be attributable to the effects of a severe infection (Lund-Sorensen et al., 2016), and given the fact that approximately 30% of the world's population is infected with *T. gondii*, the relevance of this pathogenic mechanism for suicide prevention appears to be substantial.

In addition to these epidemiological findings, an increasing number of molecular studies suggest dysregulation of the immune system and cytokines in suicidal behavior. Cytokines are small proteins that, when released from a cell, have an effect on the behavior of cells around them. They include interferons (IF), interleukins (IL), and tumor-necrosis factors (TNF), which bind to receptors and are especially important in the immune system. A substantial number of studies and meta-analyses report changes in the levels of IL and TNF in plasma, CSF, and the brain in association with suicidal behaviors (for an overview, see Brundin et al., 2015). Among the more or less heterogeneous cytokine findings, elevated interleukine-6 appears to be most robust as it appears to be associated both nonfatal and fatal suicidal behaviors (Gananção et al, 2016).

Activation of the kynurenine pathway of tryptophan catabolism is a potential neurobiological mechanism linking suicide and inflammation. As tryptophan is also the precursor of serotonin, inflammation might cause a decrease in serotonin levels by shifting the catabolism of tryptophan to breakdown via the kynurenine pathway. In addition, the tryptophan metabolite quinolinic acid increases neuronal glutamate release via NMDA receptors (Brundin et al., 2015). It is possible that serotonin levels are depleted by activated brain cells (microglia) that have enhanced metabolism of tryptophan to quinolinic acid via the kynurenine pathway, but the extent to which inflammation interferes with serotonin and glutamate neurotransmission in suicidal individuals remains to be demonstrated. In any case, in depression it appears that increased inflammation may lead to increased glutamate in the basal ganglia as measured with spectroscopy (Haroon et al., 2016). Therapeutic strategies targeting glutamate (see Chapter 10) may thus be preferentially effective in depressed patients with increased inflammation.

Microglia are cells that act as the first and main form of active immune defense in the white matter of the brain, and that respond to changes in the internal brain milieu through a sequence of activated states, each with characteristic function and morphology. They are the main producers of cytokines. Postmortem studies of the brains of suicides reveal changes: the normal dorsal–ventral difference in activated microglial density is reversed such that, with suicide, the density is greater in ventral prefrontal white matter than in dorsal prefrontal white matter, and the density of immunoreactive cells is greater in dorsal prefrontal white matter. These observations are in keeping with a stress–diathesis model of suicide, as described in Chapter 2, whereby an acute stressor activates a reactive process in the brain and creates a suicidal state in an individual at risk (Schnieder et al., 2014).

Courtet and his colleagues (2016) describe a nice and comprehensive model of the relationship between inflammation and suicidal behavior, in which many of the described inflammatory alterations are included. According to this comprehensive stress–diathesis model, childhood maltreatment, *T. gondii* infection, and sleep disturbances lead to a systemic inflammatory state, promoting HPA axis dysregulation. This low chronic inflammatory state may induce a feed-forward cycle when these subjects become exposed to stressors. The inflammatory state then leads to indoleamine-2,3-dioxygenase (IDO) activation. IDO produces kynurenine from tryptophan. Then, microglia activation (in the dorsolateral prefrontal cortex [DLPFC], anterior cingulate cortex [ACC], and mediodorsal thalamus [MDT]) leads to increased quinolinic acid production and decreased kynurenic acid production from kynurenine. This leads to increased NMDA stimulation. Also, enhanced metabolism of tryptophan results in depleted serotonin levels. Furthermore, stressors such psychiatric diseases and adverse life events interact with the vulnerability to induce suicidal behavior.

The possibility of an autoimmune basis for cases of suicide is supported by the finding that antibodies to serotonin are present in more than half of cases of major depression (compared with fewer than 10% of individuals without depression) and are found in all cases of depression with elevated proinflammatory cytokines. Presumably, an autoimmune process directed against serotonin can remove serotonergic axons or their terminals and account for deficits in serotonin neurotransmission as described earlier. This speculation is also consistent with the dorsal-ventral specificity because the transporter deficiency associated with suicide is predominantly ventral (Schnieder et al., 2014).

The inflammation hypothesis of suicide contributes substantially to the understanding and treatment of suicide risk. Inflammation enhances sensitivity to punishment versus rewards, which is a key ingredient of the neurocomputational model of suicidal behavior that will be developed in Chapter 8 (Harrison et al., 2016). Targeting the kynurenine pathway enzymes may provide attractive novel therapeutic approaches for managing suicidal behavior (Bryleva & Brundin, 2017).

4.4 Neurotrophins

Brain plasticity (from the Greek word *plastos*, meaning molded) refers to the extraordinary ability of the brain to modify its own structure and function as an adaptation to changes in the environment. Brain plasticity underlies normal brain functions, such as our ability to learn and to modify our behavior. To do so, brain cells may make new connections with each other, or reshape and mold. Plasticity is strongest during childhood, but remains a fundamental property of the brain throughout the course of life. Neurogenesis is the process of creating new brain cells. It supports many human functions, including learning and memory. In the past, it was thought that neurogenesis took place only in babies, children, and teenagers, and that it completely stopped happening at in adulthood. We now know that the generation of new nerve cells does occur in the adult brain, meaning that the brain can be strengthened and improved with the growth of new cells.

Structural and functional adaptation to environmental demands occurs through synaptic plasticity and neurogenesis, which are regulated by neurotrophins or neurotrophic factors. Of four identified neuro-trophin classes, brain-derived neurotrophic factor (BDNF) and its recep-tor, tropomyosinreceptor kinase B (TrkB), are critical mediators of plasticity, and it is hypothesized that their alteration underlies changes in plasticity observed in the brains of individuals who end their own lives.

Such changes include cortical thinning in dorsolateral prefrontal cortex neurons and fewer dentate gyrus granule neurons in depressed suicides. Volume loss suggests reduced neurogenesis, accelerated neuron loss due to apoptosis, or loss of gray matter networks of unmyelinated nerve fibers and their branches (Oquendo et al., 2014b). In general, suicides show lower BDNF protein expression in the prefrontal cortex, fewer TrkB receptors in the prefrontal cortex and hippocampus, and less BDNF and TrkB mRNA. Expression of neurotrophins in the prefrontal cortex and hippocampus of suicides is altered, indicating impairments in neurogenesis (Oquendo et al., 2014b).

Female suicides are more likely to carry the BDNF Val66Met (Val/ Met or Met/ Met) polymorphism, a gene variant associated with lower secretion of BDNF. Epigenetic changes, possibly reflecting ELAs, may also be relevant to BDNF-TrkB system dysfunction, as suicides have been reported to have higher BDNF-gene DNA methylation and, cor-respondingly, lower BDNF mRNA relative to nonsuicide comparison subjects (Oquendo et al., 2014b). Changes in the expression of Trk genes in association with suicide are well documented (Almeida & Turecki, 2016). Gene x environment interactions may play a role in the effect of BDNF and Trk genes on suicide risk, as particular polymorphisms increase the risk of suicidal behaviors in combination with exposure to (early) stressful life events such as ELAs (Mandelli & Serreti, 2016).

Thus, there is increasing evidence of a role of neuroplasticity in suicide. Interestingly, there appears to be a negative correlation between neurotrophins and inflammatory markers, stress, and suicide risk: The lower the level of neurotrophins, the higher the levels of suicide risk, stress, and inflammatory markers (Priya et al., 2016).

4.5 Cholesterol and Fatty Acids

The possible relationship between cholesterol levels and suicide risk was initially suggested when an excess mortality for suicides and injuries was observed following the use of cholesterol-lowering drugs (Hibbeln & Salem, 1996). Attention was focused on the topic even after a meta-analysis showed that deaths from suicides, accidents, and violence were not significantly increased among participants randomized to a cholesterol-lowering intervention compared with those in the control groups (Muldoon et al., 2001; De Berardis et al., 2012). Most, but not all, subsequent studies in suicide attempters confirm an association between low cholesterol serum levels and (particularly violent) suicidal behavior in depression and other psychiatric disorders. More particularly, it appears that the risk of suicide attempts increases 7-fold in men and 16-fold in women in the lowest cholesterol quartile compared with subjects in the highest quartile (Olié et al., 2011). Thus, serum cholesterol level may be a strong risk factor for suicidal behavior in patients with depressive symptoms, and may serve a useful biological marker of suicide risk (see Chapter 9).

Engelberg (1992) presented a hypothesis linking cholesterol and the serotonergic system. He hypothesized that a reduced serum cholesterol level may be accompanied by changes in viscosity and function of serotonin receptors and transporters as well as by decreased serotonin precursors that may cause an increase in suicide risk. This hypothesis is supported by findings of a significant positive correlation between serum total cholesterol and levels of CSF 5-HIAA in suicide attempters (Hibbeln et al., 2000; Jokinen et al., 2010).

Imbalances in polyunsaturated fatty acids (PUFAs, found mainly in fish, corn, and soybean oil) are associated with neuropsychiatric disorders, including depression and risk of suicide. Omega-3 (or "n-3") PUFAs are critical to brain development, mental health, and cognitive functioning, and studies have suggested a role for low omega-3 PUFA intake in suicidal behavior. Omega-3 PUFA levels are very low in suicide completers and lower in suicide attempters than nonattempters (for an overview, see Haghighi et al., 2015). An imbalance of proinflammatory omega-6 and antiinflammatory omega-3 PUFAs may be involved in an inflammatory effect on suicidal behavior (Oquendo et al., 2014b). PUFAs are not endogenously produced in humans and thus must be derived from dietary intake. However, a recent large long-term prospective cohort study in more than 200,000 individuals reveals no reduction in suicide risk in association with the intake of dietary fish and omega-3 and omega-6 PUFAs (Tsai et al., 2014). Although intake is undoubtedly a major determinant of PUFA effects since long-chain (LC)-PUFAs cannot be manufactured de novo, additional physiological factors affecting PUFA bioavailability may also mediate the clinical effects of low omega-3 PUFA levels. A recent epigenetic study shows that DNA methylation of genes involved in omega-3 PUFA biosynthesis is associated with depression and suicide risk. Long-term PUFA imbalances could thus induce changes in the epigenome that are associated with suicide (Haghighi et al., 2015). The observed link between plasma PUFA levels, DNA methylation, and suicide risk may have implications for the modulation of disease-associated epigenetic marks by nutritional intervention.

4.6 Sex Hormones

Although differences in testosterone concentrations could contribute to the gender differences in suicide epidemiology that were described in Chapter 1, remarkably few studies have looked at a possible role of testosterone in suicidal behavior. Given the close relationship between stress response and testosterone levels and their correlation with aggression and impulsivity, this hormone could nevertheless be a key biomarker of suicidal behavior. CSF and plasma testosterone levels are higher in young male (but not female) suicide attempters than in age-matched healthy volunteers. In male suicide attempters, the CSF testosterone/cortisol ratio shows a significant positive correlation with impulsivity and aggressiveness (Stefansson et al., 2016).

With regard to female sex hormones, results of studies have not been equivocal, and it is currently unclear to what extent changes in levels of sex hormones account for the female preponderance among suicide attempters or for the low rate of suicide (but not suicide attempts) among pregnant women. In general, it appears that the occurrence of suicide does not vary significantly over the menstrual cycle, but that suicide attempts are relatively more common during the premenstrual and menstrual phases.

4.7 Neuropeptides

Given the precipitating and protective roles of interpersonal stress and social support, respectively, in the development of suicide risk, there are good reasons to consider an important role of the neuropeptide oxytocin (OT) in the development of suicide risk. OT plays a seminal role in social affiliation, attachment, social support, maternal behavior, and trust, and protects against stress and anxiety. The association of lower adult CSF OT levels with childhood trauma (Heim et al., 2009) might indicate that alterations in central OT function may be involved in the adverse outcomes of childhood adversity such as suicidal behavior. Lower CSF levels of OT are indeed found in suicide attempters when compared with healthy controls, correlating significantly with suicidal intent (Jokinen et al., 2012). NMDA receptor antagonism may explain, at least in part, the effects of OT on brain and behavior.

A few other neuropeptides appear to be associated with suicidal behavior. More particularly, levels of corticotropin-releasing factor (CRF), VGF, cholecystokinin, substance P, and neuropeptide Y (NPY) differ between individuals who have attempted or completed suicide compared with healthy controls or those dying from other causes (Serafini et al., 2013). The precise role of these neuropeptides is not yet clear, but their function as key modulators of both the response to stress and emotional processing is well documented.

Chapter 4 Summary

- There are many ways in which molecular changes are associated with suicidal behavior. Molecular characteristics may predispose individuals to such behavior, or changes may precipitate suicidal crises.
- The study of molecular characteristics contributes substantially to our understanding of the dynamics of suicide. For example, molecular studies have revealed the mechanism by means of which early-life adversity may affect behavioral reactions to stressors in later life by epigenetic processes. This is generally a stable process over long periods of time (probably at least up to 20 years) that is involved in long-term gene silencing.
- Candidate gene studies have associated cortex DNA methylation changes in several genes with suicidal behavior. There is increasing evidence that methylation status could be a clinical biomarker for suicidal behavior, and epigenetic management of suicide risk is likely to be a fruitful future approach to suicide prevention.
- Quite a few of molecular changes appear to be interdependent and involved in similar processes. There is a relationship between inflammation, decreased serotonin, and increased glutamate levels, and between inflammatory markers, stress, and suicide risk. The effect of low cholesterol on suicide risk may well be mediated by the serotonergic system. Increased methylation of the 5-HT transporter is associated with decreased cortisol secretion in response to stressful situations, thus indicating a link between serotonergic functioning and the HPA axis (Ouellet-Morin et al, 2013).

• The study of the molecular basis of the pharmacological agents (see Chapter 10) may shed further light on the molecular basis of suicidal behavior. For example, lithium appears to exert its antisuicidal effect independent of its mood-stabilizing effect by modulating dopaminergic, glutamatergic, and GABAergic pathways as well as by up-regulating neuroprotective factors such as BDNF, and by down-regulating apoptotic factors regulating neuronal cell death (Turecki, 2014b). In this context, it is intriguing to note that the use of lithium is associated with increases in the volume of the same brain areas in which suicidal behavior is associated with decreased volumes, as will be described in Chapter 6.

Review Questions

1. Is suicide a normal reaction to an abnormal situation, or is the opposite true?
2. What is brain plasticity, and why is it fundamental to suicide prevention?
3. What are gene x environment interactions, and how can they influence suicide risk?
4. How are infections and dietary habits related to suicide?
5. How is it possible that early-life adversity increases suicide risk during adulthood?

Further Reading

Black, C. & Miller, B. J. (2015). Meta-analysis of cytokines and chemokines in suicidality: Distinguishing suicidal versus non-suicidal patients. *Biological Psychiatry, 78*, 28–35.

Roy, B. & Dwivedi, Y. (2017). Understanding epigenetic architecture of suicide neurobiology: A critical perspective. *Neuroscience and Biobehavioral Reviews, 72*, 10–27.

van Heeringen, K. & Mann, J. J. (2014). The neurobiology of suicidal behaviour. *Lancet Psychiatry, 1*, 63–72.

I Think, Therefore I Do Not Want to Be

The Cognitive Neuroscience of Suicidal Behavior

Learning Objectives

- Which cognitive characteristics may predispose individuals to suicidal behavior?
- What is autobiographical memory, and how might it be involved in suicidal behavior?
- What is the Suicide Stroop, and why is it important?
- What are potential causes of cognitive dysfunctions in relation to suicidal behavior?
- Describe three ways in which cognitive neuroscience can contribute to suicide prevention.

Introduction

The core question in suicide prevention is: Why does a person in a particular situation want to take his or her own life, while another person in the same situation would react in a different way and perhaps seek help? In this chapter we will investigate to what extent and in which way cognitive neuroscientific studies contribute to finding an answer to this question.

Cognition can be defined as information processing (the term comes from the Latin *cognoscere*, which means "to conceptualize," "to know," or "to recognize"). Processing information from the outside world and determining how to use that information increases adaptive strength (Robinson et al., 2013). Changes in such processing and determining may have an opposite effect, and thus may lead to premature death. Cognitive scientists make a broad distinction between "hot cognition," which involves affective (i.e., emotionally valenced) information, and " cold cognition," which involves affectively neutral information. Across both of these cognitive categories, a distinction is also made between (1) sensory-perceptual processes (early processing and detection of stimuli), (2) attention/control (the ability to attend to some stimuli and ignore others), (3) memory (maintenance and retrieval of information),

Textbox 5.1 Cognition and Suicide: Valerie as an Example

We have seen in Chapter 2 that sensitivity to particular social stimuli is considered an important part of the vulnerability to suicide. The story of Valerie in the Preface provides a compelling example of how a seemingly banal confrontation may lead to extreme consequences: Confrontation with the angry face of her uncle urged her to try to kill herself. Such a sensitivity could, in theory, be due to changes in attention, perception, memory, or other cognitive functions. If someone pays attention only to those environmental stimuli that signal defeat, this environment may become a frightening source of feeling like a loser. Another individual, however, may pay attention to completely different stimuli and experience the same environment in a different and nonthreatening way. Or is the sensitivity to particular social stimuli the consequence of past negative experiences which are stored in our memories? Or is memory not functioning well, due to which only negative connotations of particular stimuli are remembered? These are just a few examples to show how cognitive characteristics may influence the way in which we think about ourselves, the world, and the future. Such cognitive changes may render individuals suicidal, and cognitive studies aim at quantifying these changes.

and (4) executive function (complex integrative and decision-making processes). These functions are presented in order of, broadly speaking, ascending phylogenetic "complexity": Perceptual processes occur rapidly, largely in subcortical and posterior cortical circuits, and attention, higher-order learning, and executive processes require progressively more complex integration of cortically processed information (Robinson et al., 2013). These four broad divisions form the hierarchical structure for this chapter. For the sake of readability, references will be listed at the end of the chapter, per cognitive category. Textbox 5.1 describes how cognitive characteristics may have led to suicidal behavior in the case of Valerie (see the Preface).

5.1 Sensory Perception

Perception is the brain's process of organizing and interpreting sensory information to give it a meaning. It is a complex process that refers to the relatively immediate, intrapersonal response to sensory environmental and social stimuli. In essence, the term "perception" thus refers to the extraction of information from environmental stimulation. In his highly influential "cry of pain" model, which was described in Chapter 2, Mark Williams (Williams et al., 2015) refers to perceptual pop-out, in which a stimulus that is of great interest to a person appears to jump at them. This explains one's ability to hear one's own name at a party, even across a crowded room (hence called the "cocktail party phenomenon"). This is a normal perceptual process, ensuring that no information that is important for one's well-being is missed. Research has shown that such a pop-out is almost completely involuntary. For someone who is sensitive to failure (or has been made sensitive by circumstances), the world will appear to have many more aspects that refer to defeat and rejection. At exactly the point in their lives when people need relief from stress, they are bombarded with stimuli signaling that they are "losers."

Further perceptual suicide studies focus mostly on visual perception, and more particularly the perception of emotions on faces. In his 1865 book, *Expression of Emotions in Man and Animals*, Charles Darwin first proposed an evolutionary explanation for the human fascination with faces. He argued that important social cues are expressed through facial emotions during situations of extreme fear and excitement, strongly suggesting that the face is an important feature of our social communication. The study of reaction to emotional faces can thus be used to assess the reactivity to social rejection as a component of the vulnerability to suicide (see Chapter 2).

5.2 Attention

Attention can be defined as the amount of effort exerted in focusing on certain portions of an experience, such as sensory perception. Perception and attention both contribute to the ability to consciously control and direct the mental processes related to external stimuli, whereby perception refers to the ability to make sense of the environment, while attention is the ability to concentrate on perceived stimuli. Both cognitive functions thus contribute to the ability to choose which stimuli attention should be allocated to.

There are many different definitions of attention, but a very early definition by William James in his 1901 book *The Principles of Psychology* includes the main basic features. James defined attention as "the taking possession by the mind, in clear and vivid form, of one out of what seem several simultaneous possible objects or trains of thought." The term "attention" thus refers to a process of selection, namely, the selection of information and thoughts. Or, as James put it: "focalization,

green	**blue**	**yellow**	blue
blue	red	**yellow**	red
yellow	yellow	**green**	**red**
yellow	green	**blue**	yellow
green	**red**	blue	**green**
blue	**yellow**	**blue**	red

Figure 5.1 The Stroop test. See color plate 10.

concentration of consciousness are of its essence. It implies withdrawal from some things in order to deal effectively with others." In Chapter 8 we will see how crucially important this definition of attention is for our understanding of the development of suicidal thoughts and feelings.

The Continuous Performance Test (CPT) and the Stroop test (Figure 5.1) are the most commonly used measures of attention in cognitive studies of suicidal behavior. The CPT measures sustained attention and distractibility by presenting participants with a repetitive, boring task during which focus must be maintained for a period of time in order to respond to targets. The Stroop test assesses selective attention, the ability to respond to certain environmental stimuli while ignoring others. There are different variants of the Stroop test, but all versions have at least two numbers of subtasks. In the classic Stroop task, an individual is asked to identify the presented color of a series of color words – some of which are color congruent (e.g., the word "red" written in red color) and others that are color incongruent (the word "red" written in blue color).

The cognitive interference caused by the automated reading of linguistic stimuli is calculated by subtracting the average response time for the color-congruent words from the average response time for the color-incongruent words. The Stroop effect thus is the degree of difficulty people have with naming the color of the ink rather than the word itself: there is an interference between the color of the ink and the word meaning because naming colors requires more attention than reading words. In the "emotional Stroop test" the response of participants to name colors of negative emotional words is examined. For instance, depressed individuals will be slower to name the color of depressing words than nondepressing words. A few studies have particularly applied a suicide-specific variant of the emotional Stroop test by using suicide-related words, such as "suicide," "death," and "funeral," to study attentional bias in relation to suicidal behavior. This test is called the Suicide Stroop.

Sustained attention and distractibility, as assessed with the CPT, appear not to be deficient in association with suicidal behavior. A completely different picture emerges from the Stroop studies: Performance is poor in depressed individuals but even worse in those with a history of suicidal behavior. Depression-related impairments of attention, especially susceptibility to interference, are accentuated in individuals with a history of suicidal behavior (Keilp et al., 2008). Moreover, it was thought that deficits became evident without any type of explicit emotional provocation or emotionally biased stimuli, suggesting that attentional control mechanisms themselves are dysfunctional and not susceptible to specific types of emotional arousal. However, more recent studies (including a meta-analysis) using emotional Stroop tests show an interference effect with suicide-related words, and particularly the word "suicide," in the so-called Suicide Stroop, that has good predictive validity for suicidal behavior. An attentional bias toward such words, but not toward negatively valenced words in general, could thus well be a cognitive marker of suicide risk.

5.3 Memory

Theoretically, characteristics of memory, which is the capacity to encode, store, and retrieve information, may contribute to the development of suicide risk. For example, people may develop a negative vision of the world because they particularly remember the bad things that have happened during their lifetimes. Consequently, memory has been studied quite extensively in the context of suicidal behavior, focusing on divergent aspects such as short-term memory, long-term memory, autobiographical memory, and working memory. Dozens of studies have been carried out, including systematic reviews and a meta-analysis. In particular, studies that compare individuals with a history of psychiatric problems and suicidal behavior with those with only psychiatric problems are relevant for our understanding of the cognitive vulnerability to suicidal behavior, and will be discussed in this chapter.

Such studies have revealed no deficiencies in short-term memory functions in association with suicidal behavior as assessed with, for example, the Auditory Verbal Learning Test. Studies of long-term memory have produced different results, thus making it difficult to draw conclusions. Equally reflecting memory of past experiences is autobiographical memory, which encompasses our recollections of specific

personal events. Autobiographical memory is tested with the Autobiographical Memory Test (AMT). In the AMT, five positive words (*happy,
safe, interested, successful,* and *surprised*) and five negative words (*sorry,
angry, clumsy, hurt* (emotional), and *lonely*) are successively presented
to the participant. Subjects are given one minute to produce a specific
personal memory in response to each word. Responses are usually
audiorecorded. The specificity of the memories is then determined based
on the details given to describe the event. Research over the past three
decades and a recent meta-analysis indicate an association with suicidal
behavior: The specificity of autobiographical memory is decreased in
individuals with a history of attempted suicide, as shown by their tendency to generalize and summarize categories of events rather than
retrieving a single episode.

Concerning working memory, research findings are divergent, but a
meta-analysis indicates that past suicide attempters perform more poorly
on working memory tasks than nonattempters when both groups are in
the same clinical depressive state.

5.4 Executive Functions

5.4.1 Fluency

The first studies of characteristics of fluency date back to the early 1990s,
and were performed in the context of the study of executive functioning
in relation to suicidal behavior. Noteworthy findings have prompted
researchers to further study the characteristics of fluency in relation with
suicidal behavior. In the standard versions of fluency tasks, participants
are given one minute to produce as many unique words as possible
within a semantic category ("category fluency," e.g., categories of
animals or fruits) or starting with a given letter ("letter fluency," e.g.,
words starting with the letters F, A, and S). The participant's score in
each task is the number of unique correct words. The Future Thinking
Task (FTT) is designed to specifically target valence differences in
individuals' cognitions about the future. Administering the FTT involves
explicitly asking participants to generate potential events for the future,
including positive events that the individual is "looking forward to" and
negative events that the individual is "not looking forward to."

Studies of verbal fluency yield divergent results, but a meta-analysis
identifies lower fluency scores for the "animals" category, but not for the
FAS semantic fluency, among suicide attempters than among mood-
disordered controls (Richard-Devantoy et al., 2014). Concerning future

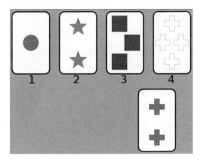

Figure 5.2 The Wisconsin Card Sorting Test: screenshot from computerized version. See color plate 11.

thinking, decreased positive future thinking, but no increase in negative future thinking, is common in suicide attempters in comparison with controls.

5.4.2 Cognitive Flexibility

Cognitive flexibility, which is defined as the ability to switch thinking between different concepts and to simultaneously think about multiple concepts, is a complex cognitive characteristic. It involves cognitive processes such as strategic planning, organized searching, using environmental feedback to shift cognitive sets, directing behavior toward achieving a goal, and modulating impulsive responding. The Wisconsin Card Sorting Test (WCST; Figure 5.2) is the most commonly used neuropsychological test to measure this characteristic. In this test, cards are presented to the participants, with figures on the cards differing with respect to color, quantity, and shape.

The participants are told to match the cards, but not which information to use for matching; however, they are told whether a particular match is right or wrong. The test generates psychometric scores, including numbers, percentages, and percentiles of categories achieved, trials, errors, and perseverative errors. This measure particularly assesses "set-shifting," i.e., the ability to display flexibility in the face of changing schedules of reinforcement. As such, the WCST relies on cognitive functions including attention, working memory, and visual processing. The Trail Making Test (TMT) also is a commonly used test of cognitive flexibility.

In general, high-lethality suicide attempters perform significantly worse than nonattempters, low-lethality attempters, and healthy controls on the

WCST, independent of an effect of depression. Low-lethality suicidal behavior including self-injurious behavior is not associated with WCST deficits. In addition, current cognitive inflexibility as measured with the WCST may increase suicidal ideation over a 6-month period, but only in suicide attempters.

5.4.3 Problem Solving

Problem solving is commonly regarded as one of the most complex neurocognitive characteristics. In relation to suicidal behavior, problem solving has been studied mainly by means of the Means-Ends Problem Solving (MEPS) procedure. This test taps the ability to orient oneself to and conceptualize a means of moving toward a goal. The MEPS consists of ten items, which require participants to imagine themselves as the protagonist in a problem situation. Participants are asked to produce a story in which the protagonist successfully resolves the problem to achieve a specified ending. Figure 5.3 shows an example problem-solving vignette from the MEPS.

Less commonly, social problem solving is assessed using the Social Problem-Solving Inventory, which measures adaptive problem-solving dimensions (positive problem orientation and rational problem solving) and dysfunctional dimensions (negative problem orientation, impulsivity/carelessness, and avoidance).

The cross-sectional and longitudinal studies of (social) problem solving in general population and clinical samples provide clear evidence that poor problem-solving ability is associated with increased suicide risk, i.e., suicidal ideation and suicidal behavior. Closer inspection of the MEPS studies suggests that individuals who are suicidal report less relevant means, are more passive in their problem-solving strategies, and are less effective in their problem-solving strategies.

In general, suicidal behavior is associated with the production of a smaller number of problem-solving strategies that are also less effective.

Mrs. C. had just moved in that day and didn't know anyone. Mrs. C. wanted to have friends in the neighborhood.

The story ends with Mrs. C. having many friends and feeling at home in the neighborhood. You begin the story with Mrs. C. in her room, immediately after arriving in the neighborhood.

Figure 5.3 Example problem-solving vignette from the MEPS.

Psychiatric disorders such as depression appear to increase this deficiency by adding a component of passivity to impaired problem solving. Passivity in problem solving may not be uniquely associated with suicidal behavior, but its combination with a smaller number and less effective alternatives appears to increase the vulnerability to suicidal behavior. It thus appears that poor problem solving is diathesis-related, as deficits in social problem-solving skills may predispose an individual under chronic stress to suicidal behavior.

Elderly individuals who attempted suicide with strong suicidal intent appear to perceive life problems as more threatening and unsolvable than nonsuicidal depressed elderly in a social problem-solving inventory (Gibbs et al., 2009).

5.4.4 Implicit Association

The implicit association test (IAT) can be used to assess whether individuals who have decided to kill themselves reveal stronger implicit cognitions associating self with death/suicide and whether the strength of such an association may predict actual suicide attempts. The IAT measures people's reaction times when classifying semantic stimuli to measure the automatic mental associations they hold about various topics, such as self-cutting or life and death/suicide (Greenwald et al., 2003).

In the "death/suicide IAT," participants classify stimuli representing the constructs of *death* (i.e., *die*, *dead*, *deceased*, *lifeless*, and *suicide*) and *life* (i.e., *alive*, *survive*, *live*, *thrive*, and *breathing*) and the attributes of *me* (i.e., *I*, *myself*, *my*, *mine*, and *self*) and "not me" (i.e., *they*, *them*, *their*, *theirs*, and *other*) (Nock & Banaji, 2007). The relative strength of each participant's association between *death* and *me* is reflected by faster responding on the *death/me* blocks relative to the *life/me* blocks), and negative scores represent a stronger association between life and self. A longitudinal study shows that the "death/suicide IAT" identifies an implicit association between death/suicide and self as a behavioral marker that distinguishes suicide attempters from other psychiatrically distressed patients and predicts future suicide attempts.

5.4.5 Decision Making

Decision making is the cognitive process of identifying and choosing alternatives based on values and preferences, resulting in the selection of a belief or a course of action among several alternative possibilities.

The Iowa Gambling Task (IGT) is the most commonly used measure of decision making. The task requires a variety of cognitive and emotional functions, including affective processing of ongoing somatic feedback, working memory, attention, response inhibition, planning, and rule detection. The task factors aspects involved in complex real-life decisions, including immediate rewards and delayed punishments, risk, and uncertainty of outcomes. The IGT is a computerized task involving four decks of cards, A, B, C, and D. Each time a participant selects a card, a specified amount of play money is awarded. However, interspersed among these rewards are probabilistic punishments (monetary losses with different amounts). Two of the decks of cards, A and B, produce high immediate gains, but, in the long run, these two decks will take more money than they give, and are therefore considered to be the disadvantageous decks. The other two decks, C and D, are considered advantageous, as they result in small, immediate gains, but will yield more money than they take in the long run. Each game consists of 100 card choices. Figure 5.4 shows a screenshot from a computerized version of the IGT.

Net scores for the gambling task are calculated by subtracting the number of disadvantageous choices (decks A and B) from the number of advantageous choices (decks C and D). Higher net scores therefore signify better performance on the task. Optimal performance on the IGT requires that participants begin to learn the contingencies in each deck as the task progresses, and to shift their strategies accordingly (choosing from advantageous decks mostly).

Individual studies, systematic reviews, and meta-analyses consistently document decision-making deficiencies in association with suicidal behavior. These deficiencies appear to exist independent of mood disturbances and persist beyond episodes of depression. Some studies indicate worse performance in cases of a history of violent suicide attempts than nonviolent attempts. Remarkably, individuals with a history of suicide attempts and affective controls less often than healthy controls understand the contingencies of the task (namely, which options yielded higher gains or losses). Understanding is associated with better performance in healthy and affective controls but not in suicide attempters, who apparently show a disconnection between what they know and what they do.

A recent study focuses on divergent components of the decision-making process using the Adult Decision-Making Competence (A-DMC) task. It appears that suicide attempters, first, are unable to resist sunk costs (the inability to abort an action for which costs are irrecoverable), as they persist with failing plans despite irrecoverable investments. The inability

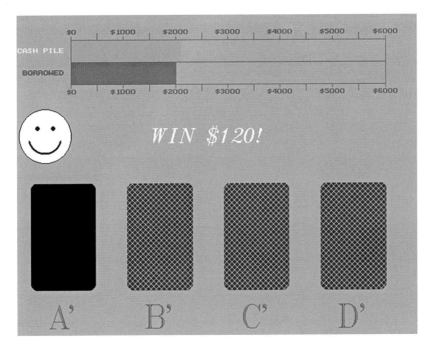

Figure 5.4 The Iowa Gambling Task: Screenshot from a computerized version.
See color plate 12.

to resist sunk costs can be thought of as a form of entrapment, suggesting that suicide attempters' decisions may be driven by their stronger focus on painful past experiences. Second, suicide attempters appear to be prone to a framing bias, reflecting an inability to conceptualize the problem at a higher abstract level, which may inhibit the search for alternative solutions in a suicidal crisis. The results thus resonate with the entrapment and no escape features of cognitive psychological models of the vulnerability to suicidal behavior as described in Chapter 2.

It is unclear to what extent dysfunctions in basic neuropsychological functions (such as attention) contribute to or are responsible for impairments in more complex neuropsychological functions (such as decision making and problem solving). Indeed, decision processes may be corrupted by a failure to adequately focus attention and control the information on which they are based (Keilp et al., 2008). At least one study found that poor decision-making task performance using the IGT was associated with impairments of selective attention and memory (Hardy et al., 2006). Impaired selective attention performance may underlie the "cognitive rigidity" that is a common clinical feature of suicide attempters (Pollock & Williams, 1998). Furthermore, correlations between (overgeneral) autobiographical memory and (less effective) problem-solving strategies are found (Pollock & Williams, 2001; Kaviani et al., 2003; Kaviani et al., 2004; Kaviani et al., 2005; Arie et al., 2008). Indications for a correlation between autobiographical memory and future thinking are also found. Williams (1996) examined whether the specificity with which suicidal patients and healthy controls retrieve episodes from their past determines the specificity with which they imagine the future. Suicidal subjects' memory and future responses are more generic, and specificity level for the past and the future is correlated for both groups. A recent neuroimaging study showed that evocation of past and future events involves highly similar patterns of brain activation (Botzung et al., 2008). Thus, neuropsychological (dys-)functions may tend to cluster, which suggests that they are manifestations of a common underlying substrate of suicidal behavior. On the other hand, studies in suicide attempters suggest that alterations in decision making are largely independent of cognitive control (including cognitive flexibility, cognitive control, and working memory) and are not related to attention deficits, as no association was found between performances on the Stroop test and IGT. However, a few studies examining decision making and cognitive inhibition in suicide attempters using Go/No-Go commission errors (Westheide et al., 2008) or the Stroop task (Legris et al., 2012) show a significant correlation between the IGT net score and attention, working memory, or cognitive flexibility. In addition, we will see further in this chapter that interventions aiming at increasing attentional control may improve decision-making competence. Overall, this review thus only partially supports the separability between decision making on the IGT and cognitive abilities such as attentional control (Toplak et al., 2010).

Such a separability nevertheless is in keeping with the suggestion (as described earlier) that the neurocognitive vulnerability to suicidal behavior may rely on impairments in two distinct anatomical systems, one processing value-based decision making (associated with ventromedial prefrontal cortex, among others) and one underlying cognitive control (associated with more dorsal prefrontal regions). Chapter 6 will discuss the functional and structural neuroanatomy of the vulnerability to suicide in detail, and point at functional correlations with neurocognitive characteristics.

Taken together, it can be hypothesized that a vulnerability to suicidal acts results from a combination of alterations in value-based/motivational processes (supporting decision making as measured by the IGT), on one side, and in cognitive control processes (as measured by fluency and Stroop tasks), on the other side (Jollant et al., 2011). Cognitive control refers to mechanisms that orchestrate thought and action in accordance with internal goals and, therefore, encompass multiple functions from task switching, response inhibition, error detection, response conflict, and working memory (Richard-Devantoy et al., 2014).

A clinical translation of this cognitive model could be that vulnerable individuals are more likely to strongly value negative life events, such as signals of social rejection, which, when they happen, lead to an intense negative state involving severe mental pain (see Chapter 1). Their difficulty in controlling this response, coupled with a preexisting difficulty envisioning the long-term consequences of some options, may limit the extent of their choices and lead them to consider suicide as the only possible way to escape this painful state (Richard-Devantoy et al., 2014).

Chapter 5 Summary

- This chapter reviews findings from more than 80 studies and reveals cognitive disturbances in association with suicidal behavior including attention, memory, and executive functions such as future fluency, problem solving, and decision making.
- Recent studies particularly demonstrate clear alterations in value-based decision-making processes.
- Hopelessness is a robust predictor of suicidal behavior; it is related to deficiencies in problem solving and verbal fluency (reduced inability to generate positive future events, rather than the higher propensity to generate negative future events).
- Deficits in attention, memory, fluency, and mental flexibility are more marked in high-lethality than low-lethality suicidal behavior, and reverse causality (the deficiencies as a consequence of self-injurious behaviors) is unlikely.
- Common third factors (related to both suicidal behavior and cognitive dysfunction), such as IQ (see Chapter 1) or depression, may play a role.
- Concerning depression, an interference effect on the Stroop task reflecting attentional deficits may occur or be exacerbated during a depressive state, due to which suicide risk may increase in parallel with more difficulties in monitoring and controlling attention, notably to suicidal thoughts. Regarding autobiographical memory, impairment may be one of the mechanisms through which depression increases an individual's vulnerability to suicidal behavior. Concerning problem

solving and future fluency, findings suggest that small changes in mood may reinstate deficits. An important clinical implication is that a small change in mood may thus lead to a simultaneous increase in hopelessness and a decrease in problem-solving ability, thus fueling a suicidal crisis.

- Methodological issues include unclear definitions of (non-)suicidal behaviors and small sample sizes.
- Nevertheless, a causal effect of cognitive deficiencies is possible and supported by the convergent nature of the findings using different study populations including longitudinal designs, and the existence of a biological gradient (more severe deficiencies in more lethal suicidal behavior).
- The causes of demonstrated cognitive deficits are yet unclear, and may include the following:
  - Genetics: heritability of cognitive functioning is considerable; for example, the heritability of Stroop Task performance is up to 50%. First-degree relatives of suicides appear to have similar cognitive deficiencies, as assessed with the WCST and IGT, as suicide attempters, but intact cognitive control, which may protect them from suicidal behavior (McGirr et al., 2013; Hoehne et al., 2015).
  - Restricted fetal growth is a documented risk factor for suicidal behavior that may be associated with disturbed development of the brain and thus constitute an intrauterine determinant of the diathesis for suicide (see Chapter 1). Prenatal maternal stress is associated with attention deficits in offspring (Weinstock, 2008).
  - Stress: perceived defeat, a common stressor precipitating suicidal behavior, impairs memory functions (Johnson et al., 2008). The administration of cortisol, i.e., the stress hormone of which the concentration may be increased in depressed suicidal individuals, is associated with impaired recall of pleasant words, while recall of unpleasant words is not affected (Tops et al., 2004).
- An important conclusion from this review of cognitive studies is that treatment of suicide risk should not focus only on state-dependent characteristics. Hopelessness and risk of suicide may disappear when depressed mood normalizes, but remain ready to be reactivated when depression returns and underlying neuropsychological disturbances persist. Williams and colleagues (2008) have pointed out that focusing on reducing hopelessness itself is not sufficient, nor does a lower level of hopelessness or suicidal ideation at the end of treatment provide reassurance that the underlying vulnerability has been treated. There is the danger that clinicians will see a patient's reduction in hopelessness

as indicating treatment success but fail to see that the underlying neuropsychological impairments resulting in, e.g., cognitive reactivity has not changed. The introduction of a relapse prevention task near the end of treatment is therefore a promising approach (Brown et al., 2005). The objective is to prime thoughts and feelings associated with prior suicide attempts and to determine whether patients are able to respond to their problems in an adaptive way. Successful completion of the task justifies completion of treatment.

• Cognitive deficits are amenable to treatment. Antidepressants such as paroxetine and bupropion may normalize cognitive deficits in the attention and memory domains in depressed suicidal individuals, whether or not in parallel with an improvement of depression severity (Gorlyn et al., 2015). Mindfulness meditation can improve decision-making competence by improving resistance to sunk-cost bias through decreased focus on past and future and decreased negative affect (Hafenbrack et al., 2014). Interventions may thus decrease the attentional information processing bias and widen suicidal individuals' attention away from suicide and toward alternatives, such as hope and reasons to live.

Review Questions

1. Describe the major cognitive deficits in association with suicidal behavior.
2. Is suicide risk associated with dysfunctions in "hot" or "cold" cognitive domains?
3. How may a depressed state and longer-term cognitive disturbances interact to increase suicide risk?
4. How may interventions aimed at increasing attentional control improve decision-making competences?
5. Give three potential causes of cognitive deficiencies in suicidal individuals.
6. Describe implications of cognitive deficiencies for the treatment and prevention of suicidal behavior.

Further Reading

Jollant, F., Lawrence, N. L., Olié, E., Guillaume, S. & Courtet, P. (2011). The suicidal mind and brain: A review of neuropsychological and neuroimaging studies. *The World Journal of Biological Psychiatry, 12*, 319–39.

Richard-Devantoy, S., Berlim, M. T. & Jollant, F. (2014). A meta-analysis
    of neuropsychological markers of vulnerability to suicidal
    behavior in mood disorders. *Psychological Medicine, 44,*
    1663–73.
van Heeringen, K., Bijttebier, S. (2016). Understanding the suicidal brain: A
    review of neuropsychological studies of suicidal ideation and behavior.
    In R. C. O'Connor & J. Pirkis (Eds.), *The international handbook of
    suicide prevention* (2nd edition). Chichester: Wiley.
Williams, J. M. G. (2001). *Suicide and attempted suicide.* London: Penguin
    Books.

References per Cognitive Category
Perception

Seymour et al., 2016; Williams et al., 2015.

Attention

Williams & Broadbent, 1986; Becker et al., 1999; King et al., 2000; Keilp
et al., 2001; Marzuk, 2005; Harkavy-Friedman et al., 2006; Raust et al.,
2007; Dombrovski et al., 2008; Keilp et al., 2008; Ohmann et al., 2008;
Rüsch et al., 2008; Westheide et al., 2008; Malloy-Diniz et al., 2009; Cha
et al., 2010; Keilp et al., 2013; Dixon-Gordon et al., 2014; Drabble et al.,
2014; Keilp et al., 2014; Tsafrir et al., 2014; Chung & Jeglic, 2016; Steward
et al., 2017.

Memory

Williams & Broadbent, 1986; Williams & Dritschel, 1988; Evans et al., 1992;
Sidley et al., 1997; Kaviani et al., 2003; Kaviani et al., 2004; Kaviani et al.,
2005; Williams et al., 2005a; Williams et al., 2005b; Leibetseder et al., 2006;
Sinclair et al., 2007; Williams et al., 2007; Arie et al., 2008; Johnson et al.,
2008; Rasmussen et al., 2008; Rüsch et al., 2008; Westheide et al., 2008;
Williams et al., 2008; Malloy-Diniz et al., 2009; Delaney et al., 2012; Keilp
et al., 2013, 2014; Richard-Devantoy et al., 2014.

Implicit Association Test

Nock et al., 2010.

Fluency

Bartfai et al., 1990; MacLeod et al., 1993; MacLeod et al., 1997; Audenaert et al., 2002; Conaghan & Davidson, 2002; Hunter & O'Connor, 2003; Tops et al., 2004; Hepburn et al., 2006; O'Connor et al., 2008; Williams et al., 2008.

Mental Flexibility

McGirr et al., 2012; Miranda et al., 2013.

Problem Solving

Sidley et al., 1997; Pollock & Williams, 1998; Pollock et al., 1998; Pollock & Williams, 2001; Kaviani et al., 2004; Pollock & Williams, 2004; Williams et al., 2005a; Arie et al., 2008; Nock et al., 2008; Gibbs et al., 2009; Oldershaw et al., 2009.

Decision Making

Jollant et al., 2005; Jollant et al., 2007; Oldershaw et al., 2009; Dombrovski et al., 2010; Clarke et al., 2011; Dombrovski et al., 2011; Martino et al., 2011; Bridge et al., 2012; Chamberlain et al., 2013; Gorlyn et al., 2013; Jollant et al., 2013; Ackerman et al., 2015; Hoehne et al., 2015; Szanto et al., 2015; Richard-Devantoy et al., 2016c; Pustilnik et al., 2017.

Treatment and Prevention

Hafenbrack et al., 2014; Gorlyn et al., 2015.

CHAPTER SIX

Images of the Suicidal Brain

Systems Neuroscience and Suicide

Learning Objectives

- Describe the main structural and functional brain imaging techniques and show how they can contribute to our insights in the development of suicide risk.
- Describe the main gray and white matter components of the frontothalamic circuitry that is involved in suicidal behavior.
- What is the Cyberball game? What can we learn about suicidal behavior from neuroimaging studies using this game?
- Which mechanisms relate disturbed decision making to suicidal behavior, and what can we learn from imaging studies about these mechanisms?
- What are possible causes of structural and functional brain changes in suicidal behavior?

Introduction

Systems neuroscience focuses on the function of neural circuits and systems that give rise to relatively higher-level functions such as those described in the previous cognitive neuroscience chapter. Primary tools are brain imaging techniques, such as molecular imaging with PET and functional, structural, and connectivity imaging with MRI. The focus is on identifying brain circuits that are involved in suicidal behavior to understand the systems-level neurobiological mechanisms that lead to individual variability in its occurrence.

This individual variability in occurrence poses a major problem for suicide prevention, and systems neuroscience can thus be expected to contribute significantly. More particularly, individual variability translates into limitations in the accuracy of risk assessment and prediction of treatment response, which constitute two major barriers to effective suicide prevention. Clinicians are unable to predict the occurrence of suicidal behavior at the level of the individual. Depressed patients are very often frightened by their suicidal thoughts, and even they often cannot predict whether these thoughts will lead them to take their own lives. In addition, when suicide risk is considered high, its management is challenging because of the poor evidence base. For instance, we cannot predict the individual response to treatment in terms of decrease in suicide risk, and interventions, be they pharmacological or psychothera-peutic, may even be associated with an increased risk of suicidal behav-ior. Even if there is a positive response to treatment in terms of a reduction in suicide risk, we do not know how and why this happens. This chapter will discuss the potential contribution of brain imaging to overcome these barriers to effective suicide prevention through the identification of brain circuits and systems that may function as biomar-kers of suicide risk and targets of treatment.

But there is more to be expected from brain imaging studies of suicide risk. Together with cognitive studies (see Chapter 5), neuroimaging provides a window to the brain, and thus much can be learned from imaging studies about the dynamics of suicide, or the cognitive pathways to suicidal behavior that constitute the suicidal mind. Integration of the insights in cognitive processes and their neuroanatomical basis sheds light on these neurocognitive pathways, and provides a firm basis for the development of new models of suicide risk, such as the computa-tional model in Chapter 8. For the sake of readability references will be listed at the end of the chapter, per brain imaging technique.

6.1 Images of the Suicidal Brain

6.1.1 Structural Imaging Studies of Suicidal Behavior

Structural imaging studies of suicidal behavior, using MRI (see Chapter 3 for technical details), have focused on lesions in gray and white matter. Brain MRI studies consistently show disturbances in association with suicidal behavior, the so-called hyperintensities in gray matter (GMH) and in white matter (WMH). In general, white matter hyperintensities can be caused by a variety of factors including restrictions in blood supply and loss or deformation of the myelin sheath (demyelinization), bleeding, or hypertrophy of glial cells. Figure 6.1 shows an example of periventricular white matter hyperintensities in association with suicidal behavior (Pompili et al., 2008).

Hyperintensities are usually seen in normal aging, but elderly suicide attempters show more WMH than elderly patient controls, and the pres-ence of WMH indicates increased risk of suicide attempts in depressed children and adolescents. WMH are one of the most replicated findings in

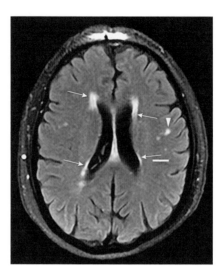

Figure 6.1 Periventricular white matter hyperintensities.

imaging studies of suicidal behavior, independent of age group, but the interpretation of the WMH findings is difficult, as will be addressed later.

Structural characteristics of white matter in association with suicidal behavior have been studied using DTI (see Chapter 3 for technical issues). The main finding is white matter abnormalities in frontothalamic circuits passing through the left internal capsule, in left orbitofrontal white matter, and in the thalamus. Detailed tract-based spatial statistical analysis of whole-brain DTI data has been developed to assess changes in white matter using multiple measures. This approach can be used to study white matter correlates of suicidal behavior in individuals with psychiatric problems such as schizophrenia and panic disorder when compared with healthy controls. The results are remarkably similar across these studied populations, with suicide attempters showing significantly higher fractional anisotropy (FA, measuring the directionality of water diffusion, reflects the extent to which white matter fibers have the same direction and are intact as an important index of structural connectivity; see Chapter 3 for technical details) in the left corona radiata, thalamic radiations, internal capsule, and sagittal stratum than nonattempters. Attempters show significantly lower axial diffusivity (AD) but normal mean diffusivity (MD) in similar areas such as the left internal capsule, thalamic radiation, and the sagittal stratum, suggesting axonal abnormalities in these regions. Suicide attempters differ substantially from nonattempters in DTI fiber tracking estimates of the number of fibers projecting to the left medial frontal cortex, orbitofrontal cortex, and left thalamus and of fibers traversing through the left anterior limb of the internal capsule (ALIC) (Jia et al., 2014).

Such findings provide new detail regarding specific alterations in fronto-thalamic loops, where anatomic abnormalities in thalamocortical and corticothalamic pathways may contribute to functional disruption of neural circuits that influence behavioral control in ways that increase the risk for suicidal behavior in depressed patients. A possible specific role of these thalamocortical loops in the development of suicide risk will be elaborated in Chapter 8.

Taken together, studies of white matter show the following changes in association with suicidal behavior:

• increased connectivity (as indicated by increased FA) in left internal capsule, thalamic radiations, corona radiata, and sagittal stratum
• decreased connectivity (decreased FA, or decreased number of stream-lines) in left orbitofrontal and bilateral dorsomedial frontal lobe
• decreased mean percentage of fibers in the left internal capsule projecting to the thalamus and the orbitofrontal cortex.

These findings are consistent with the described white matter hyperinten-sities in the frontal, temporal, and parietal lobes. It is remarkable that DTI studies appear to reveal white matter changes in the left hemisphere only, but their meaning is yet unclear. Increased connectivity may lead to greater or more rapid transmission of information, and thus lead to aberrant salience of particular sensory information or to enhanced top-down cognitive control (see Chapter 8).

Other studies focus on morphometric differences in cortical and sub-cortical gray matter areas, thus looking at volumes and thickness of the cortex. Volumes of areas of the prefrontal cortex are reduced in association with suicidal behavior, including the orbitofrontal, ventrolateral, medial and dorsomedial (including the anterior cingulate cortex) and dorsolateral prefrontal cortex. It is noteworthy that these differences are found independently of psychiatric diagnoses such as unipolar and bipolar mood disorders, schizophrenia, and borderline personality disorder.

Importantly, and as discussed in more detail in Chapter 10, treatment with lithium appears to reverse the volume reductions found in suicide attempters. Reduced cortical volumes are also found in the insular, parietal, temporal, and occipital lobes and the cerebellum. Pronounced cortical thinning is found in the right dorsolateral prefrontal cortex, the insular cortex, and superior temporal cortex. Few studies find increased

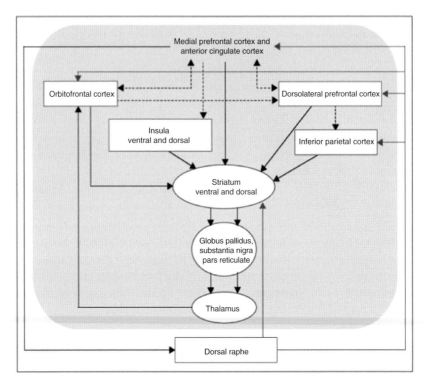

Figure 6.2 Frontothalamic circuitry and suicidal behavior: Findings from structural imaging studies (Reprinted from *The Lancet Psychiatry*, 1, van Heeringen K & Mann JJ, The neurobiology of suicide, 63–72, copyright 2014, with permission from Elsevier). See color plate 13.

volumes: increased white matter volume in inferior frontal gyri and increased temporal cortical volume.

Quite a few subcortical nuclei show a reduced volume in individuals with a history of suicidal behavior including the basal ganglia. Studies of the thalamus reveal inconsistent findings ranging from increased to reduced volumes. Inconsistencies appear to be related to genetic characteristics involving the serotonin transporter gene (enlargement in ss phenotypes; see Chapter 4) and antidepressant influences. Reduced right hippocampal volumes are reported in recent suicide attempters. Amygdala volumes appear to be increased according to some studies. Finally, some, but not all, studies find a reduced volume of the posterior third of the corpus callosum, a wide bundle of myelinated axons that connects the left and right hemisphere. Figure 6.2 summarizes the findings from comparative structural imaging studies of the suicidal brain, depicting the thalamocortical circuit in which changes are found in association with suicidal behavior.

6.1.2 Functional Imaging Studies of Suicidal Behavior

6.1.2.1 Resting State Imaging

Resting state imaging is a method of functional brain imaging that can be used to evaluate regional interactions that occur when a subject is not performing an explicit task. This resting brain activity is observed through changes in the blood flow or metabolic activity in the brain that can be measured using fMRI, PET, or SPECT. (See Chapter 3 for technical details.) Because brain activity is present in the absence of an externally prompted task, any brain region will have spontaneous fluctuations. The resting state approach is useful to explore the brain's functional organization, including functional connectivity, the connectivity between brain regions that share functional characteristics.

A comparative PET study shows relatively lower brain activity in the ventral, medial, and lateral prefrontal cortex of depressed high-lethality suicide attempters when compared with depressed low-lethality attempters. This difference is more pronounced after administration of fenfluramine, a serotonin receptor agonist, and correlates with the lethality of the suicide attempt. Another PET study shows that, after placebo, regional brain activity in attempters is lower in right dorsolateral prefrontal regions and higher in ventromedial regions than in nonattempters. After fenfluramine is taken, areas of relatively reduced activity enlarge. The findings concerning serotonin confirm the involvement of the neurotransmitter serotonin as described in Chapter 4. Alterations in glucose metabolism in specific brain regions associated with a history of suicidal behavior are thus related to altered serotonergic function and vary across a continuum from lowest to highest suicide risk.

Resting-state functional MRI reveals increased connectivity in the left cerebellum and decreased connectivity in the right superior parietal lobe (the "precuneus") in suicide attempters. Another fMRI study shows that suicide attempters have relatively increased activity in the right superior temporal gyrus and lower activity in the right ventral medial frontal gyrus relative to nonattempters.

Brain SPECT scans reveal that resting-state activity is relatively lower in the motor cortex, corpus callosum, subgenual cingulate, and anterodorsal cortex in individuals who took their own lives after the scan than in depressed and healthy controls who did not die due to suicide.

A significant area of low activity is the nucleus accumbens, extending into the ventromedial prefrontal cortex and the left and right putamen.

Brain activity during resting state – as measured with PET scans (see Chapter 3 for details about this study approach) – is lower in the right middle frontal gyrus and the right inferior parietal lobe (Brodmann area 10 and 39) in depressed individuals with concrete suicide plans than in those with suicide thoughts. Suicide plans in depressed individuals appear to be associated with reduced activity in brain areas that are involved in decision making and choice, more particularly in exploratory behavior, as will be discussed in detail in Chapter 8.

Neuropharmacological characteristics can be mapped using functional neuroimaging techniques such as PET and SPECT. The serotonergic neurotransmission system has been studied most. PET studies of the serotonin transporter show reduced binding in the midbrain. Concerning the 5-HT$_{2A}$ receptor binding, study results are divergent. Suicide attempters and nonattempters do not differ in 5-HT$_{1A}$ receptor binding in the prefrontal cortex and the brainstem raphe nuclei, but raphe nuclei receptor binding is 45% greater in higher-lethality attempters than in lower-lethality attempters. In a 2-year follow-up PET study of 100 depressed patients, higher raphe nuclei 5-HT$_{1A}$ binding predicts greater lethality of subsequent suicidal behavior during follow-up. Exploratory analyses suggest that 5-HT$_{1A}$ binding in the insula, anterior cingulate, and dorsolateral prefrontal cortex are also predictive of lethality. Thus, greater raphe nuclei 5-HT$_{1A}$ binding potential predicts more lethal suicidal behavior during a 2-year period. This effect may be mediated through decreased serotonin neuron firing and release.

Regional serotonin synthesis in the brain can be studied with PET and α-(^{11}C)-methyl-L-tryptophan trapping. When compared with healthy controls, high-lethality suicide attempters show reduced serotonin synthesis in the orbital and ventromedial prefrontal cortices, and α-(^{11}C)-methyl-L-tryptophan trapping in these regions correlates negatively with suicide intent. Low serotonin synthesis in the prefrontal cortex may thus lower the threshold for high-lethality suicidal behavior.

6.1.2.2 Spectroscopy

As described in Chapter 3, spectroscopy uses MRI to measure the concentration of molecules such as glutamate, GABA, n-acetyl-aspartate (NAA), creatinine and myo-inositol. A demonstrated reduced NAA/creatinine ratio in the left hippocampus of suicide attempters, when compared with healthy controls, probably is more reflective of a depressive state (as no depressed control group was available) than indicative of a neurobiological vulnerability to suicidal behavior. Another spectroscopy study found no differences in the concentration of nine molecules (including glutamate, GABA, and NAA) in the right dorsal prefrontal cortex between suicide attempters and a depressed control group. A potential role of NAA in suicide risk will be discussed later in the context of risk factors and in a discussion of possible causes of white matter abnormalities.

6.1.3 Imaging Studies of Suicide Risk Factors

As described in Chapter 1, suicidal behavior is the consequence of an interaction between proximal and distal risk factors. Proximal risk factors, or state-dependent characteristics associated with an increased risk of suicidal behavior, include psychiatric disorders such as depression, schizophrenia, and substance use disorders. As the vast majority of individuals suffering from these disorders will not show suicidal behavior, the specificity of these disorders with regard to suicide risk is limited. The imaging literature concerning these disorders will therefore not be reviewed in this chapter. However, other state-dependent characteristics are more specifically associated with an increased risk of suicidal behavior, including mental pain and hopelessness. Imaging studies of these state-dependent clinical correlates of suicidal behavior will therefore be reviewed later, as they may inform suicide risk assessment and treatment. Distal risk factors may include trait-dependent characteristics such as aggression and impulsivity and disturbances in emotion processing and decision making. Imaging studies have addressed these potential markers of suicide risk in studies of suicide attempters.

6.1.3.1 Mental Pain

The reading of personal scripts describing the mental pain experienced just before a suicide attempt and during the attempt itself can be used to evoke brain responses and thus assess brain areas involved in this strong emotional experience. Recall of suicidal episodes, that is, mental pain plus actual suicidal behavior, compared with neutral activity, is associated with deactivation in the prefrontal cortex (BA 6, 10, and 46), as reflected by decreased contrast during fMRI scanning. Recall of suicidal behavior, however, compared with mental pain, is associated with increased activity in the medial prefrontal cortex, the anterior cingulate cortex, and the hippocampus. The findings suggest that mental pain triggering suicidal behavior has the quality of traumatic stress, associated with decreased prefrontal activity. Planning and the suicidal behavioral response to mental pain, however, is associated with increased activity in the frontal cortex, suggesting that goal-directed suicidal behavior is associated with a reduction of mental pain. A comparative SPECT study of depressed individuals who score high on a measure of the level of mental pain and depressed individuals who score low reveals that those with high levels of mental pain show an increased score on the suicide item of the Beck Depression Inventory and a relatively increased activity in the right dorsolateral prefrontal cortex, occipital cortex, and inferior frontal gyrus and in the left inferior temporal gyrus. A spectroscopy study shows that levels of mental pain correlate negatively with NAA concentrations in prefrontal brain regions.

6.1.3.2 Pain and Affect Regulation

Numerous studies have shown that affect regulation is a common motivation for NSSI. It remains unclear how a painful and thus aversive physical stimulus becomes appetitive and reinforcing such that it becomes a repeated act. Also unclear is how a painful stimulus can precipitate a subjective sense of "relief" in the individual experiencing it, as is common in NSSI. The neurocircuitry of pain and reward processing involves overlapping components. Acute somatic pain activates pathways involving periaqueductal gray (PAG), thalamus, insula, striatum, cerebellum, and anterior cingulate cortex (ACC). Reward-processing neurocircuitry involves activation of regions such as the ventral tegmental area (VTA), nucleus accumbens (NAc), substantia nigra, and orbitofrontal cortex (OFC). Additionally, affect regulation of either painful or rewarding stimuli appears to be mediated by the insula, OFC, ACC, and other areas of the prefrontal cortex (PFC), and amygdala-cortical connections are critical for both affect and pain regulation (Osuch et al., 2014).

A painfully cold stimulus leads to greater subjective relief in individuals with NSSI than in non-NSSI controls when it is administered by themselves (and not by experimenters). Relief (suggesting reward) correlates significantly with the amount of pain during self-administered cold in NSSI individuals. Functional MRI shows greater response among NSSI-individuals than controls in right midbrain, amygdala, parahippocampal, inferior frontal and superior temporal gyri, and OFC. The correlation between response and relief is greater in NSSI patients in areas associated with reward/pain, including thalamus, dorsal striatum, and anterior pre-cuneus. The functional connectivity between right OFC and ACC is reduced in NSSI youth, implying possible deficits in the neuroregulation of emotional behavior. Self-administered pain thus appears to be associated with reward among NSSI individuals but not among non-NSSI individuals.

Interestingly, experimenter-administered incision in the forearm leads to a greater reduction of subjective and objective (task-induced) stress in individuals with borderline personality disorder (who frequently show NSSI) than in healthy controls. Resting state fMRI shows decreased amygdala activation and normalized functional connectivity with the superior frontal gyrus after incision in the borderline personality disorder group. Decreased stress levels and amygdala activity after incision support the assumption of an influence of NSSI on emotion regulation in individuals with borderline personality disorder and aids in understanding why these patients use self-inflicted pain to reduce inner tension.

6.1.3.3 Hopelessness

A few imaging studies have investigated brain correlates of hopelessness, and more particularly its association with serotonergic disturbances. Using SPECT and a selective 5-HT_{2A} receptor ligand, the binding index of 5-HT_{2A} receptors in the frontal cortex of attempted suicide patients and normal controls can be measured, indicating the density of such receptors and their affinity to the ligand (see Chapter 3 for technical issues). Levels of hopelessness can be assessed reliably using Beck's Hopelessness Scale, so that the association between 5-HT_{2a} receptor binding index and hopelessness can be studied. When compared with healthy controls, attempted suicide patients have a significantly lower binding potential of frontal 5-HT_{2A} receptors, suggesting a lower density of such receptors and higher levels of hopelessness. A significant correlation is found between hopelessness and binding index in the population of suicide attempters. Lower central serotonergic function and hopelessness thus are interrelated phenomena, which appear to increase the probability of suicidal behavior.

PET can be used to measure the relationship between brain serotonin receptor binding and negativistic dysfunctional attitudes during depression. Dysfunctional attitudes are negatively biased assumptions and beliefs regarding oneself, the world, and the future, and can be assessed reliably with the Dysfunctional Attitudes Scale (DAS). An early study of the role of serotonin in the development of dysfunctional attitudes had three main findings. First, dysfunctional attitudes decrease after administration of d-fenfluramine, which selectively induces the release of serotonin from neurons, in healthy subjects. The second finding is that higher levels of dysfunctional (more pessimistic and hopeless) attitudes during major depressive episodes are associated with higher 5-HT$_2$ binding potential in the cortex. The third main finding is that patients with major depressive episodes and high levels of dysfunctional pessimistic and hopeless attitudes have higher 5-HT$_2$ binding potential in the cortex compared with healthy subjects. The magnitude of regional 5-HT$_2$ binding potential thus may provide a vulnerability to low levels of extracellular serotonin and extremely negativistic dysfunctional attitudes.

6.1.3.4 Impulsivity

The association between white matter integrity, impulsivity, and suicide risk can be measured using DTI. Such studies show that fractional anisotropy (FA) values (reflecting fiber density, axonal diameter, and myelination in white matter) correlate with current suicidal thoughts. Another study using DTI finds lower FA values in the left orbital frontal white matter in association with a history of suicide attempts, which correlate with levels of motor impulsivity.

Using SPECT and the monoamine transporter ligand ^{123}I-β-CIT, the binding potentials of the serotonin transporter (5-HTT) and the dopamine transporter (DAT) can be measured. Suicide attempters show a significant correlation between high impulsiveness and low 5-HTT binding potential in the right inferior orbitofrontal and bilateral temporal cortical regions, subcortically in the midbrain, thalamus, and bilateral basal ganglia, and in the left cerebellar hemisphere.

6.1.3.5 Aggression

Neural correlates of aggression have been scarcely studied in relation to suicidal behaviors. Prefrontal regions primarily associated with regulation of affect and impulsive-aggressive behavior are correlated with aggression in high-lethality attempters, while aggression in low-lethality attempters is associated with limbic areas involved in empathy, social acceptance, and cooperation. High-lethality suicide attempts are characterized by a subjective intent to die, while low-lethality attempts are generally regarded as coping strategies, which may, however, include communicative gestures.

6.1.3.6 Sensitivity to Social Stressors

In a pivotal study, Jollant and colleagues (2008) were the first to use fMRI to look at functional neurobiological abnormalities underlying the vulnerability to suicidal behavior. They measured neural activity in response to angry and happy versus neutral faces in currently euthymic men with a history of major depressive disorder and suicidal behavior and currently euthymic men with a history of major depressive disorder but not of suicidal acts (affective comparison subjects) and healthy male comparison subjects. Suicide attempters show greater activity, relative to the affective comparison subjects, in the right lateral orbitofrontal cortex (Brodmann area 47) and decreased activity in the right superior frontal gyrus (area 6) in response to prototypical angry versus neutral faces.

Suicide attempters thus are distinguished from nonsuicidal patients by responses to angry and happy faces that may suggest increased sensitivity to others' disapproval, higher propensity to act on negative emotions, and reduced attention to mildly positive stimuli. These patterns of neural activity and cognitive processes may represent vulnerability markers of suicidal behavior in men with a history of depression. The specific sensitivity to angry faces was replicated in another sample of suicide attempters by showing similar relatively increased responses in the orbitofrontal cortex. The role of an angry face in the story of Valerie as described in the Preface is a compelling example of how such signs of others' disapproval may precipitate suicidal behavior.

A subsequent fMRI study investigated neural reactivity to neutral, mild, or intense emotion face morphs in two separate emotion-processing runs (happy and angry) in adolescent suicide attempters, affective controls, and healthy volunteers. To 50% intensity angry faces, attempters showed significantly greater activity than affective controls in anterior cingulate gyral-dorsolateral prefrontal cortical attentional control circuitry, primary sensory, and temporal cortices, and significantly greater activity than healthy volunteers in the primary sensory cortex. To neutral faces during the angry emotion-processing run, attempters had significantly lower activity than affective controls in the fusiform gyrus. Attempters also showed very significantly lower activity than healthy volunteers to 100% intensity happy faces in the primary sensory cortex, and to neutral faces in the happy run in the anterior cingulate and left medial frontal gyri. Psychophysiological interaction analyses revealed significantly reduced anterior cingulate gyral-insula functional connectivity to 50% intensity angry faces in attempters versus affective controls or healthy volunteers. Many of the significant findings are found in the dorsal anterior cingulate gyrus, suggesting that suicide attempters attend more to 50% intensity angry faces than nonattempters. The dorsal anterior cingulate gyrus supports attention processing, emotion processing, salience of emotion, and generation and regulation of emotional response. Furthermore, there is diminished functional connectivity from the anterior cingulate cortical region to bilateral posterior insulae in attempters relative to nonattempters. In attempters, the increased dorsal anterior cingulate gyral and other cortical activity, and reduced functional connectivity between this region and insulae, in response to 50% intensity angry faces may indicate inefficient strategies to regulate attention to, process the salience of, and select contextually appropriate behavioral responses to these stimuli. Elevated activity in attention control circuitry and reduced anterior cingulate gyral-insula functional connectivity in response to 50% intensity angry faces in attempters when compared with other groups suggest that attempters show inefficient recruitment of attentional control neural circuitry when regulating attention to mild intensity angry faces, which may represent a potential biological marker for suicide risk.

The findings suggest that greater recruitment of the anterior cingulate gyrus with emotion (following exposure to social stressors) may indicate an increased risk of suicide attempt in adolescence.

Sensitivity to social rejection can also be studied using the Cyberball paradigm and fMRI. Cyberball is a well-established experimental tool to elicit feelings of social exclusion under laboratory settings. Participants play a virtual ball-tossing game, during which they are made to believe that they play against two other real players, while in fact the other players are operated by a computer. Usually, an "Inclusion" condition, where participants receive one-third of all tosses, and an "Exclusion" condition, where participants no longer receive the ball, are conducted.

Functional MRI shows enhanced activation in the anterior insula, the ventrolateral prefrontal cortex (vlPFC), and the medial prefrontal cortex (mPFC) when contrasting the exclusion condition against the inclusion condition in healthy adolescents and adults. In adolescents suffering from NSSI, activations in the mPFC and the vlPFC are relatively increased when compared with depressed adolescents without NSSI, although subjective feelings of being excluded are equal in groups. The results point toward divergent processing of social exclusion in depressed adolescents with NSSI as compared with adolescents with mere depression in brain regions previously related to the processing of social exclusion. Further study using the Cyberball game in women with a history of suicidal behavior shows decreased contrast in the left insula and

Age-standardized suicide rates (per 100 000 population), both sexes, 2015

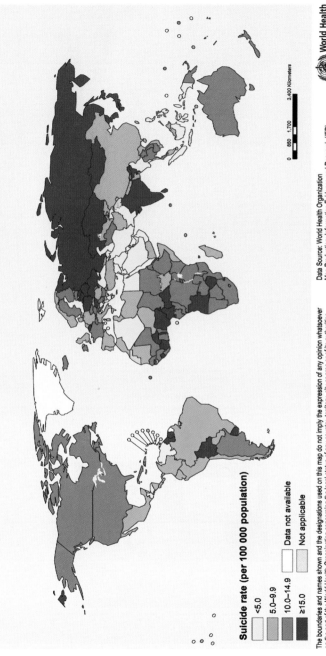

Suicide rate (per 100 000 population)

- <5.0
- 5.0–9.9
- 10.0–14.9
- ≥15.0
- Data not available
- Not applicable

0   850   1,700   3,400 Kilometers

The boundaries and names shown and the designations used on this map do not imply the expression of any opinion whatsoever on the part of the World Health Organization concerning the legal status of any country, territory, city or area or of its authorities, or concerning the delimitation of its frontiers or boundaries. Dotted and dashed lines on maps represent approximate border lines for which there may not yet be full agreement.

Data Source: World Health Organization
Map Production: Information Evidence and Research (IER)
World Health Organization

World Health
Organization

Plate 1 Suicide rates in the world.

Rank	10–14	15–24	25–34	35–44	45–54	55–64	65+
1	Unintentional Injury 763	Unintentional Injury 12,514	Unintentional Injury 19,795	Unintentional Injury 17,818	Malignant Neoplasms 43,054	Malignant Neoplasms 43,054	Heart Disease 507,138
2	Malignant Neoplasms 428	Suicide 5,491	Suicide 6,947	Malignant Neoplasms 10,909	Heart Disease 34,248	Heart Disease 76,872	Malignant Neoplasms 419,389
3	Suicide 409	Homicide 4,733	Homicide 4,863	Heart Disease 10,387	Unintentional Injury 21,499	Unintentional Injury 19,488	Respiratory disease 131,804
4	Homicide 158	Malignant Neoplasms 1,469	Malignant Neoplasms 3,704	Suicide 6,936	Liver Disease 8,874	Respiratory disease 17,457	Cerebro-vascular 120,156
5	Congenital Anomalies 156	Heart Disease 997	Heart Disease 3,522	Homicide 2,895	Suicide 8,751	Diabetes Mellitus 14,166	Alzheimer's Disease 109,495
6	Heart Disease 125	Congenital Anomalies 386	Liver Disease 844	Liver Disease 2,861	Diabetes Mellitus 6,212	Liver Disease 13,728	Diabetes Mellitus 56,142
7	Respiratory disease 93	Respiratory disease 202	Diabetes Mellitus 798	Diabetes Mellitus 1,986	Cerebro-vascular 5,307	Cerebro-vascular 12,116	Unintentional Injury 51,395
8	Cerebro-vascular 42	Diabetes Mellitus 196	Cerebro-vascular 567	Cerebro-vascular 1,788	Respiratory disease 4,345	Suicide 7,739	Influenza & Pneumonia 48,774
9	Influenza & Pneumonia 39	Influenza & Pneumonia 184	HIV 529	HIV 1,055	Septicemia 2,542	Septicemia 5,774	Nephritis 41,258
10	Benign Neo, or Septicemia 33	Cerebro-vascular 186	Congenital Anomalies 443	Septicemia 829	Nephritis 2,124	Nephritis 5,452	Septicemia 30,817

Plate 2 Ten leading causes of death, United States, 2015.

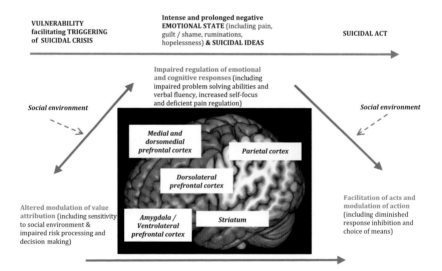

Plate 3 A neurocognitive model of suicidal behavior (Jollant, 2017).

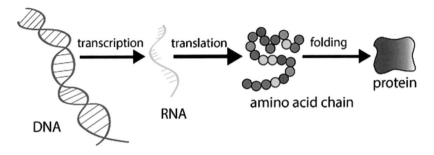

Plate 4 Gene expression: from DNA to proteins (Carmichael, 2014).

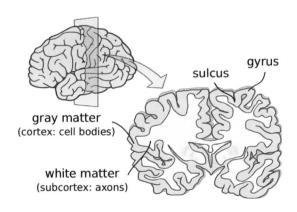

Plate 5 Gray and white matter in the brain (Budday et al., 2014).

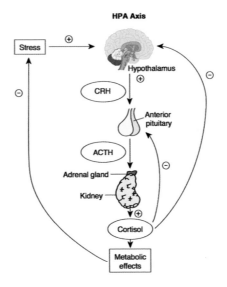

Plate 6 The hypothalamo–pituitary–adrenal (HPA) axis.

Generic Neurotransmitter System

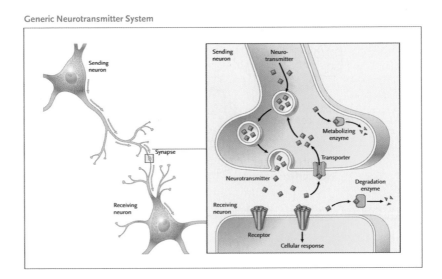

Plate 7 Neurotransmission system.

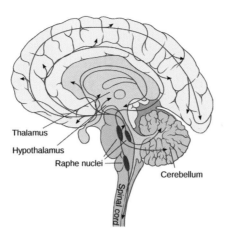

Plate 8 Serotonin neurotransmission system (Lynch, 2010).

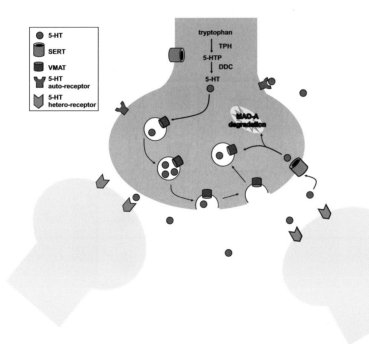

Plate 9 Serotonin neurotransmission (Daubert & Condron, 2010).

green	blue	yellow	blue
blue	red	yellow	red
yellow	yellow	green	red
yellow	green	blue	yellow
green	red	blue	green
blue	yellow	blue	red

Plate 10 The Stroop test.

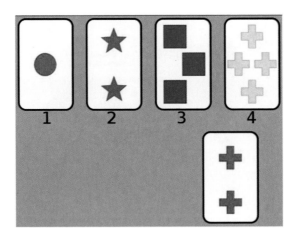

Plate 11 Wisconsin Card Sorting Test: screenshot from computerized version.

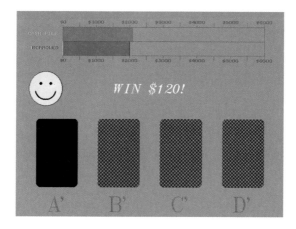

Plate 12 The Iowa Gambling Task: Screenshot from a computerized version.

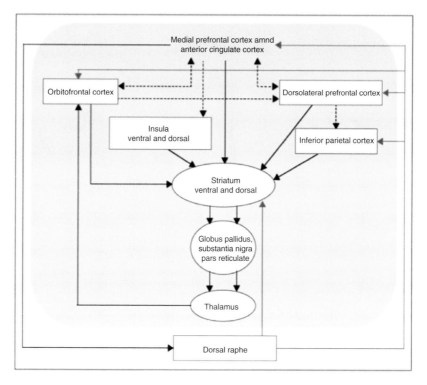

Plate 13 Frontothalamic circuitry and suicidal behavior: Findings from structural imaging studies (van Heeringen & Mann, 2014).

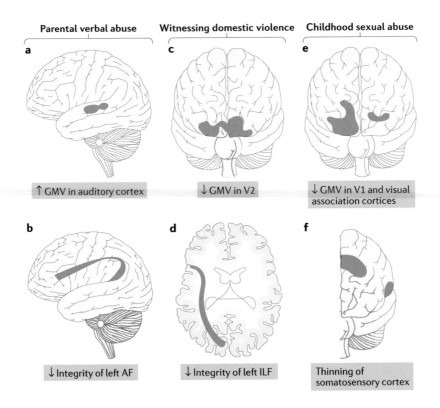

Parental verbal abuse

a

↑ GMV in auditory cortex

b

↓ Integrity of left AF

Witnessing domestic violence

c

↓ GMV in V2

d

↓ Integrity of left ILF

Childhood sexual abuse

e

↓ GMV in V1 and visual association cortices

f

Thinning of somatosensory cortex

Plate 14 The effects of childhood maltreatment on brain structures and connectivity (Teicher et al., 2016).

supramarginal gyrus during the exclusion versus inclusion condition, after controlling for number of depressive episodes, medication, mood disorder type, or social phobia. Brain responses to social exclusion in euthymic female suicide attempters thus appear to be impaired in regions previously implicated in pain tolerance and social cognition. These findings suggest sustained brain dysfunctions related to social perception in suicide attempters.

6.1.3.7 Decision Making

Suicide can be viewed as an escape from unendurable punishment at the cost of any future rewards (Dombrovski et al., 2013). Could faulty estimation of these outcomes predispose to suicidal behavior? In behavioral studies, many of those who have attempted suicide misestimate expected rewards on gambling and probabilistic learning tasks. As discussed in Chapter 5, cognitive studies using, e.g., reinforcement learning tasks and the Iowa Gambling Task (IGT) indeed demonstrate a link between impairments in decision making and suicidal behavior. Neuroimaging approaches are used to further our understanding of the neurocognitive mechanisms of these impairments, which could facilitate the development of effective treatments.

Self-injuring adolescents exhibit less activation in striatum (putamen), amygdalae, and orbitofrontal cortex regions during anticipation of reward in a monetary incentive task than controls. Central nervous system reward dysfunction is thus observed among self-injuring adolescent girls.

Elderly depressed suicide attempters have lower putamen gray matter voxel counts than elderly depressed nonattempters and nondepressed controls. Suicide attempters with lower putamen gray matter voxel counts display higher delay discounting but not delay aversion. Further study of reward learning using a reinforcement-learning task shows that suicide attempters' decision making aligns with the profile of their real-life suicidal behavior. Specifically, individuals with a history of poorly planned suicide attempts demonstrate a shortsighted preference for immediate over delayed rewards. In contrast, individuals who carefully plan their suicide attempts demonstrate greater willingness to wait for larger rewards and thus show an intact ability to delay gratification. A history of suicide attempts (particularly poorly planned ones) is associated with a weakened expected reward signal in the paralimbic cortex (a group of interconnecting brain structures that are involved in the functions of emotion processing, goal-setting, motivation, and self-control), particularly the ventromedial prefrontal cortex (vmPFC).

Thus, impulsivity and poorly planned suicide attempts are paralleled by altered value signals in the paralimbic cortex, particularly the vmPFC. A subsequent fMRI study shows, first, that a high level of premeditation is paralleled by reduced dorsolateral PFC responses to relative increases in value favoring immediate prospect. This result is consistent with the behavioral finding (see Chapter 5) that immediate rewards have less incentive value for individuals with a history of premeditated suicidal behavior. Second, suicide attempters show a blunted parahippocampal response to remote prospects. This finding may represent a neural substrate of impaired prospection in suicidal individuals, potentially undermining alternative solutions during the suicidal crisis.

Taken together, these findings suggest that distinct alterations in the way time is integrated into decision making in the brain may mark different cognitive pathways to suicidal behavior.

The neural basis of poor decision-making ability in association with the vulnerability to suicidal behavior, as discussed in Chapter 5, can be studied further using the IGT and fMRI. A group of currently not depressed males, some of whom had a history of suicidal acts (suicide attempters) while others had none (affective controls), performed an adapted version of the IGT during fMRI. Task-related functional regions of interest were independently defined in 15 male healthy controls performing the same task. In comparison to affective controls, suicide attempters showed (1) poorer performance on the gambling task, (2) decreased activation during risky relative to safe choices in left lateral orbitofrontal and occipital cortices, and (3) no difference for the contrast between wins and losses. Altered processing of risk under conditions of uncertainty, associated with left lateral orbitofrontal cortex dysfunction, could explain the decision-making deficits observed in suicide attempters. These impaired cognitive and neural processes may represent future predictive markers and therapeutic targets in a field where identification of those at risk is poor and specific treatments are lacking. These results also add to our growing understanding of the role of the orbitofrontal cortex in decision making and psychopathology.

In a replication study in another sample of suicide attempters and affective controls, these results were not found. Instead, suicide attempters showed a relatively lower response of left dorsolateral prefrontal cortex during risky versus safe choices and a higher response of the anterior cingulate, orbitofrontal, and dorsolateral prefrontal cortices, mainly on the right side, to wins versus losses. The discrepancies may be related to differences in the anatomical definition of involved brain regions or to characteristics of the study samples. An integrative interpretation may be that inadequate valuation of outcomes by both ventral and dorsal prefrontal cortex may lead suicide attempters to estimate long-term risk in the dorsolateral prefrontal cortex inadequately.

Possible changes in decision-making processes in association with suicidal behavior are also studied in adolescents using the IGT and fMRI. Surprisingly, when compared with nonattempters, attempters thereby appear to perform better on the IGT, as they choose significantly more low-risk choices than the other two groups. During low-risk decisions, nonattempter controls, but not attempters, show greater left hippocampal and middle temporal activation than healthy controls. During high-risk decisions, attempters show less activation in the right thalamus, and during low-risk decisions, attempters show greater activation in the left caudate. Thus, nonattempters but not attempters are differentiated from healthy controls during performance of the IGT. Functional abnormalities in neural circuitry implicated in learning in the context of risk may underlie risk for major depressive disorder, but not risk for suicide attempt, in adolescence. This finding, in combination with a relatively better performance on the task by suicide attempters, may thus indicate less cognitive impairment in adolescent suicide attempters than in adolescent nonattempters. Together with findings on cognitive functions in adolescent suicide attempters (see earlier discussion), suicide attempts during adolescence may thus not be associated with abnormal activity in neural circuitry supporting cognitive tasks (response inhibition and decision making in the context of risk). Potentially different neural mechanisms may thus underlie risk for suicide attempt versus major depressive disorder in adolescence. It is possible that other contributors, for example, neural circuitry supporting emotion as demonstrated in adult males with a history of suicide attempt, may underlie depression with suicidal behavior versus depression alone.

6.1.3.8 Cognitive Control and Response Inhibition

As described in Chapter 5, impaired cognitive control is found across ages in suicide attempters. Cognitive inhibition, a major component of cognitive control, refers to active suppression mechanisms that limit the processing of irrelevant stimuli. Cognitive inhibition deficits among suicide attempters may thus underlie inadequate regulation of emotional and cognitive responses. Cognitive inhibition can be measured with a go/no-go task, and it is subserved by cingular-frontal-parietal neural circuitry in healthy individuals. When compared with depressed adolescent controls and healthy controls, depressed adolescent suicide attempters perform similarly in terms of accuracy. Concerning brain activation, attempters, like healthy controls, show a reduced activation in the right anterior cingulate gyrus during the task when compared with depressed controls. Contrary to what can be expected, adolescent suicidal behavior thus is not associated with abnormal neuronal activation in the response inhibition circuit. Rather, attempters appear to be able to perform the task well without the need for recruitment of additional neural circuitry. The meaning of this finding is not yet clear. A similar study in adults shows that deficits in cognitive inhibition – related to the inferior frontal gyrus, thalamus, orbitofrontal cortex, and parietal cortex – are associated with the depressive state more than vulnerability to suicidal behavior. These findings suggest that depression-related deficits in cognitive inhibition may add up to trait-like cognitive alterations associated with the vulnerability to suicidal behavior to increase the risk of suicidal behavior.

6.2 What Can We Learn from the Systems Neuroscience Approach to Suicidal Behavior?

The overall picture emerging from structural imaging studies in association with suicidal behavior is the following:

- Frontal cortex volumes are decreased for gray matter but increased for white matter.
- Subcortical gray matter volumes are decreased for striatum; results are discrepant with regard to thalamus volumes.
- Connectivity is increased in left white matter tracts including ALIC (with, however, a decreased mean percentage of fibers projecting to the thalamus and the orbitofrontal cortex) and thalamic radiations, and decreased in left orbitofrontal and bilateral dorsomedial lobes.

Functional imaging studies reveal numerous neurophysiological alterations associated with the neurocognitive manifestations of the vulnerability to suicidal behavior, as described in Chapter 5. More specifically, these studies demonstrate that suicidal behavior is associated with disturbances in the attribution of importance to stimuli, leading to giving undue importance to signals of others' disapproval and insufficient importance to risky choices. Second, changes in the prefrontal-striatal network are associated with changes in the representation of value to different outcome options, which may lead to the choice of immediate reward over abstract and delayed reward in the process of decision making. The development of unbearable emotional pain following perception of signals of others' disapproval may be associated with a choice for immediate alleviation of pain, not taking into account the possibility of a better future. Disturbed intertemporal reward discounting may thus play an important role in the vulnerability to suicidal behavior. As the serotonergic neurotransmission system is involved in the modulation of this process of delay discounting, this may explain the demonstrated association between prefrontal serotonergic dysfunctioning and levels of hopelessness in suicide attempters. In addition to disturbed reward discounting, a relative increase of the effect of negative information on decision making could well be involved. In Chapter 8 we will see how this interpretation provides a fascinating opportunity to relate suicidal behavior with the structural and functional neuroimaging findings (this chapter) and with the neurocognitive findings (Chapter 5) in a computational model of suicidal behavior.

A number of methodological issues need to be addressed because they may influence findings and their interpretation. The comparability of findings from different studies is relatively limited because of variations in imaging and analytic techniques. Radioligands differ in their binding specificity, and, in spite of the use of solid statistical processes (statistical parametric mapping) in many studies, anatomical localization of findings is often imprecise. Small sample sizes limit the power of studies to detect group differences or can tend to amplify individual differences due to biological heterogeneity. In this context, it is noteworthy that a recent meta-analysis involving data on more than 3,000 depressed individuals shows a nearly 3% smaller volume within the skull among those with suicidal plans or attempts, but no difference regarding specific brain volume measures (Renteria et al., 2017). Other potential biases may be due to the lack of (e.g., healthy or psychiatric) comparison groups. In many studies, individuals showing suicidal behavior and their controls are not matched for potentially biasing characteristics, such as demographic variables, psychiatric (co-)morbidity, nature and severity or chronicity of associated disorders, treatment, and exposure to risk and protective factors. Generalizability of findings may be limited due to inclusion of only male or female individuals or patients with particular disorders such as schizophrenia. Many studies use a region-of-interest (ROI) approach and thus look only at predefined regions. Finally, in the majority of studies, assessment of imaging is not blind to behavioral history.

Taking these methodological issues into account, the findings reviewed in this chapter suggest that suicidal behavior is associated with changes in the frontostriatothalamic network, depicted in Figure 6.2.

Recent neuroscientific research outside the suicidological domain has clearly demonstrated the major role of this network in processes of emotion processing and cognitive control that is relevant for our understanding of suicidal behavior, namely the attribution of importance to stimuli and the representation of value to different outcome options. Attention appears to play a central role in these processes, as is also indicated by the well-documented attentional deficiencies found in relation to suicidal behavior (see Chapter 5). Three independent aspects of attentional control have been linked to separate brain regions (Petersen & Posner, 2012). These include "alerting" in the frontoparietal cortex and thalamus, "orienting" in the bilateral parietal cortex, and "executive control" in superior frontal and fusiform gyri. The anterior cingulate cortex appears to be involved in all three aspects (Petersen & Posner, 2012). A substantial number of reviewed studies suggest a crucial role of changes in these attentional control processes and their neurobiological substrate in relation to suicidal behavior.

With regard to alerting, the "cocktail party phenomenon" was discussed in Chapter 5, while neurobiological correlates of increased attention to angry faces and reduced attention to happy faces are clearly demonstrated in suicidal individuals. These findings suggest that these individuals experience relatively more difficulty in finding positive factors in their environment based on particular attentional characteristics (Jollant et al., 2008). These findings link attentional deficits to the sensitivity to particular social stimuli in suicide attempters. This concept of vulnerability will be elaborated in the computational model of suicidal behavior in Chapter 8. Deficits in orienting may, for example, account for the problems in shifting attention from immediate to delayed gratification. Many studies, as reviewed in this chapter, document deficits in attentional control and their neuroanatomical correlates in association with suicidal behavior. Attentional control is inversely related to attentional bias, which may cause individuals to process emotionally negative information preferentially over emotionally positive information.

One can only speculate about the causes of the volumetric changes in association with suicidal behavior. In general, causes of changes in gray and white matter volumes of identified brain areas have been identified, many of which play an important role in the stress–diathesis model of suicidal behavior, as described in the introductory chapters of this book. Causes of gray and white matter reductions include neuro-inflammation (Zhang et al., 2016), acute and cumulative stress (Ansell et al., 2012), early life stress, childhood maltreatment and abuse (Coplan et al., 2010; Van Dam et al., 2014; Walsh et al., 2014; Philip et al., 2016), and genetics

(Kremen et al., 2010). NAA (see earlier discussion for spectroscopy findings in suicidal behavior) is a source of acetyl groups that are incorporated in myelin; it has been suggested that deregulation underlies changes in white matter integrity. Genetic variation in the NTRK1 gene (see also Chapter 4), which is associated with nervous system development and myelination, also predicts FA in healthy volunteers (Tkachev et al., 2007).

There is putative genetic moderation of the liability for a neural effect of childhood abuse. For example, polymorphisms in the serotonin transporter promoter region genotype are found in some though not all studies (Walsh et al., 2014). Estimates of heritability for brain volumes range from 40% to more than 80%, whereby lower heritability estimates are generally found for smaller brain structures relative to larger global or lobar structures (although estimates of whether one structure has a higher heritability than another need to be interpreted with care) (Strike et al., 2015). Candidate genes that have received considerable attention are those encoding for brain-derived neurotrophic factor (BDNF) and catechol-O-methyltransferase (COMT), both of which have been implicated in cognitive and emotional processing. Neurotrophin receptor genes such as NTRK3 are important for white matter integrity (Braskie et al., 2013). Of note, a postmortem study of suicides shows thalamic volume enlargement, particularly in the pulvinar nucleus, associated with the ss genotype of the serotonin transporter gene (Young et al., 2008). The pulvinar processes information related to social threat (such as in facially expressed emotion), and relays this information via the limbic system to the anterior cingulate cortex, a brain area involved in emotional responses to pain and attention to negative consequences (Young et al., 2008). Pulvinar-related attentional processes play a central role in the computational model of suicidal behavior, as will be discussed in Chapter 8. Binding to the serotonin transporter is significantly correlated to the size of the caudate nucleus and globus pallidus (Vang et al., 2010). These few examples indicate that the serotonin transporter clearly plays a role in determining the size of brain areas that are particularly relevant for suicidal behavior. Until now, genome-wide association studies (see Chapter 3) do not shed further light on genetic effects on brain morphology (Strike et al., 2015).

As causes of white and gray matter volume changes appear to overlap, it may come as no surprise that white and gray matter abnormalities co-occur: Volumes of white matter hyperintensities and gray matter volume of the lingual gyrus and bilateral hippocampus are negatively correlated. In addition, the volume of white matter hyperintensities is negatively associated with gray matter blood flow in left anterior putamen, subcallosal, accumbens, anterior caudate, orbitofrontal, anterior insula, and frontal pole (Crane et al., 2015). A number of white and gray matter abnormalities thus appear to coexist.

Importantly, long-term lithium treatment appears to lead to increased gray matter volumes in brain areas where suicidal behavior is associated with decreased volumes: dorsolateral prefrontal cortex, orbitofrontal cortex, anterior cingulate, superior temporal cortex, parietooccipital cortex, and basal ganglia (Benedetti et al., 2011). Antidepressant treatment appears to normalize thalamus and white matter volumes in patients with major depression (Young et al., 2008; Zeng et al., 2012).

The meaning of changes in circuitry, particularly the frontothalamic network depicted in Figure 6.2, in terms of a vulnerability to suicidal behavior is not yet clear. Reviewed DTI studies mainly show increased connectivity in the left hemisphere of suicidal brains, particularly in white matter tracts passing through the left anterior limb of the internal capsule (ALIC), which mainly involve thalamocortical loops. Such exacerbated connectivity is thought to reflect excessive salience and/or focus on irrelevant stimuli (Toranzo et al., 2011). Of note, the anterior thalamic radiation and the medial forebrain bundle run in close proximity to each other though the ALIC, but suicide-related white matter changes appear to involve the anterior thalamic radiations and not the medial forebrain bundle. Differences between these two white matter tracts in the kind of information that they convey are becoming clear: While the medial forebrain bundle is a key structure of the reward circuit, the anterior thalamic radiation appears to convey particularly negative information and thus is involved in sadness and mental pain (Coenen et al., 2012). A second connectivity disturbance is found consistently in relation to NSSI and suicidal behavior and involves connections of the left inferior frontal gyrus, particularly with the anterior cingulate cortex. As will be discussed in Chapter 8, this connection (again) is important in the processing of negative information: Dysfunction of the left inferior frontal gyrus appears to enhance the inclination to adjust one's beliefs when confronted with negative information (Sharot et al., 2012).

Taken together, white matter changes seen in relation to suicidal behavior appear to contribute substantially to the excessive salience of negative information. Salience of negative information is a central component of the computational model of suicidal behavior that will be described in Chapter 8. Consequences for treatment, for example in terms of brain stimulation, will be discussed in Chapter 10. Concerning causes, early life stress predicts left frontothalamic hyperconnectivity

(Philip et al., 2016), thus pointing at the potential impact of developmental influences, which will be discussed in detail in Chapter 7.

Chapter 6 Summary

- Nearly 100 brain imaging studies document changes in the structure and/or function of the brains of people with a history of suicidal behavior.
- In general, structural gray matter changes include reduced volumes of prefrontal cortical areas and increased volumes of subcortical nuclei.
- Structural white matter changes reveal (mainly left-sided) disturbances in the connectivity between cortical and subcortical brain areas, such as the prefrontal cortex and the thalamus.
- Functional brain disturbances include changes in connectivity and activation during cognitive tasks such as emotional face recognition and facets of decision making.
- Taken together, suicidal behavior appears to be associated with changes in a frontostriatothalamic network that subserves attentional processes and decision making.
- Potential causes of these changes involve genetics and early life adversity, which may lead to developmental disturbances as discussed in Chapter 7.

Further Reading

van Heeringen, K. & Mann, J. J. (2014). The neurobiology of suicide. *The Lancet Psychiatry*, *1*, 63–72.

van Heeringen, K., Bijttebier, S., Desmyter, S., Vervaet, M. & Baeken, C. (2014). Is there a neuroanatomical basis for the vulnerability to suicidal behavior? A coordinate-based meta-analysis of structural and functional MRI studies. *Frontiers in Human Neuroscience*, *208*, e824.

References per Neuroimaging Category

Structural Imaging of Suicidal Behavior

Ahearn et al., 2001; Ehrlich et al., 2004; Ehrlich et al., 2005; Monkul et al., 2007; Pompili et al., 2007; Aguilar et al., 2008; Pompili et al., 2008; Rusch et al., 2008; Hwang et al., 2010; Matsuo et al., 2010; Vang et al., 2010; Benedetti et al., 2011; Cyprien et al., 2011; Goodman et al., 2011; Serafini et al., 2011; Spoletini et al., 2011; Wagner et al., 2011; Dombrovski et al.,

2012; Mahon et al., 2012; Nery-Fernandes et al., 2012; Soloff et al., 2012; Giakoumatos et al., 2013; Lopez-Larson et al., 2013; Jia et al., 2014; Olvet et al., 2014; Sachs-Ericsson et al., 2014; Bijttebier et al., 2015; Colle et al., 2015; Kim et al., 2015; Besteher et al., 2016; Gosnell et al., 2016; S. J. Lee et al., 2016; Y. J. Lee 2016.

Functional Imaging Studies of Suicidal Behavior

Audenaert et al., 2001; Meyer et al., 2003; Oquendo et al., 2003; Lindstrom et al., 2004; Cannon et al., 2006; Leyton et al., 2006; Ryding et al., 2006; Soloff et al., 2007; Li et al., 2009; Willeumier et al., 2011; Marchand et al., 2012; Fan et al., 2013; Miller et al., 2013; Nye et al., 2013; Sublette et al., 2013; Sullivan et al., 2015; Yeh et al., 2015; Oquendo et al., 2016; S. Zhang et al., 2016; Jollant et al., 2017; van Heeringen et al., 2017.

Imaging Studies of Suicide Risk Factors

Keilp et al., 2001; Meyer et al., 2003; van Heeringen et al., 2003; Lindstrom et al., 2004; Ryding et al., 2006; Jollant et al., 2008; Keilp et al., 2008; Jollant et al., 2010; Reisch et al., 2010; van Heeringen et al., 2010; Dombrovski et al., 2011; Jollant et al., 2011; Pan et al., 2011; Yurgelun-Todd et al., 2011; Dombrovski et al., 2012; Mahon et al., 2012; Dombrovski et al., 2013; Pan et al., 2013a; Pan et al., 2013b; Osuch et al., 2014; Soloff et al., 2014; Olié et al., 2015; Reitz et al., 2015; Richard-Devantoy et al., 2015; Sauder et al., 2015; Groschwitz et al., 2016; Richard-Devantoy et al., 2016a; Vanyukov et al., 2016; Jollant et al., 2017; Olié et al., 2017.

"In my end is my beginning"

A Neurodevelopmental Perspective on Suicidal Behavior*

Learning Objectives

- How can early-life experiences lead to suicidal behavior much later in life?
- What are epigenetics?
- Can brain changes in individuals who were exposed to childhood abuse be interpreted as adaptive?
- Can genes make people more or less vulnerable to the effects of adverse early-life experiences?

Introduction

How can distal risk factors increase the risk of suicide much later in life? What mechanisms make it possible that paternal or maternal characteristics or adverse early life experiences make people decide decades later to end their own lives? In other words, how do vulnerability factors come into existence, and how can they become manifest many years later? This chapter will show that neuroscience contributes substantially to finding answers to these intriguing questions, which are so important for suicide prevention. If we are able to reliably assess vulnerability factors that are amenable to interventions, we can prevent self-destructive behaviors before any damage is done.

Consistent genetic epidemiological data, as reviewed in Chapter 3, point at a genetic variation that is thought to account for part of the familial aggregation of suicide and that is partially independent from the familial clustering of mental disorders (Turecki et al., 2012). But there is another distal risk factor, of which the importance for suicide risk is becoming more and more clear: early life adversity (ELA). ELAs constitute a distal factor with strongest effects on suicide risk (Brezo et al., 2007; Fergusson et al., 2008). Neuroscientific research clearly shows the devastating consequences of ELAs, leaving scars in the brain that induce or increase the vulnerability to suicidal behavior.

---

* "In the end is my beginning" quoted from T. S. Eliot (1940), "East Coker", *New English Weekly* & the *New Age: A Review of Public Affairs, Literature and the Arts*, 16, no. 22, March 21.

7.1 Early Life Adversity: The Nature and Scope of the Problem

ELAs are common, but estimated frequencies of their occurrence differ due to differences in definitions. The estimated prevalence of childhood maltreatment in Western societies is between 10% and 15%. The WHO World Mental Health Surveys in 21 countries show that nearly 40% of the 52,000 respondents report ELAs, among which maltreatment in the form of childhood physical abuse (CPA) is the second most commonly reported (8%), after parental death (12.5%). Neglect (4.4%) and child-hood sexual abuse (CSA; 1.6%) are less commonly reported but are devastating ELAs (Kessler et al., 2010). The incidence of CSA, however, probably is far greater than reported, due to shame and stigma. More-over, the impact of differences in definitions is substantial: In the United States, each state has its own definitions of child abuse and neglect that are based on standards set by federal law. However, most states recognize four major types of maltreatment: neglect, physical abuse, psychological maltreatment, and sexual abuse. The Child Abuse Preven-tion and Treatment Act defines child abuse and neglect as, at a min-imum: "Any recent act or failure to act on the part of a parent or caretaker which results in death, serious physical or emotional harm, sexual abuse or exploitation; or an act or failure to act, which presents an imminent risk of serious harm."

Maltreatment in general, and CSA in particular, constitutes a major problem at a global level, as can be learned from the meta-analysis of findings from 65 studies in 22 countries (Perada et al., 2009). The main findings of the meta-analysis are shown in Textbox 7.1.

Textbox 7.1 Global Data on Early-Life Adversity Including Childhood Sexual Abuse

- An estimated 8% of males and 20% of females universally face sexual abuse before the age of 18 years.
- The highest prevalence rate of CSA is seen in Africa (34.4%).
- Europe, America, and Asia have prevalence rates of 9%, 10%, and 24%, respectively.
- With regard to females, seven countries report prevalence rates as being more than one-fifth, i.e., 38% in Australia, 32% in Costa Rica, 31% in Tanzania, 31% in Israel, 28% in Sweden, 25% in the United States, and 24% in Switzerland

In the United States, an estimated 4.4 million referrals, involving the alleged maltreatment of approximately 7.2 million children, were received by child protection services agencies in 2015. Three-fifths of reports of alleged child abuse and neglect were made by professionals. One-fifth of these children were found to be victims. More than 80% of victims are maltreated by a parent, acting alone or with someone else. More than one-third of victims are maltreated by their mother acting alone. One-fifth of victims are maltreated by their father acting alone. One-fifth of victims are maltreated by both parents. Thirteen percent of victims are maltreated by a perpetrator who is not a parent of the child (US Department of Health and Human Services, 2017).

In Canada, 32% of the adult population has experienced physical abuse, sexual abuse, and/or exposure to intimate partner violence in childhood (Afifi et al., 2014).

There is a strong link between ELAs and negative mental health outcomes (Lutz & Turecki, 2014). Maltreatment during early development is among the strongest predictors of psychiatric pathology and the severity of its clinical course, including early onset of illness, poor treatment response, increased comorbidity, and chronic health care utilization. ELAs are strongly linked with obesity, personality disorders, depression, substance use disorders, aggression and violence, and suicidal behavior.

7.2 ELAs and Suicidal Behavior

7.2.1 Epidemiological Studies

Although most individuals who show suicidal behavior do not have a history of ELA, a significant minority ranging from 10% to 40% does (Turecki et al., 2012). In a similar way, most individuals with a history of ELA will not show suicidal behavior, but the risk is significantly increased: victims of CSA, compared with the general population, are nearly 20 times more likely to end their own lives. Relative risks are higher for female than male victims, and CSA victims who take their own lives are predominantly aged in their 30s at time of death (Cutajar et al., 2010). Further epidemiological data are available from general and clinical populations and from psychological autopsy studies. (see Chapter 3 for technical details.)

CSA, CPA, emotional abuse, and neglect are associated with suicidal behavior across community, clinical, and high-risk samples. These adverse events are a major contributor to nonfatal and fatal suicidal behavior, as shown in multiple studies and reviews including, for example, an analysis of the occurrence of suicidal behavior following CSA in more than 65,000 subjects in 177 studies (Maniglio, 2011). In most studies, these associations remain significant when controlling for potential confounding factors such as demographics, mental health, family, and peer-related variables. (For a review, see Miller et al., 2013.) The WHO World Mental Health Surveys show that the risk of suicidal behavior increases with the number of ELAs (odds ratio ranging from 1 to 6), independently of lifetime psychiatric disorders (Bruffaerts et al., 2010).

According to the Adverse Childhood Experiences (ACEs) study, sponsored by the Centers for Disease Control and Prevention (CDC), exposure to one or more maltreatment-related ELAs accounts for 67% of the population attributable risk (PAR) for suicide attempts (Dube et al., 2003), PAR being the reduction in incidence of suicide attempts that would be observed if the population were entirely unexposed to ACEs. Individuals exposed to six or more ELAs have a 20-year reduction in lifespan (Brown et al., 2009).

Gender, age, frequency of the abuse, the identity of the abuser, and the type of ELA appear to influence the link between ELAs and suicidal behavior. The association between CSA, and to a lesser degree CPA, and suicide attempts may be stronger for males than females (Miller et al., 2013). At a population level, the prevalence of CSA, however, is much higher among women, so that the disease burden of suicide caused by CSA is likely to be higher in females. Calculations suggest that approximately 20% of suicidal behavior in women can be attributed to CSA exposure. In men, approximately 10% of suicidal behavior probably can be attributed to CSA exposure. At the individual level, young men who have experienced CSA may need increased attention to avoid suicidal outcomes (DeVries et al., 2014).

A growing body of research shows that the relationship between ELAs and increased suicide risk continues throughout the life span (Sachs-Ericsson et al., 2013). Specifically, Bruffaerts and colleagues (2010) found that ELA in a broader sense (including CPA and CSA, parental loss, financial adversity, illness) has the strongest associations with suicide attempts in childhood, decreasing during teen years and young adulthood, and increasing again in later adulthood. Among adolescents, timing of first exposure has no effect on the occurrence of suicidal behavior (Gomez et al., 2017).

Frequency of the abuse and the identity of the abuser are important moderators of suicide risk (Turecki et al., 2012). Abuse perpetrated by an immediate family member carries greater risk of suicidal behavior than abuse committed by an extended family member or an unrelated individual, suggesting that it is the psychological trauma associated with the maltreatment rather than the actual physical or sexual experience that confers the lifelong increased risk of suicidal behavior. Close family members are the main source of support during development and are essential to provide healthy attachment patterns, appropriate emotional regulation to environmental stimuli, and stress resilience. Thus, the experience of repeated acts of abuse by parental figures, caregivers, or other close relatives signals a hostile and unreliable environment to which the organism may try to adapt by adjusting key response systems, such as brain networks involved in reactivity to stress (see later discussion). The WHO World Mental Health Surveys show that CSA and CPA are consistently the strongest risk factors for both the onset and persistence of suicidal behavior following ELAs, especially during adolescence (Bruffaerts et al., 2010). Studies that have investigated effects of different forms of ELA suggest that CSA may be relatively more important in explaining suicidal behavior than CPA or neglect. A meta-analysis specifically looking at the effects of CSA using data from seven longitudinal and two twin studies shows an estimated odds ratio of approximately 2.5 for suicidal behavior in CSA victims (Devries et al., 2014).

7.2.2 Psychological Autopsy Studies

Probably the largest psychological autopsy study (see Chapter 3 for technical details), involving more than 200 suicides, shows that a number of risk factors in the first 10 years of life appear to be common to all investigated suicides. For example, close to 40% are victims of physical and/or sexual abuse during the first 10 years of their lives (Séguin et al., 2007, 2014). The data from this important study further reveal two developmental models of suicide trajectories. The first one is experienced by 40% of the suicides: Individuals are plagued with adversities very early on in life (0–4 years of age) and accumulate a great number of developmental difficulties very rapidly, thus creating a greater burden of adversity as time passes. Examples of adversity include parent alcohol misuse, physical or sexual abuse, neglect, and tension with parents. These are followed by changes of residence and by the development of psychopathology leading to suicide. Clearly, not all individuals in this trajectory experience all these adversities, but most of them have a rapid increase in the burden of adversity, and 80% die by suicide during the 20–24 age period. Individuals who follow the second trajectory, accounting for 60% of the suicides, have a similar burden of adversity very early on in life (0–4 years of age), but are essentially exposed to overall low to moderate adversity during their whole lifetimes. There is a sharp increase in the burden of adversity taking place following the 20–24 age period, and death by suicide occurs at a time when the burden is still somewhat moderate or low. Of note is that 55% of participants die on their first suicide attempt.

The information collected with the psychological autopsies sheds light on the sequence of difficulties from early risk variables (physical and sexual aggression, neglect, and tension) to variables emerging during the teenage years (conduct and behavioral difficulties, and social and school difficulties) and those emerging during young adulthood (end of a love relationship and suicide attempt). In the first trajectory, almost every sphere of the lives of the suicides is affected by adversity, and they die at a very young age, indicating again the importance of and the difficulties in screening for and identifying these types of disruptive, at-risk individuals earlier in the developmental process and differentiating between the need for low-intensity and high-intensity intervention.

Individuals in the second trajectory, who constitute 60% of the investigated suicides, are exposed to the same common factors associated with suicide, but have a lower burden of adversity throughout their lives. In some cases, early sexual abuse translates into long-term marital violence, but other spheres of life – academic or professional – may be unharmed. This second trajectory is marked by a slower decline over time and is accompanied and compounded by psychiatric disorders, such as mood disorders. As events accumulate in the course of their lives and mental health problems create more and more suffering and adversity, these individuals' ability to resist feelings of despair crumble. These individuals, who do not have a high burden of adversity, may fly under the radar of clinicians, co-workers, and, in some cases, close relatives. Perhaps the challenge with this population is to help them access mental health services in a timely manner (Séguin et al., 2014).

7.3 Neurobiological Mechanisms Linking ELAs and Suicidal Behavior

Increasing evidence points at a series of neurobiological changes resulting from ELA that may explain the increased occurrence of suicidal behavior. Such changes may become manifest as stable cognitive, emotional, and behavioral characteristics (so-called phenotypes), such as early maladaptive schemas and cognitive distortions (e.g., catastrophizing, overgeneralization, black-and-white thinking, and hopelessness), maladaptive coping strategies, and emotion regulation deficiencies. Neurobiological underpinnings of these phenotypical expressions include changes at molecular and systems levels.

7.3.1 Molecular Changes

7.3.1.1 Inflammatory Markers

Adults who experienced childhood trauma exhibit HPA-axis dysregulation and an associated systemic proinflammatory state (Tyrka et al., 2013), with increased levels of C-reactive protein (CRP), fibrinogen, and proinflammatory cytokines (Coelho et al., 2014). Such inflammatory markers are linked to an increased risk of suicidal behavior, as described in Chapter 4, possibly via an effect of inflammation on brain structure and functions. Concerning brain structures, effects may include microglial activation and a decrease in neurotrophins such as BDNF, leading to decreased neuronal repair, decreased neurogenesis, and an increased glutamatergic activity, which may contribute to apoptosis. Such mechanisms are very relevant for our understanding of structural brain changes linked with suicidal behavior (such as reduced gray matter volumes; see Chapter 6), possibly as mediators of the association between ELAs and suicidal behavior (see later discussion). From a functional point of view, inflammation appears to enhance particularly the sensitivity to negative information versus positive information, which is a crucial component in the computational model of suicidal behavior that will be elaborated in Chapter 8 (Harrison et al., 2016).

7.3.1.2 Genetics

The disparate findings in genetic association studies of suicidal behavior (see Chapter 4) may in part be attributable to differences in environmental characteristics (Mann & Currier, 2016). It is therefore not surprising that the sizable literature documenting the preeminent role of ELAs as a major environmental risk factor for suicidal behavior has driven the field toward investigating gene–environment interactions (Nemeroff, 2016). The search for an answer to the question as to whether specific genetic polymorphisms can be identified to interact with the environmental risk factor of ELAs to mediate risk of suicide has yielded some remarkable results.

Concerning suicide and gene–environment interactions, a report investigating the association between child abuse history, the serotonin transporter genotype, and suicide attempts among substance use dis-order patients showed that those with low expression genotypes had more suicide attempters when they had experienced more child abuse (Roy et al., 2007). However, a later study found no association with the genotype or with gene–environment interaction (Coventry et al., 2010). Another study documents an increased risk of suicidal behavior with the interaction between ELAs and the opposite variant of the 5HT transporter gene, the ll genotype, in depressed individuals exposed to childhood abuse (Shinozaki et al., 2013). Taken together, these findings suggest that the interactive effect on suicidal behavior is specific in the context of a preexisting psychiatric disorder. Gene–environment inter-action studies involving other serotonergic genes, such as the 1A and 2A receptor genes and the TPH1 and TPH2 genes, have also yielded incon-sistent results (for an overview, see Mandelli & Seretti, 2016).

It is likely that interaction effects exist with genes related to other neurobiological systems involved in suicidal behavior such as the stress-response system and neurotrophins. There are mixed results from stud-ies of an interaction effect between the CRH receptor 1 gene and ELA, although there might be a decreased risk of suicidal behavior associated with one genetic variant in early traumatized individuals (Ben-Efraim et al., 2011). Variants of FKBP5, a stress-related gene that is also involved in inflammatory processes, interact with ELAs in increasing the risk of suicidal behavior (Roy et al., 2010, 2012). Importantly, the FKBP5 TT genotype predisposes subjects who have experienced child-hood abuse to widespread structural brain changes in the subcortical and cortical emotion-processing brain areas, as will be discussed later (Grabe et al., 2016).

Concerning neurotrophins, a common variant of the NTRK2 gene appears to increase the risk of suicidal behavior in individuals exposed to early trauma (Murphy et al., 2011).

7.3.1.3 Epigenetics

Epigenetic processes emerge as crucial mediators of the long-term neurobiological embedding of ELAs (Lutz & Turecki, 2014). The term "epigenetics" refers to the chemical and physical processes that program the genome to express its genes in a time-dependent manner. As described in Chapter 3 in detail, epigenetic processes convey information in the absence of a change in the DNA sequence. The epigenome is responsive to developmental, physiological, and environmental cues. As such, epigenetics explains how the environment regulates the genome, and epigenetic mechanisms are well suited to mediate the effects of early environmental factors, potentially throughout the lifespan. This section will focus on DNA methylation, as this is the epigenetic mark that received by far the most interest in the field of ELAs (Lutz & Turecki, 2014). More particularly, the focus will be on the epigenetics of the stress-response system and the neurotrophins.

ELAs have been proposed to impose long-term effects on behavior at least partly by altering the neural circuits involved in the regulation of stress. The effects of ELAs on HPA axis activity are impacted by several factors including, but not limited to, the following:

- the type and number of ELAs, age at first ELA, and chronicity
- social support and presence of traumatic events in adulthood
- family history of major psychiatric disorders
- genetic and epigenetic factors. (Nemeroff, 2016)

Groundbreaking research investigating the consequences of variations in maternal care in offspring in the rat found that the frequency of maternal pup licking and grooming (LG) over the first week of life programs the expression of genes that regulate behavioral and endocrine responses to stress (Turecki et al., 2012). One of the most robust effects involves the expression of the glucocorticoid receptor (GR) gene in the hippocampus. The offspring of high LG mothers have increased hippocampal GR expression and more modest responses to stress compared with the offspring of low LG mothers (Liu et al., 1997). Maternal behavior is thus associated with an epigenetic modification of a neuron-specific promoter of the GR gene in the offspring. More specifically, increased maternal LG leads to decreased promoter methylation and higher expression of GRs in the hippocampus (Weaver et al., 2004). Variations in the quality of maternal care thus directly regulate epigenetic states and, thus, exert sustained effects on gene transcription (Turecki et al., 2012). There are important parallels between behavioral and molecular changes observed in the rodent models of parent–offspring interactions and behavioral and neurobiological alterations that associate with a history of ELA in humans (Turecki et al., 2012). Pups reared by low LG mothers show increased behavioral and HPA responses to mild stress. In humans, such effects involve HPA dysfunction, as observed in individuals who have been exposed to childhood abuse (Heim et al., 2010). As described in detail in Chapter 4, such a dysfunction is closely related to an increased vulnerability for suicide.

Evidence of an effect of ELA on the epigenetic state of the human genome was first observed by investigating the methylation state of the

GR gene in the hippocampus in postmortem studies of individuals who died by suicide and had histories of ELA (see Figure 4.2; McGowan et al., 2009). These individuals, when compared with normal controls and suicides with no histories of ELA, show decreased mRNA expression levels of total GR and a GR exon variant that is homologous to a rat exon in the hippocampus.

This finding was subsequently extended to other transcripts of the GR in the brains of suicides (Labonté et al., 2012b). In sharp contrast to these widespread effects on the hippocampus, no change in DNA methylation or in GR expression is detectable in the cingulate cortex, another important site for the regulation of the HPA axis. Epigenetic adaptations to ELAs thus appear to be specific to particular brain regions.

Further investigations demonstrated epigenetic effects of ELAs in the form of GR promoter methylation in peripheral blood samples from individuals who were exposed to varying forms of ELAs. (For an overview, see Nemeroff, 2016, and Turecki, 2016.) In a large population of individuals diagnosed with borderline personality disorder, depression or posttraumatic stress disorders, all of which have been previously associated with histories of ELAs, CSA was associated with increased GR promoter DNA methylation in the peripheral blood (Perroud et al., 2011). In addition, the severity of child abuse correlated positively with methylation levels. In another study, Tyrka and colleagues (2012) investigated the DNA methylation status of the GR gene, demonstrating increased methylation of the GR gene in circulating leukocytes from subjects with histories of ELA. Increased levels of GR methylation were also associated with decreased sensitivity in the dexamethasone suppression test, a marker of HPA axis hypersensitivity (see Chapter 4), suggesting a functional relationship between peripheral GR methylation and HPA axis activity. Findings using peripheral tissues are thus consistent with results observed in postmortem studies of individuals who took their own lives. It remains unclear, however, how and why ELAs impact the GR methylation state in some (hippocampus, blood leukocytes), but not all (cingulate cortex) tissues.

The activity of the HPA axis is also controlled by mechanisms other than GR negative feedback. At the intracellular level, FKBP5 is a chaperone protein that inhibits GR ligand binding and translocation of the GR–ligand complex to the nucleus and thus is an important regulator of the stress-response system (see Chapter 4). Several glucocorticoid response elements are present at the FKBP5 gene, so that expression of FKBP5 is stimulated by glucocorticoids and represents an intracellular short negative feedback loop. As described earlier, genetic polymorphisms in

FKBP5 interact with a history of ELAs to predict suicide attempts in adulthood (Roy et al., 2010). Subsequent investigations show that a functional polymorphism of the FKBP5 gene increases the risk of developing stress-related psychiatric disorders in adulthood by allele-specific, childhood trauma–dependent DNA demethylation in functional glucocorticoid response elements of FKBP5. This demethylation is linked to increased stress-dependent gene transcription followed by a long-term dysregulation of the stress hormone system and a global effect on the function of immune cells and brain areas associated with stress regulation (Klengel et al., 2013). Thus, molecular mechanisms of long-term environmental reactivity are increasingly identified.

Important and interesting epigenetic findings are also reported for neurotrophins, and particularly for the brain-derived neurotrophic factor (BDNF) gene and its high-affinity receptor, tyrosine receptor kinase type B (TRKB). As described in Chapter 4, BDNF is a widely expressed neurotrophin, which supports the survival of existing neurons and encourages the growth and differentiation of new neurons, synaptogenesis, and synaptic function and plasticity. Maternal maltreatment decreases BDNF mRNA expression in the prefrontal cortex of adult rats, which is associated with site-specific hypermethylation in promoters of the BDNF gene (see Turecki, 2016). Interestingly, site-specific hypermethylation seems to follow a developmental pattern, with one promoter hypermethylation occurring immediately after the maltreatment, whereas another promoter methylation increases gradually to reach significantly altered levels only at adulthood.

To examine a possible association between epigenetic BDNF changes and suicidal behavior, the methylation state of BDNF can be assessed in postmortem brain tissue and in peripheral white blood cells. Methylation appears to be significantly increased in the Wernicke area of the brains of suicides when compared with controls (Keller et al., 2010). Study of the methylation state of the BDNF gene in white blood cells from borderline personality patients shows that peripheral levels of DNA methylation in the BDNF promoter increase as a function of the number of ELAs (Perroud et al., 2013). A history of suicidal behavior in depressed individuals is also associated with greater methylation of the BDNF promoter (Kang et al., 2013). Of note, the level of methylation predicts the likelihood of improvement of suicidal thoughts during treatment such that greater methylation predicts less improvement.

BDNF DNA methylation in the blood may thus well represent a biomarker for the early detection of suicide risk, as will be discussed in more detail in Chapter 9.

But there is more: Epigenetic changes in the stress-response system can be influenced by psychological therapies. In borderline personality disorder individuals, BDNF methylation significantly decreases in responders to 4 weeks of intensive cognitive behavior therapy (dialectical behavior therapy), with changes in methylation status significantly correlating with changes in depression scores, hopelessness scores, and impulsivity (Perroud et al., 2013). Similarly, change in FKBP5 DNA methylation is associated with response to cognitive behavior therapy. Individuals with the greatest reduction in severity show decreases in percentage of DNA methylation during treatment, whereas those with little or no reduction in severity increase in percentage of DNA methylation (Roberts et al., 2015).

As discussed earlier, serotonin also acts as a mediator between early adverse life experience and subsequent behavior, shaping individual differences in susceptibility to mental health or illness. Variations in 5-HT signaling, due to genetic variations, epigenetic modifications, or antidepressant drugs, set developmental pathways that predispose some individuals to succumb in the face of contextual adversity while permitting others to benefit from an advantageous environment. Some, but not all, studies suggest that ELAs, and particularly CSA, are linked to DNA methylation of the 5HT transporter gene promoter region (for an overview, see Turecki, 2016). Methylation of the 5HT2A receptor gene appears to be increased in white blood cells of individuals with suicidal thoughts, but not significantly decreased in the prefrontal cortex of suicides (De Luca et al., 2009). 5HT thus may act as a mediator between ELA and suicidal behavior via both genetic variations (see earlier discussion) and epigenetic modifications. It turns out to be essential to take the genotype into consideration when investigating the epigenetic profile of the 5HT system after ELA: Increased methylation of the transporter promoter region is associated with increased risk of unresolved trauma in people carrying the l allele, while the opposite is true for carriers of the two short alleles (Van IJzendoorn et al., 2010).

It is possible that the effect of ELAs on suicidal behavior is not limited to epigenetic changes in specific genes, but that the whole genome is affected. Several genome-wide association studies (GWAS) have shown epigenetic regulation effects of ELAs (see Turecki, 2016). Such studies are now beginning to show genome-wide DNA methylation changes in peripheral tissues in association with ELAs and suicidal behavior. Labonté and colleagues (2012b) were the first to show genome-wide promoter DNA methylation changes in postmortem hippocampal tissue of suicides, linked with a history of childhood abuse: A total of

362 promoters are differentially methylated in the abused group, with hypermethylation in 248 promoters and hypomethylation in 114 promoters. Of note, the methylation changes mainly occur in neurons and in genes that are implicated in neural plasticity. Further GWAS investigation of DNA methylation levels within the ventral prefrontal cortex shows that DNA methylation increases throughout the lifespan, but that suicides showed an 8-fold greater number of methylated sites relative to controls, with greater DNA methylation changes over and above the increased methylation observed in normal aging (Haghighi et al., 2014).

7.3.2 Systems Mediators

A link between ELAs and alterations in brain structure, function, connectivity, or network architecture is documented in more than 180 original reports. Alterations in specific regions (e.g., the adult hippocampus or the anterior cingulate cortex [ACC]) and pathways (such as the corpus callosum) have been consistently associated with childhood maltreatment across laboratories and populations. Hence, connecting ELAs to brain changes is strongly supported.

Many studies using structural MRI have scrutinized gray and white matter volumes in individuals with ELAs, showing that ELAs are associated with reduced volumes of the ACC, orbitofrontal cortex, hippocampus, and caudate nuclei (Nemeroff, 2016). A recent meta-analysis reported widespread reductions in gray matter volumes in ELA victims in several brain regions, including the prefrontal cortex, hippocampus, parahippocampus, striatum, and orbitofrontal cortex (Lim et al, 2014). Of note, most studies have not found volumetric changes in the amygdalae.

Regarding white matter, the most consistent finding is that of alterations in the corpus callosum, characterized by reduced midsagittal area volumes or decreased fractional anisotropy (diminished integrity) on DTI scans (see Chapter 3 for technical details) (Teicher & Samson, 2013). Animal data indicate that the anterior limb of the internal capsule (ALIC; see Figure 6.2) is affected by early life stress during development resulting in significant reductions in fractional anisotropy in the ALIC (Coplan et al., 2010). Global-based connectivity (GBC), the connectivity of each voxel with every other voxel of the brain, can be pathologically restricted (i.e., reduced GBC) or broadened (i.e., increased GBC) in large-scale network synchronization. GBC studies show that the severity of childhood trauma predicts left thalamic hyperconnectivity, which thus can be regarded as a biomarker of exposure to ELAs (Philip et al., 2016).

Functional neuroimaging approaches can be expected to contribute to our understanding of how ELAs may lead to suicidal behavior. A prominent finding in relation to exposure to ELAs is reduction of resting state functional connectivity (RSFC) in the default mode network (DMN). Other key findings include disruptions in emotional processing networks in subjects with ELAs, such as reduced integration between the left amygdala and frontal regions. RSFC changes within the executive network have also been implicated in ELAs: Dorsolateral prefrontal cortex (DLFPC) connectivity correlates negatively with ELA severity, while ELA is associated with greater anticorrelated RSFC between the DLPFC and the DMN, indicating a deterioration in the intrinsic relationships associated with healthy function. ELA is also associated with reduced negative connectivity between the amygdala and DMN, as well as with decreased RSFC between regions of the salience network and hippocampus (reviewed in Philips et al., 2016).

The study of brain activation following exposure to emotional face expressions using fMRI has contributed significantly to our understanding of a neural basis of suicidal behavior, as we saw in the previous chapter. Functional MRI investigations show that higher levels of childhood trauma are associated with stronger differentiation in brain responses to negative compared with positive faces in clusters comprising the right angular gyrus, supramarginal gyrus, middle temporal gyrus, and the lateral occipital cortex. Childhood trauma is associated with reporting negative faces as more negative, and positive faces as less positive (Aas et al., 2017). It thus appears that functional brain consequences of exposure to ELA appear to overlap with those in relation to suicidal behavior, possibly reflecting cognitive changes underlying suicidal behavior (see Chapter 5), such as altered attentional allocation toward negative stimuli and increased negativity bias.

Three final issues need to be mentioned concerning imaging findings and ELA, namely, the age-dependent induction and appearance of changes in brain structure, and the effect of type of ELA. There appear to be potential sensitive periods of exposure to CSA in brain development. Hippocampus volume is reduced in association with CSA at 3–5 years and 11–13 years, maltreatment particularly affecting dendritic arborization of pyramidal cells in CA3 and neurogenesis in the dentate gyrus. Corpus callosum volume is reduced with CSA at 9–10 years, and frontal cortex volume is attenuated in subjects with CSA at 14–16 years. Brain regions apparently have unique windows of vulnerability to the effects of childhood maltreatment (Andersen et al., 2008; Pechtel et al., 2014). The effects of maltreatment on brain functioning may not appear immediately following exposure. For example, reductions in the gray matter volume of the hippocampus are reported in adults with ELA histories but not in maltreated children. This pattern of results is consistent with translational studies showing that effects of early stress on the hippocampus first emerge during the transition between puberty and adulthood. The delay between exposure to ELA and neurobiological change may be particularly relevant, as a comparable time lag occurs between exposure and suicidal behavior.

The effect of type of abuse is remarkable, as shown in Figure 7.1. Parental verbal abuse is associated with changes in auditory areas, while witnessing domestic violence is linked with changes in visual areas.

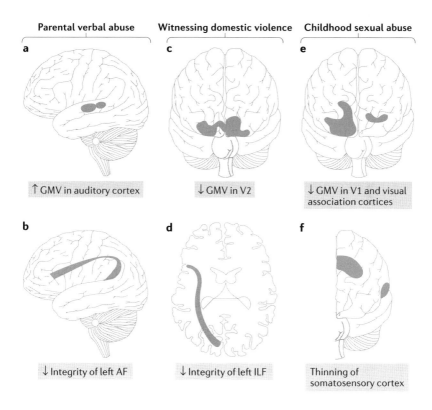

Figure 7.1 The effects of childhood maltreatment on brain structures and connectivity (Reprinted by permission from Macmillan Publishers Ltd: *Nature Reviews Neuroscience*, Teicher et al., The effects of childhood maltreatment on brain structure, function and connectivity, copyright 2016). See color plate 14.

Exposure to childhood sexual abuse is associated with gray matter reduction in parts of the visual cortex involved in facial recognition and with thinning of portions of somatosensory cortex involved in processing tactile sensations from the genitals (Teicher et al., 2016). This remarkable phenomenon suggests that identified brain changes are to be regarded not only as damage following exposure to ELAs but perhaps as adaptations to environmental threats, which will be discussed in more detail later.

7.3.3 Imaging Genetics

In addition to the described molecular and brain system changes, imaging genetic approaches point at possible relationships between them. In other words, genetic characteristics may predispose individuals to particular brain system changes when exposed to ELAs. One recent study indeed provides evidence for such an interactive effect of the FKBP5 genotype. The FKBP5 gene is a key regulator of HPA-axis sensitivity and activity as described in Chapter 4 and earlier: Cortisol induces FKBP5 gene expression by activation of glucocorticoid-response elements, and, in turn, FKBP5 binding to the GR reduces GR affinity for cortisol and diminishes the amount of activated GRs being translocated to the cell nucleus. High-expression-inducing T alleles of the FKBP5 gene are associated with relative GR resistance. ELAs lead to dysregulated HPA-axis function, as discussed earlier, especially in genetically predisposed subjects carrying the TT genotype. Based on findings in animal models, it can be expected that an exaggerated cortisol response may then impair neuroplasticity and trigger structural brain changes. Structural brain imaging indeed shows reduced gray matter volumes comprising the bilateral insula, the superior and middle temporal gyrus, the bilateral hippocampus, the right amygdala, and the bilateral anterior cingulate cortex in abused TT carriers. The results thus support the hypothesis that the FKBP5 TT genotype predisposes subjects who have experienced childhood abuse to widespread structural brain changes in the subcortical and cortical emotion-processing brain areas (Grabe et al., 2016).

Postmortem tissue can also be used to study epigenetic effects of childhood adversity, showing that such a history is associated with cell-type specific changes in DNA methylation of oligodendrite genes and a global impairment of the myelin-related transcriptional program in the anterior cingulate cortex. These effects are not present in depressed suicides without a history of child abuse. Adult suicides with a history of childhood abuse show selective and significant reductions in the thickness of myelin sheaths around small-diameter axons in the anterior cingulate cortex. Such findings suggest that childhood abuse, in part through epigenetic reprogramming of oligodendrocytes, may lastingly disrupt cortical myelination, a fundamental feature of cerebral connectivity (Lutz et al., 2017).

7.4 "In my end is my beginning": The Delayed and Lethal Consequences of Early-Life Adversity

The huge amount of information described in this chapter reflects the devastating and potentially lethal consequences of early life adversities (ELAs) such as sexual and physical abuse. Epidemiological findings clearly demonstrate a significant increase in the risk of suicidal behavior following exposure to ELA, and we are now beginning to see the mediating mechanisms underlying this lethal link. Up to 40% of individuals with suicidal behavior have a history of ELA. The molecular and brain system correlates of exposure to ELAs overlap considerably with those of suicidal behavior, to such an extent that the study of the neurobiological sequelae of ELA contributes to our understanding of the development of suicide risk. The overlap in molecular changes includes the involvement of the stress-response system and the serotonin neurotransmission system.

Overlapping brain system changes include structural and functional brain characteristics, such as a reduced size of the corpus callosum, decreased gray matter volumes of the prefrontal cortex, and thalamo-cortical hyperconnectivity. The well-documented reduction in hippocampal volume following childhood sexual abuse, however, is not so commonly found in association with suicidal behavior. This discrepancy can possibly be explained by the moderating effect of age: A reduction in hippocampal volume is mainly found following exposure to sexual abuse at a very young age, and it could well be that suicidal behavior is particularly linked to sexual abuse at a later age, for example when the corpus callosum is implicated at 9–10 years of age. Concerning overlapping functional brain changes, increased reactivity to facial expressions of anger is found following ELAs and in association with suicidal behavior. It remains to be demonstrated whether such reactivity explains the link between ELA and suicidal behavior, particularly in individuals in which ELA consisted of exposure to anger and aggression.

The phenotypical expression of such overlaps requires further study, but may include sensitivity to particular stressors due to the interaction between neurobiological and neurocognitive alterations. The influence of ELAs on hypothalamic-pituitary-adrenal response to psychological stressors has been evaluated in a series of studies using the Trier Social Stress Test (for an overview, see Teicher & Samson, 2013). While it was first reported that women with a history of CSA or CPA had an increased cortisol response to stress challenge, subsequent studies have increasingly shown a blunting of cortisol response in adults with ELA. Thus, some individuals may show an augmented response, consistent with an enhanced fight/flight reaction, while others may show a blunted response, consistent with freezing. This divergent pattern of response may be influenced by type and timing of ELA, but also by genetic characteristics. For example, reappraisal ability (the success of using reappraisal to down-regulate negative affect) is influenced by a BDNF Val66Met genotype × ELA interaction, with Met carriers showing both the lowest level of reappraisal ability in ELA-exposed individuals and the highest level of reappraisal ability in non-ELA individuals. The BDNF Val66Met polymorphism thus moderates the link between ELA and emotion regulation ability (Miu et al., 2017).

Concerning the type of ELA, Van Orden and colleagues (2010) hypothesize that the experience of ELA that is physically painful or associated with physical injury may be uniquely connected with habituation to pain and, thus, an acquired capacity for lethal suicidal behavior (see Chapter 2 for a description of the interpersonal theory of suicide, in which acquired capacity plays an important role). Indeed, adolescents who have more invasive sexual abuse experiences that involve sexual contact or intercourse are more likely to have a history of a suicide attempt than those who did not experience contact in the context of the abusive experience and those who were not sexually abused. Further, as research suggests that boys may be more likely than girls to experience severe pain and injury in the context of sexual abuse, this may help explain the apparently stronger link between childhood sexual abuse and suicide attempts in boys as compared with girls (see Miller et al., 2013).

The fact that the link between ELA and suicidal behavior has been demonstrated in a huge amount of studies using a wide diversity of study designs and populations suggests a causal effect of ELA. Nevertheless, alternative interpretations have been suggested (for an overview, see Teicher et al., 2016). For example, alterations in brain structure or function may predispose to both sexual abuse and suicidal behavior. Many abused children evidence brain damage, even without an apparent or reported head injury, and it has been suggested that these children are more vulnerable to being sexually abused by family members because of their neurological handicap. Following this line of reasoning, and given the demonstrated neuroanatomical changes linked with suicidal behavior, it could be that such neurological damage also predisposes to suicidal behavior in later life. Such an interpretation may be possible in individual cases, but it is highly unlikely to explain the link between ELAs and suicidal behavior in the vast majority of cases.

The extent to which mediating molecular and brain system changes are to be regarded as damage due to ELA or as adaptive mechanisms is much less clear. Stress is harmful for the brain and particularly harmful for the developing brain. Stress-induced programming of the glucocorticoid stress response system and stress-induced release of neurotransmitters affect basic processes including neurogenesis, synaptic overproduction and pruning, and myelination during sensitive periods in genetically susceptible individuals. These effects target specific stress-susceptible brain regions including hippocampus, amygdala, neocortex, cerebellum, and white matter tracts. Brain structures likely to be especially vulnerable to the effects of ELA would have one or more of the following features: (11) a protracted postnatal development, (2) a high density of glucocorticoid receptors, and (3) some degree of postnatal neurogenesis (Teicher & Samson, 2016).

An alternative view is that the brain is modified by early stress in a potentially adaptive way. "Adaptive" in this sense means that the alterations are experience-dependent responses to the environment and not simply nonspecific stress-induced impairments. Many of the ELA-related findings appear to make sense as neuroplastic adaptive responses. These include alterations in auditory cortex and arcuate fasciculus in children experiencing verbal abuse, in visual cortex and visual-limbic pathway in subjects visually witnessing domestic violence, and in thinning of genital representation areas in the somatosensory cortex of sexually abused females. Also, enhanced amygdala response to emotional faces and diminished striatal response to anticipated reward also makes sense as adaptations that would tip the balance in approach-avoidance situations toward avoidance. In this case, psychopathology may emerge due to the mismatch between the world the brain was modified to survive in and the world it finds itself in during subsequent developmental stages (Teicher & Samson, 2016). These two hypotheses are not mutually exclusive. There may be types of exposure that trigger adaptive responses and experiences that are so horrible as to damage the brain in nonadaptive ways. It is also likely that polymorphisms that influence the expression of molecules involved in neurotransmission, stress response, or brain development may render some individuals more susceptible to both the positive and negative impacts of early experience (Teicher & Samson, 2016).

Development sets a forecast for a place in the world ahead. Early life experiences contribute to the development of a blueprint of the world in the brain that may or may not be adapted to living in the "real world" as an adolescent or adult. For example, developmental changes in serotonergic functioning, either directly associated with allelic 5HT transporter variations or via early adverse experiences, may amplify a positive response to a nurturing environment but at the same time increase the sensitivity to adverse information. Importantly, developmental changes in 5HT signaling appear to particularly affect thalamocortical axonal pathways (Brummelte et al., 2017). Of note, such a sensitivity to negative information and thalamocortical communication play crucial roles in the computational model of suicidal behavior, which will be developed in the next chapter.

Chapter 7 Summary

- Epidemiological studies clearly demonstrate an increased risk of suicidal behavior following exposure to early life adversity (ELA).
- This devastating effect is moderated by age, gender, timing and frequency of the exposure, identity of the abuser, and genetic characteristics.
- Molecular changes involving the stress-response system, inflammation, and neurotrophic factors mediate the relationship between ELAs and suicidal behavior.
- ELAs may change the expression of genes, without changing the DNA, via epigenetic mechanisms.
- ELAs may increase the risk of suicidal behavior via structural and functional brain changes that interfere with emotion regulation and decision making.

Review Questions

1. What can we learn from epidemiological studies about the relationship between early life adversities and suicide risk?
2. There are no animal models of suicidal behavior, but what can be learned from such models about the ways in which the early environment programs responses to stress that may precipitate suicidal behavior in humans?

3. Which epigenetic mechanisms may explain the increased risk of suicide in later life following early life adversity?
4. How can changes in the structure and function of the brain following
   exposure to early life adversity play an adaptive role?

Further Reading

Nemeroff, C. B. (2016). Paradise lost: The neurobiological and clinical
       consequences of child abuse and neglect. *Neuron, 89*, 892–909.
Teicher, M. H. & Samson, J. A. (2013). Childhood maltreatment and
       psychopathology: A case for ecophenotypic variants as clinically and
       neurobiologically distinct subtypes. *American Journal of Psychiatry,
       170*, 1114–33.
    (2016). Enduring neurobiological effects of childhood abuse and neglect.
       Journal of Child Psychology and Psychiatry, 57, 241–66.
Turecki, G. (2016). Epigenetics of suicidal behaviour. In W. P. Kashka & D.
       Rujescu (Eds.), *Biological aspects of suicidal behaviour*. Basel, Karger.
Turecki, G., Ernst, C., Jollant, F., Labonté, B. & Mechawar, N. (2012). The
       neurodevelopmental origins of suicidal behavior. *Trends in
       Neurosciences, 35*, 14–23.

CHAPTER EIGHT

I Predict, Therefore I Cannot Be

A Predictive Coding Account of Suicidal Behavior

Learning Objectives

- Which brain processes underlie the optimism bias in healthy people?
- What is belief updating, and how is it influenced by the certainty of our beliefs?
- How could the ancient and omnipresent neurotransmitter serotonin be related to suicide as a relatively contemporary and uniquely human phenomenon?
- What is the central role of the thalamus in a predictive coding account of suicidal behavior?
- How may neurostimulation change our beliefs about the future?

Introduction

Our understanding of how the brain works has expanded enormously in recent decades. Nevertheless, neuroscience is still looking for a model of brain function that enables the integratation of findings from the divergent approaches that were described in the previous chapters in the context of suicidal behavior, such as the cognitive, developmental, and systems approaches. The predictive coding hypothesis may well provide such a unifying model. The production of false beliefs and their behavioral consequences are a central issue in this model. As hopelessness is an example of such false beliefs that dramatically increase the risk of suicidal behavior, a predictive coding model of suicidal behavior may provide new insights and badly needed new avenues to treatment and prevention.

This chapter will describe a computational predictive coding model of suicidal behavior, in which findings from the cognitive, neuroimaging, neurobiological, developmental, and neuropsychological studies as described in the previous chapters can be integrated. This model leads to a new understanding of suicide and, consequently, to new approaches to its prevention.

In contrast with the previous chapters, this chapter describes a purely theoretical and hypothetical view, in which recent insights based on predictive coding are used to develop an understanding of suicidal behavior as the choice of individuals in their social contexts. Predictive coding is a metaphor for message passing in the brain and addresses a central feature of psychiatric problems, the production and maintenance of false beliefs (Friston et al., 2014). As false beliefs about ourselves, the world, and the future are at the core of suicidal thoughts and behavior, the change of such beliefs is crucial to suicide prevention. Recent findings from predictive coding research offer an understanding of the development of these beliefs, how they relate to disturbances in brain structures and functions, and how they may be changed.

8.1 Predictive Coding and Suicidal behavior

As we have seen in previous chapters, many theoretical frameworks have been developed to understand suicidal behavior and to guide detection and treatment of suicide risk. Such frameworks are solid and evidence-based, and have been developed mainly against a neurobiological or psychological background. However, there is currently no unifying model of suicidal behavior in which neurobiological and psychological characteristics can be integrated. For example, we have seen in Chapter 4 that the relationship between suicidal behavior and changes in serotonin neurotransmission is among the most replicated findings in biological psychiatry. As a neurotransmitter, serotonin is also present in plants and animals, and is estimated to be at least 700 million years old. So how can we understand an effect of such an omnipresent and evolutionarily old neurotransmitter on the occurrence of a uniquely human and relatively contemporary phenomenon such as suicidal behavior?

People have views of themselves, the future, and the world. In cognitive psychology, these views are recognized as schemas, or patterns of thoughts, while in predictive coding models such views are described in terms of predictions or (prior) beliefs. In everyday life, people update their beliefs about the world, the future, and themselves based on what they perceive: Bottom-up sensory inputs are compared with top-down beliefs, and mismatches are signaled as prediction errors. Cortical activations (such as those described in functional neuroimaging studies of suicidal behavior in Chapter 6) reflect the production of prediction errors as mismatches between existing beliefs and new perceptual information. These errors can be minimized in two ways: Beliefs can be updated or sensory input can be attenuated by, for example, withdrawal into oneself or escape from the world. Neurobiological correlates of belief updating are increasingly demonstrated. If something goes wrong in the process of updating beliefs, false beliefs may develop and persist despite perceptual proof of the opposite.

The central hypothesis in this chapter is that suicide can be explained by one seemingly simple abnormality, i.e., an imbalance in the certainty of beliefs and the certainty of contextual sensory input. More particularly, it is hypothesized that suicide risk is associated with increased certainty of particular predictions (due to which they cannot be updated) and a (possibly compensatory) relative increase in the certainty of particular sensory input. This association may explain why suicidal individuals are, for example, impervious to positive information but hypersensitive to signals of defeat, and unable to change their negative predictions of the future by considering positive outcomes, and thus become hopeless. A predictive coding account may be very appropriate to explain suicidal behavior related to false predictions; the meaning of "predict" derives from its origin in Latin – *pre* (before or in front of) plus *dicere* (to speak), in other words, "to declare what will happen in the future" (Friston, 2012). Faulty inferences can easily lead to false predictions in the form of beliefs of hopelessness, a crucial risk factor for suicidal behavior. Predictive coding models have recently been developed for, among others, autism (Lawson et al., 2014), schizophrenia (Horga et al., 2014), and functional somatic symptoms (Edwards et al., 2012). As a predictive coding approach yields new insights in the development of suicidal behavior, it can be expected to contribute substantially to the prediction and treatment of suicide risk.

Predictive coding states that the brain continually generates models of the world to predict sensory input. In terms of brain processing, a predictive model of the world is created in higher cortical areas and communicated through feedback connections to hierarchically lower sensory areas. In contrast, feed-forward connections convey sensory input and project an error signal when there is a mismatch between the predicted information and the actual sensory input. Prediction errors are important because they signal that the current "internal" model of the world is not up to the task of explaining the "outside" world. Once a prediction error has been signaled, the system must decide what to do with that signal: Some errors may be spurious and uninformative, e.g., in an uncertain environment, while other prediction errors must be taken very seriously and thus lead to updating of the model of the world. Prediction errors can be dealt with by means of changing the sensory input (action) or by changing the predictions (perception). Action minimizes prediction errors through a selective sampling of input to ensure it conforms to our predictions, for example, by means of withdrawing into oneself. Perception is the process of minimizing prediction errors by providing better top-down predictions through the updating of prior beliefs.

The process of perception is influenced by two characteristics, i.e., the valence of sensory information and the relative precision of prior beliefs and sensory information. Whether new information is positive or negative is important in determining the extent to which it will alter beliefs. In general, healthy people tend to alter beliefs more in response to favorable than to unfavorable information, indicating the fundamental roles of emotion and the weighing of information in decision making (Sharot et al., 2011; Sharot & Garrett, 2016). The influence of prior beliefs, relative to bottom-up sensory evidence, is controlled by the precision accorded to prior beliefs and such sensory information. Precision corresponds to the confidence or certainty associated with a belief or with bottom-up information. A high sensory precision will increase the influence of ascending prediction errors by turning up the "volume" of sensory channels in which more confidence is placed. Conversely, high precision of prior beliefs will bias perception toward these beliefs and inhibit their updating. The balance of the precision ascribed to bottom-up information relative to prior beliefs determines the extent to which prior beliefs can or need to be updated. Negative beliefs about the self, the world, or the future can become impervious to positive contextual influences. For example, negative beliefs or predictions about the future may be changed by positive information about the beneficial effects of time and treatment, but severely suicidal individuals may not able to do so, and thus show high levels of hopelessness. The predictive coding hypothesis states that this is due to an imbalance in the estimation of precision (or certainty): Negative beliefs are held with relatively high precision, while the estimated precision of positive information is low. Thus, estimations of precision are particularly important in this process, and inappropriate estimation of precision can easily create and maintain false inference (Adams et al., 2014). Cortical abnormalities may reduce precision at higher levels of the inferential hierarchy, and thus bias inference toward sensory input due to which prior beliefs are more likely to be updated. Similarly, brain abnormalities may decrease the precision of sensory input and limit the likelihood that their perception will lead to an update of beliefs.

Precision is a belief about a belief, a belief about the validity of our own thoughts about ourselves, the world, and the future, and the updating of precision is just as important as the updating of predictions. Attention can be understood as the process whereby the brain optimizes precision estimates: By enhancing the precision, attention increases the weight that is put on prior beliefs or sensory input. This is equivalent to proposals of attention selecting channels that convey precise or salient information and optimizing perceptual inference using the expected precision of processing streams (Feldman & Friston, 2010). We will return to this later in this chapter, when potential neuromodulatory mechanisms are discussed.

Insight into the neural, neuronal, and neurobiological mechanisms of belief updating, including the updating of precision beliefs, is increasing rapidly. Belief updating is thought to be mediated by neural coding of prediction errors in response to positive information in the left inferior frontal gyrus (IFG) and bilateral superior frontal gyrus (SFG) and to negative information in the right IFG and the right inferior parietal lobule (IPL). Intact mental health is linked to a relatively attenuated neural coding of negative information in the right IPL (Garrett et al., 2014). Valence, which is the intrinsic positivity or negativity of beliefs or sensory input, thus affects belief updating. This supposes a close inter-action and thus connectivity between brain regions involved in complex cognitive functions, such as the prefrontal cortex, and key structures for emotion such as the striatum. This supposition is clearly supported by neuroimaging findings: Stronger white matter connectivity of the left IFG with left regions involved in emotion regulation is associated with greater change in belief for favorable information but with reduced change in beliefs for unfavorable information in healthy individuals (Moutsiana et al., 2015).

Undesirable information appears to be underweighted in healthy individuals (Sharot & Garrett, 2016), suggesting a decreased encoding of the precision or certainty of such information. Concerning precision beliefs, activity in the ventromedial prefrontal cortex and the frontopolar cortex, and the strength of their connectivity, appear to be related to the estimation of precision beliefs (De Martino et al., 2013; McGuire et al, 2014). Further study implicates corticothalamic loops in "precision engineering," particularly involving the pulvinar, a thalamic nucleus that regulates relationships between cortical regions and is implicated in attentional control (Kanai et al., 2015). There thus is empirical evidence in favor of the replication principle in precision control: For every direct connection between two cortical regions, there is a parallel, indirect corticothalamic pathway that goes through thalamic nuclei that contain relay neurons (see Figure 8.1).

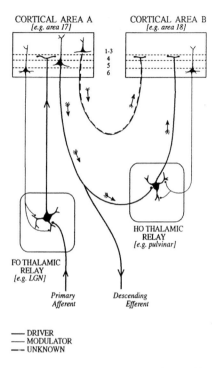

CORTICAL AREA A
[e.g. area 17]

CORTICAL AREA B
[e.g. area 18]

1-3
4
5
6

HO THALAMIC
RELAY
[e.g. pulvinar]

FO THALAMIC
RELAY
[e.g. LGN]

Primary
Afferent

Descending
Efferent

—— DRIVER
—— MODULATOR
––– UNKNOWN

Figure 8.1 Schema to illustrate cortical and thalamic pathways (Sherman & Guillery, 1998). Two thalamic nuclei are shown: a first-order (FO) relay on the left and a higher order (HO) relay on the right. A first-order relay receives its driver inputs on proximal dendrites from subcortical sources via ascending pathways, whereas a higher order relay receives its driver inputs from cells in cortical layer 5. The first-order relay sends a driver input to layer 4 of cortical area A (thick line), and that same cortical area sends a modulator input (thin line) with small terminals onto distal dendrites of the thalamic relay cell) from layer 6 back to the same first-order thalamic nucleus. Cortical area A in turn sends a driver input from layer 5 to the higher order thalamic relay. This higher order relay sends its thalamocortical axons (shown as drivers) to cortical area B and receives a modulator input back from layer 6 of cortical area B. Note that there are two paths by which cortical area A can influence area B. One is the transthalamic path, shown by small arrows and drawn as thick lines indicative of a driver pathway. The other is the direct corticocortical pathway (a "feed-forward" pathway), and this is shown by small arrows. (Copyright (1998) National Academy of Sciences, U.S.A.)

The relay neuron is the functional unit of the thalamus, and these cells receive two general types of afferents: drivers and modulators. Driver inputs are considered the main conduits of information. In contrast, modulator inputs modify how driver inputs are processed: They fine-tune the message relayed by thalamic cells and control the probability of its transmission (the so-called gating of information) by adjusting cellular and synaptic mechanisms. First-order relays receive subcortical driver inputs (e.g., visual input to a thalamic nucleus), while higher order relays (pulvinar and posterior medial or medial dorsal nuclei) receive driver input from (layer 5 of) the cortex and thus participate in cortico-thalamo-cortical (or transthalamic) circuits. According to the replication principle, direct corticocortical connections are paralleled by transthalamic ones, by means of which information can be modulated or gated by thalamic circuitry in ways unavailable to direct corticocortical pathways (Sherman, 2016). The encoding of precision in higher order relay neurons thus may be achieved by modulating the gain of corticocortical communication via thalamocortical projections. Neurons in the pulvinar exhibit features of selective attention and respond more strongly to behaviorally relevant stimuli than to unattended stimuli. The notion of precision estimation in parallel corticothalamic pathways thus integrates seemingly disparate aspects of attention and precision (Kanai et al., 2015). In other words, thalamic amplification of functional cortical connectivity may sustain attentional control (Schmitt et al., 2017).

Insight into the neuropharmacology of precision estimation is increasing (Adams et al., 2014). Postsynaptic gain gates the influence of presynaptic inputs on postsynaptic outputs and is determined by activation of receptors including NMDA receptors and classical neuromodulator receptors such as serotonin (5-HT). The precision of sensory input appears to be regulated via NMDA-excitatory influence of corticothalamic neurons, while inhibitory effects on thalamic cells occur mainly via GABAergic synapses (Crandall et al., 2016). The NMDA receptor antagonist ketamine, which appears to have strong antisuicidal effects (see later discussion and Chapter 10 for details), may exert such effects by influencing the excitatory-inhibitory balance of thalamocortical communication.

Beyond single sensory events, adaptive perception and action rest on the accurate estimation of fluctuations in the precision of possible environmental events. Classical neuromodulators such as 5-HT may thereby putatively track the volatility in the environment across time, and this information globally scales the weight that one should place on bottom-up evidence relative to prior beliefs (Lawson et al., 2015). As stated earlier, prediction errors arising from such bottom-up information from an uncertain environment are relatively less likely to lead to updating of beliefs due to reduced precision estimation.

Given the well-documented association between 5-HT disturbances and suicidal behavior (see Chapter 4), it is particularly relevant in the context of this chapter to take a close look at the role of 5-HT in precision estimation, but unfortunately this is not yet fully understood. In line with early theories of 5-HT functions (Deakin & Graeff, 1991), contemporary accounts of the function of 5-HT focus on behavioral inhibition, in which thoughts can be considered as actions leading from one belief state to the next, and in which 5-HT directly and reflexively inhibits chains of thoughts predicted to lead toward negative outcomes (Dayan & Huys, 2008). Thoughts leading to a negative outcome may thus engender a (5-HT-mediated Pavlovian reflexive) withdrawal response, which leads to their termination. Such a natural tendency to inhibit thoughts leading to aversive states may protect from psychopathology ("the serotonergic crutch"; Montague et al., 2012), while a failure to show this type of inhibition may lead to enhanced negative thoughts (Crocket & Cools, 2015). 5-HT may thus inhibit the updating of beliefs in a negative direction, and lowering 5-HT may induce negative cognitive biases because of paying relatively more attention to negative than positive information (Dayan & Huys, 2008). Attentional weighting of negative prediction errors may thus be related to 5-HT functioning, and several lines of research indeed support a role of 5-HT in attentional control via gating. Reduced 5-HT activity and decreased Stroop interference are linked, presumably via enhanced attentional control (Scholes et al., 2007). Acute tryptophan depletion, which is thought to reduce 5-HT in the brain, may increase the salience of negative information via deficient inhibitory control (Hitsman et al., 2007). Reducing inhibition and improving tonic cortical gating of information could well be the mechanism underlying this association. Conversely, serotonergic hallucinogens affect gating in corticothalamic loops and lead to imprecise bottom-up signaling in the context of preserved and perhaps enhanced top-down processing (Corlett et al., 2009). Reduced 5-HT functioning may thus increase the motivational influence of aversive information on behavior via increased precision and improved gating of aversive information relative to the precision of top-down control.

Disturbed Pavlovian behavioral inhibition may have far more deleterious effects via Pavlovian-instrumental transfer (PIT), thus not only enhancing negative thoughts but also influencing choices and behavioral consequences. Normally, aversive Pavlovian cues invigorate goal-directed withdrawal from aversive outcomes. Increasing evidence shows that this PIT-effect is associated with pruning of the decision tree in one's mind. Goal-directed actions are chosen through exploration of a branching set of possible future situations, which is also known as "tree search" (Daw et al., 2005). Such trees can be pruned in a valence-dependent way by excising poor decision subtrees from consideration, and it is becoming clear that the propensity to prune increases in the face of negative outcomes in healthy individuals (Huys et al., 2012). Behavioral inhibition may thus be associated with pruning negative parts of the tree, which is reflected in the optimistic bias that characterizes healthy individuals. Compromised behavioral inhibition, on the other hand, may lead to maladaptive pruning, with aversive chains being insufficiently deselected (Dayan & Huys, 2008).

While valence thus affects internal considerations and choice, recent findings indicate a role of precision or certainty in this process, particularly involving the precision of beliefs (or predictions) about the future. Exploration of possible future situations, i.e. tree search, is based on predictions of long-term outcomes by chaining together short-term predictions about the immediate consequences of each action in a sequence. People may strategically explore as a function of the relative uncertainty about the expected value of options (Badre et al., 2012). The certainty (precision) of negative predictions (beliefs) may preclude exploration of alternative strategies. This may explain the perseverative answers and lack of alternative strategies (i.e., lack of belief updating) shown by suicide attempters during neuropsychological tasks, as will be discussed later. The frontopolar cortex (FPC) tracks changes in relative uncertainty, and thus guides the cognitive process of branching (Badre et al., 2012; Hyafin & Koechlin, 2016). The brain indeed uses certainty about (or precision of) preexisting beliefs to adjust the influence of new observations on belief updating, and the relative precision of existing beliefs thereby correlates positively with neural activity in the FPC, in parallel with the posterior parietal cortex (McGuire et al., 2014). This functional connectivity pattern is consistent with contributions to precision estimation in the parietal cortex. Relative uncertainty about existing beliefs correlates negatively with vmPFC and medial temporal lobe neural activity, consistent with previously reported effects of subjective confidence in these regions (De Martino et al., 2013; McGuire et al., 2014).

Reductions in serotonin selectively enhance aversive PIT, i.e., the motivational influence of aversive stimuli on goal-directed behavior (Hebart & Glätscher, 2015). Aversive Pavlovian cues modulate connectivity between the ventromedial prefrontal cortex (vmPFC) and the caudate nucleus: Greater aversive Pavlovian inhibition of goal-directed approach responding is associated with reduced connectivity between vmPFC and the caudate nucleus during aversive stimuli (Geurts et al., 2013). Compromised 5-HT neurotransmission may thus increase the motivational influence of aversive information on goal-directed behavior, perhaps via increased connectivity between vmPFC and the caudate nucleus.

8.2 Precision, Valence, and Suicide Risk

This chapter aims at explaining the vulnerability to suicidal behavior in terms of deficiencies in the estimation of the precision of prior beliefs and environmental input related to their valence. First, it is hypothesized that a relatively high precision of negative (prior) beliefs about the self, the world, and the future makes these beliefs impervious to positive information. Such positive information may, for example, concern hope and potential beneficial effects of time and treatment. Second, a relatively high precision of negative sensory input may explain the sensitivity to aversive social stimuli as it has been described in neurobiological (see Chapters 4 and 6) and cognitive psychological (see Chapter 5) models of the vulnerability to suicidal behavior. A failure to attenuate sensory precision may thus lead to a failure to suppress and contextualize prediction errors pertaining to negative social input such as signals of defeat.

If we fail to update models of the world that are necessary for interaction and survival, and if we fail to minimize prediction errors following aversive social input, we might consider avoiding (input from) this world and retire "to a dark and quiet room" (Friston et al., 2012). The updating of beliefs and consequent minimization of prediction errors thereby depends on the relative precision attributed to beliefs and social input. An aberrant precision account of the vulnerability to suicidal behavior may accommodate many of the experimental findings that support existing psychological and neurobiological theories of suicidal behavior. The next section will address such findings and theories.

8.3 Integrating Suicide-Related Systems and Molecular and Cognitive Changes in a Predictive Coding Account of Suicidal Behavior

8.3.1 Brain Systems Changes

The review of neuroimaging studies in Chapter 6 identifies changes in a frontothalamic network in the brain in association with suicidal behavior. Structural brain changes involve both gray matter volumes and white matter connections between (sub-)cortical regions, including thalamocortical pathways.

Given the association between connectivity of the left IFG and belief updating for positive information, as described earlier, the reduced left IFG connectivity as found in suicide attempters may well be related to reduced belief updating for positive information (Bijttebier et al., 2015). Notably, increasing left IFG connectivity using neurostimulation is associated with reduced feelings of hopelessness in depressed individuals, as we will see in more detail in Chapter 10 (Baeken et al., 2017). The identification of deficiencies in a thalamocortical network using structural neuroimaging is in keeping with the role of parallel corticothalamic pathways in attention and precision estimation as noted earlier. Impaired corticothalamic circuitry has indeed been demonstrated in relation to suicidal behavior in a substantial number of studies (see Chapter 6). Of note, postmortem studies find an increased volume of the thalamus in suicides (and not in depressed individuals who died due to other causes), particularly involving the pulvinar in individuals with the ss genotype of the serotonin transporter gene. These ss-genotype individuals show a 20% increase in pulvinar neuron number and volume (see Chapter 4 for the link between this phenotype and suicidal behavior; Young et al., 2007; 2008).

Cortical responses are generally considered an index of precision-weighted prediction errors (Friston, 2005). Functional imaging studies have investigated such cortical responses to (aversive) social stimuli in association with suicidal behavior. As described earlier, a failure to attenuate the precision of aversive information can be expected to be associated with increased activity in the right orbitofrontal cortex, which was indeed shown in fMRI studies of suicide attempters following exposure to aversive facial emotions (see, e.g., Jollant et al., 2008). Of note, EEG measures of frontal electrical activity during a guessing task show an increased neural response to loss (and not to gains) in children of suicide attempters when compared with demographically and clinically matched children of parents without suicidal behavior. An increased neural response to negative information might thus represent one of the potential pathways of the familial transmission of suicide risk (Tsypes et al., 2017).

8.3.2 Molecular Changes

8.3.2.1 Serotonin

The relationship between changes in the serotonin (5-HT) neurotransmission system and suicidal behavior probably is one of the most replicated findings in biological psychiatry (for a detailed overview, see Chapter 4). Findings include indices of enhanced serotonin synthesis capacity, including more 5-HT and serotonergic neurons in the raphe nuclei, perhaps in response to decreased serotonergic tone, and deficits in serotonin transporter binding in ventromedial prefrontal cortex and anterior cingulate regions, possibly as a homeostatic adaptation to the decreased tone. Studies of levels of 5-HIAA, a metabolite of 5-HT, suggest that the serotonergic impairment in association with suicidal behavior involves neurotransmission rather than synthesis (Oquendo et al., 2014b). The interpretation of findings is a matter of debate. In line with a proposed central role of the serotonin-1A (5-HT_{1A}) receptor in the regulation of brain serotonergic activity (Popova & Naumenko, 2013), it has recently been suggested that the up-regulation of 5-HT_{1A} (auto-)receptors as demonstrated in postmortem and neuroimaging studies plays a central role in explaining changes in the serotonin system in association with suicidal behavior (Menon & Kattimani, 2015). The up-regulation of these receptors may well be associated with homeostatic up-regulation of mechanisms aimed at increasing central serotonin bioavailability, thus explaining compensatory increases in serotonergic activity as reflected by, e.g., more serotonergic neurons and decreased transporter binding (Menon & Kattimani, 2015). Support for this hypothesis was found recently in a prospective study showing an association between greater index 5-HT_{1A} receptor binding in the raphe nucleus, more subsequent suicidal ideation, and greater lethality of subsequent suicidal behavior during a 2-year follow-up of depressed individuals (Oquendo et al., 2016). The 5-HT_{1A} system is involved in prefrontal cortical functions, particularly attention.

8.3.2.2 Neurobiological Stress Response

Suicidal behavior is associated with abnormalities in the neurobiological stress response system (the hypothalamic-pituitary-adrenal [HPA] axis; see Chapter 4 for a detailed discussion). Studies of cortisol reactivity to laboratory stressors have yielded conflicting results showing both increased and decreased cortisol production, but blunted cortisol reactivity to stress appears to be a (possibly heritable) trait diathesis factor in suicidal behavior (McGirr et al., 2011; O'Connor et al., 2017). This can be explained by an altered sensitivity of corticoid receptors, including a decreased sensitivity of glucocorticoid receptors (Oquendo et al., 2014b). Many studies have shown epigenetic glucocorticoid receptor gene methylation in brain tissue in relationship to experiences of trauma and psychopathology. (For a review, see Chapters 4 and 7, and Figure 4.2.)

8.3.2.3 GABA and Glutamate

Several studies point at epigenetic reduction in the expression of the GABA A receptor gene in the frontopolar cortex in suicides (Poulter et al., 2008; Yin et al., 2016). Concerning glutamate, some but not all studies have found decreased NMDA receptor binding in the prefrontal cortex of suicides, while glutamate levels in brain regions apparently do not differ between suicides and comparison subjects (Oquendo et al., 2014b). The involvement of glutamatergic dysfunction is supported by the potential antisuicidal properties of the glutamate antagonist keta-mine, but the role of glutamatergic alterations in suicide is yet unclear and requires urgent further study.

8.3.3 Cognitive Changes

Studies, systematic reviews, and meta-analyses indicate an association between neuropsychological dysfunctions and suicidal behavior. (For an overview, see Chapter 5.) More particularly, deficiencies in future think-ing, attentional control, and decision making have been documented in association with a history of suicidal behavior.

8.3.3.1 Future Thinking

Hopelessness is characterized by low levels of positive future thinking, rather than the preponderance of negative future thinking (MacLeod et al., 1993; O'Connor et al., 2008; O'Connor & Nock, 2014). Low endorse-ment of a positive interpretation of ambiguous situations predicts suicidal ideation (Beard et al., 2017), via its effect on hopelessness (Beevers & Miller, 2004). Hopelessness predicts suicidal behavior independently of depression, and appears to be more important than depression in explain-ing thoughts about suicide (Beck et al., 1993; O'Connor & Nock, 2014).

Beyond this important role of valence-related content of future expectancies, their precision – or the probability that a particular out-come will occur – also appears to be influential. The determining role of inevitability has been highlighted already in early definitions of hope-lessness (Andersen et al., 1992). More than a decade later, MacLeod and colleagues (2005) demonstrated that the extent to which suicide attempters rated their negative predictions as likely outcomes correlated positively with levels of hopelessness. Pessimistic certainty also appears to explain why a history of suicide attempts confers risk of future suicidal behavior (Krajniak et al., 2013). These findings thus suggest a unique contribution of precision of the prediction of a positive future to the development of suicide risk, beyond valence-related characteristics. Sargalska and colleagues (2011) examined the cognitive content of future expectancies in relation to suicidal ideation in more detail in a nonclinical population. They found that the certainty about an absence of positive outcomes predicts suicidal ideation, beyond the effects of simple pessimism about positive or negative outcomes. Thus, it appears that it is particularly the certainty (or precision) of negative predictions that determines levels of hopelessness.

8.3.3.2 Attentional Control

Studying the role of sensitivity to sensory input, such as signals of defeat, in the vulnerability to suicidal behavior more than 20 years ago, Williams (2001) already demonstrated the "perceptual pop-out" of stimuli signaling loser status using the emotional Stroop task (EST) in suicide attempters. As described in Chapter 5 (see also Figure 5.1), in this task the person sees a series of words that are printed in colored inks. Their task is to call out the colors in which the words are printed, as fast as possible but making as few errors as possible. If the meaning of the word is salient, there will be interference with the naming of the color. The EST is based on the assumption that individuals who use suicide schema exhibit delayed responding to suicide-related stimuli because of their increased salience. Recent cross-sectional and prospective studies and a meta-analysis of emotional Stroop tests show an interference effect with, and thus an attentional bias toward, suicide-related words, particularly the word "suicide." The Suicide Stroop has good predictive validity for suicidal behavior in clinical and nonclinical populations (Cha et al., 2010; Chung & Jeglic, 2016).

8.3.3.3 Decision Making

Studies, reviews, and a meta-analysis consistently show that suicide attempters perform significantly worse on decision-making tasks such as the Iowa Gambling Task (IGT) than depressed or healthy comparison subjects (for a review and meta-analysis, see Richard-Devantoy et al., 2014). The IGT involves aspects of complex real-life decisions, including immediate rewards and delayed punishments, risk, and uncertainty of outcomes. Attempters apparently fail to learn during the task, picking approximately the same proportion of disadvantageous cards in the first and final blocks of the task. The interpretation of this replicated finding is unclear. Attempters may fail to integrate reinforcement history, i.e., past experiences, and make decisions largely on their present state. According to an alternative interpretation, as stated earlier, the perseverative answers and lack of alternative strategies (i.e., lack of belief updating) shown by suicide attempters during IGT tasks may be due to the certainty (precision) of negative predictions. Consequently, exploration of alternative strategies may be reduced.

8.4 A Predictive Coding Account of Suicidal Behavior

The outlined computational framework describes the importance of the optimal integration of prior beliefs and sensory evidence for individuals to survive in a dynamic and uncertain environment (Adams et al., 2013). As precision describes the relative certainty of each source of information, its accurate representation is crucial for this integration. The hypothetical predictive coding account of suicidal behavior suggests that aberrant precision encoding may interfere with survival to such an extent that it leads to premature and self-chosen death. Suicide is conceptualized as the consequence of an imbalance in the relative precision of prior beliefs and sensory input. More particularly, suicide-related beliefs about the self, the world, and the future are regarded as negatively biased beliefs that are held with undue precision, and thus become impervious to positive information. The vulnerability to suicide appears to be associated with an inability to incorporate positive information in beliefs about the future, reflecting an imbalance between the weight of such information and that of prior beliefs, to such an extent that prior beliefs are not updated. Suicidal states of mind may thereby be triggered by adverse life events via increased precision (or decreased attenuation) of sensory input such as signals of defeat. Such an increased precision of sensory input may be compensatory, as it ensures that relevant sensory information gets sufficient weight and is not subordinate to higher cognitive control mechanisms. Suicide risk can thus be formulated in terms of a valence-dependent imbalance in the encoding of precision of prior beliefs and contextual input.

The aberrant precision hypothesis for suicidal behavior is based on false inference in the context of the predictive brain. However, we have also appealed to notions like Pavlovian instrumental transfer, optimism bias, and pruning in tree searches. These heuristic notions may, in the next few years, be reconciled within the false inference formulation. For example, valence has been formulated in terms of prior preferences in the setting of active inference, which also mandates an optimism bias when reconciling beliefs about hidden states of the world and policies that one should be pursuing. Furthermore, notions of pruning and exploration can also be considered in the context of predictive model selection and models of active inference (Friston et al., 2015). Formal models that are currently being introduced into computational psychiatry may thus be usefully applied to choice behavior in people at risk of suicide to test the specific claims of the above hypothesis.

8.4.1 Implications for Understanding Suicidal Behavior

The outlined predictive coding account of suicidal behavior is hypothetical, as it has not yet been studied directly. However, experimental findings from neuropsychological, neurobiological, and neuroimaging studies of suicidal behavior appear, in general, to support such an account, which offers a remarkable opportunity to integrate and understand these findings. For example, the outlined framework offers an intriguing way to understanding the association between the relatively contemporary and uniquely human phenomenon of suicide and changes in the functions of serotonin, the neurotransmitter that is millions of years old and ubiquitously present in plants, animals, and humans. Serotonin plays a key role in (Pavlovian) linking aversive predictions with behavioral inhibition. The basic idea is that evolution has endowed even simple organisms with powerful, prespecified behavioral programs whereby predictions of aversive outcomes elicit innate, preparatory avoidance responses. Such Pavlovian responses are useful by preparing the organism to interact optimally with its environment, for example, by means of withdrawal. Reduced 5-HT functioning may thus increase the motivational influence of aversive information on behavior via improved gating of aversive information relative to the precision of top-down control. Dysfunctional inhibition may influence choice behavior via maladaptive pruning of decision trees. The proposed account thus may explain how neurobiological (such as serotonergic) dysfunctions affect motivational and volitional components of suicidal behavior by increasing the motivational influence of aversive information and redefining goal-directed behavior in terms of ending this influence. It thus appears that the "response space" (Spence, 2009) of suicidal individuals is widened to include negative and self-destructive responses, as if suicidal individuals dwell in dark and negative parts of this space, where nonsuicidal individuals do not go (thanks to behavioral inhibition). In this chapter, we have described the neuroanatomical, neurobiological, and cognitive characteristics that potentially determine the constraints of the response space of suicidal individuals. However, these constraints are not static and thus may be amenable to change via, e.g., psychological and pharmacological interventions.

8.4.2 Implications for Treatment and Prevention

Given the proposed central role of precision and valence in this hypothetical computational account of suicidal behavior, interventions targeting these issues may well play an important role in suicide prevention. Three potential approaches are discussed later, from a neurobiological, neuropsychological, and functional neuroanatomical point of view, respectively.

The acute beneficial effects of ketamine on suicide risk may well be due to its blocking effect on NMDA receptors (surmised to be involved in top-down predictions) and enhancement of AMPA receptors (involved in bottom-up signaling) (Den Ouden et al., 2012; Whalley, 2016). Beneficial effects of ketamine may thus be due to restoring the imbalance in the relative precision of sensory evidence and top-down beliefs (Vinckier et al., 2016).

Given that precision is determined by attention, a change in attentional bias or an amelioration of attentional deficits may be important in reducing the vulnerability to suicidal behavior. An intervention aimed at the modification of suicide-specific attentional bias appears to have no impact on this bias or on suicidal ideation, but preliminary data indicate that the beneficial effects of mindfulness-based cognitive therapy on suicide risk factors are associated with a decrease in Stroop interference (Cha et al., 2016; Chesin et al., 2016).

Transcranial magnetic stimulation (TMS) has the potential to change belief updating, apparently by influencing precision estimation: TMS interference to the activity of the right inferior frontal gyrus (IFG) causes healthy individuals to be more optimistic, apparently by increasing the precision of positive information: They judge the probabilities that good things will happen to them in the future higher than their own estimations without TMS (Sharot, 2012). When TMS is applied to the left IFG, the optimism bias disappears and estimations resemble an overly pessimistic thinking (Sharot et al., 2012). TMS may also alter sensory precision at lower hierarchical levels, as application to the visual cortex, while performing a visual task, induces changes in precision (Rahnev et al., 2012). Dorsolateral rTMS apparently has no beneficial effect on the severity of suicidal ideation when compared with sham stimulation (Desmyter et al., 2016), but is associated with a decrease in levels of hopelessness, notably paralleled by an increase in left IFG connectivity (Baeken et al., 2017). The extent to which TMS may influence the precision of sensory input and prior beliefs in suicidal individuals remains to be demonstrated, taking into account gray and white matter changes that may interfere with connectivity between hierarchical levels.

8.4.3 Implications for Further Study

This aberrant precision account of suicidal behavior may generate falsifiable hypotheses that can be tested using clinical, behavioral, pharmacological, neuropsychological, neuroimaging, and computational modeling methods (Lawson et al., 2014). Neurostimulation may thereby play a prominent role. For example, given the role of the frontopolar cortex in precision estimation, it can be expected that frontopolar stimulation may influence choice behavior to such an extent that more uncertain options are selected. Anodal transcranial direct current stimulation (tDCS) of the right frontopolar cortex indeed causes individuals to make more exploratory choices by up-regulating neuronal excitability, thus enhancing encoding of precision (Beharelle et al., 2015). The precision of value-based choices thereby appears to depend on the synchronous communication between the frontopolar and the parietal cortex. Oscillatory desynchronization using transcranial alternating current stimulation (tACS) specifically affects the precision of value-based choices (Beharelle et al., 2015). The effects of such localized neurostimulation interventions on precision estimation and choice behavior in suicidal individuals clearly need to be studied. Such investigations could thereby target oscillatory synchrony as a mechanism of attentional control in the identified thalamocortical network, and its deficiencies such as thalamocortical dysrhythmia, involved in depression and pain.

Chapter 8 Summary

- The dynamics of life and survival in times of adversity require updating of beliefs, acquired during upbringing and built on a base of genetic preparedness, in order to cope with changing circumstances.
- The updating of beliefs is influenced by the valence and the relative precision (or certainty) of these beliefs and the information regarding these circumstances: Healthy people tend to update their beliefs more

readily in the case of positive than negative information, which is thought to reflect the effect of the estimation of precision based on valence.

• Suicidal behavior can be explained as a consequence of deficiencies in valence-based precision estimation. First, negative prior beliefs about the self, the world, and the future are held with undue precision and thus become impervious to positive information. Second, increased estimated precision hampers attenuation of particular negative sensory information (e.g., signals of defeat).

• It is hypothesized that a relatively simple deficiency in (e.g., serotonergic) neuromodulation and implicit encoding of precision may lead to a failure to acquire internal models that are necessary for interaction with the world.

• Central to the hypothesis is a deficiency in behavioral inhibition, which favors the updating of beliefs in a negative direction, which consequently has an undue influence on behavioral choices.

• The outlined conceptualization offers a remarkable opportunity to integrate findings from cognitive, neuroimaging, and neurobiological studies in a model of suicidal behavior that provides urgently needed potential new avenues to the treatment and prevention of suicide risk.

Further Reading

Dayan, P. & Huys, Q. J. M. (2008). Serotonin, inhibition, and negative mood. *PLoS Computational Biology*, *4*(2): e4.

Dayan, P. & Seymour, B. (2009). Values and actions in aversion. *Neuroeconomics*, 175–91.

Friston, K. J., Stephan, K. E., Montague, R. & Dolan, R. J. (2014). Computational psychiatry: The brain as a phantastic organ. *The Lancet Psychiatry*, *1*, 148–58.

Spence, S. A. (2009). *The actor's brain: Exploring the cognitive neuroscience of free will.* Oxford: Oxford University Press.

CHAPTER NINE

Predicting the Unpredictable

Neuroscience Contributions to Suicide Prediction

Learning Objectives

- Understand the problems and possibilities in predicting suicidal behavior at the individual level.
- Learn what biomarkers are, why they are particularly important for suicide prediction, and which neurobiological characteristics may serve as biomarkers for suicidal behavior.
- Identify appropriate research approaches to the development of accurate biomarkers.
- Learn the opportunities and limitations of statistical approaches using big data, e.g., from social media.

Introduction

Sometimes depressed individuals visit their doctors because they are afraid that they will hurt or kill themselves. Subsequent conversations reveal that they are scared because they cannot predict whether their suicidal thoughts and wishes will lead them to take their own lives. During supervision sessions, trainees in psychiatry often say that they consider the estimation of suicide risk one of the most difficult tasks when they are working in emergency departments, the more so as many suicidal individuals will not talk about their suicidal wishes because they do not want help; they want to die. The magnitude of the difficulties in estimating suicide risk is in sharp contrast with the very limited value of available predictive tools and with the consequences in case of mistakes. The overall picture emerging from studies of the performance of predictive tools and questionnaires is that prediction may only be slightly better than chance. In other words, one could as well flip a coin to decide whether there is a risk of suicide.

The "prediction" topic logically follows the previous chapter, which focused on the kind of information that suicidal individuals may (not) use in updating their beliefs (predictions) about themselves, the world, and the future, and that may motivate them to end their own lives. This chapter addresses the kind of information that health care staff may take into account in order to update their beliefs or predictions about the risk of suicide in their patients. This chapter will review the problems in the prediction of suicidal behavior, but also identify possibilities and opportunities from a neuroscientific point of view.

9.1 The Prediction of Suicidal Behavior

In fact, it is not surprising that suicidal behavior is difficult to predict. The base rate of suicide is low. Many people may think that life is not worth living, but fewer people think about ending their own lives. Far fewer people engage in self-injurious or suicidal behavior, and only a minority of those people will do so with the intent to die. In addition, suicidal individuals are not inclined to talk about their thoughts and feelings because of shame and taboos, but particularly because they do not want help; they want to die. The World Health Organization recommends that all people over the age of 10 years with a mental disorder or other risk factor should be asked about thoughts or plans of self-harm within the past month. However, even when asked, suicidal individuals may deny the existence of suicidal thoughts and wishes. One study found that almost 80% of people who eventually died by suicide denied suicidal thoughts in their last verbal communication (Busch et al., 2003). Health care staff commonly are reluctant to ask depressed people about suicidal thoughts because they are afraid that talking about suicide will lower the threshold for suicidal behavior. There is no scientific evidence, however, showing that talking about suicide leads to suicidal behavior (Dazzi et al., 2014). Inquiring about suicidal thoughts and feelings may, on the contrary, offer a possibility to reduce the social isolation and fears that may accompany suicidal thoughts. Talking about such thoughts makes it possible to determine the severity of the threat of suicide, and collect the information that is necessary to predict the occurrence of suicidal behavior.

The important question here is, Which information is needed to predict such behavior in a reliable way? An optimal prediction model for suicide requires high sensitivity to minimize so-called false negatives, that is, undetected suicides, and, preferably but less critically, high specificity to reduce the number of false positives, which may overburden limited resources (Mann et al., 2006). Definitions of relevant terms can be found in Figure 9.1.

		Presence of condition	
		Condition present	Condition absent
	Positive	True positive (A)	False positive (B)
Test outcome			
	Negative	False negative (C)	True negative (D)

Sensitivity = A / (A+C)   Positive predictive value (PPV) = A / (A+B)
Specificity = D / (B+D)   Negative predictive value (NPV) = D / (C+D)

Figure 9.1 Sensitivity-specificity diagram.

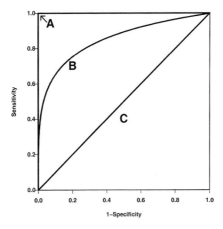

Figure 9.2 ROC curves.

In the context of suicide prevention, it is important to maximize sensitivity to avoid missing as few cases as possible. However, such an approach risks the inclusion of an overwhelming number of nonsuicides unless specificity is very high. A major problem in predicting suicide is that most suicide risk factors, when assessed as screening tests, have low specificity and that consequently the number of false positives is substantial. Low specificity combined with the low base rate of suicide makes the positive predictive value of individual risk factors low. For a marker of suicide risk to be clinically useful, it must have high sensitivity (>90%) and specificity (>90%). Markers should also show strong predictive value.

Figure 9.2 shows so-called receiver operating characteristic (ROC) curves, which are a statistical relationship with regard to limits of detection and screening. The curves on the graph demonstrate the inherent trade-off between sensitivity and specificity. Curve A in Figure 9.2

reflects a test that would be perfectly sensitive and have no false positives (100% specific).

Determining the area under the curve (AUC) allows one to compare different tests. The greater the area under the curve (up to the maximum 1.0), the more accurate the test is (both better sensitivity and specificity). AUC values may range from 0.5 (curve C in Figure 9.2; no discriminating ability) to 0.9–1 (curve A; excellent accuracy).

A meta-analysis of 37 relevant longitudinal cohort studies (see Chapter 1 for definitions) of suicide risk assessment based on clinical suicide-related variables and conducted over 40 years, involving more than 300,000 people of whom more than 3,000 died by suicide, reveals a statistically strong association between high-risk strata and death by suicide. However, the meta-analysis of the sensitivity of suicide risk categorization shows that about half of all suicides are likely to occur in lower-risk groups, and the meta-analysis of positive predictive value (PPV) suggests that 95% of high-risk patients will not take their own lives (Large et al., 2016). A systematic review of studies looking at the prediction of suicide following nonfatal suicidal behavior using risk factors and risk scales concludes that such an approach to suicide risk assessment may be falsely reassuring and thus is not useful as a basis of treatment decisions (Chan et al., 2016).

The following sections will address the question whether a neuro-scientific approach to risk prediction may contribute to suicide prevention by means of the identification of biomarkers.

9.2 Biomarkers

The term "biomarker," a portmanteau of "biological marker," refers to an objective indication of a particular state, which can be measured accurately and reproducibly. Theoretically, biomarkers may aid health care staff in the prediction of suicidal behavior. As discussed extensively in previous chapters, quite a few neurobiological characteristics have been proposed as risk factors for suicidal behavior. Figure 9.3 gives an overview of identified biomarkers and shows how they may relate to structural and functional brain systems changes.

However, the vast majority of studies are cross-sectional, and the identified characteristics thus may qualify only as neurobiological correlates and not as (causal) risk factors. In addition, quite a few findings from longitudinal studies have been contradictory. Meta-analyses of longitudinal studies that have investigated whether neurobiological factors predict suicidal behavior can be used to resolve such discrepancies.

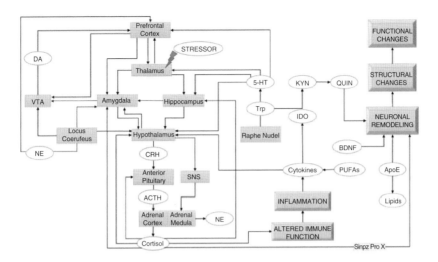

Figure 9.3 Model of connections between biomarkers associated with suicidal behavior (*Current Psychiatry Reports*, Biomarkers of suicide attempt behavior: towards a biological model of risk, 19(6), 2017, Sudol K & Mann JJ. With permission of Springer.). 5-HT, serotonin; ACTH, adrenocorticotropic hormone; ApoE, apolipiprotein E; BDNF, brain-derived neurotrophic factor; CRH, corticotropin-releasing hormone; DA, dopamine; IDO, indoleamine 2,3- dioxygenase; KYN, kynurenine; NE, norepinephrine; PUFAs, polyunsaturated fatty acids; QUIN, quinolinic acid; SNS, sympathetic nervous system; Trp, tryptophan; VTA, ventral tegmental area.

The following sections will summarize findings from, as much as possible, longitudinal and meta-analytic studies of biomarkers of suicide risk.

9.2.1 Single Biomarkers

9.2.1.1 Cognitive Biomarkers

As discussed in Chapter 5, the implicit association test (IAT) is an established psychological test that measures a person's unconscious beliefs on a subject or motivations toward a specific behavior. A computer displays an image (in this case relative to suicidal behavior) or a neutral image, and the subject presses a key to indicate whether or not they view the image as related to self. The reaction time in this task provides the measure of their propensity for suicidal behavior. Cohort studies of patients in psychiatric emergency departments show that a specific death/life IAT test predicts future suicidal behavior within 3 and 6 months, independently of the person's voiced intention and the clinician's belief of future suicidal behavior (sensitivity 50%, specificity 81%, PPV 32%, negative predictive value (NPV) 90%). Of note, the accuracy of the IAT is improved when used with other variables such as a history of suicidal behaviors, depression with psychosis, and educational level (Nock et al., 2010; Randall et al., 2013).

9.2.1.2 Neurobiological Biomarkers

A first meta-analysis using the stress–diathesis model of suicidal behavior (see Chapter 2) included longitudinal studies of serotonergic dysfunction (as a marker of the presence of the diathesis) and HPA-axis dysfunction (as a marker of acute stress response). Meta-analyses of the results of 25 identified longitudinal studies of 5-hydroxyindoleacetic acid in the cerebrospinal fluid (CSF 5-HIAA; see Chapter 4) and the dexamethasone-suppression test (DST; also see Chapter 4) in mood disorder patients (thus with a higher suicide base rate than the general population) yield odds ratios for prediction of suicide of 4.5 and 4.7, respectively. Individuals in the low CSF 5-HIAA group and DST non-suppressors thus have a more than 4-fold risk of suicide compared with the high CSF 5-HIAA group and nonsuppressors. A prediction model that requires either DST or CSF 5-HIAA tests to be positive results in 88% sensitivity and 28% specificity and has a positive predictive value of 10% (Mann et al., 2006). A sensitivity of 88% means that, for example, in a sample of 1,000 persons with a base rate of suicide of 5%, about 18 out of 20 suicides would be detected, which is a very good result. The "cost" of this success, however, would be that, with a specificity of 28%, 705 individuals would incorrectly be identified as potential suicides and they would receive intensive preventive treatment unnecessarily (Mann et al., 2006). As we will show later, the combined use of both neurobiological measures yields quite different predictive values.

A more recent meta-analysis uses findings from longitudinal studies of a large number of neurobiological factors, as shown in Table 9.1. The analyses reveal that these neurobiological factors have a weak and, in most cases, nonsignificant association with subsequent suicide attempt or death by suicide. Only two specific neurobiological factors remain significant, cytokines and low levels of fish oil nutrients, but only one study examining each of these factors could be included in the meta-analysis. It should be noted that meta-analyses of the CSF serotonin metabolite and the DST yield significant odds ratios of 2.15 and 1.75, respectively, but publication bias analyses indicate that studies with findings below the mean are missing, and adjusted odds ratios are not significant. The

---

Table 9.1 Neurobiological factors studied in meta-analysis

- Blood-related factors: glucose, cholesterol, serum tryptophan ratio, plasma oxytocin
- Cerebrospinal fluid metabolite: serotonin, dopamine, oxytocin, norepinephrine, cortisol-releasing hormone, DHEA
- Cytokines: monocyte chemotactic protein-1, tumor necrosis factor-α, vascular endothelial growth factor, interleukin-10
- Genes: serotonin synthesis (tryptophan hydroxylase gene), serotonin transporter and receptor polymorphisms
- Hormone challenges/tests: DST nonsuppression (or lowered suppression), fenfluramine challenge
- Molecule binding: platelet serotonin [3H] paroxetine binding
- Nutrients: serum cholesterol level, omega-3 and omega-6 monosaturated fatty acid, saturated fatty acid intake and serum levels
- Peripheral physiology: systolic blood pressure, lung test

---

meta-analysis shows no evidence of protective effects for any of the examined neurobiological factors (Chang et al., 2016).

This finding suggests that neurobiological factors may not substantially increase or decrease the risk of future suicidal behavior when studied individually. For example, the CSF serotonin metabolite analyses produce a weighted odds ratio of 2.15 for suicide death (before accounting for publication bias). In terms of absolute risk for suicide death for a given individual over a 1-year period, low CSF serotonin metabolites would increase risk from 0.013 per 100 people to 0.028 per 100 people, and thus provide limited improvement in clinical prediction. However, it is of utmost importance in interpreting these findings to note that nearly all studies include long follow-up intervals, measure factors as trait-like entities, and test putative risk factors in isolation. It is possible that, in the context of several other risk factors (e.g., other neurobiological factors, stressful life events, low social support, prior history of self-injury, and hopelessness), sudden shifts in certain neurobiological factors may be associated with greatly increased risk for a few hours, days, or weeks. These findings highlight a need for studies that examine potential neurobiological risk factors over short intervals, in conjunction with other potential risk factors, and in a state-like manner (Chang et al., 2016). Later we will see examples of studies that focus on the predictive value of combinations of neurobiological characteristics, with or without clinical risk factors.

In suicide prevention, it is particularly impractical to directly access the target organ – the brain – in live individuals, and even its proxy fluid, the cerebrospinal fluid, is less accessible for routine use than blood. Although the blood of course is not the brain, there are common neurobiological mechanisms and environmental and medication effects that can be identified across tissues with convergent approaches. The identification of blood biomarkers for disease risk has emerged as an important area of translational research in medicine, particularly in cancer and cardiovascular medicine, in the quest for precision and individualization of prevention and treatment (Niculescu et al., 2015a).

In Chapter 4 we have seen that genetic studies of suicidal behavior have identified the involvement of quite a few genes in suicidal behavior. Genetic tests that assess, for example, allelic distributions (such as the ss, sl, or ll genotypes of the serotonin transporter gene; see Chapter 4) could therefore be useful, the more so as they can be done early in life so that suicide risk can be estimated already at a young age. Given the stress–diathesis model, however, it can be expected that gene expression biomarkers better reflect the gene–environment interactions that lead to suicide risk than genetic characteristics. Le-Niculescu and colleagues (2013) studied biomarkers for "suicidality" looking at the expression of genes in the blood of the following:

1. live male bipolar patients with and without suicidal thoughts, to generate a list of differentially expressed genes, from which relevant genes are identified using a convergent functional genomics approach
2. suicides, to study whether expression levels of the blood biomarkers identified in the live bipolar subject cohort are actually altered in the blood in an age-matched cohort of suicides
3. live cohorts of bipolar disorder and psychosis subjects, to show that the blood levels of the identified top biomarker SAT1 (spermidine/spermine N1–acetyltransferase 1) differentiates future as well as past hospitalizations with suicidality.

Expression of three other genes (PTEN, MARCKS, and MAP3K3) shows similar but weaker effects. Taken together, retrospective and prospective hospitalization data suggest SAT1 (and to a lesser extent PTEN, MARCKS, and MAP3K3) as a biomarker of suicidality. In Chapter 4, SAT1 is discussed in the context of the polyamine stress response system. In a similar study in females, decreased expression of the BCL2, PIK3C3, and GSK3B genes accurately predicts future hospitalizations for suicidality (Levey et al., 2016). These genes have antiapoptotic and neurotrophic effects and are known targets of the antisuicidal mood stabilizer drug lithium, which increases their expression and/or activity. Furthermore, circadian clock genes are overrepresented among the top markers. Notably, PER1 (increased in expression in suicidality) and CSNK1A1 (decreased in expression) accurately predict future hospitalizations. Circadian clock abnormalities are related to mood disorder, and sleep abnormalities have been implicated in suicide. Signaling of the omega-3 fatty acid docosahexaenoic acid is one of the top biological pathways overrepresented in validated biomarkers, which is of interest given the potential therapeutic and prophylactic benefits of omega-3 fatty acids. Some of the top biomarkers from this study in females show changes in expression (increase versus decrease) similar to those described earlier in the study in males, whereas others have changes in opposite directions, underlying the issue of biological context and differences in suicidality between the two genders.

A subsequent investigation of blood expression levels of the SAT1, PTEN, MAP3K3, and MARCKS genes and changes in the experience of suicidal ideation during a 12-week antidepressant treatment reveals no significant change in the expression of these four genes over the course of the study, despite increasing suicidal ideation or initiation of anti-depressant treatment (Mullins et al., 2014). Comparison of the groups shows that gene expression does not differ between patients with or without treatment-related suicidality. This independent study apparently does not support the validity of the biomarkers proposed by Le-Niculescu and colleagues (2013; see earlier discussion). The within-subject analysis used to compare gene expression at different moments during treatment in the same person is a powerful design, as it removes the possible influence of genetics and other patient-specific factors. However, the samples used in the two studies differ regarding gender and psychiatric disease, which may at least in part explain the differences in findings. Guintivano and colleagues (2014) employed genome-wide DNA methylation profiling separately on neuronal and glial nuclei in three cohorts of postmortem brains to identify associations with suicide. Validation was conducted in postmortem prefrontal cortical tissue and in peripheral blood from three living groups. Functional associations with gene expression, stress and anxiety, and salivary cortisol were assessed. The DNA methylation scan identified an additive epigenetic and genetic association with suicide at a region of the SKA2 gene independently in the postmortem brain cohorts. This finding was replicated with suicidal ideation in blood from three live cohorts. SKA2 gene expression was significantly lower in suicide decedents and was associated with genetic and epigenetic variation. Analysis of salivary cortisol measurements suggested that SKA2 epigenetic and genetic variation may modulate cortisol suppression, consistent with its implicated role in glucocorticoid receptor transactivation. In Chapter 4, SKA2 is described as a chaperone protein that is involved in the translocation of the glucocorticoid receptor. In the current study, SKA2 significantly interacted with anxiety and stress to explain about 80% of suicidal behavior and progression from suicidal ideation to suicide attempt. These gene expression findings thus identify SKA2 as a genetic and epigenetic target, and support its involvement in the etiology of fatal and nonfatal suicidal behavior. Analysis of genetic and epigenetic effects on suicidal behavior and gene expression separately indicates that DNA methylation alone may be the primary factor conferring risk (Guintivano et al., 2014).

This hypothetical interpretation is supported by findings from a subsequent study showing that levels of DNA methylation at the previously implicated SKA2 locus predict higher rates of current suicidal thoughts and behaviors, even after including well-established psychiatric risk factors for suicide in the model. Genetic variation at the methylation-associated SNP is not related to any of the suicide phenotypes examined. This study thus confirms that SKA2 methylation levels explain unique variance in suicide risk not captured by clinical symptom interviews, providing further evidence of its potential utility as a biomarker of suicide risk (Sadeh et al., 2016).

A further study develops a suicide prediction model using only SKA2 DNA methylation to predict suicidal behavior (Clive et al., 2016). While the interpretation of findings is hampered by quite a few methodological issues (such as a small and biased study sample), the authors generate an epigenetic biosignature of a stress state using brain, saliva, and whole-blood DNA methylation data of several cohorts. A statistically oriented approach that analyses cross-tissue epigenetic reprogramming by cortisol and interaction with the previous reported SKA2 suicide biomarker yields a biosignature that predicts suicide consistently across multiple, highly variable populations. This biosignature is cross-tissue in that it predicts suicidal behavior in both blood and saliva samples and is based on probes that are associated with suicide in prefrontal neurons. The results are consistent with a model whereby suicide-associated HPA-axis dysregulation causes an overproduction of circulating cortisol, which causes DNA methylation changes in various tissues, resulting in behavioral changes through the actions of DNA methylation in the brain, while leaving measurable marks in the periphery that enable the biomarker-based prediction of suicidal ideation and behaviors.

Depressed individuals with suicidal ideation show DNA hypermethylation and reduced expression of stress-related genes (BDNF, FKBP5, and NR3C1) in peripheral blood mononuclear cells when compared with healthy controls, while the depressed patients without suicidal ideation are not different. Depressed individuals with or without suicidal ideation are not different from each other, likely owing to a relatively small sample size. The findings underline the importance of epigenetic modifications of stress-associated genes in depression and, possibly, suicidal behavior (Roy et al., 2017).

9.2.2 Combined Biomarkers

As has become clear in Chapter 1, there never is one single explanation or cause for a suicide; there always are interacting causal factors that increase the risk of suicidal behavior. It is therefore not surprising that the use of one single predictor of suicidal behavior leads to low specificity. This problem of a lack of specificity of individual risk factors might thus be reduced if risk factors could be used in combination such that each additional risk factor introduces significant new risk information and updates risk estimates (known as the sequential updating of prior beliefs or predictions; see Chapter 8). To accomplish this, the risk factors chosen need to be somewhat independent of each other. The stress–diathesis model (see Chapter 2) is an evidence-based model to explain the occurrence of suicidal behavior as the consequence of the interaction between state-dependent and diathesis-related characteristics, and this model is compatible with such a combination approach. The distribution of the stressor risk factors in the population is believed to be largely independent of the diathesis risk factors, and thus, overall risk is factored into (largely) independent risk categories.

9.2.2.1 Combined Neurobiological Markers

Candidate biological markers have been proposed for each of these categories, serotonergic dysfunction as a marker of the presence of the diathesis, and HPA-axis dysfunction as a marker of acute stress response (Mann et al., 2006). While the predictive model using CSF 5-HIAA "OR" DST yields limited improvement in clinical prediction of suicidal behavior (see earlier discussion), the predictive model using "AND" to combine DST and CSF 5-HIAA tests clearly increases the specificity of prediction. When the biological tests are applied in combination, or sequentially, specificity rises from 55% (DST alone) to 88% (combination of DST and CSF 5-HIAA). However, this model, while it achieves greater specificity and thus reduces the number of false positives (from 38 to 10), does so at a heavy cost of sensitivity, which declines to 38%. It would thus fail to identify 5 out of 8 suicides.

A subsequent prospective study of clinically accessible measures of disturbances in the stress response system and the serotonin system, the DST and fasting serum cholesterol levels, confirms that individuals with an abnormal DST result are significantly more likely to die by suicide during follow-up. Low cholesterol values are associated with subsequent suicide when age is included as a covariate. These results indicate that, with the use of age-appropriate thresholds, serum cholesterol concentrations may be combined with DST results to provide a clinically useful estimate of suicide risk (Coryell & Schlesser, 2007).

9.2.2.2 Combined Clinical and Neurobiological Markers

Le-Niculescu and colleagues (2013) use multidimensional approaches in the prediction of suicidal behavior in their bipolar cohort, in addition to the gene expression investigations that were discussed earlier. The authors sequentially add data about mood and anxiety using two simple visual analogue scales to the expression levels of the biomarkers. They thus investigate the accuracy of predicting future hospitalizations for suicidal behavior for increasingly complex models (SAT1, SAT1 + anxiety, SAT1 + anxiety + mood). In this way, the investigators show that the accuracy for future hospitalizations with suicidality increases progressively from poor (with SAT1 alone) to good (with SAT1, anxiety, and mood). In other words, they substantially enhance their capability to predict hospitalizations with suicidality by combining genetic and clinical factors.

In a further study Niculescu and colleagues (2015b) use RNA biomarkers from blood samples along with newly developed questionnaires in the form of an app, which enables them to predict which individuals in a group of patients being seen for a variety of psychiatric illnesses would experience significant suicidal ideation with approximately 92% accuracy. Among patients with bipolar disorder, the accuracy reaches 98%. The combination of biomarkers and the app is also accurate in predicting which of the patients would be hospitalized for suicidality in the year following testing (71% across all diagnoses, 94% for bipolar disorder). One of the apps assesses levels of mood and anxiety, while the other asks questions related to life issues including physical and mental health, addictions, cultural factors, and environmental stress. Neither app asks whether the individual is thinking of suicide. The questionnaires by

themselves, implemented as apps on tablets, predict the onset of significant suicidal thoughts with more than 80% accuracy. There are a few
limitations to this study that require additional research. First, all participants in this study were men. In addition, the research was based on
work with people with psychiatric diagnoses. How well the biomarkers
would work among people who have not been diagnosed with a psychiatric disease is not known.

A further example of the beneficial effects of combing (epi-)genetic
and clinical data on the accuracy of predicting suicidal behavior is
provided by a study of the SKA2 gene (Kaminsky et al., 2015). The
authors show that SKA2 methylation interacts with scores on the Child
Trauma Questionnaire (CTQ) to predict lifetime suicide attempt in
saliva and blood with 70%–80% accuracy. Moreover, the interaction
mediates the suppression of cortisol following DST (see Chapter 3).
Cumulatively, the findings suggest that epigenetic variation at SKA2
mediates vulnerability to suicidal behaviors through dysregulation of
the HPA axis in response to stress.

9.3 Predicting the Unpredictable?

The concept of suicide risk assessment is controversial and much
debated in suicide research. National suicide prevention guidelines provide recommendations for risk assessment, but unfortunately there is no
widely accepted standard of care. What constitutes a risk assessment is
also an important question. While risk assessment is often synonymous
with risk assessment tools or scales, at its most basic it represents an
encounter where an individual is asked about suicidal thoughts and plans
(Bolton et al., 2015). A collaborative, therapeutic alliance between clinician and patient is important when conducting the assessment. Even a
single mental health assessment in the emergency department has been
associated with a reduced risk of repeat suicidal behavior, which may be
as high as 40% in the short term (Kapur et al., 2013).

Despite the fascinating findings from sophisticated research as described
in the previous sections, suicide risk assessment continues to pose a major
challenge. An early longitudinal study showed that 96% of high-risk
predictions were false positives, and that more than half of suicides
occurred in the low-risk group and were hence false negatives (Pokorny,
1983). Pokorny's complaint that the overwhelming number of false positives renders suicide risk assessment unfeasible is perhaps less valid
now than in 1983, but similar findings have been reported since then in
subsequent longitudinal epidemiological studies. This poses a huge

challenge to mental health services that have been developed around a model of identifying and managing risk. Consequently, it is suggested to abandon attempts to design interventions based on risk stratification and instead aim to provide an adequate standard of care to all patients: Every individual should have access to timely, individualized, high-quality treatment for psychiatric disorder (Nielsen et al., 2017).

The prediction problem is not limited to suicidal behavior or psychiatry; it is a common problem in medicine. Studies outside the area of suicidology yield promising findings. For example, the Framingham Risk Score is a widely used tool to assess risk for cardiovascular diseases. Closer to the topic of this book are studies concerning the prediction of bipolar disorder from which we can learn. As in suicidal behavior a positive family history is a strong predictor for bipolar disorder. Risk for bipolar disorder is thus elevated in bipolar offspring, but affected families and clinicians want to know an individual risk estimate so that monitoring frequency and timing of intervention strategies can be adapted to calculated individual risks. Using data from a longitudinal cohort of bipolar offspring, it has been possible to develop a "risk calculator" to predict, at the individual level, the risk of developing bipolar spectrum disorder in youth at familial risk for the disorder with an AUC of 0.76, indicating good discrimination (see Section 9.1 and Figure 9.2), comparable to risk calculators used clinically in other areas of medicine (Hafeman et al., 2017).

The study findings as reviewed in this chapter suggest that, as with the bipolar risk calculator, the accuracy in predicting suicidal behavior increases with the use of multiple sources of information. One step further in that respect is the use of big data that might provide accurate predictive models (Passos et al., 2016). Big data is a broad term used to denote volumes of large and complex measurements. Beyond genomics and other "omic" fields, big data may include clinical, sociodemographic, administrative, molecular, environmental, and even social media information. Machine learning, also known as pattern recognition, represents a range of techniques used to analyze big data by identifying patterns of interaction among variables. Compared with traditional statistical methods that provide primarily average group-level results, machine-learning algorithms allow predictions and stratification of clinical outcomes at the level of an individual subject by integrating multiple risk factors into a predictive tool. For example, gene expression biomarkers and clinical information can be integrated to develop a risk assessment tool able to predict suicide risk at an individual subject level across major psychiatric disorders. The study by Le-Niculescu and colleagues (2013) as described earlier in this chapter reports excellent accuracy with an AUC of 0.92 using such biomarkers and clinical information. Further machine-learning studies use dynamic characteristics like verbal and nonverbal communication, termed "thought markers." Machine learning and natural language processing thereby successfully identify differences in retrospective suicide notes, newsgroups, and social media such as tweets, text messages, web forums, and blogs. (For an overview of study findings, see Pestian et al., 2017.) Suicidal thought markers are also studied prospectively using interviews with suicidal and control subjects, and include acoustic (vocal and prosodic) and linguistic (identification of words and word-pairs) marker features. Machine learning algorithms can be trained to automatically identify the suicidal subjects in a group of suicidal subjects and psychiatric and healthy controls. The inclusion of acoustic characteristics appears to be most helpful when classifying between suicidal and psychiatric control subjects, which is most relevant for assessing suicide risk (Pestian et al., 2017). AUCs in these studies are in the range of 0.85–0.90, indicating excellent accuracy.

The application of machine learning to neuroimaging data has changed direction in recent years and is now increasingly applied to, for example, predicting individual disease course and outcome. Relevant for suicide prediction are findings from studies in depression showing that individual trajectories can be predicted using fMRI characteristics such as neural responses to emotional faces (see Chapter 6 for findings concerning suicidal behavior) with a promising accuracy of 73% (Schmaal et al., 2015). Computational neuroimaging strategies, whether or not combined with machine learning, have great potential for outcome prediction in individual patients (Stephan et al., 2017). Given the huge unmet needs, such approaches are urgently needed to increase our abilities to accurately predict suicidal behavior at the individual level.

It goes without saying that machine learning has its limitations as well: Data commonly are collected for other reasons and therefore may not include relevant characteristics such as, in the case of suicide prediction, relational and social characteristics. Nevertheless, this chapter makes clear that there is considerable room for (an urgently needed) improvement in the accuracy of suicide prediction. Artificial intelligence may thereby prove to be "smarter" than human practitioners (Chen & Asch, 2017). However, no machine will ever be capable of preventing suicide. It is what makes us human that will help us to prevent people from taking their lives.

Chapter 9 Summary

- The prediction of suicidal behavior is a crucial component of suicide prediction but one of the most difficult tasks for health care staff.
- Even with the use of specifically developed scales and tools, prediction may be only slightly better than chance.
- Biomarkers show great promise as predictors of suicidal behavior, as they may detect underlying vulnerability.
- As a cognitive biomarker, implicit association tests show good predictive accuracy in longitudinal studies.
- A few single genetic biomarkers show promise in suicide prediction, particularly involving the SAT1 and SKA2 genes.
- Combinations of biomarkers and clinical characteristics substantially increase the accuracy of predicting suicidal behavior.
- The future of suicide prediction has already begun, with the use of big data and machine learning using multiple sources of information showing excellent accuracy.

Review Questions

1. Give three reasons why the prediction of suicidal behavior is so difficult.
2. Explain why the accuracy of suicide risk assessment increases with the number of used sources of information.
3. Explain what a cognitive biomarker is, and give an example of a cognitive biomarker of suicide risk.
4. What is a risk calculator, and what kind of research data are needed to develop such a tool for the prediction of suicide risk at the individual level?
5. What are the possibilities and limitations in using machine learning for suicide prediction?

Further Reading

Bolton, J. M., Gunnell, D. & Turecki, G. (2016). Suicide risk assessment and intervention in people with mental illness. *British Medical Journal*, *351*, h4978.

Chen, J. H. & Asch, S. M. (2017). Machine learning and prediction in medicine – beyond the peak of inflated expectations. *New England Journal of Medicine*, *376*, 2507–9.

Mann, J. J., Currier, D., Stanley, B., Oquendo, M. A., Amsel, L. V. & Ellis, S. P. (2006). Can biological tests assist prediction of suicide in mood disorders? *International Journal of Neuropsychopharmacology*, *9*, 465–74.

Niculescu A. B., Levey, D., Le-Niculescu, H., Niculescu, E., Kurian, S.M. & Salomon, D. (2015). Psychiatric blood biomarkers: Avoiding jumping to premature negative or positive conclusions. *Molecular Psychiatry*, *20*, 286–8.

CHAPTER TEN

The Treatment of Suicide Risk

Neuroscience Aspects

Learning Objectives

- Understand the benefits and dangers of antidepressants concerning suicide risk.
- What makes lithium a strong anti-suicidal drug?
- Why may ketamine be important for suicide prevention?
- Describe neurostimulation techniques and their role in suicide prevention.
- What is the neuroscientific basis of the effects of psychotherapy?
- Why is a distinction between biological and psychological treatment approaches obsolete?

Introduction

There are no medications that will keep all suicidal individuals from taking their own lives. On the contrary, drugs may increase the risk of suicide, and people may use prescribed medications as a means of suicide via an overdose. Similarly, there are no words or psychotherapeutic interventions that prevent self-destructive behaviors. Like medication, psychotherapy may even lead to an increased suicide risk. Due to interventions such as the nonsuicide contract, health care professionals may feel safe, but this will not stop individuals from taking their own lives when overwhelmed with suicidal feelings. This chapter will review the problems, possibilities, and opportunities in the treatment of suicide risk from a neuroscientific point of view. The focus will be on neurobiological treatments, highlighting intriguing innovations such as neurostimulation. In addition, it will be made clear that the distinction between biological and psychological treatment approaches is obsolete: Learning and top-down processes such as the updating of beliefs and goals (see Chapter 8) are crucial to the success of psychotherapy, while they are the primary drivers of neural functioning and synaptic plasticity in the brain.

10.1 Medication

The National Confidential Inquiry into Suicide and Homicide by People with Mental Illness (2014) in the United Kingdom found that almost half of a large group of suicides had been prescribed psychotropic medication in the 12 months prior to their suicide. Antidepressants were most commonly prescribed (selective serotonin antidepressants 25%, tricyclic antidepressants 12%, other antidepressants 12%). Benzodiazepines (19%) and other hypnotics and anxiolytics (14%) were also common. Antidepressant drugs are involved in 20% of self-poisoning suicides in the United Kingdom. The relationship between medication and suicide prevention thus is not straightforward.

10.1.1 Antidepressants

We have seen in Chapter 1 that at least 50% of suicides occur in the context of a depressive episode, and one therefore would expect that the adequate treatment of the depression automatically leads to a decrease in suicide risk. This is not always the case, however, and the effects of antidepressant drugs on suicidal behavior have been a matter of debate for decades. Many epidemiological and clinical studies of these effects have been published, reporting often contradictory findings. Such studies includeepidemiological and clinical studies, and randomized controlled trials (RCTs) (for detailed overviews of these epidemiological and clinical studies, see Brent, 2016, and Tondo & Baldessarini, 2016).

Epidemiologic studies find relationships between a greater number of sales or prescriptions of antidepressants and lower suicide rates in the United States and European countries but not in all other studied countries and regions. There is an inverse relationship between sales of selective serotonin-reuptake inhibitors (SSRIs), such as fluoxetine (Prozac) and escitalopram (Lexapro), and suicide, with the strongest findings among youth younger than 25 (Ludwig & Marcotte, 2005). There is also an inverse relationship between number of prescriptions of SSRIs and number of suicides in a county-by-county analysis in the United States (Gibbons et al., 2005). This relationship is found only for prescriptions of SSRIs; the higher the proportion of prescriptions of the older and less selective tricyclic antidepressants among the total antidepressants prescribed, the higher the suicide rate. In the period from 1990 to 2000, there was a drop in the suicide rate of 0.23 per 100,000 for every 1% increase in antidepressant prescriptions (Olfson et al., 2003). Studies of large cohorts of depressed patients and case-control comparisons yield inconsistent and inconclusive findings. A nonsystematic review of a series of clinical cohort studies shows risk reductions of between 40% and 81% in nonfatal and fatal suicidal behavior among depressed patients taking antidepressant drugs (Rihmer & Gonda, 2013). An observational study from Finland shows that current use of antidepressants is associated with a 39% increased risk of suicide attempts but a 32% reduced rate of suicide compared with periods without antidepressant use (Tiihonen et al., 2006). The risk of attempted suicide apparently is 2.5 times higher in the month before starting an antidepressant compared with the period of antidepressant use (Simon, 2006).

Discrepancies in epidemiological studies can be explained, at least in part, by an effect of age. A propensity-matching study (meaning that all characteristics that predict receiving the treatment are taken into account) in nearly 25,000 depressed adolescents finds no increased risk of a suicide attempt in those who start taking an antidepressant, and shows that longer duration of treatment (>180 days) is protective against suicide attempts relative to shorter treatment (<55 days) (Valuck et al., 2004). A prospective follow-up of a Finnish cohort of more than 15,000 hospitalized suicide attempters indicates that SSRI use is associated with a higher rate of suicide attempts but a lower rate of suicide in both adolescents and adults (Tiihonen et al., 2006).

Suicidal thinking or behavior usually is recorded as an incidental event or adverse secondary effect in observational studies, which thus should tell us something about the effect of antidepressants on suicidal thinking and behavior. However, the interpretation of such findings is difficult: Without randomized controls, it could well be that antidepressants are more likely to be prescribed to more severely ill subjects also at presumably greater suicidal risk. Randomized controlled trials should provide the best information on effects of antidepressant treatment on suicidal risks, but individual trials are limited in number and exposure times, whereas outcome events are relatively rare. Moreover, the identification of such risks has been based on incidental and passively acquired, non-explicit assessments of suicidal outcomes and typically after having made efforts to exclude potentially suicidal subjects (Tondo & Baldessarini, 2016). A meta-analysis of randomized placebo controlled trials of antidepressants registered by the Food and Drug Administration (FDA) finds an increased risk of suicidal thoughts and nonfatal suicidal behavior in participants younger than 25 years, but a protective effect on suicide in older individuals in association with the use of antidepressants (Stone et al., 2009). A meta-analysis of 27 youth antidepressant RCTs shows an increased rate of suicidal events with a risk difference of 0.7% (meaning

WARNING: SUICIDALITY AND ANTIDEPRESSANT DRUGS

Antidepressants increased the risk compared to placebo of suicidal thinking and behavior (suicidality) in children, adolescents, and young adults in short-term studies of Major Depressive Disorder (MDD) and other psychiatric disorders. Anyone considering the use of [Insert established name] or any other antidepressant in a child, adolescent, or young adult must balance this risk with clinical need. Short-term studies did not show an increase in the risk of suicidality with antidepressants compared to placebo in adults beyond age 24; there was a reduction in risk with antidepressants compared to placebo in adults aged 65 and older. Depression and certain other psychiatric disorders are themselves associated with increases in the risk of suicide. Patients of all ages who are started on antidepressant therapy should be monitored appropriately and observed closely for clinical worsening, suicidality, or unusual changes in behavior. Families and caregivers should be advised of the need for close observation and communication with the prescriber.

Figure 10.1 Black-box warning.

the rate of suicidal events in the medication group is higher than the placebo group by 0.7%), thus with a 1.7-fold increase in suicidal events (Bridge et al., 2007). In addition, 11 times more depressed adolescents respond to an antidepressant in terms of a reduction in depressive symptoms than experience a suicidal event, with even higher benefit–risk ratios for those with obsessive compulsive or anxiety disorders. A Cochrane review of adolescent depression RCTs finds similarly increased risks for suicidal events with the prescription of newer generation antidepressants (odds ratio 1.58), with approximately 4.5 times as many youth attaining clinical remission as experiencing suicidal events (Hetrick et al., 2012).

Given the reports of increases in nonfatal suicidal behavior in antidepressant-treated adolescents, the FDA issued the so-called black-box warning affixed to all antidepressants about the risk of suicidal events associated with antidepressants in youth in 2004 (see Figure 10.1). Interestingly, the introduction of this warning can be regarded as a natural experiment (Brent, 2016). In comparing the period before and after the warning, the introduction is followed by drops in antidepressant prescriptions for youth in the United States, but also in the Netherlands, Canada, and the United Kingdom, accompanied by a decline in the rate of diagnosis of depressive disorders, number of visits for the treatment of depressive disorders, and increases in suicide in all the previously noted countries but the United Kingdom. (For an overview of studies, see Brent, 2016.) Epidemiological data also show, however, that rates of suicide among people 10–34 years of age increase gradually between 1999 and 2010, without any sudden changes around the time of the FDA warnings, suggesting little evidence that actual suicide rates have

Table 10.1 Possible mechanisms involved in an increased risk of suicidal behavior with antidepressant treatment

- uneven resolution of symptoms (energizing behavior with persistent depressed mood)
- unrecognized mixed episode in context of bipolar disorder
- jitteriness and akathisia
- paradoxical worsening of depression
- insomnia due to stimulating antidepressants
- SSRI induced left-right asymmetry of combined EEG theta and alpha power
- comorbid borderline personality disorder with impulsiveness
- acute reduction of BDNF/dysfunction of the TrkB pathway (see Chapter 4)
- genetic factors, e.g., 5-HT transporter gene polymorphism
- long half-life of antidepressant.

changed in the wake of the advisory (MMWR, 2013). Nevertheless, the FDA was obviously mindful of the need to balance the small risk associated with antidepressant treatment against its proven benefits. An expanded black-box warning issued in 2007 states that depression itself is associated with an increased risk of suicide. Has this well-intended warning accomplished its task – to educate clinicians about risk without discouraging appropriate treatment of depression (Friedman, 2014)? The overall data indicate that the risk posed by untreated depression, in terms of morbidity and mortality, is far greater than the small risk associated with antidepressant treatment. Ten years after the expanded black box warning, there appear to be sufficient arguments to suggest removing the warning completely.

How antidepressants might increase the risk of (nonfatal) suicidal behavior is not definitely known. Progression of underlying depression reflecting ineffective drug treatment could be an initial consideration. However, in clinical trials demonstrating their efficacy, antidepressants are associated with increased rates of (nonfatal) suicidal behavior. Thus, drug ineffectiveness is insufficient to explain an association of anti-depressants with risk of suicidality compared with placebo, and several other mechanisms have been proposed (see Table 10.1; Reeves & Ladner, 2010).

One additional contributing mechanism can be suggested based on the predictive coding model described in the previous chapter. Patients' predictions or expectancies can substantially affect the results of clinical

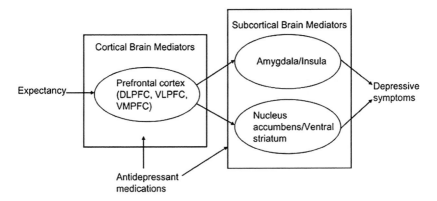

Figure 10.2 Antidepressants and expectancies: Brain mediators (Rutherford et al., 2010. Reprinted with permission for Bentham Science Publishers).

trials, and managing them is an important part of clinical care. Expectancies are a class of psychological and neurobiological processes that may be responsible for part of the improvement observed with (psychiatric) treatments (Rutherford et al., 2010; Figure 10.2).

Figure 10.2 shows a model of expectancy effects in the treatment of depression (Rutherford et al., 2010). Pathological decreases in prefrontal cortex (PFC) function, increases in limbic activity, and disordered connectivity between these regions all have been observed in depression. Available evidence suggests that antidepressant medications may function by normalizing these pathological changes and increasing functional connectivity between PFC and subcortical regions. For example, decreased amygdala activation is observed with effective antidepressant treatment and predicts the extent of attenuation of negative affect following reappraisal. The model predicts that higher expectancy will be associated with greater therapeutic improvements in these brain areas, leading to improvement in depressive symptoms by reversing depressed patients' excessive sensitivity to negative environmental cues and reduced responsivity to positive cues (Rutherford et al., 2010).

Meta-analyses of antidepressant trials show that placebo response rates are high (typically ~30%) and often larger than the difference in response rates between drug and placebo (typically ~10%). Antidepressant effects of the same drug are more marked if the drug is provided in an open design (with people knowing that they receive the drug) than if the drug or a placebo is received in a randomized controlled design (with a 50% chance of receiving the active drug) (Rutherford et al., 2017). Much of the improvement on placebo treatment appears to be due to active neurobiological processes related to expectancy, and higher expectation of therapeutic improvement leads to greater improvement in psychiatric symptoms, particularly in depression. Some depressed patients appear more prone to the effects of expectancy than others – for example, placebo responses decrease with increasing severity of baseline depression scores. Depressed patients who experience substantial early improvement (presumably due to positive expectancies instilled by knowing effective treatment has begun) are likely to experience a substantial worsening when their expectancies are diminished.

It can be hypothesized that suicidal and nonsuicidal depressed individuals differ regarding expectancy effects. Expectancies are beliefs about the future, and expectancy-based placebo effects are dependent on intact cognition to generate placebo response (Rutherford et al., 2014). In Chapter 8, we noted that suicidal individuals commonly are impervious to positive information, and it was hypothesized that suicide is related to an inability to change beliefs about the self, the world, and the future using positive information. Hopelessness, the clinical manifestation of this inability, is an expectancy, and increased levels of hopelessness are considered the most robust clinical predictor of suicide in depressed individuals. On the contrary, hope is central to the placebo effect and reflects positive expectancies. It could thus well be that suicidal depressed individuals are less prone to the effects of positive expectancies. Optimizing expectancy should thus be explored as a useful therapeutic technique in the clinical treatment of depressed and suicidal patients (Rutherford et al., 2014).

Comparative studies looking at differences between antidepressants in terms of negative and positive effects have yielded some interesting findings. A large observational study using a general practitioner database of antidepressant prescriptions in more than 200,000 patients (aged 20–64) shows that rates of suicide and attempted suicide or self-harm are similar during periods of treatment with SSRIs and tricyclic and related antidepressants, but worse with mirtazapine, trazodone, and venlafaxine (Coupland et al., 2014). It should be noted that there is always the potential for a selection bias and/or reversed causality in observational studies. One randomized clinical trial of suicidal patients shows that a selective serotonin-reuptake inhibitor has a better antidepressant effect and leads to greater reduction in suicidal ideation than a noradrenergic-dopaminergic drug, and that this therapeutic advantage is greatest in patients with the most severe suicidal ideation (Grunebaum et al., 2012).

10.1.2 Mood Stabilizers

In their update of systematic reviews and meta-analyses, Cipriani and colleagues (2013) show that lithium is an effective treatment reducing the risk of suicide in people with unipolar and bipolar mood disorders. It may exert its antisuicidal effect by reducing relapse of mood disorder, but additional mechanisms are considered. Neurobiological research has focused on lithium's influence on neurotransmitters such as serotonin, noradrenalin, GABA, and dopamine, on the cortisol stress hormone system, second messenger systems such as the inositol metabolism, glycogen synthase kinase 3, and more. The most common hypothesis is that lithium leads to a decrease in impulsivity and aggression via several influences within the nerve cell. It could be that lithium, through its serotonin agonistic properties, counteracts serotonin deficiency at the neurotransmitter level (Lewitzka et al., 2015). More recent studies point at an antiapoptotic effect of lithium, thereby stimulating neurogenesis. Its use in long-term treatment is indeed associated with increased gray matter volume in brain areas that show reduced volumes in association with suicidal behavior, effects that might decrease suicide risk (Benedetti et al., 2011).

Despite the large number of studies showing evidence of lithium's antisuicidal effects, there are some limitations of these studies that are worth noting. Several studies investigated a selective group of patients, as good adherence is a prerequisite of lithium treatment. These selective patients may possess protective factors such as better coping with long-term treatment or treatment in specialized settings, while other patients (with worse adherence) may not. However, there are observational studies showing that discontinuation of lithium medication increases the risk of suicide considerably, even after long episodes of treatment. It is unlikely that this phenomenon is a withdrawal effect (Lewitzka et al., 2015).

The well-documented antisuicidal effect of lithium is supported by the finding of an inverse correlation between lithium levels in drinking water and suicide rates in many regions of the world, as described in Chapter 1. The mean lithium concentration in drinking water reported in the studies reviewed is in the range of 0.01 mg/l; this would require thousands of liters to match the amount of lithium present, for instance, in a single 300-mg tablet of lithium carbonate. Explanations of the findings that even very low levels of lithium provided in drinking water may reduce the risk of suicide are, at present, only speculative. Even very low but long-lasting lithium exposure may enhance neurotrophic mechanisms, neuroprotective factors, and/or neurogenesis, which may account eventually for a reduced risk of suicide (Vita et al., 2015). It will be interesting to study brain correlates of lithium levels in drinking water in the general population and in diathetic individuals.

The effect of other mood stabilizers such as anticonvulsants on the occurrence of suicidal behavior is less clear. In 2008, the FDA issued a controversial warning and alerted health care providers to an increased risk of suicidal thoughts and behaviors in patients taking antiepileptic drugs (AEDs). The FDA's safety alert was based on an analysis of suicidality data from 199 randomized, placebo-controlled trials of 11 AEDs. Subsequently, major methodological problems with the analysis were identified. For example, the analysis was a retrospective analysis of spontaneous reports of suicidal thoughts and behaviors, rather than being based on systematically collected data. Only a minority of included patients suffered from epilepsy, and the drugs were commonly prescribed for other conditions such as pain, migraine, and depression with an increased risk of suicidal behavior. Adverse effects of AEDs on the risk of suicide may thus have been overestimated (van Heeringen & Mann, 2014).

10.1.3 Hypnotic and Anxiolytic Medications

Retrospective and prospective epidemiological studies suggest that hypnotics (including benzodiazepines and the so-called Z-drugs such as zolpidem) are associated with an increased risk of suicide. However, none of these studies adequately controls for depression or other psychiatric disorders that may be linked with insomnia. A recent review of epidemiological and toxicological studies indicates that hypnotic medications are associated with suicidal ideation (McCall et al., 2017). Another review of studies (including controlled trials and naturalistic observational studies) shows that benzodiazepines are associated with increased risk of fatal and nonfatal suicidal behavior (Dodds, 2017). As described in Chapter 5, cognitive impairment, and more specifically problems with decision making and executive function, is common in suicidal individuals. Such cognitive impairment may be increased due to hypnotic drug effects, so that the intake of these drugs may increase the risk of suicidal behavior. The risk appears to be higher if the drug is consumed with alcohol, if it is taken at a dosage higher than recommended, or if the patient does not go to bed or fall asleep soon after ingestion or awakens a few hours after ingestion. The possibility remains open that judicious prescription of hypnotics, when taken appropriately, might reduce (not increase) the risk of suicide (McCall et al., 2017). The same line of reasoning appears to be applicable to anxiolytic drugs. Alprazolam is approved as a benzodiazepine anxiolytic, and a meta-analysis of alprazolam clinical trials shows that alprazolam is no more likely than placebo to be associated with the emergence of worsening of suicidal ideation. Moreover, alprazolam is more likely than placebo to be associated with an improvement in preexisting suicidal ideation (Jonas et al., 1996).

10.1.4 Antipsychotic Drugs

In 2003, the antipsychotic clozapine was the first psychiatric drug to be approved by the FDA in the United States for the reduction of suicidal behavior in psychosis. The regulatory approval was largely based on the International Suicide Prevention Trial (InterSePT), a randomized trial showing that suicidal behavior (measured by suicide attempts, hospitalizations, and rescue interventions) was significantly decreased in patients treated with clozapine (Meltzer et al., 2003). More recent observational studies (such as Tiihonen et al., 2011) in large samples of schizophrenia patients confirm this finding and show that maximum antisuicide benefit is seen with higher antipsychotic doses, suggesting a causal beneficial effect of the drug. As stated earlier, in observational studies there is always the potential for a selection bias and/or reversed causality. For example, it is possible that patients who become suicidal – for whatever reason – stop taking their antipsychotic medications, rather than becoming suicidal because they stopped the medications. Moreover, the singularities of clozapine, such as the safety restrictions and intensive follow-up associated with its use, may have influenced the outcome. A recent thorough review of the antisuicidal effects of antipsychotic drugs concludes (1) that except for clozapine, no antipsychotic treatment has been established to be useful in reducing suicide risk, but also (2) that recent data suggest that this antisuicidal effect could be extended to other second-generation antipsychotic drugs (Iglesias et al., 2016).

10.1.5 Pain Killers

Given the important role of mental or emotional pain in the development of suicide risk (see Chapter 2), and given the indications that the brain does not differentiate between physical and emotional pain (Eisenberger, 2012), the impact of pain killers on suicide risk is worth investigating. Could mental pain be treated like physical pain, and would a reduction in mental pain lead to a decrease in suicidal thoughts?

Acetaminophen (or paracetamol) is a physical pain suppressant that acts through central (rather than peripheral) neural mechanisms, and its effects on behavioral and neural responses to social rejection have recently been studied. In two experiments, participants took acetaminophen or placebo daily for 3 weeks. Acetaminophen was found to reduce reports of social pain on a daily basis and also decreased neural responses to social rejection in brain regions previously associated with distress caused by social pain and the affective component of physical pain (dorsal anterior cingulate cortex, anterior insula). Thus, acetaminophen reduces behavioral and neural responses associated with the pain of social rejection, demonstrating substantial overlap between social and physical pain (DeWall et al., 2010). A recent placebo-controlled trial in severely depressed and suicidal individuals (of whom nearly two-thirds had made at least one suicide attempt) addresses the intriguing possibility that physical pain suppressants may reduce suicide risk. Individuals who receive an ultra-low dose of the opioid buprenorphine show a greater reduction in suicidal ideation than those who receive placebo, after 2 and 4 weeks. Reduction of mental pain as measured with a simple mental pain assessment is similarly significantly different between study groups. It should be noted that the larger reduction in suicidal ideation is already apparent during the first week of treatment but reaches levels of significance at the end of week 2. Of note, the magnitude of reduction in depressive symptoms is smaller than that of the reduction in suicidal ideation. Proportions of individuals taking antidepressant or antipsychotic medication or suffering from borderline personality disorder (with outspoken sensitivity to social rejection) were similar in both study groups. No withdrawal symptoms are reported after treatment discontinuation at the end of the trial (Yovell et al., 2016). Thus, the pharmacological findings of this study support the view that suicidal ideation and depression may be distinct, although related, phenomena, as was already suggested in Chapter 2.

10.1.6 Ketamine

There is increasing support for ketamine as a treatment for depressive symptoms, and particularly suicidal ideation. Ketamine is a drug used illicitly as a party drug and clinically as an anesthetic since the 1970s. Add-on open-label (which means that ketamine is given in addition to antidepressants in noncontrolled conditions) studies suggest that intravenous ketamine is associated with rapid reductions in suicidal thoughts, even in cases in which antidepressive effects are limited, and thus may act as an antisuicidal agent. While early studies focused on immediate effects, showing reductions in suicidal ideation within 24 hours, subsequent studies show that repeated administration may lead to sustained antisuicidal effects during months of follow-up (Ionescu et al., 2016).

The benefits of ketamine for suicidal ideation may outweigh associated risks. But while there are indeed reasons for optimism, there is also a need for great caution. Unfortunately, the scientific evidence supporting the clinical use of ketamine for suicidal ideation is still to be regarded as preliminary: The interpretation of studies, in general, is hampered by methodological issues such as small sample sizes and biased inclusion. Regarding study sample sizes, it is interesting to look at meta-analyses of ketamine effects on suicidal ideation. Several such meta-analyses of clinical trials have been performed and in general support the findings from individual studies. For example, a meta-analysis of five studies including 99 subjects shows a large and consistent decrease of suicidal ideation, confirming the efficacy across different time points. However, the conclusion remains that the level of relevant, emerging evidence should be considered as "very low" so far (Bartoli et al., 2017). Randomized, controlled, and adequately powered trials are clearly needed.

Acknowledging that ketamine might be beneficial to some individuals suffering from mood disorders, limitations of the available data and the potential risk associated with the drug have led the American Psychiatric Association to publish a consensus statement to facilitate clinical decision making and use of the drug (Sanacora et al., 2017).

Ketamine reduces neuronal excitation by blocking NMDA receptors, resulting in increased AMPA-mediated glutamatergic signaling, which in turn triggers activation of intracellular synaptogenic pathways. In addition to NMDA antagonism, ketamine affects many of the molecular correlates of suicidal behavior that are described in detail in Chapter 4. (For an overview, see Li & Vlisides, 2016.) These include the inhibition of calcium channels and serotonin reuptake; an increase of (hippocampal) BDNF, perhaps via epigenetic mechanisms; an increase in prefrontal acetylcholine; and stimulation of noradrenergic neurons in the medial prefrontal cortex. Ketamine's potential antisuicidal effect mechanisms are linked to interruption of the kynurenine pathway and modulating proinflammatory cytokine exacerbation.

From a systems point of view (see Chapter 6), and more particularly with the predictive coding model in mind (see Chapter 8), it is important to note that ketamine modulates corticocortical and thalamocortical connectivity. Ketamine administration leads to inhibited corticocortical information transfer, but also to increased thalamocortical connectivity (Höflich et al., 2015). Disruption of a frontoparietal network and a decrease in gain of parietal pyramidal with subanesthetic doses of ketamine is correlated with self-reports of a blissful state. The effects of ketamine may thus depend on its ability to change the balance of frontoparietal connectivity patterns (Muthukumaraswamy et al., 2015).

From a cognitive point of view, ketamine appears to play an active role in strategic attention shifts away from a peripheral stimulus (Fuchs et al., 2015). A randomized controlled study of ketamine and the anesthetic control midazolam shows that explicit suicidal cognitions and implicit associations, as assessed with the Implicit Association Test (see Chapters 5 and 9), are reduced with ketamine but not midazolam (Price et al., 2014). Single subanesthetic administration of ketamine in healthy individuals leads to increased glutamate activity in the anterior cingulate cortex paralleled by a marginally poorer performance on the Stroop task (see Chapter 5 for Stroop performance and suicidal behavior) (Rowland et al., 2005).

Although ketamine thus appears to be a promising therapeutic option in a context of great unmet needs for patients at imminent risk of suicide, it goes without saying that additional randomized trials are needed to substantiate the pattern of positive findings, particularly among people selected for high suicide risk such as those with personal or familial histories of suicidal behaviors. Additional future directions for the field to substantiate the scientific basis for the use of ketamine for acutely suicidal individuals include potential mechanisms or biomarkers of response, clinical correlates, and the relationship of ketamine to suicidal behaviors such as suicide attempts and death by suicide. Other drugs acting on the NMDA receptor, such as D-cycloserine, may well have an antisuicidal effect. D-cycloserine may also enhance beneficial effects of psychotherapy (see later discussion).

10.1.7 Other Pharmacological Agents

Effects of medications on suicide risk are not limited to the described psychotropic and analgesic drugs. The FDA has issued warnings for increased suicide risk with varenicline, a drug used to help individuals stop smoking. There have been postmarketing reports of serious mental health issues in patients who use the drug, including suicidal thoughts, suicide attempts, and suicide. Medication for the treatment of prostatic enlargement (5-alpha-reductase inhibitors) may increase the risk of self-harming behavior (Welk et al., 2017). Interferon therapy for, e.g., multiple sclerosis may be associated with an increased risk of suicidal behavior (Fragoso et al., 2010). Evidence in support of the initial worry about suicide-inducing effects of isotretinoine as a treatment for acne is not convincing.

The neuropeptide oxytocin has long been known as the hormone that promotes feelings of love, social bonding, and well-being, and thus may protect against suicidal behavior. Levels of oxytocin are indeed lower in the cerebrospinal fluid of suicide attempters and in women exposed to childhood abuse and in the plasma of individuals with an increased risk of suicidal behavior, namely those suffering from a borderline personality disorder (Heim et al., 2009; Lee et al., 2009; Bertsch et al., 2013). A large body of evidence has implicated oxytocin in the modulation of human neural activity underlying social cognition, including the negative emotion processing that was discussed in Chapters 2, 5, and 8 as a crucial component of the diathesis of suicidal behavior. A placebo-controlled study shows that, under placebo, a preferential response to negative social feedback compared with positive social feedback is evoked in brain regions putatively involved in pain processing and the identification of emotionally important visual cues in social perception, which weakens with oxytocin administration (Gozzi et al., 2017). Oxytocin thus appears to reduce neural responses to receiving negative social feedback so that they are not significantly greater than those to positive social feedback. There is a clear need for studies of the effect of oxytocin on suicide risk.

10.2 Neurostimulation

10.2.1 Electroconvulsive Therapy

Since the 1940s, electroconvulsive therapy (ECT) has been considered the most effective intervention for severe mood disorders, and several long-term follow-up studies have suggested that patients who receive ECT have reduced mortality of all causes when compared with non-ECT control patients (Sackeim, 2017). In contrast with more recent neurostimulation techniques (see later discussion), no sham (inactive condition)-controlled studies have been performed, but open-label studies indicate rapid resolution of suicide risk. (For an overview of studies, see Fink et al., 2014.) The use of ECT, however, is inhibited by fear of electricity, unreasoned prejudice, legislative restrictions, and the limited availability of trained professionals and adequate facilities. Fears of memory loss also play a role, as the most severe and persistent adverse cognitive effect of ECT pertains to memory for past events (retrograde amnesia). With the advances in ECT technique that reduce recovery time, there is a parallel decrease in the severity of long-term retrograde amnesia. Recent work fails to detect any adverse effect of high-dose, ultrabrief pulse right unilateral ECT on memory or other cognitive assessments conducted within days of ECT course termination. A large multisite study in geriatric depression shows that this form of ECT nevertheless results in a 62% remission rate. (For an overview of studies, see Sackheim, 2017.) The present practice of recommending ECT as a last resort in expert treatment algorithms thus appears to unnecessarily put depressed suicidal individuals at substantial risk. Similar to pharmacotherapy, the neurobiological mechanisms underlying symptom improvement remain unclear. Molecular studies point at increased BDNF, increased monoamine turnover, and normalization of the HPA axis. From a systems point of view, a controlled neuroimaging study shows that ECT leads to widespread neuroplasticity in neocortical, limbic, and paralimbic regions and that changes relate to the extent of antidepressant response. Variations in thickness of the anterior cingulate cortex, which discriminate treatment responders and predict response early in the course of ECT, may represent a biomarker of overall clinical outcome. ECT-related increases in thickness may be attributable to neuroplastic processes affecting the size and/or density of neurons and glia and their connections (Pirnia et al., 2016). Magnetic resonance spectroscopy (see Chapter 3 for technical details) suggests a role of normalization of glutamate/glutamine levels in the anterior cingulate cortex in clinical improvement (Njau et al., 2017).

Given the apparently beneficial effects of a single infusion of ketamine on suicide risk, the use of ketamine as an anesthetic drug for ECT seems a logical next step in the treatment of acutely suicidal individuals. Preliminary evidence suggesting an accelerated improvement and an alleviation of cognitive adverse effects of the ECT–ketamine combination is not confirmed in a large randomized controlled trial, which unfortunately does not include suicide risk as an outcome measure (Anderson et al., 2017).

10.2.2 Transcranial Magnetic Stimulation

Repetitive transcranial magnetic stimulation (rTMS) has well-documented positive effects on depression without major side effects.

A review of the literature indicates that rTMS improves cognitive functions associated with suicide risk, including memory, attention, executive functioning, and choice behavior such as choosing immediate reward over larger, delayed rewards. Moreover, rTMS is thought to have molecular effects similar to those seen with ECT (see earlier discussion). It is therefore not surprising that preliminary noncontrolled studies suggest a rapid beneficial effect of rTMS on suicidal thoughts. (For more details, see Desmyter et al., 2016.) A first rTMS study that used a sham control found a significant decrease in suicide risk but no significant difference between the TMS and the sham group (George et al., 2014). Intermittent theta burst stimulation (iTBS; a variant of rTMS) uses bursts of high-frequency stimulation at repeated intervals and is thought to affect brain function more thoroughly when compared with classic rTMS. A sham-controlled study of iTBS applied to the left dorsolateral prefrontal cortex shows a decrease of suicide risk following accelerated iTBS in treatment-resistant unipolar depressed patients, however, without statistically significant difference between the effect of active and the sham treatment. The antisuicidal effect lasts up to 1 month after baseline and appears to be independent of the antidepressant effect (Desmyter et al., 2016). The beneficial effect of sham treatment on suicidal ideation is remarkable, as it suggests that hopeless suicidal individuals can have positive expectancies regarding treatment. Interestingly, resting-state functional neuroimaging indicates that response to iTBS in depressed individuals is associated with increased functional connectivity between the left medial orbitofrontal cortex and the anterior cingulate cortex. Increased functional connectivity is associated with a decrease in feelings of hopelessness (Baeken et al., 2017). This important observation fits nicely in the predictive coding model of suicidal behavior that was developed in Chapter 8: Stronger connectivity of the left inferior frontal gyrus with left regions involved in emotion regulation is associated with greater change in belief for favorable information but with reduced change in beliefs for unfavorable information in healthy individuals. Chapter 8 clearly describes how improved incorporation of positive information in beliefs can be expected to prevent suicidal behavior.

10.2.3 Magnetic Seizure Therapy

As a potential alternative to ECT, magnetic seizure therapy (MST) demonstrates clinical efficacy in patients with treatment-resistant depression and has a more benign cognitive adverse effect profile. With MST, electrical current is induced directly in brain tissue through fluctuating magnetic fields that, unlike the electric currents of ECT, are not shunted by the skull. Thus, compared with ECT, MST stimulates a much smaller region of the cortex and elicits seizures with a weaker induced electric field, which may explain why MST produces fewer cognitive adverse effects. An open-label study shows a significant decrease in suicidal thoughts after MST in treatment-resistant depressed individuals. Cortical inhibition measures were thereby assessed by combined TMS and electroencephalography (TMS-EEG) in the left DLPFC (N100 and LICI). These measures have been shown to be reliable indices of GABAergic interneuron function, and they predict remission of suicidal thoughts as a response to MST with an AUC of 0.90, reflecting excellent accuracy. (See Chapter 9 for a discussion of AUC.) Cortical inhibition may thus be used to identify patients with treatment-resistant depression, who are most likely to experience remission of suicidal ideation following a course of MST. Stronger inhibitory neurotransmission at baseline may reflect the integrity of transsynaptic networks that are targeted by MST for optimal therapeutic response (Sun et al., 2016).

10.2.4 Other Neurostimulation Techniques

Given the changes in gray and white matter brain areas related to suicidal behavior, which are described extensively in Chapter 6, neurostimulation of these areas might theoretically contribute to the prevention of such behavior. Encouraging antidepressant results have been found in depressed individuals using deep brain stimulation (DBS) of the subcallosal cingulate gyrus, the anterior limb of the internal capsule (ALIC; see Chapter 6), and the reward system (the nucleus accumbens and the medial forebrain bundle). Beneficial effects on suicide risk remain unclear, but suicide and suicide attempts are reported as side effects. DBS in these areas therefore does not appear to be the way forward in suicide prevention, even in treatment-resistant depressed individuals.

Transcranial direct current stimulation (tDCS) is a noninvasive neurostimulation technique that affects neuronal firing and synaptic efficacy. It is used to enhance cognitive performance in demanding situations by the army and athletes. Conventional tDCS montages produce diffuse current through the brain, making it difficult to establish causality between stimulation of any one given brain region and resulting behavioral changes. Recently, high-definition tDCS (HD-tDCS) methods have been developed to target brain regions with increased focality relative to conventional tDCS. The study of the effects of tDCS on depression is

---

Textbox 10.1 Quote from the Internet

I don't have much to say, except that a few hours ago I was suicidal, and now that I have plugged in, I am feeling better.

I was so depressed that I couldn't leave my bed, I didn't even have the motivation to use this device. I asked my mum to make me a cup of coffee, that gave me a bit of kick, I immediately used it to put on tDCS, and now I can make a post on it.

I just hope that people are actively doing research on it and other devices that could make my life better, because meds don't really help me.

---

still in its infancy (Szymkowicz et al., 2016), but beneficial effects on related cognitive characteristics including response inhibition and valence-based choice behavior (see Chapter 5 for more details) are increasingly reported. Available small open-label studies and individual patient reports (see, e.g., Textbox 10.1) suggest promising effects on depressive symptoms including suicidal thoughts.

Transcranial alternating current stimulation (tACS) is similar to tDCS, but instead of applying a direct electrical current, tACS oscillates a sinusoidal current at a chosen frequency to interact with the brain's natural cortical oscillations. The precision of beliefs and value-based choices plays an important role in the computational model of suicidal behavior that is developed in Chapter 8. The precision of value-based choices thereby appears to depend on the synchronous communication between the frontopolar and parietal cortexes. Oscillatory desynchronization using tACS specifically affects the precision of value-based choices (Beharelle et al., 2015). The effects of such localized neurostimulation interventions on precision estimation and choice behavior in suicidal individuals clearly need to be studied. Such investigations could thereby target oscillatory synchrony as a mechanism of attentional control in the identified thalamocortical network, and its deficiencies such as thalamo-cortical dysrhythmia, involved in depression and pain.

10.3 Psychotherapy: Neuroscientific Aspects

As with medication and neurostimulation, psychotherapy may contribute to suicide prevention, but caution is needed. The point of view that, unlike antidepressants and neurostimulation, psychotherapy is free of adverse effects is not correct and highly misleading. Suicidal ideation and (even fatal) suicidal behavior are recognized adverse effects with psychotherapy (Bridge et al., 2005; Stone, 1971). A brief psychotherapeutic intervention with suicide attempters in the emergency department appears, in general, to have no effect on the repetition of suicidal behavior, but there is evidence of a harmful effect in those without a history of multiple episodes of self-harm (O'Connor et al., 2017). It appears that psychological interventions have the potential to increase rumination and negative affect, and potentially self-harm repetition, by serving as unhelpful reminders of negative experiences in the lead-up to the index self-harm event or during hospital treatment (Witt, 2017).

Nevertheless, there is increasing evidence of protective effects of psychotherapy on suicide risk, but apparently only if this therapy focuses on suicide-specific issues. This observation fits in the concept of "precision medicine," highlighting the vital importance of tailoring treatments to individual patients, which in this case means the presence of suicide risk. This approach is supported by findings from systematic reviews and a meta-analysis of studies on psychotherapy for depression showing that effects on suicidal ideation and suicide risk are small and not statistically significant. There is thus insufficient evidence for the assumption that suicide risk in depressed patients can be reduced with psychotherapy for depression (Cuijpers et al., 2013).

Tailored approaches in individuals at risk of suicidal behavior appear to be more effective. A meta-analysis shows that cognitive therapy significantly reduces subsequent fatal and nonfatal behavior among suicide attempters (Hawton et al., 2016). Unique Danish register-based data on more than 65,000 individuals show that deliberate self-harm patients (for a discussion of terminology, see Chapter 1) receiving psychosocial therapy (8–10 sessions of mainly client-centered psychotherapy) at specialized suicide prevention clinics have significantly lower odds of dying by suicide (and other diseases and medical conditions) than those receiving standard care (Birkbak et al., 2016).

An RCT comparing psychological pain theory–based cognitive therapy (PPTBCT) with usual psychological care in depressed individuals shows that measures of depression, suicidal ideation, psychological pain, and automatic thoughts decrease in both groups at the post-intervention and 4-week follow-up time points. Suicidal ideation, however, is significantly less severe at follow-up in the treatment group than in the usual psychological care group. PPTBCT may thus effectively reduce suicide risk in patients with major depressive disorder (Zou et al., 2017).

A neuroscience-based psychotherapeutic approach targets the neuro-cognitive biases that are associated with suicide risk (see Chapter 5). One form of cognitive bias modification tailored to reduce disorder-specific attentional bias is attention bias modification (ABM), which reduces engagement with negative stimuli among depressed individuals. It essentially interferes in the cycle of attending toward negative cues that may underlie the predictive coding deficiency, as described in the previous chapter. Positive effects of ABM on depression have been shown across distinct behavioral and neurobiological measures of attentional bias. While specific attentional biases have been identified using the suicide Stroop task (see Chapter 5; Cha et al., 2010), beneficial effects of ABM targeting suicide-specific attentional biases on suicide risk, however, have not yet been demonstrated. Experiments in community-based individuals with suicidal thoughts and in suicidal inpatients using a computerized ABM intervention find no effects on suicide-specific attentional biases or severity of suicidal thoughts, perhaps due to the (too) small number of sessions or applied methods of attention training (Cha et al., 2017).

Changes in psychological processes are paralleled by changes in the functions or structures of the brain. The neurobiological/psychosocial treatment distinction between pharmacotherapy and psychotherapy is incorrect and obsolete, because the target of both therapies is disturbed neural functioning. Their difference lies only in their method for delivering therapeutic neurobiological changes. On the one hand, pharmacotherapy uses a broad modulation of neurochemistry through a chemical agent that is designed to help facilitate the reorganization of the brain in a way that frees the patient from pathological neural processes. On the other hand, psychotherapy, particularly cognitive behavioral therapy (CBT), uses a tailored modulation of neurochemistry through a patient–therapist relationship that counteracts (e.g., learned emotional or behavioral responses), eliminates (e.g., ruminative thoughts), and/or restructures (e.g., depressogenic schemas) the forces that drive pathological neural processes. Evidence for the thesis that psychotherapy, in essence, is a neurobiological treatment comes from neuroimaging studies that suggest that, across major psychiatric disorders, psychotherapy normalizes and/or reorganizes neural functioning, and that these neural changes are associated with symptom improvement (Prosser et al., 2016). More than 20 studies document adaptive brain changes involving neural reorganization following (particularly cognitive) psychotherapy for depression and anxiety disorders.

Furthermore, psychotherapy and pharmacotherapy affect the brain in both similar and different manners, suggesting that their neural mechanisms of therapeutic action are not wholly overlapping, which may explain why combined therapy, in general, is superior to monotherapy. For example, an increase in prefrontal function, which is involved in cognitive control, and its connectivity with subcortical areas could well be the mechanism behind the effectiveness of cognitive therapy for depressed individuals, while antidepressant medications operate more directly on the amygdala, which is involved in the generation of negative emotion. At a molecular level, psychotherapy leads to changes in gene expression through learning, by altering the strength of synaptic connections between nerve cells and inducing morphological changes in neurons. Remarkably, (psychodynamic) psychotherapy, and not the SSRI antidepressant fluoxetine, increases $5\text{-}HT1_A$ receptor density (Karlsson et al., 2010). The important role of the $5\text{-}HT1_A$ receptor for suicidal behavior is highlighted in Chapters 4 and 8, but the implications for the treatment of suicide risk are not yet clear. Another example of the potential benefits of combined treatments is the addition of D-cycloserine to cognitive behavior therapy. D-cycloserine is a partial NMDA agonist and its addition to cognitive behavior therapy for anxiety disorder is associated with a small augmentation effect, which indicates a beneficial effect of this compound on learning (Mataix-Cols et al., 2017). It goes without saying that potential beneficial additive effects of psychotherapy and neurobiological treatments urgently need to be studied in the context of suicide prevention.

There are indications that individual characteristics that may predispose to suicidal behavior influence the effect of treatment. Childhood maltreatment is an important example, in the context of this book, because it unequivocally predicts poor treatment outcome. It appears that maltreated depressed patients may respond preferentially to cognitive psychotherapies that are less effective for their nonmaltreated depressed peers, while the latter may respond more favorably to antidepressant drugs (Teicher & Samson, 2013).

Neurobiological mechanisms may interfere with the success of psychological treatment. For example, stress disrupts the ability to benefit from prior knowledge during learning, and glucocorticoid activation is sufficient to produce this effect. In other words, the updating of beliefs, a core issue in suicide prevention, as described in Chapter 8, is hampered by activation of the glucocorticoid stress response system (Kluen et al., 2016). Increased methylation of the BDNF gene (see Chapter 4) due to early life adversities is associated with nonresponse to behavior therapy but decreases in responders, parallel with decreases in severity of depression and hopelessness (Perroud et al., 2013).

10.4 The Treatment of Suicide Risk: Treating the Untreatable?

Resistance to treatment is a popular and persistent myth about suicidal individuals, as was already noticed in Chapter 1 (see Textbox 1.1): Those who want to take their own lives will do so, whether or not they get treatment. This chapter describes many studies that show the opposite: Suicide can be prevented, and effective treatments do exist. Antidepressants, lithium, clozapine, and suicide-specific psychotherapy are examples of interventions that work. However, apart from the fact that caution is needed because of (initial) threshold-lowering effects of medication and psychotherapy on suicide risk, there are urgent needs in the treatment of suicide risk. Most drugs take (often too much) time before they may exert their positive effects. For example, antidepressants may take 3 or more weeks before any effect on suicide risk may be noticed. Neurostimulation by means of ECT may have beneficial effects within a couple of days, which can be life-saving. It is not correct and even dangerous to consider ECT a last resort treatment for depressed and suicidal individuals.

Results with more recent and refined neurostimulation approaches are promising, but placebo effects hamper the assessment of their specific effects on suicide risk. For example, the rapid decrease in suicide risk seen with rTMS is similar in actively treated and sham-treated individuals. The mere fact that suicidal individuals show placebo effects is surprising. Much of the improvement on placebo treatment appears to be due to active neurobiological processes related to positive expectancy. While such expectancies are an important ingredient of placebo effects, negative views of the future, which are impervious to positive information, are a major driver of suicidal thoughts and wishes. Brain mediators of expectancies are well defined, and it will be interesting and important for suicide prevention to study the effects of neurostimulation on these brain mediators. In this context, it is of interest to note that deep brain stimulation of the anterior limb of the internal capsule (the ALIC that is involved in the brain system changes associated with suicidal behavior; see Chapter 6) appears to show an antidepressant effect in treatment-resistant depressed individuals that is independent of a placebo-response (Bergfeld et al., 2016).

Will we ever live in a suicide-proof society? Nobody knows, but it is highly unlikely. Suicide is a very complex phenomenon, to which many very distinct factors contribute. These factors range from genes and epigenetic changes to societal taboo-related characteristics that lead to shame and that interfere with seeking help. Knowledge of the neuroscientific basis of suicidal behavior may thus be a necessary though insufficient condition for effective suicide prevention. However, translation of neuroscientific knowledge into effective treatments of suicide risk may contribute to eliminating one of the most persistent and dangerous myths concerning suicide, namely, that suicide risk cannot be treated and that suicide cannot be prevented. This book shows the opposite. Many effective treatments are available, and exciting new developments hold great promise for the future.

In any case, there should be no more stories like Valerie's in the Preface to this book. The lethal combination of a depression and a familial loading of suicide should alert general practitioners and specialists, but also school teachers, parents, and peers. Screening tools are now available, even for peers and parents. Everybody should now know that depression and suicide risk in adolescents exist, but can be treated effectively.

And, by the way, Valerie is fine now.

Chapter 10 Summary

- The effects of antidepressants on suicide have been a matter of debate for decades, but a protective effect has clearly been demonstrated, particularly among the elderly.
- Clozapine and lithium have strong antisuicidal properties.
- Psychotropic drugs that target NMDA receptors appear to have rapid antisuicidal effects.
- Electroconvulsive therapy has a strong and rapid protective effect on suicide risk, and its position as a last-resort treatment in guidelines is not correct.
- More refined neurostimulation treatment approaches are becoming available, but the assessment of their specific antisuicidal effects is hampered by substantial placebo effects.
- The occurrence of a placebo effect, reflecting positive expectancies, in suicidal individuals is surprising, as these individuals are characterized by marked negative views of the future.
- Caution is needed when treating suicidal individuals with medication, psychotherapy, or neurostimulation, because these treatments may (initially) lower the threshold for suicidal behavior.

- A basic contribution of neuroscience to suicide prevention lies in the elimination of the persistent and dangerous myth that suicide risk cannot be treated and that suicide cannot be prevented. This book shows the opposite by describing the interventions that work and the mechanisms by means of which neurobiological or psychological interventions that target the brain are effective in preventing people from taking their own lives.

Review Questions

1. What are popular myths about the possibility of treating suicide risk, and how can neuroscience contribute to their elimination?
2. Why may doctors show reluctance in prescribing antidepressant medications to depressed suicidal individuals?
3. What mechanisms are possibly involved in the antisuicidal effect of lithium?
4. Why is the distinction between psychological therapies and neurobiological treatments obsolete?
5. What are the opportunities and problems in the use of novel neurostimulation techniques when compared with ECT?
6. Will there ever be a society without suicide?

Glossary

Allele. One of the alternative forms of a gene that is located at a specific location on a specific chromosome.

Association study. Genetic association studies are used to find candidate genes or genome regions that contribute to suicidal behavior by testing for a correlation between such behavior and genetic variation.

Autism. A complex neurodevelopment disorder with a range of various cognitive and behavioral symptoms often referred to as a spectrum of disorders.

Autoimmune. Autoimmunity is the system of immune responses of an organism against its own healthy cells and tissues.

Base pairs. Building blocks formed by pairing adenine (A), guanine (G), cytosine (C), and thymine (T) that link the two strands of DNA like rungs on a ladder. There are an estimated 3 billion base pairs in human DNA.

Brain-derived neurotropic factor (BDNF). A protein implicated in learning and several aspects of neuron health and development.

Brodmann areas. A system for using numbers to define brain areas by anatomical location, originally based on autopsy studies of neuron structures.

Chromosome. Thread-like structure that carries DNA in genes. Humans have 23 pairs of chromosomes.

Cohort study. The observational study of a group of people with defined characteristics who are followed up to determine incidence of, or mortality from, some specific disease, all causes of death, or another outcome such as suicidal behavior.

Cortisol. A steroid hormone in the glucocorticoid class of hormones that is produced in the adrenal gland and released in response to stress.

Cross-sectional study. A research study design that uses different subjects at different time points to establish a trend (see also **longitudinal study**).

CT scan. Computerized tomography is a procedure that uses X-rays to image body tissues and structures. These images provide no information about the functioning of tissues.

Cytokines. Small proteins (including interferons and interleukins) that are produced by immune cells (such as lymphocytes) and that are especially important in the immune system.

Decision making. The cognitive process resulting in the selection of a belief or a course of action among several alternative possibilities.

Deep brain stimulation (DBS).   A neurosurgical procedure involving the implantation of a device called a neuro-stimulator that delivers controlled mild electrical shocks to targeted brain areas.

Default network.   The network of brain areas that is active while a person is not engaged in any mental activity.

Diathesis.   A constitutional predisposition toward a particular state or condition.

Diffusion tensor imaging (DTI).   An MRI technique that uses water diffusion patterns to image white matter fibers.

Distal risk factor.   A risk factor that represents an underlying vulnerability for a particular condition, event, disease, or behavior.

Dizygotic twins.   Two offspring produced by the same pregnancy, developing from two different eggs. Each twin is fertilized by its own sperm cell.

DNA.   Deoxyribonucleic acid is a self-replicating material present in nearly all living organisms as the main constituent of chromosomes. It is the carrier of genetic information.

EEG.   An electroencephalogram is a technique that measures the electrical activity of the brain by using electrodes attached to the scalp.

Endophenotype.   A hereditary characteristic that is associated with some condition but is not a direct symptom of that condition.

Epigenetics.   The field of study that investigates how genetic expression may be influenced by external factors.

False positive.   A test result that erroneously indicates something that turns out to be untrue.

Fractional anisotropy (FA).   A measure of water diffusion derived from MRI and used to image white matter fibers and assess their integrity.

Frontothalamic loop.   Circuit in the brain that connects the prefrontal cortex and the thalamus.

Functional MRI (fMRI).   A neuroimaging procedure using MRI that measures regional brain activity by detecting aspects of blood flow.

GABA.   Gamma-aminobutyric acid is a major inhibitory neurotransmitter in the brain.

Gene.   A hereditary unit consisting of a DNA sequence at a specific location on a chromosome.

Gene expression.   The process by which genetic instructions start or stop creating proteins.

Genome.   The entire set of DNA base pairs; all the genetic material of an organism.

Genome-wide association study (GWAS).   A method that searches the genome for small variations (see **single nucleotide polymorphisms**) that occur more frequently in people with a disease or trait. Each study can look at hundreds or thousands of SNPs at the same time (see **microarrays**).

Glutamate. An amino-acid neurotransmitter that plays a major role in neural activation.

Haplotype. A group of genes that is inherited together from a single parent.

Heritability. A statistical estimate of how much variation in behavior in a population is due to genetic influences.

HPA axis. The hypothalamus-pituitary-adrenal axis is an interactive neuroendocrine unit comprised of the hypothalamus, the pituitary gland, and the adrenal glands. The hypothalamus is located in the brain and the pituitary at the base of it, whereas the adrenals are on top of the kidneys. The HPA axis plays key roles in the response to stress. The major pathway of the axis results in the secretion of cortisol.

Learned helplessness. Occurs when a subject endures repeatedly aversive stimuli that it is unable to escape or avoid. After such experience, a subject often fails to learn or accept "escape" or "avoidance" in new situations where such behavior would likely be effective. The subject thus learns that it is helpless in situations where there is a presence of aversive stimuli, has accepted that it has lost control, and thus gives up trying.

Ligand. A molecule that binds to a receptor. In neuroimaging, ligands are commonly labeled with a radioactive substance, so that receptor binding can be measured.

Linkage study. A family-based method to map a characteristic to a genomic location by demonstrating co-segregation of a disease with genetic markers of known chromosomal localization.

Longitudinal study. A study where each subject is followed over time to investigate any changes (contrast with **cross-sectional study**).

Lymphocyte. One of the subtypes of white blood cells in the immune system.

Meta-analysis. A quantitative statistical analysis that combines the results of multiple separate but similar individual studies to test the pooled data for statistical significance.

Methylation. A chemical process that can change DNA; of special interest in epigenetic investigations.

Microarray. A tool used to determine whether the DNA from a particular individual contains a mutation in genes (SNPs). Thousands of SNPs can be studied simultaneously.

Monozygotic (MZ) twins. Identical twins who have 100% of their genes in common.

MRI. Magnetic resonance imaging is a medical imaging technique to form pictures of structures and functions in the body using strong magnetic fields.

mRNA. Messenger ribonucleic acid carries a portion of the DNA to other parts of the cell for processing.

Neurocognition. A form of cognition that is associated with the functioning of one or more specific areas of the brain.

Neuropsychology. The study of the relationship between behavior, emotions, and cognition, on the one hand, and brain function, on the other.

Neuroticism. A stable personality characteristic reflecting the likelihood to experience feelings such as anxiety, worry, and fear.

Neurotransmission. The process by which signaling molecules (neurotransmitters) are released by a nerve cell (the presynaptic neuron), and bind to and activate receptors of another neuron (the postsynaptic neuron).

Nonshared environment. Unique experiences that contribute to the environmental influences on heritability.

Oligodendrocytes. Cells in the nervous system that provide support and insulation to projections (axons) of nerve cells (neurons) by creating myelin sheets.

Phenotype. The composite of observable characteristics resulting from the expression of the genetic code (genotype) and the influence of environmental factors and the interactions between the two.

Population-attributable risk. The reduction in incidence that would be observed if the population were entirely unexposed to a risk factor, compared with its actual exposure pattern.

Positron emission tomography (PET). A technique to image body tissue functioning based on detecting the accumulation of low-level radioactive labels.

Predisposition. A genetic characteristic that influences the phenotypic development under the influence of environmental conditions.

Proteomics. The study of proteins and how they work.

Proximal risk factor. The risk factor in the causal chain that actually precipitates disease, as distinguished from predisposing or distal risk factors.

Psychache. Psychological pain that is so intense that it can be a risk factor for suicide.

Region of interest (ROI). A brain area defined for neuroimaging analysis.

RNA. Ribonucleic acid plays an important role in transferring information from DNA to the protein-forming system in cells.

Rumination.   Compulsively focused attention on the symptoms of distress, and on its possible causes and consequences, as opposed to its solutions.

Serotonin.   A neurotransmitter derived from tryptophan.

Shared environment.   Common experiences that contribute to the environmental influences on heritability.

Single nucleotide polymorphism (SNP, pronounced "snip").   A change or variation in a base pair substituting one base for another. SNPs may be associated with traits or diseases and can be hints for identifying relevant genes.

SNP.   See **single nucleotide polymorphism**.

Spectroscopy, or magnetic resonance spectroscopic imaging (MRSI).   A noninvasive imaging method that provides spectroscopic information about cellular or metabolic activity in addition to the image that is generated by MRI alone. Spectroscopy analyzes molecules such as hydrogen ions or, more commonly, protons.

Structural MRI (sMRI).   An MRI technique that visualizes the make-up of tissue but contains no functional information.

Transcranial alternating current stimulation (tACS).   A noninvasive technique for applying weak alternating electrical current through the skull to stimulate brain areas.

Transcranial direct current stimulation (tDCS).   A noninvasive technique for applying weak constant electrical current through the skull to stimulate brain areas.

Transcranial magnetic stimulation (TMS).   A procedure that uses magnetic fields placed over the scalp to stimulate or suppress brain activity.

Val66Met.   A gene associated with brain-derived neurotropic factor.

Valence.   The "goodness" (positive valence) or "badness" (negative valence) of a stimulus or situation.

Volition.   The act of making a conscious decision or choice.

Voxel.   The smallest unit in a neuroimage; a three-dimensional pixel.

Voxel-based-morphometry (VBM).   A technique for measuring brain characteristics at the level of individual voxels.

References

Aas, M., Kauppi, K., Brandt, C. L., Kaufmann, T., Steen, N. E., Agartz, I.,
    Westlye, L. T., Andreassen, O. A. & Melle, I. (2017). Childhood
    trauma is associated with increased brain responses to emotionally
    negative as compared to positive faces in patients with psychotic
    disorders. *Psychological Medicine*, *417*, 669–79.
Ackerman, J. P., McBee-Strayer, S. M., Mendoza, K., Stevens, J., Sheftall,
    A. H., Campo, J. V. & Bridge, J. A. (2015). Risk-sensitive decision-
    making deficit in adolescent suicide attempters. *Journal of Child and
    Adolescent Psychopharmacology*, *25*, 109–13.
Adams, R. A., Brown, H. R. & Friston, K. J. (2014). Bayesian inference,
    predictive coding and delusions. *AVANT*, *V*, 51–88.
Adams, R. A., Stephan, K. E., Brown, H. R., Frith, C. D. & Friston, K. J.
    (2013). The computational anatomy of psychosis. *Frontiers in
    Psychiatry*, 4, 47.
Afifi, T. O., Enns, M., Cox, B., Asmundson, G., Stein, M. & Sareen, J. (2008).
    Population attributable fractions of psychiatric disorders and suicide
    ideation and attempts associated with adverse childhood experiences.
    American Journal of Public Health, *98*, 946–52.
Afifi, T. O., MacMillan, H. L., Boyle, M., Taillieu, T., Cheung, K. & Sareen,
    J. (2014). Child abuse and mental disorders in Canada. *Canadian
    Medical Association Journal*, *186*, E324–E332.
Aguilar, E. J., Garcia-Marti, G., Marti-Bonmati, L., Lull, J. J., Moratal, D.,
    Escarti, M. J., Robles, M., Gonzales, J. C., Guillamon, M. I. & Sanjuan,
    J. (2008). Left orbitofrontal and superior temporal gyrus changes
    associated to suicidal behavior in patients with schizophrenia.
    Progress in Neuropsychopharmacology and Biological Psychiatry,
    32, 1673–6.
Ahearn, E. P., Jamison, K. R., Steffens, D. C., Cassidy, F., Provenzale, J. M.,
    Lehman, A., Weisler, R. H., Carroll, B. J. & Krishnan, K. R. (2001).
    MRI correlates of suicide attempt history in unipolar depression.
    Biological Psychiatry, *50*, 266–70.
Almeida, D. & Turecki, G. (2016). A slice of the suicidal brain: What have
    post-mortem molecular studies taught us? *Current Psychiatry Reports*,
    18, 98.
Amen, D. G., Prunella, J. R., Fallon, J. H., Amen, B. & Hanks, C. (2009).
    A comparative analysis of completed suicide using high resolution

brain SPECT imaging. *Journal of Psychiatry and Clinical Neuroscience*, *21*, 430–9.

Andersen, S. L., Tomada, A., Vincow, E. S., Valente, E., Polcari, A. & Teicher, M. H. (2008). Preliminary evidence for sensitive periods in the effect of childhood sexual abuse on regional brain development. *Journal of Neuropsychiatry and Clinical Neuroscience*, *20*, 292–301.

Andersen, S. M., Spielman, L. A. & Bargh, J. A. (1992). Future-event schemas and certainty about the future: Automaticity in depressives' future-event predictions. *Journal of Personality and Social Psychology*, *63*, 711–23.

Anderson, I. M., Blamire, A., Branton, T., Clark, R., Downey, D., Dunn, G., Easton, A., Elliott, R., Elwell, C., Hayden, K., Holland, F., Karim, S., Loo, C., Lowe, J., Nair, R., Oakley, T., Prakash, A., Sharma, P. K., Williams, S. R., McAllister-Williams, R. H. & Ketamine-ECT Study team. (2017). Ketamine augmentation of electroconvulsive therapy to improve neuropsychological and clinical outcomes in depression (Ketamine-ECT): a multicentre, double-blind, randomised, parallel-group, superiority trial. *Lancet Psychiatry*, *4*, 365–77.

Andersson, L., Allebeck, P., Gustafsson, J. E. & Gunnell, D. (2008). Association of IQ scores and school achievement with suicide in a 40-year follow-up of a Swedish cohort. *Acta Psychiatrica Scandinavica*, *118*, 99–105.

Andriessen, K., Rahman, B., Draper, B., Dudley, M. & Mitchell, P. B. (2017). Prevalence of exposure to suicide: A meta-analysis of population-based studies. *Journal of Psychiatric Research*, *88*, 113–20.

Anestis, M. D. & Houtsma, C. (2017). The association between gun ownership and statewide overall suicide rates. *Suicide and Life-Threatening Behavior*. Epub ahead of print.

Anguelova, M., Benkelfat, C. & Turecki, G. (2003). A systematic review of association studies investigating genes for serotonin receptors and the serotonin receptor: II. Suicidal behavior. *Molecular Psychiatry*, *8*, 646–53.

Ansell, E. B., Rando, K., Tuit, K., Guarnaccia, J. & Sinha, R. (2012). Cumulative adversity and smaller gray matter volume in medial prefrontal, anterior cingulate, and insula regions. *Biological Psychiatry*, *72*, 57–64.

Antypa, N., Serretti, A. & Rujescu, D. (2013). Serotonergic genes and suicide: A systematic review. *European Neuropsychopharmacology*, *23*, 1125–42.

Arie, M., Apter, A., Orbach, I., Yefet, Y. & Zalsman, G. (2008). Autobiographical memory, interpersonal problem solving, and suicidal behaviour in adolescent inpatients. *Comprehensive Psychiatry*, *49*, 22–9.

Arsenault-Lapierre, G., Kim, C. & Turecki, G. (2004). Psychiatric diagnoses in 3275 suicides: A meta-analysis. *BMC Psychiatry*, *4*, 37.

Asarnow, J. R., Porta, G., Spirito, A., Emslie, G., Clarke, G., Wagner, K. D., Vitiello, B., Keller, M., Birmaher, B., McCraken, J., Mayes, T., Berk, M. & Brent, D. A. (2011). Suicide attempts and nonsuicidal self-injury in the Treatment of Resistant Depression in Adolescents: Findings from the TORDIA study. *Journal of the American Academy of Child and Adolescent Psychiatry*, *50*, 772–81.

Åsberg, M., Träskman, L. & Thoren, P. (1976). 5-HIAA in the cerebrospinal fluid: A biochemical suicide predictor? *Archives of General Psychiatry*, *33*, 1193–7.

Audenaert, K., Goethals, I., Van Laere, K., Lahorte, P., Brnas, B., Versijpt, J., Vervaet, M., Beelaert, L., van Heeringen, K. & Dierckx, R. (2002). SPECT neuropsychological activation procedure with the Verbal Fluency Test in attempted suicide patients. *Nuclear Medicine Communications*, *23*, 907–16.

Audenaert, K., Van Laere, K., Dumont, F., Slegers, G., Mertens, J., van Heeringen, K. & Dierckx, R. (2001). Decreased frontal serotonin 5-HT2a receptor binding index in deliberate self-harm patients. *European Journal of Nuclear Medicine*, *28*, 175–82.

Badre, D., Doll, B. B., Long, N. M. & Frank, M. J. (2012). Rostrolateral prefrontal cortex and individual differences in uncertainty-driven exploration. *Neuron*, *73*, 595–607.

Baeken, C., Duprat, R., Wu, G. R., De Raedt, R. & van Heeringen, K. (2017). Subgenual anterior cingulate functional connectivity in medication-resistant major depression: A neurobiological marker for accelerated intermittent Theta Burst Stimulation treatment? *Biological Psychiatry: Cognitive Neuroscience and Neuroimaging*, 2, no. 7, 556–65.

Baklan, A. V., Huber, R. S., Coon, H., Gray, D., Wilson, P., McMahon, W. M. & Renshaw, P. F. (2015). Acute air pollution exposure and risk of suicide completion. *American Journal of Epidemiology*, *181*, 295–301.

Baldacara, L., Nery-Fernandes, F., Rocha, M., Quarantini, L. C., Rocha, G. G., Guimaraes, J. L., Araujo, C., Oliveira, I., Miranda-Scippa, A. & Jackowski, A. (2011). Is cerebellar volume related to bipolar disorder? *Journal of Affective Disorders*, *135*, 305–9.

Baldessarini, R. J. & Hennen, J. (2004). Genetics of suicide: An overview. *Harvard Review of Psychiatry*, *12*, 1–13.

Barker, A., Hawton, K. & Fagg, J. (1994). Seasonal and weather factors in parasuicide. *British Journal of Psychiatry*, *165*, 375–80.

Bartfai, A., Winborg, I. M., Nordström, P. & Asberg, M. (1990). Suicidal behavior and cognitive flexibility: Design and verbal fluency after attempted suicide. *Suicide and Life-Threatening Behavior*, *20*, 54–66.

Bartoli, F., Riboldi, I., Crocamo, C., Di Brita, C., Clerici, M. & Carrà, G. (2017). Ketamine as a rapid-acting agent for suicidal ideation: A meta-analysis. *Neuroscience and Biobehavioral Reviews*, *77*, 232–6.

Bastiampillai, T., Sharfstein, S. S. & Allison, S. (2016). Increase in US suicide rates and the critical decline in psychiatric beds. *Journal of the American Medical Association*, *24*, 2591–2.

Beard, C., Rifkin, L. S. & Björgvinsson, T. (2017). Characteristics of interpretation bias and relationship with suicidality in a psychiatric hospital sample. *Journal of Affective Disorders*, *207*, 321–6.

Beck, A. T., Steer, R. A., Beck, J. S. & Newman, C. F. (1993). Hopelessness, depression, suicidal ideation and clinical diagnosis of depression. *Suicide & Life-Threatening Behavior*, *23*, 139–45.

Becker, E. S., Strohbach, D. & Rinck, M. (1999). A specific attentional bias in suicide attempters. *Journal of Nervous and Mental Disorders*, *187*, 730–5.

Beckman, K., Mittendorfer-Rutz, E., Lichtenstein, P., Larsson, H., Almqvist, C., Runeson, B. & Dahlin, M. (2016). Mental illness and suicide after self-harm among young adults: Long-term follow-up of self-harm patients, admitted to hospital care, in a national cohort. *Psychological Medicine*, *46*, 3397–405.

Beevers, C. G. & Miller, L. W. (2004). Perfectionism, cognitive bias, and hopelessness as prospective predictors of suicidal ideation. *Suicide & Life-Threatening Behavior*, *34*, 126–37.

Beharelle, A. R., Polania, R., Hare, T. A. & Ruff, C. C. (2015). Transcranial stimulation over frontopolar cortex elucidates choice attributes and neural mechanisms used to resolve exploration-exploitation trade-off. *Journal of Neuroscience*, *35*, 14544–56.

Bellivier, F., Belzeaux, R., Scott, J., Courtet, P., Goimard, J. L. & Azorin, J. M. (2017). Anticonvulsants and suicide attempts in bipolar I disorders. *Acta Psychiatrica Scandinavica*, *13*, 470–8.

Ben-Efraim, Y. J., Wasserman, D. & Wasserman, J. (2011). Gene environment interactions between CRHR1 variants and physical assault in suicide attempts. *Genes, Brain and Behavior*, *10*, 663–72.

Benedetti, F., Radaelli, D., Poletti, S., Locatelli, C., Falini, A., Colombo, C. & Smeraldi, E. (2011). Opposite effects of suicidality and lithium on gray matter volumes in bipolar depression. *Journal of Affective Disorders*, *135*, 139–47.

Bergfeld, I. O., Mantione, M., Hoogendoorn, M. L., Ruhé, H. G., Van Laarhoven, J., Visser, I., Figee, M., De Kwaasteniet, B. P., Horst, F.,

Schene, A. H., Van den Munckhof, P., Beute, G., Schuurman, R. & Denys, D. (2016). Deep brain stimulation of the ventral anterior limb of the internal capsule for treatment-resistant depression: A randomized clinical trial. *JAMA Psychiatry*, *73*, 456–64.

Bertsch, K., Schmidinger, I., Neumann, I. D. & Herpertz, S. C. (2013). Reduced plasma oxytocin levels in female patients with borderline personality disorder. *Hormones and Behavior*, *673*, 424–9.

Besteher, B., Wagner, G., Koch, K., Schachtzabel, C., Reichenbach, J. R., Schlösser, R., Sauer, H. & Schultz, C. C. (2016). Pronounced prefronto-temporal cortical thinning in schizophrenia: Neuroanatomical correlate of suicidal behavior? *Schizophrenia Research*, *176*, 151–7.

Bijttebier, S., Caeyenberghs, K., Van den Ameele, H., Achten, E., Rujescu, D., Titeca, K. & van Heeringen, K. (2015). The vulnerability to suicidal behavior is associated with reduced connectivity strength. *Frontiers in Human Neuroscience*, *9*, 632.

Birkbak, J., Stuart, E. A., Lind, B. D., Qin, P., Stenager, E., Larsen, K. J., Wang, A. G., Nielsen, A. C., Pedersen, C. M., Winslov, J. H., Langhoff, C., Mühlmann, C., Nordentoft, M. & Erlangsen, A. (2016). Psychosocial therapy and causes of death after deliberate self-harm: A register-based nationwide multicentre study using propensity score matching. *Psychological Medicine*, *46*, 4319–3427.

Björkholm, C. & Monteggia, L. M. (2016). BDNF – a key transducer of antidepressant effects. *Neuropsychopharmacology*, *102*, 72–9.

Bolton, J. M., Gunnell, D. & Turecki, G. (2015). Suicide risk assessment and intervention in people with mental illness. *British Medical Journal*, *351*, h4978.

Bostwick, J. M., Pabbati, C., Geske, J. P. & McKean, A. J. (2016). Suicide attempts as a risk factor for completed suicide: Even more lethal than we knew. *American Journal of Psychiatry*, *173*, 1094–1100.

Botzung, A., Denkova, E. & Manning, L. (2008). Experiencing past and future events: Functional neuroimaging evidence on the neural bases of mental time travel. *Brain and Cognition*, *66*, 202–12.

Bourgeois, M. (1987). Existe-t-il des modèles animaux du suicide? [Are there animal models of suicidal behavior?]. *Psychologie Medicale*, *19*, 739–40.

Braskie, M. N., Kohannim, O. & Jahanshad, N. (2013). Relation between variants in the neurotrophin receptor gene NTRK3, and white matter integrity in healthy young adults. *Neuroimage*, *82*, 146–53.

Brenner, B., Cheng, D., Clark, S. & Camargo, C.A. (2011). Positive association between altitude and suicide in 2584 US counties. *High Altitude Medicine & Biology*, *12*, 31–5.

Brent, D. (2009). In search of endophenotypes for suicidal behavior. *American Journal of Psychiatry*, *166*, 1087–8.

Brent, D. A. (2016). Antidepressants and suicidality. *Psychiatry Clinics*, *39*, 503–12.

Brezo, J., Klempan, T. & Turecki, G. (2008a). The genetics of suicide: A critical review of molecular studies. *Psychiatric Clinics of North America*, *31*, 179–203.

Brezo, J., Paris, J., Barker, E. D., Tremblay, R., Vitaro, F., Zoccolillo, M., Hébert, M. & Turecki, G. (2007). Natural history of suicidal behaviors in a population-based sample of young adults. *Psychological Medicine*, *37*, no. 11, 1563–74.

Brezo, J., Paris, J., Vitaro, F., Hébert, M., Tremblay, R. E. & Turecki, G. (2008b). Predicting suicide attempts in young adults with histories of childhood abuse. *British Journal of Psychiatry*, *193*, 134–9.

Bridge, J. A., Barbe, R. P. & Birmaher, B. (2005). Emergent suicidality in a clinical psychotherapy trial for adolescent depression. *American Journal of Psychiatry*, *162*, 2173–5.

Bridge, J. A., Iyengar, S. & Salary, C. B. (2007). Clinical response and risk for reported suicidal ideation and suicide attempts in pediatric antidepressant treatment: A meta-analysis of randomized controlled trials. *JAMA*, *297*, 1683–96.

Bridge, J. A., McBee-Strayer, S. M., Cannon, E. A., Sheftall, A. H., Reynolds, B., Campo, J. V., Pajer, K. A., Barbe, R. P. & Brent, D. A. (2012). Impaired decision making in adolescent suicide attempters. *Journal of the AmericanAcademy of Child and Adolescent Psychiatry*, *51*, 394–403.

Brown, D. W., Anda, R. F., Tiemeier, H., Felitti, V. J., Edwards, V. J., Croft, J. B. & Giles, W. H. (2009). Adverse childhood experiences and the risk of premature mortality. *American Journal of Preventive Medicine*, *37*, 389–96.

Brown, G. K., Beck, A. T., Steer, R. A. & Grisham, J. R. (2000). Risk factors for suicide in psychiatric outpatients: A 20-year prospective study. *Journal of Consulting and Clinical Psychology*, *68*, 371–7.

Brown, G. K., Ten Have, T., Henriques, G. R., Xie, S. X., Hollander, J. E. & Beck, A. T. (2005). Cognitive therapy for the prevention of suicide attempts: A randomized controlled trial. *JAMA*, *294*, 563–70.

Bruffaerts, R., Demyttenaere, K., Borges, G., haro, J. M., Chiu, W. T., Hwang, I., Karam, E. G., Kessler, R. C., Sampson, N., Alonso, J., Andrade, L. H., Angermeyer, M., Benjet, C., Bromet, E., de Girolamo, G., De Graaf, R., Florescu, S., Gureje, O., Horiguchi, I., Hu, C., Kovess, V., Levinson, D., Posada-Villa, J., Sagar, R., Scott, K., Tsang, A., Vassilev, S. M., Williams, D. R. & Nock, L. K. (2010). Childhood adversities as risk factors for onset and persistence of suicidal behaviour. *British Journal of Psychiatry*, *197*, 20–7.

Brummelte, S., Mc Glanaghy, E., Bonnin, A. & Oberlander, T. F. (2017). Develomental changes in serotonin signalling: Implications for early brain function, behaviour and adaptation. *Neuroscience*, *3423*, 212–31.

Brundin, L., Erhardt, S., Bryleva, E. Y., Achtyes, E. D. & Postolache, T. T. (2015). The role of inflammation in suicidal behaviour. *Acta Psychiatrica Scandinavica*, *132*, 192–203.

Brunner, R., Parzer, P., Haffner, J., Steen, R., Roos, J., Klett, M. & Resch, F. (2007). Prevalence and psychological correlates of occasional and repetitive deliberate self-harm in adolescents. *Archives of Pediatric and Adolescent Medicine*, *161*, 641–9.

Bryleva, E. Y. & Brundin, L. (2017). Kynurenine pathways metabolites and suicidality. *Neuropharmacology*, *112*, 324–30.

Budday, S., Raybaud, C. & Kuhl, E. (2014). A mechanical model predicts morphological abnormalities in the developing human brain. *Science Reports*, *4*, 5644.

Busch, K. A., Fawcett, J. & Jacobs, D. G. (2003). Clinical correlates of inpatient suicide. *Journal of Clinical Psychiatry*, *64*, 14–19.

Canner, J. K., Giuliano, K., Selvarajah, S., Hammond, E. R. & Schneider, E. B. (2016). Emergency department visits for attempted suicide and self-harm in the USA: 2006–2013. *Epidemiology and Psychiatric Services*. Epub ahead of print.

Cannon, D. M., Ichise, M., Fromm, S. J., Nugent, A. C., Rollis, D., Gandhi, S. K. & Drevets, W. C. (2006). Serotonin transporter binding in bipolar I disorder assessed using [11C] DASB and positron emission tomography. *Biological Psychiatry*, *60*, 207–17.

Caplan, R., Siddarth, P., Levitt, J., Gurbani, S., Shields, W. D. & Sankar, R. (2010). Suicidality and brain volumes in pediatric epilepsy. *Epilepsy and Behavior*, *18*, 286–90.

Carmichael, A. G. (2014). BioSocial Methods Collaborative: Central Dogma Enhanced [Digital image]. Available at http://biosocialmethods.isr.umich.edu/epigenetics-tutorial/epigenetics-tutorial-gene-expression-from-dna-to-protein/.

Caspi, A., Sugden, K., Moffitt, T. E., Taylor, A., Craig, I. W., Harrington, H., McClay, J., Mill, J., Martin, J., Braithwaite, A. & Poulton, R. (2003). Influence of life stress on depression: Moderation by a polymorphism in the 5-HTT gene. *Science*, *301*, 386–9.

Cavanagh, J. T., Carson, A. J., Sharpe, M. & Lawrie, S. M. (2003). Psychological autopsy studies of suicide: A systematic review. *Psychological Medicine*, *33*, 395–405.

Cha, C. B., Najmi, S., Amir, N., Matthews, J. D., Deming, C. A., Glenn, J. J., Calixte, R. M., Harris, J. A. & Nock, M. (2017). Testing the efficacy of Attention Bias Modification for suicidal thoughts: Findings from two experiments. *Archives of Suicide Research*, *21*, 33–51.

Cha, C. B., Najmi, S., Park, J. M., Finn, C. T. & Nock, M. K. (2010). Attentional bias toward suicide-related stimuli predicts suicidal behavior. *Journal of Abnormal Psychology*, *119*, 616–22.

Chachamovich, E., Haggarty, J., Cargo, M., Hicks, J., Kirmayer, L. J. & Turecki, G. (2013). A psychological autopsy study of suicide among Inuit in Nunavut: Methodological and ethical considerations, feasibility and acceptability. *International Journal of Circumpolar Health*, *72*, 20078.

Chamberlain, S. R., Odlaug, B. L., Schreiber, L. R. N. & Grant, J. E. (2013). Clinical and neurocognitive markers of suicidality in young adults. *Journal of Psychiatric Research*, *47*, 586–91.

Chan, M. K., Bhatti, H., Meader, N., Stockton, S., Evans, J., O'Connor, R. C., Kapur, N. & Kendall, T. (2016). Predicting suicide following self-harm: Systematic review of risk factors and risk scales. *British Journal of Psychiatry*, *357*, 277–83.

Chang, B. P., Franklin, J. C., Ribeiro, J. D., Fox, K. R., Bentley, K. H., Kleiman, E. M. & Nock, M. K. (2016). Biological risk factors for suicidal behaviors: A meta-analysis. *Translational Psychiatry*, *6*, e887.

Chen, J. H. & Asch, S. M. (2017). Machine learning and prediction in medicine: Beyond the peak of inflated expectations. *New England Journal of Medicine*, *376*, 2507–9.

Chen, Z., Zhang, H., Jia, Z., Zhong, J., Huang, X., Du, M., Chen, L., Kuang, W., Sweeney, J. A. & Gong, Q. (2015). Magnetization transfer imaging of suicidal patients with major depressive disorder. *Scientific Reports*, *5*, 9670.

Cheng, A. T. (1995). Mental illness and suicide: A case-control study in east Taiwan. *Archives of General Psychiatry*, *52*, 594–603.

Chesin, M. S., Benjamin-Philip, C. A., Keilp, J., Fertuck, E. A., Brodsky, B. S. & Stanley, B. (2016). Improvements in executive attention, rumination, cognitive reactivity, and mindfulness among high-suicide risk patients participating in adjunct mindfulness-based cognitive therapy: Preliminary findings. *Journal of Alternative Complementary Medicine*, *22*, 642–9.

Ching, E. (2016). The complexity of suicide: Review of recent neuroscientific evidence. *Journal of Cognition and Neuroethics*, *3*, 27–40.

Cho, H., Guo, G. & Iritani, B. J. (2006). Genetic contribution to suicidal behaviors and associated risk factors among adolescents in the U.S. *Preventive Science*, *7*, 303–11.

Cho, S. S., Pellechia, G., Ko, J. H., Ray, N., Obeso, I., Houle, S. & Strafela, A.P. (2012). Effect of continuous theta burst stimulation of the right dorsolateral prefrontal cortex on cerebral blood flow changes during decision making. *Brain Stimulation*, *5*, 116–23.

Christodoulou, C., Douzenis, A., Papadopoulos, F. C., Papadopoulo, A., Bouras, G, Gourbellis, R. & Lykouras, L. (2012). Suicide and seasonality. *Acta Psychiatrica Scandinavica*, *125*, 127–46.

Chung, Y. & Jeglic, E. L. (2016). Use of the Modified Emotional Stroop Task to detect suicidality in college population. *Suicide & Life-Threatening Behavior*, *46*, 55–66.

(2017). Detecting suicide risk among college students: A test of the predictive validity of the modified emotional Stroop task. *Suicide & Life-Threatening Behavior*, *47*, 398–409.

Cipriani, A., Hawton, K., Stockton, S. & Geddes, J. R. (2013). Lithium in the prevention of suicide in mood disorders: Updated systematic review and meta-analysis. *British Medical Journal*, *364*, 346.

Clark, L., Dombrovski, A. Y., Siegle, G. J., Butters, M. A., Shollenberger, C. L., Sahakian, B. J. & Szanto, K. (2011). Impairment in risk-sensitive decision-making in older suicide attempters with depression. *Psychology and Aging*, *26*, no. 2, 321–30.

Clayden, R. C., Zaruk, A., Meyre, D., Thabane, L. & Samaan, Z. (2012). The association of attempted suicide with genetic variants in the SLC6A4 and TPH genes depends on the definition of suicidal behavior: A systematic review and meta-analysis. *Translational Psychiatry*, *2*, e166.

Clive, M. L., Boks, M. P., Vinkers, C. H., Osborne, L. M., Payne, J. L., Ressler, K. J., Smith, A. K., Wilcox, H. C. & Kaminsky, Z. (2016). Discovery and replication of a peripheral tissue DNA methylation biosignature to augment a suicide prediction model. *Clinical Epigenetics*, *8*, 113.

Coelho, R., Viola, T. W., Walss-Bass, C., Brietzke, E. & Grassi-Oliveira, R. (2014). Childhood maltreatment and inflammatory markers: A systematic review. *Acta Psychiatrica Scandinavica*, *129*, 180–92.

Coenen, V. A., Panksepp, J., Hurwitz, T. A., Urbach, H. & Mädler, B. (2012). Human medial forebrain bundle (MFB) and anterior thalamic radiation (ATR): Imaging of two major subcortical pathways and the dynamic balance of opposite affects in understanding depression. *Journal of Neuropsychiatry and Clinical Neuroscience*, *24*, 223–36.

Colle, R., Chupin, M, Cury, C., Vandendrie, C., Gressier, F., Hardy, P., Falissard, B., Colliot, C., Ducreux, D. & Corruble, E. (2015). Depressed suicide attempters have smaller hippocampus than depressed patients without suicide attempts. *Journal of Psychiatric Research*, *61*, 13–18.

Conaghan, S. & Davidson, K. M. (2002). Hopelessness and the anticipation of positive and negative future experiences in older parasuicidal adults. *British Journal of Clinical Psychology*, *41*, 233–42.

Conner, K. R., Conwell, Y. & Duberstein, P. R. (2001). The validity of proxy-based data in suicide research: A study of patients 50 years of age and older who attempted suicide. II. Life events, social support and suicidal behavior. *Acta Psychiatrica Scandinavica*, *104*, 452–7.

Coplan, J. D., Abdallah, C. G., Tang, C. Y., Mathew, S. J., Martinez, J., Hof, P. R., Smith, E. L., Dwork, A. J., Perera, T. D., Pantol, G., Carpenter, D., Rosenblum, L. A., Shungu, D.C., Gelernter, J., Kaufman, A., Jackowski, A., Kaufman, J. & Gorman, J. M. (2010). The role of early life stress in the development of the anterior limb of the internal capsule in non-human primates. *Neuroscience Letters*, *480*, 93–6.

Corlett, P. R., Frith, C. D. & Fletcher, P. C. (2009). From drugs to deprivation: A Bayesian framework for understanding models of psychosis. *Psychopharmacology*, *206*, 515–30.

Coryell, W. & Schlesser, M. (2007). Combined biological tests for suicide prediction. *Psychiatry Research*, *150*, 187–91.

Coste, C. P., Sadaghiani, S., Friston, K. J. & Kleinschmidt, A. (2011). Ongoing brain activity fluctuations directly account for intertribal and indirectly for intersubject variability in Stroop task performance. *Cerebral Cortex*, *21*, 2612–19.

Coupland, C., Hill, T., Morriss, R., Arthur, A., Moore, M. & Hippisley-Cox, J. (2014). Antidepressant use and risk of suicide and attempted suicide or self-harm in people aged 20 to 64: Cohort study using a primary care database. *British Medical Journal*, *350*, 517.

Courtet, P., Giner, L., Seneque, M., Guillaume, S., Olie, E. & Ducasse D. (2016). Neuroinflammation in suicide: Toward a comprehensive model. *The World Journal of Biological Psychiatry*, *17*, 564–86.

Coventry, W. L., James, M. R., Eaves, L. J., Gordon, S. D., Gillespie, N. A., Ryan, L., Heath, A. C., Montgomery, G. W., Martin, N. G. & Wray, N. R. (2010). Do 5HTTLPR and stress interact in risk for depression and suicidality? Item response analyses of a large sample. *American Journal of Medical Genetics Part B: Neuropsychiatric Genetics*, *153*, 757–65.

Crandall, S. R., Cruikshank, S. J. & Connors, B. W. (2016). A corticothalamic switch: Controlling the thalamus with dynamic synapses. *Neuron*, *86*, 768–82.

Crane, D. E., Black, S. E., Ganda, A., Mikulis, D. J., Nestor, S. M., Donahue, M. J. & MacIntosh, B. J. (2015). Gray matter blood flow and volume are reduced in association with white matter hyperintensity lesion burden: A cross-sectional MRI study. *Frontiers in Aging Neuroscience*, *7*, 131.

Crocket, M. J. & Cools, R. (2015). Serotonin and aversive processing in affective and social decision-making. *Current Opinion in Behavioral Sciences*, *5*, 64–70.

Cuijpers, P., De Beurs, D., Van Spijker, B., Berking, M., Andersson, G. & Kerkhof, A. (2013). The effects of psychotherapy for adult depression on suicidality and hopelessness: A systematic review and meta-analysis. *Journal of Affective Disorders*, *144*, 183–90.

Curtin, S.C., Warner, M. & Hedegaard, H. (2016). Increase in suicide rates in the United States, 1999–2014. NCHS data brief, no. 241. Hyattsville, MD: National Center for Health Statistics.

Cutajar, M. C., Mullen, P. E., Ogloff, J. R. P., Thomas, S. D., Wells, D. L. & Spataro, J. (2010). Suicide and fatal drug overdose in child sexual abuse victims: A historical cohort study. *Medical Journal of Australia*, *192*, 184–7.

Cutler, G. J., Flood, A., Dreyfus, J. & Ortega, H. W. (2015). Emergency department visits for self-inflicted injuries in adolescents. *Pediatrics*, *136*, 28–34.

Cyprien, F., Courtet, P., Malafosse, A., Maller, J., Meslin, C., Bonafé, A., Le Bars, E., de Champfleur, N. M., Ritchie, K. & Artero, S. (2011). Suicidal behavior is associated with reduced corpus callosum area. *Biological Psychiatry*, *70*, 320–6.

Daubert, E. A. & Condron, B. G. (2010). Serotonin: A regulator of neuronal morphology and circuitry. *Trends in Neurosciences*, *33*, 424–34.

Daw, N. D., Niv, Y. & Dayan, P. (2005). Uncertainty-based competition between prefrontal and dorsolateral systems for behavioral control. *Nature Neuroscience*, *8*, 1704–11.

Daw, N. D., O'Doherty, J. P., Dayan, P., Seymour, B. & Dolan, R. J. (2006). Cortical substrates for exploratory decisions in humans. *Nature*, *441*, 876–9.

Dayan, P. & Huys, Q. J. M. (2008). Serotonin, inhibition, and negative mood. *PLoS Computational Biology*, *4*, e4.

Dayan, P. & Seymour, B. (2009). Values and actions in aversion. *Neuroeconomics*, 175–91.

Dazzi, T., Gribble, R. & Wessely, S. (2014). Does asking about suicide and related behaviours induce suicidal ideation? What is the evidence? *Psychological Medicine*, *44*, 3361–63.

De Berardis, D., Marini, S., Piersanti, M., Cavuto, M., Perna, G., Valchera, A., Mazza, M., Fornaro, M., Iasevoli, F., Martinotti, G. & Di Giannantonio, M. (2012). The relationships between cholesterol and suicide: An update. *ISRN Psychiatry*, 387901.

De Catanzaro, D. (1980). Human suicide: A biological perspective. *Behavioral and Brain Sciences*, *3*, 265–72.

De Luca, V., Viggiano, E., Dhoot, R., Kennedy, J. L. & Wong, A. H. (2009). Methylation and QTDT analysis of the 5-HT2A receptor 102C allele: Analysis of suicidality in major psychosis. *Journal of Psychiatric Research*, *43*, 532–7.

De Martino, B., Fleming, S. M., Garrett, N. & Dolan, R. J. (2013). Confidence in value-based choice. *Nature Neuroscience*, *16*, 105–10.

Deakin, J. & Graeff, F. (1991). 5HT and mechanisms of defense. *Journal of Psychopharmacology*, *5*, 305–15.

Delaney, C., McGrane, J., Cummings, E., Morris, D. W., Tropea, D., Gil, M., Corvin, A. & Donohoe, G. (2012). Preserved cognitive function is associated with suicidal ideation and single suicide attempts in schizophrenia. *Schizophrenia Research*, *140*, 232–6.

Den Ouden, H. E. M., Kok, P. & De Lange, F. P. (2012). How prediction errors shape perception, attention and motivation. *Frontiers in Psychology*, *3*, 548.

Deshpande, G., Baxi, M. & Robinson, J. L. (2016). A neural basis for the acquired capability for suicide. *Frontiers in Psychiatry*, *7*, 125.

Desmyter, S., Bijttebier, S., van Heeringen, K. & Audenaert, K. (2013). The role of neuroimaging in our understanding of the suicidal brain. *CNS & Neurological Disorders Drug Targets*, *12*, 921–9.

Desmyter, S., Duprat, R., Baeken, C., Van Autreve, S., Audenaert, K. & van Heeringen, K. (2016). Accelerated intermittent theta burst stimulation for suicide risk in therapy-resistant depressed patients: A randomized, sham-controlled trial. *Frontiers in Human Neuroscience*, *10*, 480.

Desmyter, S., van Heeringen, K. & Audenaert, K. (2011). Structural and functional neuroimaging studies of the suicidal brain. *Progress in Neuro-Psychopharmacology and Biological Psychiatry*, *35*, 796–808.

Desrochers, T. M., Chatham, C. H. & Badre, D. (2015). The necessity of rostrolateral prefrontal cortex for higher-level sequential behavior. *Neuron*, *87*, 1357–68.

Devries, K. M., Mak, J. Y. T., Child, J. C., Falder, G., Bacchus, L. J., Astbury, J. & Watts, C. H. (2014). Childhood sexual abuse and suicidal behaviour: A meta-analysis. *Pediatrics*, *133*, e1331–e1344.

DeWall, C. N., MacDonald, G., Webster, G. D., Masten, C. L., Baumeister, R. F., Powell, C., Combs, D., Schurtz, D. R., Stillman, T. F., Tice, D. M. & Eisenberger, N. I. (2010). Acetaminophen reduces social pain: behavioral and neural evidence. *Psychological Science*, *21*, 931–7.

Dhingra, K., Boduszek, D. & O'Connor, R. C. (2016). A structural test of the Integrated Motivational-Volitional Model of suicidal behaviour. *Psychiatry Research*, *239*, 169–78.

Dickerson, F., Wilcox, H., Adamos, M., Katsafanas, E., Kushalani, S., Origoni, A., Savage, C., Schweinfurth, L., Stallings, C., Sweeney, K. & Yolken, R. (2017). Suicide attempts and markers of immune response in individuals with serious mental illness. *Journal of Psychiatric Research*, *87*, 37–43.

Dixon-Gordon, K. L., Gratz, K. L., McDermott, M. J. & Tull, M.T. (2014). The role of executive attention in deliberate self-harm. *Psychiatry Research*, *218*, 113–17.

Dodds, T. J. (2017). Prescribed benzodiazepines and suicide risk: A review of the literature. *Primary Care Companion CNS Disorders*, *19*, 16r02037.

Dombrovski, A. Y., Butters, M. A., Reynolds, C. F., Houck, P. R., Clark, L., Mazumbar, S. & Szanto, K. (2008). Cognitive performance in suicidal depressed elderly: Preliminary report. *American Journal of Geriatric Psychiatry*, *16*, 109–115.

Dombrovski, A. Y., Clark, L., Siegle, G. J., Butters, M. A., Ichikawa, N., Sahakian, B. J. & Szanto, K. (2010). Reward/punishment learning in older suicide attempters. *American Journal of Psychiatry*, *167*, 699–707.

Dombrovski, A. Y., Siegle, G. J., Szanto, K., Clark, L., Reynolds, C. F. & Aizenstein, H. (2012). The temptation of suicide: Striatal gray matter, discounting of delayed rewards, and suicide attempts in late-life depression. *Psychological Medicine*, *42*, 1203–15.

Dombrovski, A. Y., Szanto, K., Clark, L., Reynolds, C. F. & Siegle, G. J. (2013). Reward signals, attempted suicide, and impulsivity in late-life depression. *JAMA Psychiatry*, *70*, 1020–1030.

Dombrovski, A. Y., Szanto, K., Siegle, G. J., Wallace, M. L., Forman, S. D., Sahakian, B., Reynolds, C. F. & Clark, L. (2011). Lethal forethought: Delayed reward discounting differentiates high- and low-lethality suicide attempts in old age. *Biological Psychiatry*, *70*, no. 2, 138–44.

Dour, H. J., Cha, C. B. & Nock, M. K. (2011). Evidence for an emotion–cognition interaction in the statistical prediction of suicide attempts. *Behaviour Research and Therapy*, *49*, 294–8.

Doya, K. (2008). Modulators of decision making. *Nature Neuroscience*, *11*, 410–16.

Drabble, J., Bowles, D. P. & Barker, L. A. (2014). Investigating the role of executive attentional control to self-harm in a non-clinical cohort with borderline personality features. *Frontiers in Behavioral Neuroscience*, *8*, 274.

Dube, S. R., Feliti, V. J., Dong, M., Giles, W. H. & Anda, R. F. (2003). The impact of adverse childhood experiences on health problems: Evidence from four birth cohorts dating back to 1900. *Preventive Medicine*, *37*, 268–77.

Durkheim, E. (1897). *Suicide: A study in sociology.* Translation by John A. Spaulding and George Simpson, 1952. London: Routledge & Kegan.

Edmondson, A. J., Brennan, C. A. & House, A. O. (2016). Non-suicidal reasons for self-harm: A systematic review of self-reported accounts. *Journal of Affective Disorders, 191,* 109–17.

Edwards, M. J., Adams, R. A., Brown, H., Pareés, I. & Friston, K. J. (2012). A Bayesian account of "hysteria." *Brain, 135,* 3495–3512.

Ehrlich, S., Breeze, J. L., Hesdorffer, D. C., Noam, G. G., Hong, X., Alban, R. L., Davis, S. E. & Renshaw, P. F. (2005). White matter hyperintensities and their association with suicidality in depressed young adults. *Journal of Affective Disorders, 86,* 281–7.

Ehrlich, S., Noam, G. G., Lyoo, I. K., Kwon, B. J., Clark, M. A. & Renshaw, P. F. (2004). White matter hyperintensities and their associations with suicidality in psychiatrically hospitalized children and adolescents. *Journal of the American Academy of Child and Adolescent Psychiatry, 43,* 770–6.

Eisenberger, N. I. (2012). The neural bases of social pain: Evidence for shared representations with physical pain. *Psychosomatic Medicine, 74,* 126–35.

Engelberg, H. (1992). Low serum cholesterol and suicide. *Lancet, 339,* 727–9.

Evans, J., Williams, J. M. G., O'Loughlin, S. & Howells, K. (1992). Autobiographical memory and problem solving strategies of parasuicide patients. *Psychological Medicine, 22,* 399–405.

Fan, T., Wu, X., Yao, L. & Dong, Y. (2013). Abnormal baseline brain activity in suicidal and non-suicidal patients with major depressive disorder. *Neuroscience Letters, 534,* 35–40.

Fardet, L., Petersen, I. & Nazareth, I. (2012). Suicidal behavior and severe neuropsychiatric disorders following glucocorticoid therapy in primary care. *American Journal of Psychiatry, 169,* 491–7.

Feldman, H. & Friston, K. J. (2010). Attention, uncertainty, and free-energy. *Frontiers in Human Neuroscience, 4,* 215.

Fergusson, D. M., Boden, J. M. & Horwood, L. J. (2008). Exposure to childhood sexual and physical abuse and adjustment in early adulthood. *Child Abuse & Neglect, 32,* 607–19.

Fergusson, D. M., Woodward, L. J. & Horwood, L. J. (2000). Risk factors and life processes associated with the onset of suicidal behaviour during adolescence and early adulthood. *Psychological Medicine, 30,* 23–39.

Fink, M., Kellner, C. H. & McCall, W. V. (2014). The role of ECT in suicide prevention. *Journal of ECT, 30,* 5–9.

Finkelstein, Y., MacDonald, E. M., Hollands, S., Sivilotti, M. L. A., Hutson, J. R., Mamdani, M. M., Koren, G. & Juurlink, D. N., for the Canadian

Drug Safety and Effectiveness Research Network (CDSERN) (2015). Risk of suicide following deliberate self-poisoning. *JAMA Psychiatry*, 72, 570–5.

Fiori, L. M. & Turecki, G. (2011). Epigenetic regulation of spermidine/spermine N^1-acetyltransferase (SAT1) in suicide. *Journal of Psychiatric Research*, 45, 1229–1235.

Fitzgerald, M. L., Kassir, S. A., Underwood, M. D., Bakalian, M. J., Mann, J. J. & Arango, V. (2017). Dysregulation of striatal dopamine receptor binding in suicide. *Neuropsychopharmacology*, 42, 974–82.

Fjeldsted, R., Teasdale, T. W., Jensen, M. & Erlangsen, A. (2016). Suicide in relation to the experience of stressful life events: A population-based study. *Archives of Suicide Research.* Epub ahead of print.

Flegr, J. (2013). How and why Toxoplasma makes us crazy. *Trends in Parasitology*, 29, 156–63.

Forman, E. M., Berk, M. S., Henriques, G. R., Brown, G. K. & Beck, A. T. (2004). History of multiple suicide attempts as a behavioural marker of severe psychopathology. *American Journal of Psychiatry*, 161, 437–43.

Fountoulakis, K. N. (2016). Suicide and the economic situation in Europe: Are we experiencing the development of a "reverse stigma"? *British Journal of Psychiatry*, 208, 273–4.

Fragoso, Y. D., Frota, E. R., Lopes, J. S., Noal, J. S., Giacomo, M. C. & Gomes, S. (2010). Severe depression, suicide attempts, and ideation during the use of interferon beta by patients with multiple sclerosis. *Clinical Neuropharmacology*, 33, 312–16.

Friedman, R. A. (2014). Antidepressants' black box warning – 10 years later. *New England Journal of Medicine*, 371, 1666–8.

Friston, K. (2005). A theory of cortical responses. *Philosophical Transactions of the Royal Society B*, 360, 815–36.

Friston, K. J. (2010). The free-energy principle: A unified brain theory? *Nature Reviews Neuroscience*, 11, 21–2.

(2012). Prediction, perception and agency. *International Journal of Psychophysiology*, 83, 248–52.

Friston, K. J., Rigoli, F., Ognibene, D., Mathys, C., Fitzgerald, T. & Pezzulo, G. (2015). Active inference and epistemic value. *Cognitive Neuroscience*, 6, 187–224.

Friston, K. J., Stephan, K. E., Montague, R. & Dolan, R. J. (2014). Computational psychiatry: The brain as a phantastic organ. *Lancet Psychiatry*, 1, 148–58.

Friston, K., Thornton, C. & Clark, A. (2012). Free-energy minimization and the dark-room problem. *Frontiers in Psychology*, 3, 1–7.

Fuchs, I., Ansorge, U, Huber-Huber, C., Höflich, A. & Lanzenberger, R. (2015). S-ketamine influences strategic allocation of attention but not exogenous capture of attention. *Consciousness and Cognition, 35,* 282–94.

Ganan ça, L., Oquendo, M. A., Tyrka, A. R., Cisneros-Trujillo, S., Mann, J. J. & Sublette, M. E. (2016). The role of cytokines in the pathophysiology of suicidal behaviour. *Psychoneuroendocrinology, 63,* 296–310.

Garrett, N., Sharot, T., Faulkner, P., Korn, C. W., Roiser, J. P. & Dolan, R. J. (2014). Losing the rose-tinted glasses: Neural substrates of unbiased belief updating in depression. *Frontiers in Human Neuroscience, 8,* 639.

Geoffroy, M. C., Gunnell, D. & Power, C. (2014). Prenatal and childhood antecedents of suicide: 50-year follow-up of the 1958 British Birth Cohort study. *Psychological Medicine, 44,* 1245–56.

George, M. S., Raman, R., Benedek, D., Pelic, C., Grammer, G, Stokes, K., Schmidt, M., Spiegel, C., Dealmeida, N., Beaver, K. L., Borckardt, J. J., Sun, X., Jain, S. & Stein, M. B. (2014). A two-site pilot randomized 3-day trial of high dose left prefrontal repetitive transcranial magnetic stimulation (rTMS) for suicidal inpatients. *Brain Stimulation, 7,* 421–31.

Geulayov, G., Kapur, N., Turnbull, P., Clements, C., Waters, K., Ness, J., Townsend, E. & Hawton, K. (2016). Epidemiology and trends in non-fatal self-harm in three centres in England 2000–2012: Findings from the Multicentre Study of Self-Harm in England. *British Medical Journal Open, 6,* e010538.

Geurts, D. E. M., Huys, Q. J. M., De Ouden, H. E. M. & Cools, R. (2013). Aversive Pavlovian control of instrumental behavior in humans. *Journal of Cognitive Neuroscience, 25,* 1428–41.

Giakoumatis, C. I., Tandon, N., Shaha, J., Mathew, I. T., Brady, R. O., Clementz, B. A., pearlson, G. D., Thaker, G. K., Tamminga, C. A., Sweeney, J. A. & Keshavan, M. S. (2013). Are structural brain abnormalities associated with suicidal behaviour in patients with psychotic disorders? *Journal of Psychiatric Research, 47,* 1389–95.

Gibbons, R. D., Hur, K., Bhaumik, D. K. & Mann, J. J. (2005). The relationship between antidepressant medication use and rate of suicide. *Archives of General Psychiatry, 62,* 165–72.

Gibbs, L. M., Dombrovski, A. Y., Morse, J., Siegle, G. J., Houck, P. R. & Szanto, K. (2009). When the solution is part of the problem: Problem solving in elderly suicide attempters. *International Journal of Geriatric Psychiatry, 24,* 1396–1404.

Gilbert, P. & Allan, S. (1998). The role of defeat and entrapment (arrested flight) in depression: An exploration of an evolutionary view. *Psychological Medicine, 28,* 585–98.

Gomez, S. H., Tse, J., Wang, Y., Turner, B., Millner, A. J., Nock, M. K. & Dunn, E. C. (2017). Are there sensitive periods when child maltreatment substantially elevates suicide risk? Results from a nationally representative sample of adolescents. *Depression and Anxiety*, *34*, 734–41.

Goodman, M., Hazlett, E. A., Avedon, J. B., Siever, D. R., Chu, K. W. & New, A.S. (2011). Anterior cingulate volume reduction in adolescents with borderline personality disorder and co-morbid major depression. *Journal of Psychiatric Research*, *45*, 803–7.

Gorlyn, M., Keilp, J. G., Oquendo, M. A., Burke, A. K. & Mann, J. J. (2013). Iowa gambling task performance in currently depressed suicide attempters. *Psychiatry Research*, *207*, 150–7.

Gorlyn, M., Keilp, J., Burke, A., Oquendo, M. A., Mann, J. J. & Grunebaum, M. (2015). Treatment-related improvement in neuropsychological functioning in suicidal depressed patients: Paroxetine vs. bupropion. *Psychiatry Research*, *225*, 407–12.

Gosnell, S. N., Velasquez, K. M., Molfese, P. J., Madan, A., Fowler, J. C., Frueh, B. C., Baldwin, P. R. & Salas, R. (2016). Prefrontal cortex, temporal cortex and hippocampus volume are affected in suicidal psychiatric patients. *Psychiatry Research Neuroimaging*, *256*, 250–6.

Gozzi, M., Dashow, E. M., Thurm, A., Swedo, S. E. & Zink, C. F. (2017). Effects of oxytocin and vasopressin on preferential brain responses to negative social feedback. *Neuropsychopharmacology*, *42*, 1409–19.

Graae, F., Tenke, G., Bruder, G., Rotheram, M. J., Placentini, J., Castro-Blanco, D., Leite, P. & Towey, J. (1996). Abnormality of EEG alpha wave asymmetry in female adolescent suicide attempters. *Biological Psychiatry*, *40*, 706–13.

Grabe, H. J., Wittfeld, K., Van der Auwera, S., Janowitz, D., Hegenscheid, K., Habes, M., Homuth, G., Barnow, S., John, U., Nauck, M., Völzke, H., Meyer zu Schwabedissen, H., Freyberger, H. J. & Hosten, N. (2016). Effect of the interaction between childhood abuse and rs1360780 of the FKBP5 gene on gray matter volume in a general population sample. *Human Brain Mapping*, *37*, 1602–13.

Grandclerc, S., De Labrouhe, D., Spodenkiewicz, M., Lachal, J. & Moro M. R. (2016). Relations between non-suicidal self-injury and suicidal behavior in adolescence: A systematic review. *PLoS One*, *11*, e0153760.

Gray, A. L., Hyde, T. M., Deep-Soboslay, A., Kleinman, J. E. & Sodhi, M. S. (2015). Sex differences in glutamate receptor gene expression in major depression and suicide. *Molecular Psychiatry*, *20*, 1057–68.

Greenwald, A. G., Nosek, B. A. & Banaji, M. R. (2003). Understanding and using the Implicit Association Test: I. An improved scoring algorithm. *Journal of Personality and Social Psychology*, *85*, 197–216.

Groschwitz, R.C., Plener, P. L., Groen, G., Bonenberger, M. & Abler, B. (2016). Differential neural processing of social exclusion in adolescents with non-suicidal self-injury. *Psychiatry Research Neuroimaging, 255*, 43–9.

Grunebaum, M. F., Ellis, S. P., Duan, N., Burke, A. K., Oquendo, M. A. & Mann, J. J. (2012). Pilot randomized clinical trial of an SSRI vs bupropion: Effects on suicidal behavior, ideation, and mood in major depression. *Neuropsychopharmacology, 37*, 697–706.

Guintivano, J., Brown, T., Newcomer, A., Jones, M., Cox, O., Maher, B. S., Eaton, W. W., Payne, J. L., Wilcox, H. C. & Kaminsky, Z. A. (2014). Identification and replication of a combined epigenetic and genetic biomarker predicting suicide and suicidal behaviors. *American Journal of Psychiatry, 171*, 1287–96.

Gunnell, D., Löfving, S., Gustafsson, J. E. & Allebeck, P. (2011). School performance and risk of suicide in early adulthood: Follow-up of two national cohorts of Swedish schoolchildren. *Journal of Affective Disorders, 131*, 104–12.

Hafeman, D. M., Merranko, J., Goldstein, T. R., Axelson, D., Goldstein, B. I., Monk, K., Hickey, M. B., Sakolsky, D., Diler, R., Iyengar, S., Brent, D. A., Kupfer, D. J., Kattan, M. W. & Birmaher, B. (2017). Assessment of a person-level risk calculator to predict new-onset bipolar spectrum disorder in youth at familial risk. *JAMA Psychiatry, 74*, 841–7.

Hafenbrack, A. C., Kinias, Z. & Barsade, S. G. (2014). Debiasing the mind through meditation: Mindfulness and the sunk-cost bias. *Psychological Science, 25*, 369–76.

Hagan, C. R., Ribeiro, J. D. & Joiner, T. E. (2016). Present status and future prospects of the interpersonal-psychological theory of suicidal behavior. In R. C. O'Connor & J. Pirkis (Eds.), *The international handbook of suicide prevention*. Chichester: Wiley.

Haghighi, F., Galfalvy, H., Chen, S., Huang, Y. Y., Cooper, T. B., Burke, A. K., Oquendo, M. A., Mann, J. J. & Sublette, M. E. (2015). DNA methylation perturbations in genes involved in polyunsaturated fatty acid biosynthesis associated with depression and suicide risk. *Frontiers in Neurology, 6*, 192.

Haghighi, F., Xin, Y., Chanrion, B., O'Donnell, A. H., Ge, Y., Dwork, A. J., Arango, V. & Mann, J. J. (2014). Increased DNA methylation in the suicide brain. *Dialogues in Clinical Neuroscience, 16*, 430–8.

Hardy, D. J., Hinkin, C. H., Levine, A. J., Castellon, S. A. & Lam, M. N. (2006). Risky decision making assessed with the gambling task in adults with HIV. *Neuropsychology, 20*, 355–60.

Harkavy-Friedman, J. M., Keilp, J. G., Grunebaum, M. F., Sher, L., Printz, D., Burke, A. K., Mann, J. J. & Oquendo, M. (2006). Are BPI and BPII suicide attempters distinct neuropsychologically? *Journal of Affective Disorders, 94*, 255–9.

Haroon, E., Fleischer, C. C., Felger, J. C., Chen, X., Woolwine, B. J., Patel, T., Hu, X. P. & Miller, A. H. (2016). Conceptual convergence: Increased inflammation is associated with increased basal ganglia glutamate in patients with major depression. *Molecular Psychiatry*, *21*, 1351–7.

Harper, S., Charters, T. J., Strumpf, E. C., Galea, S. & Nandi, A. (2015). Economic downturns and suicide mortality in the USA, 1989–2010: Observational study. *International Journal of Epidemiology*, *44*, 956–66.

Harris, E. C. & Barraclough, B. (1997). Suicide as an outcome of mental disorders: A meta-analysis. *British Journal of Psychiatry*, *170*, 205–28.

Harrison, N. A., Voon, V., Cercignani, M., Cooper, E. A., Pessiglione, M. & Critchley, H. D. (2016). A neurocomputational account of how inflammation enhances sensitivity to punishments versus rewards. *Biological Psychiatry*, *80*, 73–81.

Haws, C. A., Gray, D. D., Yurgelun-Todd, D. A., Moskos, M., Meyer, L. J. & Renshaw, P. F. (2009). The possible effect of altitude on regional variation in suicide rates. *Medical Hypotheses*, *73*, 587–90.

Hawton, K. & van Heeringen, K. (2009). Suicide. *The Lancet*, *73*, 1372–81.

Hawton, K., Appleby, L., Platt, S., Foster, T., Cooper, J., Malmberg, A. & Simkin, S. (1998). The psychological autopsy approach to studying suicide: A review of methodological issues. *Journal of Affective Disorders*, *50*, 269–76.

Hawton, K., Malmberg, A. & Simkin, S. (2004). Suicide in doctors: A psychological autopsy study. *Journal of Psychosomatic Research*, *57*, 1–4.

Hawton, K., Simkin, S., Rue, J., Haw, C., Barbour, F., Clements, A., Sakarovitch, C. & Deeks, J. (2002). Suicide in female nurses in England and Wales. *Psychological Medicine*, *32*, 239–50.

Hawton, K., Witt, K. G., Taylor Salisbury, T. L., Arensman, E., Gunnell, D., Hazel, P., Townsend, E. & van Heeringen, K. (2016). Psychosocial interventions for self-harm in adults. *Cochrane Database of Systematic Reviews*, *5*, CD012189.

Hebart, M. N. & Glätscher, J. (2015). Serotonin and dopamine differentially affect appetitive and aversive general Pavlovian-to-instrumental transfer. *Psychopharmacology*, *232*, 437–51.

Heim, C., Shugart, M., Craighead, W. E. & Nemeroff, C. B. (2010). Neurobiological and psychiatric consequences of child abuse and neglect. *Developmental Psychobiology*, *52*, 671–90.

Heim, C., Young, L. J., Newport, D. J., Mietzko, T., Miller, A. H. & Nemeroff, C. B. (2009). Lower CSF oxytocin concentrations in women with a history of childhood abuse. *Molecular Psychiatry*, *14*, 954–8.

Helbich, M., Blüml, V., Leitner, M. & Kapusta, N. D. (2013). Does altitude moderate the impact of lithium on suicide? A spatial analysis in Austria. *Geospatial Health*, *7*, 209–18.

Hepburn, S. R., Barnhofer, T. & Williams, J. M. G. (2006). Effects of mood on how future events are generated and perceived. *Personality and Individual Differences*, *41*, 801–11.

Hetrick, S. E., McKenzie, J. E. & Cox, G. R. (2012). Newer generation antidepressants for depressive disorders in children and adolescents. *Cochrane Database of Systematic Reviews*, *11*, CD004851.

Hibbeln, J. R. & Salem, N. (1996). Risks of cholesterol-lowering therapies. *Biological Psychiatry*, *40*, 686–7.

Hibbeln, J. R., Umhau, J. C., George, D. T., Shoaf, S. E., Linnoila, M. & Salem, N. (2000). Plasma total cholesterol concentrations do not predict cerebrospinal fluid neurotransmitter metabolites: Implications for the biophysical role of highly unsaturated fatty acids. *American Journal of Clinical Nutrition*, *71*, 331S–338S.

Hitsman, B., Spring, B., Pingitore, R., Munafo, M. & Hedeker, D. (2007). Effect of tryptophan depletion on the attentional salience of smoking cues. *Psychopharmacology*, *192*, 317–24.

Hodgkinson, S., Steyer, J., Kaschka, W. P. & Jandl, M. (2016). Electroencephalographic risk markers of suicidal behavior. In W. P. Kaschka & D. Rujescu (Eds.), *Biological aspects of suicidal behavior*. Basel: Karger.

Hoehne, A., Richard-Devantoy, S., Ding, Y., Turecki, G. & Jollant, F. (2015). First-degree relatives of suicide completers have impaired decision-making but functional cognitive control. *Journal of Psychiatric Research*, *68*, 192–7.

Höflich, A., Hahn, A., Küblböck, M., Kranz, G. S., Vanicek, T., Windischberger, C., Saria, A., Kasper, S., Winkler, D. & Lanzenberger, R. (2015). Ketamine-induced modulation of the thalamo-cortical network in healthy volunteers as a model for schizophrenia. *International Journal of Neuropsychopharmacology*, *18*, 1–11.

Homberg, J. R. (2013). Serotonin and decision making processes. *Neuroscience and Biobehavioral Reviews*, *36*, 218–36.

Horga, G., Schatz, K. C., Abi-Dargham, A. & Peterson, B. S. (2014). Deficits in predictive coding underlie hallucinations in schizophrenia. *Journal of Neuroscience*, *34*, 8072–82.

Huber, R. S., Kim, N., Renshaw, C. E., Renshaw, P. F. & Kondo, D. G. (2014). Relationship between altitude and lithium in groundwater in the United States of America: Results of a 1992–2003 study. *Geospatial Health*, *9*, 231–5.

Hunter, E. C. & O'Connor, R. C. (2003). Hopelessness and future thinking in parasuicide: The role of perfectionism. *British Journal of Clinical Psychology*, *42*, 355–65.

Huys, Q. J. M., Eshel, N., O'Nions, E., Sheridan, L., Dayan, P. & Roiser, J. P. (2012). Bonsai trees in your head: How the Pavlovian system sculpts goal-directed choices by pruning decision trees. *PLoS Computational Biology*, *8*, e1002410.

Hwang, J. P., Lee, T. W., Tsai, S. J., Chen, T. J., Yang, C. H., Ling, J. F. & Tsai, C. F. (2010). Cortical and subcortical abnormalities in late-onset depression with history of suicide attempts investigated with MRI and voxel-based morphometry. *Journal of Geriatric Psychiatry and Neurology*, *23*, 171–84.

Hyafil, A. & Koechlin, E. (2016). A neurocomputational model of human frontopolar cortex function. *BioRxiv*. Epub ahead of print.

Iglesias, C., Saiz, P. A., Garcia-Portilla, P. & Bobes, J. (2016). Antipsychotics. In P. Courtet (Ed.), *Understanding suicide: From diagnosis to personalized treatment*. Heidelberg: Springer.

Ingram, R. E. & Luxton, D. D. (2005). Vulnerability-stress models. In B. L. Hankin & J. R. Z. Abela (Eds.), *Development of psychopathology: A vulnerability-stress perspective*. Los Angeles, CA: Sage Publications.

Ionescu, D. F., Swee, M. B., Pavone, K. J., Taylor, N., Akeju, O., Baer, L., Nyer, M., Cassano, P., Mischoulon, D., Alpert, J. E., Brown, E. N., Nock, M. K., Fava, M. & Cusin, C. (2016). Rapid and sustained reductions in current suicidal ideation following repeated doses of intravenous ketamine: Secondary analyses of an open-label study. *Journal of Clinical Psychiatry*, *77*, e719–e725.

Jee, H. J., Cho, C. H., Lee, Y. J., Choi, N., An, H. & Lee, H. J. (2017). Solar radiation increases suicide rate after adjusting for other climate factors in South Korea. *Acta Psychiatrica Scandinavica*, *135*, no. 3, 219–27.

Jia, Z., Wang, Y., Huang, X. et al. (2014). Impaired frontothalamic circuitry in suicidal patients with depression revealed by diffusion tensor imaging at 3.0 T. *Journal of Psychiatry and Neuroscience*, *38*, 130023.

Johnson, J., Tarrier, N. & Gooding, P. (2008). An investigation of aspects of the cry of pain model of suicide risk: The role of defeat in impairing memory. *Behaviour Research and Therapy*, *46*, 968–75.

Johnston, J. A., Y., Wang, F., Liu, J., Blond, B. N., Wallace, A., Liu, J., spencer, L., Cox Lippard, E. T., Purves, K. L., Landeros-Weisenbergern, A., Hermes, E., Pittman, B., Zhang, S., King, R., Martin, A., Oquendo, M. A. & Blumberg, H. (2017). Multimodal neuroimaging of frontolimbic structure and function associated with suicide attempt in adolescents and young adults with bipolar disorder. *American Journal of Psychiatry*, *174*, 667–75.

Jokinen, J. & Nordström, P. (2009). HPA axis hyperactivity and attempted suicide in young adult mood disorder inpatients. *Journal of Affective Disorders*, *116*, 117–20.

Jokinen, J., Chatzitofis, A., Hellström, C, Nordström, P., Uynas-Moberg, K. & Asberg, M. (2012). Low CSF oxytocine reflects high intent in suicide attempters. *Psychoneuroendocrinology*, *37*, 482–90.

Jokinen, J., Nordström, A. L. & Nordström, P. (2010). Cholesterol, CSF 5-HIAA, violence and intent in suicidal men. *Psychiatry Research*, *178*, 217–19.

Jollant, F., Bellivier, F., Leboyer, M., Astruc, B., Torres, S., Verdier, R., Castelnau, D., Malafosse, A. & Courtet, P. (2005). Impaired decision making in suicide attempters. *American Journal of Psychiatry*, *162*, 304–10.

Jollant, F., Guillaume, S., Jaussent, I., Bechara, A. & Courtet, P. (2013). When knowing what to do is not sufficient to make good decisions: Deficient use of explicit understanding in remitted patients with histories of suicidal acts. *Psychiatry Research*, *210*, no. 2, 485–90.

Jollant, F., Guillaume, S., Jaussent, I., Bellivier, F., Leboyer, M., Castelnau, D., Malafosse, A. & Courtet, P. (2007a). Psychiatric diagnoses and personality traits associated with disadvantageous decision-making. *European Psychiatry*, *22*, 455–61.

Jollant, F., Guillaume, S., Jaussent, I., Castelnau, D., Malafosse, A. & Courtet, P. (2007b). Impaired decision making in suicide attempters may increase the risk of problems in affective relationships. *Journal of Affective Disorders*, *99*, 59–62.

Jollant, F., Lawrence, N. S., Giampietro, V., Brammer, M. J., Fullana, M. A., Drapier, D., Courtet, P. & Philips, M. L. (2008). Orbitofrontal cortex response to angry faces in men with histories of suicide attempts. *American Journal of Psychiatry*, *165*, 740–8.

Jollant, F., Lawrence, N. S., Olié, E., O'Daly, O., Malafosse, A., Courtet, P. & Philips, M. L. (2010). Decreased activation of lateral orbitofrontal cortex during risky choices under uncertainty is associated with disadvantageous decision-making and suicidal behavior. *Neuroimage*, *51*, 1275–81.

Jollant, F., Lawrence, N.L., Olié, E., Guillaume, S. & Courtet, P. (2011). The suicidal mind and brain: A review of neuropsychological and neuroimaging studies. *The World Journal of Biological Psychiatry*, *12*, 319–39.

Jollant, F., Near, J., Turecki, G. & Richard-Devantoy, S. (2017). Spectroscopy markers of suicidal risk in depressed patients. *Progress in Neuropsychopharmacology and Biological Psychiatry*, *73*, 64–71.

Jonas, J. M. & Hearron, A. E. Jr. (1996). Alprazolam and suicidal ideation: A meta-analysis of controlled trials in the treatment of depression. *Journal of Clinical Psychopharmacology, 16*, 208–11.

Jovev, M., Garner, B., Phillips, L., Velakoulis, D., Wood, S. J., Jackson, H. J., Pantelis, C., McGorry, P. D. & Chanen, A. M. (2008). An MRI study of pituitary volume and parasuicidal behavior in teenagers with first-presentation borderline personality disorder. *Psychiatry Research Neuroimaging, 162*, 273–7.

Kaess, M., Hille, M., Parter, P., Maser-Gluth, C., Resch, F. & Brunner, R. (2012). Alterations in the neuroendocrinological stress response to acute psychosocial stress in adolescents engaging in nonsuicidal self-injury. *Psychoneuroendocrinology, 37*, 157–61.

Kaminsky, Z., Wilcox, H. C., Eaton, W. W., Van Eck, K., Kilaru, V., Jovanovic, T., Klengel, T. Bradley, B., Binder, E., Ressler, K. J. & Smith, A. K. ((2015). Epigenetic and genetic variation at SKA2 predict suicidal behaviour and post-traumatic stress disorder. *Translational Psychiatry, 5*, e627.

Kanai, R., Komura, Y., Shipp, S. & Friston, K. J. (2015). Cerebral hierarchies: Predictive processing, precision and the pulvinar. *Philosophical Transactions of the Royal Society B, 370*, 20140169.

Kang, H. J., Kim, J. M., Lee, J. Y., Kim, S. Y., Bae, K. Y. & Kim, S. W. (2013). BDNF promoter methylation and suicidal behavior in depressive patients. *Journal of Affective Disorders, 151*, 679–85.

Kapur, N., Cooper, J., O'Connor, R. C. & Hawton, K. (2013). Non-suicidal self-injury versus attempted suicide: New diagnosis or false dichotomy? *British Journal of Psychiatry, 202*, 326–8.

Kapur, N., Steeg, S., Webb, R, Haigh, M., Bergen, H, Hawton, K., Ness, J., Waters, K. & Cooper, J. (2013). Does clinical management improve outcomes following self-harm? Results from the Multicentre Study of Self-Harm in England. *PLoS One, 8*, e70434.

Karlsson, H., Hirvonen, J. & Kajander, J. (2010). Research letter: Psychotherapy increases brain serotonin 5-HT1A receptors in patients with major depressive disorder. *Psychological Medicine, 40*, 523–8.

Kaviani, H., Rahimi, M., Rahimi-Darabad, P., Kamyar, K. & Naghavi, H. (2003). How autobiographical memory deficits affect problem-solving in depressed patients. *Acta Medica Iranica, 41*, 194–8.

Kaviani, H., Rahimi, P. & Naghavi, H. R. (2004). Iranian depressed patients attempting suicide showed impaired memory and problem-solving. *Archives of Iranian Medicine, 7*, 113–17.

Kaviani, H., Rahimi-Darabad, P. & Naghavi, H. R. (2005). Autobiographical memory retrieval and problem-solving deficits of Iranian depressed patients attempting suicide. *Journal of Psychopathology and Behavioral Assessment*, *27*, 39–44.

Keilp, J. G., Beers, S. R., Burke, A. K., Melhem, N. M., Oquendo, M. A., Brent, D. A. & Mann, J. J. (2014). Neuropsychological deficits in past suicide attempters with varying levels of depression severity. *Psychological Medicine*, *44*, 2965–74.

Keilp, J. G., Gorlyn, M., Oquendo, M. A., Burke, A. K. & Mann, J. J. (2008). Attention deficit in depressed suicide attempters. *Psychiatry Research*, *159*, 7–17.

Keilp, J., Gorlyn, M., Oquendo, M. A. & Mann, J. J. (2006). Aggressiveness, not impulsiveness or hostility distinguishes suicide attempters with major depression. *Psychological Medicine*, *36*, 1779–88.

Keilp, J. G., Gorlyn, M., Russell, M. Oquendo, M. A., Burke, A. K., Harkavy-Friedman, J. & Mann, J. J. (2013). Neuropsychological function and suicidal behavior: Attentional control, memory and executive dysfunction in suicide attempt. *Psychological Medicine*, *43*, 539–51.

Keilp, J. G., Oquendo, M. A., Stanley, B. H., Burke, A. K., Cooper, T. B., Malone, K. M. & Mann, J. J. (2010). Future suicide attempt and responses to serotonergic challenge. *Neuropsychopharmacology*, *35*, 1063–72.

Keilp, J. G., Sackeim, H. A., Brodsky, B. S., Oquendo, M. A., Malone, K. M. & Mann, J. J. (2001). Neuropsychological dysfunction in depressed suicide attempters. *American Journal of Psychiatry*, *158*, 735–41.

Keilp, J. G., Stanley, B. H., Beers, S. R., Melhem, N. M., Burke, A. K., Cooper, T. B., Oquendo, M. A., Brent, D. A. & Mann, J. J. (2016). Further evidence of low baseline cortisol levels in suicide attempters. *Journal of Affective Disorders*, *190*, 187–92.

Keller, S., Sarchiapone, M., Zarrilli, F., Videtic, A., Ferraro, A. & Carli, V. (2010). Increased promoter methylation in the Wernicke area of suicide subjects. *Archives of General Psychiatry*, *67*, 258–67.

Kelly, T. M. & Mann, J. J. (1996). Validity of DSM-III-R diagnosis by psychological autopsy: A comparison with clinician ante-mortem diagnosis. *Acta Psychiatrica Scandinavica*, *94*, 337–43.

Kercher, A. & Rapee, R. M. (2009). A test of a cognitive diathesis–stress generation pathway in early adolescent depression. *Journal of Abnormal Child Psychology*, *37*, 845–55.

Kessler, R. C., Borges, G. & Walters, E. E. (1999). Prevalence of and risk factors for lifetime suicide attempts in the National Comorbidity Survey. *Archives of General Psychiatry*, *56*, 617–26.

Kessler, R. C., McLaughlin, K. A., Green, J. G., Gruber, M. J., Sampson, N. A., Zaslavsky, A. M., Aguilar-Gaxiola, S., Alhamzawi, A. O., Alonso,

J., Angermeyer, M., Benjet, C., Bromet, E., Chatterji, S., de Girolamo, G., Demyttenaere, K., Fayyad, J., Florescu, S., Gal, G., Gureje, O., Haro, J. M., Karam, E.G., Kawakami, N., Lee, S., Lépine, J. P., Ormel, J., Posada-Villa, J., Sagar, R., Tsang, A., Ustün, T. B., Vassilev, S., Viana, M. C. & Williams, D. R. (2010). Childhood adversities and adult psychopathology in the WHO World Mental Health Surveys. *British Journal of Psychiatry*, *197*, no. 5, 378–85.

Kessler, R. C., McLaughlin, K. A., Green, J. G., Gruber, M. J., Sampson, N. A., Zaslavsky, A. M., Aguilar-Gaxiola, S., Alhamzawi, A. O., Alonso, J., Angermeyer, M., Benjet, C., Bromet, E., Chatterji, S., de Girolamo, G., Demyttenaere, K., Fayyad, J., Florescu, S., Gal, G., Gureje, O., Haro, J. M, Hu, C., Karam, E. G., Kawakami, N., Lee, S., Lépine, J. P., Ormel, J., Posada-Villa, J., Roberts, S., Keers, R., Lester, K. J., Coleman, J. R., Breen, G., Arendt, K., Blatter-Meunier, J., Cooper, P., Creswell, C., Fjermestad, K., Havik, O. E., Herren, C., Hogendoorn, S. M., Hudson, J. L., Krause, K., Lyneham, H. J., Morris, T., Nauta, M., Rapee, R. M., Rey, Y., Schneider, S., Schneider, S. C., Silverman, W. K., Thastum, M., Thirlwall, K., Waite, P., Eley, T. C. & Wong, C. C. (2015a). HPA axis related genes and response to psychological therapies: Genetics and epigenetics. *Depression and Anxiety*, *32*, 861–70.

Kessler, R. C., Warner, C. H., Ivany, C., Petukhova, M. V., Rose, S., Bromet, J., Brown, M. et al. (2015b). Predicting suicides after psychiatric hospitalization in US Army soldiers: The Army Study to Assess Risk and Resilience in Service Members (Army STARRS). *JAMA Psychiatry*, *72*, 49–57.

Khan, M., Asad, N. & Syed, E. (2016). Suicide in Asia: Epidemiology, risk factors and prevention. In R. C. O'Connor & J. Pirkis (Eds.), *The international handbook of suicide prevention*. Chichester: Wiley.

Kim, B., Oh, J., Kim, M. K., Lee, S., Tae, W. S., Kim, C. M., Choi, T. K. & Lee, S. H. (2015). White matter alterations are associated with suicide attempt in patients with panic disorder. *Journal of Affective Disorders*, *175*, 139–46.

Kim, H. S., Sherman, D. K., Taylor, S. E., Sasaki, J. Y., Chu, T. Q., Ryu, C., Suh, E. M. & Xu, J. (2010). Culture, serotonin receptor polymorphism and locus of attention. *Social and Cognitive Affective Neuroscience*, *5*, 21–218.

King, D. A., Conwell, Y., Cox, C., Henderson, R. E., Denning, D. G. & Caine, E. D. (2000). A neuropsychological comparison of depressed suicide attempters and non-attempters. *Journal of Neuropsychiatry and Clinical Neurosciences*, *12*, 64–70.

Klengel, T., Mehta, D., Anacker, C., Rex Haffner, M., Prüssner, J. C., Pariante, C. M., Pace, T. W. W., Mercer, K. B., Mayberg, H. S.,

Bradley, B., Nemeroff, C. B., Holsboer, F., Heim, C. M., Ressler, K. J., Rein, T. & Binder, E. B. (2013). Allele-specific FKBP5 DNA demethylation mediates gene-childhood trauma interactions. *Nature Neuroscience*, *16*, 33–41.

Klonsky, E. D. (2011). Non-suicidal self-injury in United States adults: Prevalence, socio-demographics, topography and functions. *Psychological Medicine*, *41*, 1981–6.

Kluen, L. M., Nixon, P., Agorastos, A., Wiedermann, K. & Schwabe, L. (2016). Impact of stress and glucocorticoids on schema-based learning. *Neuropsychopharmacology*, *42*, 1254–61.

Korpi, E. R., Kleinman, J. E. & Wyatt, R. J. (1988). GABA concentrations in forebrain areas of suicide victims. *Biological Psychiatry*, *32*, 109–14.

Krajniak, M., Miranda, R. & Wheeler, A. (2013). Rumination and pessimistic certainty as mediators of the relation between lifetime suicide attempt history and future suicidal ideation. *Archives of Suicide Research*, *17*, 196–211.

Kremen, W. S., Prom-Wormley, E., Panizzon, M. S., Eyler, L. T., Fischl, B., Neale, M. C., Franz, C. E., Lyons, M. J., Pacheco, J., Perry, M. E., Stevens, A., Schmitt, J. E., Grant, M. D., Seidman, L. J., Thermenos, H. W., Tsuang, M. T., Eisen, S. A., Dale, A. M. & Fennema-Notestine, C. (2010). Genetic and environmental influences on the size of specific brain regions in midlife: The VETSA MRI study. *NeuroImage*, *49*, 1213–23.

Krishnan, V. & Nestler, E. J. (2008). The molecular neurobiology of depression. *Nature*, *455*, 894–902.

Kundakovic, M., Gudsnuk, K., Herbstman, J. B., Tang, D., Perera, F. P. & Champagne, F. A. (2015). DNA methylation of BDNF as a biomarker of early-life adversity. *Proceedings of the National Academy of Sciences*, *112*, 6807–13.

Kuo, W. H., Gallo, J. J. & Eaton, W. W. (2004). Hopelessness, depression, substance disorder, and suicidality. *Social Psychiatry and Psychiatric Epidemiology*, *39*, 497–501.

Labonté, B., Suderman, M., Maussion, G., Lopez, J. P., Narro-Sanchez, L., Yerko, V., Mechawar, N., Szyf, M., Meaney, M. J. & Turecki, G. (2013). Genome-wide methylation changes in the brains of suicide completers. *American Journal of Psychiatry*, *170*, 511–20.

Labonté, B., Suderman, M., Maussion, G., Navaro, L., Yerko, V., Mahar, I., Bureau, A., Mechawar, N., Szyf, M., Meaney, M. J. & Turecki, G. (2012a). Genome-wide epigenetic regulation by early-life trauma. *Archives of General Psychiatry*, *69*, 722–31.

Labonté, B., Yerko, V., Gross, J., Mechawar, N., Meaney, M. J., Szyf, M. & Turecki, G. (2012b). Differential glucocorticoid receptor exon 1(B),

1(C), and 1(H) expression and methylation in suicide completers with a history of childhood abuse. *Biological Psychiatry, 72*, 41–8.

Large, M., Kaneson, M., Myles, N., Myles, H., Gunaratne, P. & Ryan, C. (2016). Meta-analysis of longitudinal cohort studies of suicide risk assessment among psychiatric patients: Heterogeneity in results and lack of improvement over time. *PLoS One, 11*, e0156322.

Lawson, R. P., Friston, K. J. & Rees, G. (2015). A more precise look at context in autism. *Proceedings of the National Academy of Sciences, 112*, E5226.

Lawson, R. P., Rees, G. & Friston, K. J. (2014). An aberrant precision account of autism. *Frontiers in Human Neuroscience, 8*, 302.

Le-Niculescu, H., Levey, D. F., Ayalew, M., Palmer, L., Gavrin, L. M., Jain, N., Winiger, E., Bhosrekar, S., Shankar, G., Radel, M., Bellanger, E., Duckworth, H., Olesek, K., Vergo, J., Schweitzer, R., Yard, M., Ballew, A., Shektar, A., Sandusky, G. E., Schork, N. J., Kurian, S. M., Salomon, D. R. & Niculescu, A. B. (2013). Discovery and validation of blood biomarkers for suicidality. *Molecular Psychiatry, 18*, 1249–64.

Lee, B. H. & Kim, Y. K. (2010). The roles of BDNF in the pathophysiology of major depression and in antidepressant treatment. *Psychiatry Investigation, 7*, 231–5.

(2011). Potential peripheral biological predictors of suicidal behavior in major depressive disorder. *Progress in Neuropsychopharmacology and Biological Psychiatry, 35*, 842–7.

Lee, R., Ferris, C., Van de Kar, L. D. & Coccaro, E. F. (2009). Cerebrospinal fluid oxytocin, life history of aggression, and personality disorder. *Psychoneuroendocrinology, 34*, 1567–73.

Lee, S. J., Kim, B., Oh, D., Kim, M. K., Kim, K. H., Bang, S. Y., Choi, T. K. & Lee, S. H. (2016). White matter alterations associated with suicide in patients with schizophrenia or schizophreniform disorder. *Psychiatry Research, 248*, 23–9.

Lee, Y. J., Kim, S., Gwak, R., Kim, S. J., Kang, S. G., Na, K. S., Son, Y. D. & Park, J. (2016). Decreased regional gray matter volume in suicide attempters compared to non-attempters with major depressive disorder. *Comprehensive Psychiatry, 67*, 59–65.

Legris, J., Links, P. S., van Reekum, R., Tannock, R. & Toplak, M. (2012). Executive function and suicidal risk in women with borderline personality disorder. *Psychiatry Research, 196*, 101–8.

Leibetseder, M. M., Rohrer, R. R., Mackinger, H. F. & Fartacek, R. R. (2006). Suicide attempts: Patients with and without affective disorder show impaired autobiographical memory specificity. *Cognition and Emotion, 20*, 516–26.

Leon, A. C., Friedman, R. A., Sweeney, J. A., Brown, R. P. & Mann, J. J. (1990). Statistitical issues in the identification of risk factors for suicidal behavior: The application of survival analysis. *Psychiatry Research, 31,* 99–108.

Levey, D. F., Niculescu, E. M., Le-Niculescu, H., Dainton, H. L., Phalen, P. L., Ladd, T. B., Weber, H., Belanger, E., Graham, D. L., Khan, F. N., Vanipenta, N. P., Stage, E. C., Ballew, A., Gelbart, T., Shekhar, A., Schork, N. J., Kurian, S. M., Sandusky, G. E., Salomon, D. R. & Niculescu, A. B. (2016). Understanding and predicting suicidality in women: Biomarkers and clinical risk assessment. *Molecular Psychiatry, 21,* 768–85.

Lewitzka, U., Severus, E., Bauer, R., Ritter, P., Müller-Oerlinghausen, B. & Bauer, M. (2015). The suicide prevention effect of lithium: More than 20 years of evidence – a narrative review. *International Journal of Bipolar Disorder, 3,* 15.

Leyton, M., Paquette, V., Gravel, P., Rosa-Neto, P., Weston, F., Diksic, M. & Benkelfat, C. (2006). α-[^{11}C]Methyl-L-tryptophan trapping in the orbital and ventromedial prefrontal cortex of suicide attempters. *European Neuropsychopharmacology, 16,* 220–3.

Li, D. & He, L. (2007). Meta-analysis supports association between serotonin transporter (5-HTT) and suicidal behavior. *Molecular Psychiatry, 12,* 47–54.

Li, J., Kuang, W. H., Zou, K., Deng, W., Li, T., Gong, Q. Y. & Sun, X. L. (2009). A proton magnetic spectroscopy research on hippocampus metabolisms in people with suicide-attempted depressions (in Chinese with English abstract). *Sichuan Da Xue Xue Bao Yi Xue Ban, 40,* 59–62.

Li, L. & Vlisides, P. E. (2016). Ketamine: Fifty years of modulating the mind. *Frontiers in Human Neuroscience, 10,* 612.

Lim, L., Radua, J. & Rubia, K. (2014). Gray matter abnormalities in childhood maltreatment: A voxel-wise meta-analysis. *American Journal of Psychiatry, 171,* 854–63.

Lin, G. Z., Li, L., Song, Y. F., Shen, Y. X., Shen, S. Q. & Ou, C. Q. (2016). The impact of ambient air pollution on suicide mortality: A case-crossover study in Guangzhou, China. *Environmental Health, 15,* 90.

Lin, P. Y. & Tsai, G. (2004). Association between serotonin transporter gene promoter polymorphism and suicide: Results of a meta-analysis. *Biological Psychiatry, 55,* 1023–30.

Lindqvist, D., Isaksson, A., Träskman-Bendz, L. & Brundin, L. (2008). Salivary cortisol and suicidal behavior: A follow-up study. *Psychoneuroendocrinology, 33,* 1061–8.

Lindström, M. B., Ryding, E., Bosson, P., Ahnlide, J.A., Rosén, I. & Träskman-Bendz, L. (2004). Impulsivity related to brain serotonin transporter binding capacity in suicide attempters. *European Neuropsychopharmacology*, *14*, 295–300.

Liu, D., Diorio, J., Tannenbaum, B., Caldji, C., Francis, D., Freedman, A., Sharma, S., Pearson, D., Plotsky, P. M. & Meaney, M. J. (1997). Maternal care, hippocampal glucocorticoid receptors, and hypothalamic-pituitary-adrenal responses to stress. *Science*, *277*, 1659–62.

Lockwood, J., Daley, D., Towsend, E. & Sayall, K. (2017). Impulsivity and self-harm in adolescence: A systematic review. *European Child and Adolescent Psychiatry*, *26*, 387–402.

Lopez-Larson, M., King, J. B., McGlade, E., Bueler, E., Stoeckel, A., Epstein, D. J. & Yurgelun-Todd, D. (2013). Enlarged thalamic volumes and increased fractional anisotropy in the thalamic radiations in veterans with suicide behaviors. *Frontiers in Psychiatry*, *4*, 83.

Ludwig, J. & Marcotte, D. E. (2005). Antidepressants, suicide, and drug regulation. *Journal of Policy Analysis and Management*, *24*, 259.

Lund-Sørensen, H., Benros, M. E., Madsen, T., Sørensen, H. J., Eaton, W. W., Postolache, T. T., Nordentoft, M. & Erlangsen, A. (2016). A nationwide cohort study of the association between hospitalization with infection and risk of death by suicide. *JAMA Psychiatry*, *73*, 912–19.

Lutz, P. E. & Turecki, G. (2014). DNA methylation and childhood maltreatment: From animal models to human studies. *Neuroscience*, *264*, 142–56.

Lutz, P. E., Tanti, A., Gasecka, A., Barnett-Burns, S., Kim, J. J., Zhou, Y., Chen, G. C., Wakid, M., Shaw, M., Almeida, D., Chay, M. A., Yang, J., Larivière, V., M'Boutchou, M. N., Van Kempen, L. C., Yerko, V., Prud'homme, J., Davoli, M. A., Vaillancourt, K., Théroux, J. F., Bramouillé, A., Zhang, T. Y., Meaney, M. J., Ernst, C., Côté, D., Mechawar, N. & Turecki, G. (2017). Association of a history of child abuse with impaired myelination in the anterior cingulate cortex: Convergent epigenetic, transcriptional, and morphological evidence. *American Journal of Psychiatry*. Epub ahead of print.

Lynch, P. J. (2010). Brain human sagittal section. Wikimedia Commons. https://commons.wikimedia.org/wiki/File:Serotonergic_neurons.svg.

Maciejewski, D. F., Creemers, H. E., Lynskey, M. T., Madden, P. A. F., Heath, A. C., Statham, D. J., Martin, N. G. & Verweij, K. (2014). Overlapping genetic and environmental influences on non-suicidal self-injury and suicidal ideation: Different outcomes, same etiology? *JAMA Psychiatry*, *71*, 699–705.

MacLeod, A. K., Pankhania, B. & Mitchell, D. (1997). Parasuicide, depression and the anticipation of positive and negative future experiences. *Psychological Medicine*, *27*, 973–7.

MacLeod, A. K., Rose, G. S. & Williams, J. M. G. (1993). Components of hopelessness about the future in parasuicide. *Cognitive Therapy and Behaviour*, *17*, 441–55.

MacLeod, A. K., Tata, P., Tyrer, P., Schmidt, U., Davidson, K. & Thompson, S. (2005). Hopelessness and positive and negative future thinking in parasuicide. *British Journal of Clinical Psychology*, *44*, 495–504.

Mahon, K., Burdick, K. E., Wu, J., Ardekani, B. A. & Szeszko, P. R. (2012). Relationship between suicidality and impulsivity in bipolar I disorder: A diffusion tensor imaging study. *Bipolar Disorder*, *14*, 80–9.

Makris, G. D., Reutfors, J., Larsson, R., Isacsson, G., Ösby, U., Ekbom, A., Ekselius, L. & Papadopoulos, F. C. (2016). Serotonergic medication enhances the association between suicide and sunshine. *Journal of Affective Disorders*, *189*, 276–81.

Malloy-Diniz, L. F., Neves, F. S., Abrantes, S. S. C., Fuentes, D. & Correa, H. (2009). Suicide behavior and neuropsychological assessment of type I bipolar patients. *Journal of Affective Disorders*, *112*, 231–6.

Mandelli, L. & Serretti, A. (2016). Gene-environment interaction studies in suicidal behaviour. In W. P. Kaschka & D. Rujescu (Eds.), *Biological aspects of suicidal behavior*. Basel: Karger.

Maniglio, R. (2011). The role of childhood sexual abuse in the etiology of suicide and non-suicidal self-injury. *Acta Psychiatrica Scandinavica*, *124*, 30–41.

Mann, J. J. (2003). Neurobiology of suicidal behaviour. *Nature Reviews Neuroscience*, *4*, 819–28.

  (2013). The serotonergic system in mood disorders and suicidal behavior. *Philosophical Transactions of the Royal Society B Biological Science*, *368*, 20120537.

Mann, J. J. & Arango, V. (1992). Integration of neurobiology and psychopathology in a unified model of suicidal behavior. *Journal of Clinical Psychopharmacology*, *12*, S2–S7.

Mann, J. J. & Currier, D. (2016). Relationships of genes and early-life experience to the neurobiology of suicidal behavior. In R. C. O'Connor & J. Pirkis (Eds.), *The international handbook of suicide prevention*. Chichester: Wiley.

Mann, J. J. & Haghighighi, F. (2010). Genes and environment: Multiple pathways to psychopathology. *Biological Psychiatry*, *68*, 403–4.

Mann, J. J. & Michel, C. A. (2016). Prevention of firearm suicide in the United States: What works and what is possible. *American Journal of Psychiatry*, *173*, 969–79.

Mann, J. J., Apter, A., Bertolote, J., Beautrais, A., Currier, D., Haas, A., Hegerl, U., Lonnqvist, J., Malone, K., Marusic, A., Mehlum, L., Patton, G., Phillips, M., Rutz, W., Rihmer, Z., Schmidtke, A., Shaffer,

D., Silverman, M., Takahashi, Y, Varnik, A., Wasserman, D, Yip, P. & Hendin, H. (2005). Suicide prevention strategies: A systematic review. *JAMA*, *294*, 2064–74.

Mann, J. J., Arango, V., Avenevoli, S., Brent, D. A., Champagne, F. A., Clayton, P., Currier, D., Dougherty, D. M., Haghigi, F., Hodge, S. E., Kleinman, J., Lehner, T., McMahon, F., Moscicki, E. K., Oquendo, M. A., Pandey, G. N., Pearson, J., Stanley, B., Terwilliger, J. & Wenzel, A. (2009). Candidate endophenotypes for genetic studies of suicidal behavior. *Biological Psychiatry*, *65*, 556–63.

Mann, J. J., Currier, D., Stanley, B., Oquendo, M. A., Amsel, L. V. & Ellis, S. P. (2006). Can biological tests assist prediction of suicide in mood disorders? *International Journal of Neuropsychopharmacology*, *9*, 465–74.

Mann, J. J., Waternaux, C., Haas, G. L. & Malone, K. M. (1999). Toward a clinical model of suicidal behavior in psychiatric patients. *American Journal of Psychiatry*, *156*, 181–9.

Marchand, W. R., Lee, J. N., Johnson, S., Thatcher, J., Gale, P., Wood, N. & Jeong, E. K. (2012). Striatal and cortical midline circuits in major depression: Implications for suicide and symptom expression. *Progress in Neuropsychopharmacology and Biological Psychiatry*, *36*, 290–9.

Martino, D.J., Strejilevich, S.A., Torralva, T. & Manes, F. (2011). Decision making in euthymic bipolar I and bipolar II disorders. *Psychological Medicine*, *41*, 1319–27.

Marusic, A. (2005). History and geography of suicide: Could genetic risk factors account for the variation in suicide rates? *American Journal of Medical Genetics C Seminars in Medical Genetics*, *133*, 43–7.

Marzuk, P. M., Hartwell, N., Leon, A. C. & Portera, L. (2005). Executive functioning in depressed patients with suicidal ideation. *Acta Psychiatrica Scandinavica*, *112*, 294–301.

Mataix-Cols, D., Fernandez de la Cruz, L., Monzani, B., Rosenfield, D., Anderson, E., Perez-Viogil, A. et al. (2017). D-cycloserine augmentation of exposure-based cognitive behaviour therapy for anxiety, obsessive-compulsive, and posttraumatic stress disorders: A systematic review and meta-analysis of individual participant data. *JAMA Psychiatry*, *74*, 501–10.

Mathias, C. W., Dougherty, D. M., James, L. M., Richard, D. M., Dawes, M. A., Acheson, A. & Hill-Kapturczak, N. (2011). Intolerance to delayed reward in girls with multiple suicide attempts. *Suicide & Life-Threatening Behavior*, *41*, 277–86.

Matsuo, K., Nielsen, N., Nicoletti, M. A., Hatch, J. P., Monkul, E. S., Watanabe, Y., Zunta-Soares, G. B., Nery, F. G. & Soares, J. C. (2010).

Anterior genu corpus callosum and impulsivity in suicidal patients with bipolar disorder. *Neuroscience Letters*, *469*, 75–80.

McCall, W. V., Benca, R. M., Rosenquist, P. B., Riley, M. A., McCloud, L., Newman, J. C., Case, D., Rumble, M. & Krystal, A. D. (2017). Hypnotic medications and suicide: Risk, mechanisms, mitigation and the FDA. *American Journal of Psychiatry*, *174*, 18–25.

McGirr, A. & Turecki, G. (2007). The relationship of impulsive aggressiveness to suicidality and other depression-linked behaviors. *Current Psychiatry Reports*, *9*, 460–6.

McGirr, A., Diaconu, G., Berlim, M. T., Pruessner, J. C., Sablé, R., Cabot, S. & Turecki, G. (2010). Dysregulation of the sympathetic nervous system, hypothalamic-pituitary-adrenal axis and executive function in individuals at risk for suicide. *Journal of Psychiatry and Neuroscience*, *35*, 399–408.

McGirr, A., Diaconu, G., Berlim, M. T. & Turecki, G. (2011). Personal and family history of suicidal behaviour is associated with lower peripheral cortisol in depressed outpatients. *Journal of Affective Disorders*, *131*, 368–73.

McGirr, A., Dombrovski, A. Y., Butters, M. A., Clark, L. & Szanto, K. (2012). Deterministic learning and attempted suicide among older depressed individuals: Cognitive assessment using the Wisconsin Card Sorting Task. *Journal of Psychiatric Research*, *46*, 226–32.

McGirr, A., Jollant, F. & Turecki, G. (2013). Neurocognitive alterations in first degree relatives of suicide completers. *Journal of Affective Disorders*, *145*, 264–9.

McGowan, P. O., Sasaki, A., D'Alessio, A. C., Dymov, S., Labonte, B., Szyf, M., Turecki, G. & Meaney, M. J. (2009). Epigenetic regulation of the glucocorticoid receptor in human brain associates with childhood abuse. *Nature Neuroscience*, *12*, 342–8.

McGuire, J. T., Nassar, M. R., Gold, J. I. & Kable, J. W. (2014). Functionally dissociable influences on learning rate in a dynamic environment. *Neuron*, *84*, 870–81.

Meerwijk, E. L., Ford, J. M. & Weiss, S. J. (2013). Brain regions associated with psychological pain: Implications for a neural network and its relationship to physical pain. *Brain Imaging and Behavior*, *7*, 1–14.

Melhem, N. M., Keilp, J. G., Porta, G., Oquendo, M. A., Burke, A., Stanley, B., Cooper, T. B., Mann, J. J. & Brent, D. A. (2016). Blunted HPA axis activity in suicide attempters compared to those at high risk for suicidal behavior. *Neuropsychopharmacology*, *41*, 1447–56.

Meltzer, H. Y., Alphs, L., Green, A. I., Altamura, A. C., Anand, R., Bertoldi, A., Bourgeois, M., Chouinard, G., Islam, M. Z., Kane, J., Krishnan, R., Lindenmayer, J. P., Potkin, S. & International Suicide

Prevention Trial Study Group (2003). Clozapine treatment for suicidality in schizophrenia: International Suicide Prevention Trial (InterSePT). *Archives of General Psychiatry*, *60*, 82–91.

Menon, V. & Kattimani, S. (2015). Suicide and serotonin: Making sense of evidence. *Indian Journal of Psychological Medicine*, *37*, 377–8.

Meyer, J. H., Houle, S., Sagrati, S., Carella, A., Hussey, D. F., Ginovart, N., Goulding, V., Kennedy, J. & Wilson, A. A. (2004). Brain serotonin transporter binding potential measured with carbon 11-labeled DASB positron emission tomography: Effects of major depression episodes and severity of dysfunctional attitudes. *Archives of General Psychiatry*, *61*, 1271–9.

Meyer, J. H., McMain, S., Kennedy, S. H., Korman, L. Brown, G. M., DaSilva, J. N., Wilson, A. A., Blak, T., Eynan-Harvey, R., Goulding, V. S., Houle, S. & Links, P. (2003). Dysfunctional attitudes and 5-HT2 receptors during depression and self-harm. *American Journal of Psychiatry*, *160*, 90–9.

Miller, A. B., Esposito-Smythers, C., Weismoore, J. T. & Renshaw, K. D. (2013). The relationship between child maltreatment and adolescent suicidal behaviour: A systematic review and critical examination of the literature. *Clinical Child and Family Psychology Review*, *16*, 146–72.

Miller, J. M., Kinnally, E. L., Ogden, R. T., Oquendo, M. A., Mann, J. J. & Parsey, R. V. (2009). Reported childhood abuse is associated with low serotonin binding in vivo in major depressive disorder. *Synapse*, *63*, 565–73.

Miranda, R., Valderrama, J., Tsypes, A., Gadol, E. & Gallagher, M. (2013). Cognitive inflexibility and suicidal ideation: Mediating role of brooding and hopelessness. *Psychiatry Research*, *210*, 174–81.

Mirkovic, B., Laurent, C., Podlipski, M. A., Frebourg, T., Cohen, D. & Gerardini, P. (2016). Genetic association studies of suicidal behavior: A review of the past 10 years, progress, limitations, and future directions. *Frontiers in Psychiatry*, *7*, 158.

Mittendorfer-Rutz, E., Rasmussen, F. & Wasserman, D. (2007). Familial clustering of suicidal behaviour and psychopathology in young suicide attempters: A register-based nested case control study. *Social Psychiatry and Psychiatric Epidemiology*, *43*, 28–36.

Miu, A. C., Carnut, M., Vulturara, R., Szekelly, R. D., Bilc, M. I., Chis, A., Fernandez, K. C., Szentagotai-Tatar, A. & Gross, J. J. (2017). BDNF Val66Met polymorphism moderates the link between child maltreatment and reappraisal ability. *Genes, Brain and Behavior*, *16*, 419–26.

MMWR (2013). Suicide among adults aged 35–64 years – United States, 1999–2010. *MMWR Morbidity and Mortality Weekly Reports*, *62*, 321–5.

(2017). Average number of deaths from motor vehicle injuries, suicide, and homicide, by day of the week. *US Department of Health and Human Services/Centers for Disease Control and Prevention, 66,* 22.

Monkul, E. S., Hatch, J. P., Nicoletti, M. A., Spence, S., Brambilla, P., Lacerda., A. L. T., Sassi, R. B., Mallinger, A. G., Keshavan, M. S. & Soares, J. C. (2007). Fronto-limbic brain structures in suicidal and non-suicidal female patients with major depressive disorder. *Molecular Psychiatry, 12,* 360–6.

Monroe, S. M. & Hadjiyannakis, H. (2002). The social environment and depression: Focusing on severe life stress. In I. H. Gotlib & C. L. Hammen (Eds.), *Handbook of depression.* New York, NY: Guilford Press.

Monson, E. T., De Klerk, K., Gaynor, S. C., Wagner, A. H., Breen, M. E., Parsons, M., Casavant, T. L., Zandi, P. P., Potash, J. B. & Willour, V. L. (2016). Whole-gene sequencing investigation of *SAT1* in attempted suicide. *American Journal of Medical Genetics Part B: Neuropsychiatric Genetics, 171,* 888–95.

Montague, P. R., Dolan, R. J. & Friston, K. J. (2012). Computational psychiatry. *Trends in Cognitive Sciences, 16,* 72–80.

Moran, R. J., Campo, P., Symmonds, M., Stephan, K. E., Dolan, R. J. & Friston, K. J. (2013). Free energy, precision and learning: The role of cholinergic neuromodulation. *Journal of Neuroscience, 33,* 8227–36.

Morthorst, B. R., Soegaard, B., Nordentoft, M. & Erlangsen, A. (2016). Incidence rates of deliberate self-harm in Denmark 1994–2011. *Crisis, 37,* 256–64.

Moutsiana, C., Charpentier, C. J., Garrett, N., Cohen, M. X. & Sharot, T. (2015). Human frontal-subcortical circuit and asymmetric belief updating. *Journal of Neuroscience, 35,* 14077–85.

Muehlenkamp, J. J., Claes, L., Havertape, L. & Plener, P. L. (2012). International prevalence of adolescent non-suicidal self-injury and deliberate self-harm. *Child and Adolescent Psychiatry and Mental Health, 6,* 10.

Muldoon, M. F., Manuck, S. B., Mendelsohn, A. B., Kaplan, J. R. & Belle, S. H. (2001). Cholesterol reduction and non-illness mortality: Meta-analysis of randomised clinical trials. *British Medical Journal, 322,* 11–15.

Mullins, N., Hodgson, K., Tansey, K. E., Perroud, N., Maier, W., Mors, O., Rietschel, M., Hauser, J., Henigsberg, N., Souery, D., Aitchison, K., Farmer, A., McGuffin, P., Breen, G., Uher, R. & Lewis, C. M. (2014). Investigation of blood mRNA biomarkers for suicidality in an independent sample. *Translational Psychiatry, 4,* e474.

Mumford, D. (1992). On the computational architecture of the neocortex. II. The role of cortico-cortical loops. *Biological Cybernetics*, *66*, 241–51.

Murphy, T. M., Ryan, M. & Foster, T. (2011). Risk and protective genetic variants in suicidal behaviour: Association with SLC1A2, SLC1A3, 5-HTR1B and NTRK2 polymorphisms. *Behavioral and Brain Functions*, *7*, 22.

Muthukumaraswamy, S. D., Shaw, A. D., Jackson, L. E., Hall, J., Moran, R. & Saxena, N. (2015). Evidence that subanesthetic doses of ketamine cause sustained disruptions of NMDA and AMPA-mediated frontoparietal connectivity in humans. *Journal of Neuroscience*, *35*, 11694–706.

National Confidential Inquiry into Suicide and Homicide by People with Mental Illness. (2014). *Suicide in primary care in England: 2002–2011*. Manchester, UK. Available at www.bbmh.manchester.ac.uk/cmhr/ research/centreforsuicideprevention/nci/reports/ SuicideinPrimaryCare2014.pdf.

Nemeroff, C. B. (2016). Paradise lost: The neurobiological and clinical consequences of child abuse and neglect. *Neuron*, *89*, 892–909.

Nery-Fernandes, F., Rocha, M. V., Jackowski, A., Ladeia, G., Guimaraes, J. L., Quarantini, L. C., Araùgo-Neto, C. A., De Oliveira, I. R. & Miranda-Scippa, A. (2012). Reduced posterior corpus callosum area in suicidal and non-suicidal patients with bipolar disorder. *Journal of Affective Disorders*, *142*, 150–5.

Niculescu, A. B., Levey, D., Le-Niculescu, H., Niculescu, E., Kurian, S. M. & Salomon, D. (2015a). Psychiatric blood biomarkers: Avoiding jumping to premature negative or positive conclusions. *Molecular Psychiatry*, *20*, 286–8.

Niculescu, A. B., Levey, D. F., Phalen, P. L., Le-Niculescu, H., Dainton, H. D., Jain, N., Belanger, E., James, A., George, S., Weber, H., Graham, D. L., Schweitzer, R., Ladd, T. B., Learman, R., Niculescu, E. M., Vanipenta, N. P., Khan, F. N., Mullen, J., Shankar, G., Cook, S., Humbert, C., Ballew, A., Yard, M., Gelbart, T., Shekhar, A., Schork, N. J., Kurian, S. M., Sandusky, G. E. & Salomon, D. R. (2015b). Understanding and predicting suicidality using a combined genomic and clinical risk assessment approach. *Molecular Psychiatry*, *20*, 1266–85.

Nielsen, O., Wallace, D. & Large, M. (2017). Pokorny's complaint: The insoluble problem of the overwhelming number of false positives generated by suicide risk assessment. *British Journal of Psychiatry Bulletin*, *41*, 18–20.

Njau, S., Joshi, S. H., Espinoza, R., Leaver, A. M., Vasavada, M., Marguina, A., Woods, R. P. & Narr, K. L. (2017). Neurochemical correlates of rapid treatment response to electroconvulsive therapy in patients with major depression. *Journal of Psychiatry and Neuroscience, 42*, 6–16.

Nock, M. K. & Banaji, M. R. (2007). Assessment of self-injurious thoughts using a behavioral test. *American Journal of Psychiatry, 164*, 820–3.

Nock, M. K. & Mendes, W. B. (2008). Physiological arousal, distress tolerance, and social problem-solving deficits among adolescent self-injurers. *Journal of Consulting and Clinical Psychology, 75*, 28–38.

Nock, M. K., Borges, G., Bromet, E. J., Alonso, J., Angermeyer, M., Beautrais, A., Bruffaerts, R., Chiu, W. T., De Girolamo, G., Gluzman, S., De Graaf, R., Gureje, O., Haro, J. M., Huang, Y., Karam, E., Kessler, R. C., Lepine, J. P., Levinson, D., Medina-Mora, M. E., Ono, Y., Posada-Villa, J. & Williams, D. (2008). Cross-national prevalence and risk factors for suicidal ideation, plans and attempts. *British Journal of Psychiatry, 192*, 98–105.

Nock, M. K., Park, J. M., Finn, C. T., Deliberto, T. L., Dour, H. J. & Banaji, M. R. (2010). Measuring the suicidal mind: Implicit cognition predicts suicidal behavior. *Psychological Science, 21*, 511–17.

Nordentoft, M. (2011). Crucial elements in suicide prevention strategies. *Progress in Neuropsychopharmacology and Biological Psychiatry, 35*, 848–53.

Nordt, C., Warnke, I., Seifritz, E. & Kawohl, W. (2015). Modelling suicide and unemployment: A longitudinal analysis covering 63 countries, 2000–2011. *Lancet Psychiatry, 2*, 239–45.

NSRF (2016). *National self-harm registry Ireland: Annual report 2015*. Cork: National Suicide Research Foundation.

NVSS (2016). *National vital statistics reports*, vol. 65, no. 4.

Nye, J. A., Purselle, D., Plisson, C., Voll, R. J., Stehouwer, J. S., Votaw, J. R., Klits, C. D., Goodman, M. M. & Nemeroff, C. B. (2013). Decreased brainstem and putamen SERT binding potential in depressed suicide attempters using [11C]-zient PET imaging. *Depression & Anxiety, 30*, 902–7.

O'Connor, D. B., Ferguson, E., Green, A., O'Carroll, R. E. & O'Connor, R. C. (2016). Cortisol levels and suicidal behavior: A meta-analysis. *Psychoneuroendocrinology, 63*, 370–9.

O'Connor, D. B., Green, J. A., Ferguson, E., O'Carroll, R. E, O'Connor, R. C. (2017). Cortisol reactivity and suicidal behavior: Investigating the role of hypothalamic-pituitary-adrenal axis responses to stress in suicide attempters and ideators. *Psychoneuroendocrinology, 75*, 183–91.

O'Connor, R. C. (2011). Towards an integrated motivational-volitional of suicidal behaviour. In R. C. O'Connor, S. Platt, & J. Gordon (Eds.),

International handbook of suicide prevention: Research, policy and practice (pp. 181–98). Hoboken, NJ: Wiley Blackwell.

O'Connor, R. C. & Nock, M. (2014). The psychology of suicidal behaviour. *Lancet Psychiatry*, *1*, 73–85.

O'Connor, R. C., Ferguson, E., Scott, F., Smyth, R., McDaid, D., Park, A. L., Beautrais, A. & Armitage, C. J. (2017). A brief psychological intervention to reduce repetition of self-harm in patients admitted to hospital following a suicide attempt: A randomised controlled trial. *Lancet Psychiatry*, *4*, 541–460.

O'Connor, R. C., Fraser, L., Whyte, M. C., MacHale, S. & Masterton, G. (2008). A comparison of specific future expectancies and global hopelessness as predictors of suicidal ideation in a prospective study of repeat self-harmers. *Journal of Affective Disorders*, *110*, 207–14.

OECD (2012). *Health at a glance: Europe 2012*. Paris: OECD Publishing.

Ohmann, S., Schuch, B., König, M., Blaas, S., Fliri, C. & Popow, C. (2008). Self-injurious behavior in adolescent girls. *Psychopathology*, *41*, 226–35.

Oldershaw, A., Grima, E., Jollant, F., Richards, C., Simic, M., Taylor, L. & Schmidt, U. (2009). Decision making and problem solving in adolescents who deliberately self-harm. *Psychological Medicine*, *39*, 95–104.

Olfson, M., Shaffer, D. & Marcus, S. C. (2003). Relationship between antidepressant medication treatment and suicide in adolescents. *Archives of General Psychiatry*, *60*, 978–82.

Olié, E., Ding, Y., Le Bars, E., Menjot de Champfleur, N., Mura, T., Bonafé, A., Courtet, P. & Jollant, F. (2015). Processing of decision making and social threat in patients with history of suicide attempt: A neuroimaging replication study. *Psychiatry Research Neuroimaging*, *234*, 369–77.

Olié, E., Jollant, F., Deverdun, J., Menjot de Champfleur, N., Cyprien, F., Le Bars, E., Mura, T., Bonafé, A. & Courtet, P. (2017). The experience of social exclusion in women with a history of suicidal acts: A neuroimaging study. *Scientific Reports*, *7*, 89.

Olié, E., Picot, M. C., Guillaume, S., Abbar, M. & Courtet, P. (2011). Measurement of total serum cholesterol in the evaluation of suicidal risk. *Journal of Affective Disorders*, *133*, 234–8.

Olvet, D. M., Peruzzo, D., Thapa-Chhetry, B., Sublette, M. E., Sullivan, G. M., Oquendo, M. A., Mann, J. J. & Parsey, R. V. (2014). A diffusion tensor imaging study of suicide attempters. *Journal of Psychiatric Research*, *51*, 60–7.

Oquendo, M. A., Galfalvy, H. C., Currier, D., Grunebaum, M. F., Sher, L., Sullivan, G. M., Burke, A. K., Harkavy-Friedman, J., Sublette, M. E., Parsey, R. V. & Mann, J. J. (2011). Treatment of suicide attempters with bipolar disorder: A randomized clinical trial comparing lithium with valproate in the prevention of suicidal behavior. *American Journal of Psychiatry*, *168*, 1050–56.

Oquendo, M. A., Galfalvy, H., Russo, S., Ellis, S. P., Grunebaum, M. F., Burke, A. & Mann, J. J. (2004). Prospective study of clinical predictors of suicidal acts after a major depressive episode in patients with major depressive disorder or bipolar disorder. *American Journal of Psychiatry*, *61*, 1433–41.

Oquendo, M. A., Galfalvy, H., Sullivan, G. M., Miller, J. M., Milak, M. M., Sublette, E., Cisneros-Trujillo, S., Burke, A. K., Parsey, R. V. & Mann, J. J. (2016). Positron emission tomographic imaging study of the serotonergic system and prediction of risk and lethality of future suicidal behavior. *JAMA Psychiatry*, *73*, 1048–55.

Oquendo, M. A., Perez-Rodriguez, M. M., Poh, E., Burke, A. K., Sublette, M. E., Mann, J. J. & Galfalvy, H. (2014a). Life events: A complex role in the timing of suicidal behavior among depressed patients. *Molecular Psychiatry*, *19*, 902–9.

Oquendo, M. A., Placidi, G. P., Malone, K. M., Campbell, C., Keilp, J., Brodsky, B., Kegeles, L. S., Cooper, T. B., Parsey, R. V., Van Heertum, R. L. & Mann, J. J. (2003). Positron emission tomography of regional brain metabolic responses to a serotonergic challenge and lethality of suicide attempts in major depression. *Archives of General Psychiatry*, *60*, 14–22.

Oquendo, M. A., Sullivan, G. M., Sudol, K., Baca-Garcia, E., Stanley, B. H., Sublette, M. E. & Mann, J. J. (2014b). Toward a biosignature for suicide. *American Journal of Psychiatry*, *171*, 1259–77.

Orlando, C. M., Broman-Fulks, J. J., Whitlock, J. L., Curtin, L. & Michael, K. D. (2015). Non-suicidal self-injury and suicidal self-injury: A taxometric investigation. *Behavior Therapy*, *46*, 824–33.

Osuch, E., Ford, K., Wrath, A., Bartha, R. & Neufeld, R. (2014). Functional MRI of pain application in youth who engaged in repetitive non-suicidal self-injury vs. psychiatric controls. *Psychiatry Research Neuroimaging*, *223*, 104–12.

Ouellet-Morin, I., Wong, C. C., Danese, A., Pariante, C. M., Papadopoulos, A. S., Mill, J. & Arseneault, L. (2013). Increased serotonin transporter gene (SERT) DNA methylation is associated with bullying victimization and blunted cortisol response to stress in childhood: A longitudinal study of discordant monozygotic twins. *Psychological Medicine*, *43*, 1813–23.

Pan, L. A., Batezati-Alves, S. C., Almeida, J. R. C., Segreti, A., Akkal, D., Hassel, S., Lakdawala, S., Brent, D. A. & Philips, M. L. (2011). Dissociable patterns of neural activity during response inhibition in depressed adolescents with and without suicidal behavior. *Journal of the American Academy of Child and Adolescent Psychiatry*, *50*, 602–11.

Pan, L. A., Hassel, S., Segreti, A., Nau, S. A., Brent, D. A. & Philiups, M. L. (2013a). Differential patterns of activity and functional connectivity in emotion processing neural circuitry to angry and happy faces in adolescents with and without suicide attempt. *Psychological Medicine*, *43*, 2129–42.

Pan, L. A., Segreti, A., Almeida, J., Jollant, F., Lawrence, N., Brent, D. A. & Philips, M. L. (2013b). Preserved hippocampal function during learning in the context of risk in adolescent suicide attempt. *Psychiatry Research Neuroimaging*, *211*, 112–18.

Pandey, G. N. & Dwivedi, Y. (2010). What can postmortem studies tell us about the pathoetiology of suicide? *Future Neurology*, *5*, 701–20.

  (2012). Peripheral biomarkers for suicide. In Y. Dwivedi (Ed.), *The neurobiological basis of suicide*. Boca Raton, FL: CRC Press.

Passos, I. C., Mwangi, B. & Kapczinski, F. (2016). Big data analytics and machine learning: 2015 and beyond. *The Lancet Psychiatry*, *2016*, no. 3, 13–15.

Pechtel, P., Lyons-Ruth, K., Anderson, C. M. & Teicher, M. H. (2014). Sensitive periods of amygdala development: The role of maltreatment in preadolescence. *NeuroImage*, *97*, 236–44.

Pedersen, M. G., Mortensen, P. B., Norgaard-Pedersen, B. & Postolache, T. T. (2012). *Toxoplasma gondii* infection and self-directed violence in mothers. *Archives of General Psychiatry*, *69*, 1123–30.

Perada, N., Guilera, G., Forns, M. & Gomez-Benito, J. (2009). The prevalence of sexual abuse in community and student samples: A meta-analysis. *Clinical Psychology Review*, *29*, 328–38.

Perroud, N., Paoloni-Giacobino, A., Prada, P., Olié, E., Salzmann, A., Nicastro, R., Guillaume, S., Mouthon, D., Stouder, C., Dieben, K., Huguelet, P., Courtet, P. & Malafosse, A. (2011). Increased methylation of glucocorticoid receptor gene (NR3C1) in adults with a history of childhood maltreatment: A link with the severity and type of trauma. *Translational Psychiatry*, *1*, e59.

Perroud, N., Salzmann, A., Prada, P., Nicastro, R., Hoeppli, M. E., Furrer, S., Ardu, S., Krejci, I., Karege, F. & Malafosse, A. (2013). Response to psychotherapy in borderline personality disorder and methylation status of the BDNF gene. *Translational Psychiatry*, *3*, e207.

Pestian, J. P., Sorfter, M., Connolly, B., Bretonnel, K., McCullumsmith, C., Gee, J. T., Morency, P. P., Scherer, S. & Rohlfs, L. for the STM Research Group. (2017). A machine learning approach to identifying thought markers of suicidal subjects: A prospective multicenter trial. *Suicide & Life-Threatening Behavior, 47*, 112–21.

Petersen, S. E. & Posner, M. I. (2012). The attention system of the human brain: Twenty years after. *Annual Review of Neuroscience, 21*, 73–89.

Philip, N. S., Tyrka, A. R., Albright, S. E., Sweet, L. H., Almeida, J., Price, L. H. & Carpenter, L. L. (2016). Early life stress predicts thalamic hyperconnectivity: A transdiagnostic study of global connectivity. *Journal of Psychiatric Research, 79*, 93–100.

Pirkis, J., Mok, K., Robinson, J. & Nordentoft, M. (2016). Media influences on suicidal thoughts and behaviors. In R. C. O'Connor & J. Pirkis (Eds.), *The international handbook of suicide prevention*. Chichester: Wiley.

Pirnia, T., Joshi, S. H., Leaver, A. M., Vasavada, M., Njau, S., Woods, R. P., Espinoza, R. & Narr, K. L. (2016). Electroconvulsivbe therapy and structural neuroplasiticiy in neocortical, limbic and paralimbic cortex. *Translational Psychiatry, 6*, e832.

Plener, P. L., Zohsel, K., Hohm, A., Buchmann, A. F., Banaschewskia, T., Zimmermann, U. S. & Laucht, M. (2017). Lower cortisol level in response to a psychosocial stressor in young females with self-harm. *Psychoneuroendocrinology, 76*, 84–7.

Pokorny, A. D. (1983). Prediction of suicide in psychiatric patients: Report of a prospective study. *Archives of General Psychiatry, 40*, 249–57.

Pollock, L. R. & Williams, J. M. G. (1998). Problem solving and suicidal behavior. *Suicide and Life-Threatening Behavior, 28*, 375–87.

(2001). Effective problem solving in suicide attempters depends on specific autobiographic recall. *Suicide and Life-Threatening Behavior, 31*, 386–96.

(2004). Problem-solving in suicide attempters. *Psychological Medicine, 34*, no. 1, 163–7.

Pompili, M., Ehrlich, S., De Pisa, E., Mann, J. J., Innamorati, M., Cittadini, A., Montagna, B., Iliceto, P., Romano, A., Amore, M., Tatarelli, R. & Girardi, P. (2007). White matter hyperintensities and their associations with suicidality in patients with major affective disorders. *European Archives of Psychiatry and Clinical Neuroscience, 257*, 494–9.

Pompili, M., Innamorati, M., Mann, J. J., Oquendo, M. A., Lester, D., Del Casale, A., Serafini, G., Rigucci, S., Romano, A., Tamburello, A., Manfredi, G., De Pisa, E., Ehrlich, S., Giupponi, G., Amore, M., Tatarelli, R. & Girardi, P. (2008). Periventricular white matter hyperintensities as predictors of suicide attempts in bipolar disorders and unipolar depression. *Progress in Neuropsychopharmacology and Biological Psychiatry, 32*, 1501–7.

Pompili, M., Innamorati, M., Masotti, V., Personnè, F., Lester, D., Di Vittorio, C., Pompili, M., Longo, L., Dominici, G., Serafini, G., Lamis, D. A., Amore, M. & Girardi, P. (2016). Polyunsaturated fatty acids and suicide risk in mood disorders: A systematic review. *Progress in Neuropsychopharmacology and Biological Psychiatry*. Epub ahead of print.

Popova, N. K. & Naumenko, V. S. (2013). 5-HT1A receptor as a key player in the brain 5-HT system. *Reviews in the Neurosciences, 24*, 191–204.

Post, R. M. (1992). Transduction of psychosocial stress into the neurobiology of recurrent affective disorder. *American Journal of Psychiatry, 149*, 999–1010.

Poudel-Tandukar, K., Nanri, A., Iwasaki, L.M., Mizoue, T., Matsushita, Y., Takahashi, Y., Noda, M., Inoue, M. & Tsugane, S. and the Japan Public Health Center-Based Prospective Study Group (2011). Long chain n-3 fatty acids intake, fish consumption, and suicide in a cohort of Japanese men and women: The Japan Public Health Center-based (JPHC) prospective study. *Journal of Affective Disorders, 129*, 282–8.

Pouliot, L. & De Leo, D. (2006). Critical issues in psychological autopsy studies. *Suicide and Life-Threatening Behavior, 36*, 491–510.

Poulter, M. O., Weaver, I. C., Palkovits, M., Faludi, G., Merali, Z., Szyf, M. & Anisman, H. (2008). GABAA receptor promotor hypermethylation in the suicide brain: Implications for the involvement of epigenetic processes. *Biological Psychiatry, 64*, 645–52.

Preti, A. (2007). Suicide among animals: A review of evidence. *Psychological Reports, 101*, 831–48.

(2011). Animal models and neurobiology of suicide. *Progress in Neuro-Psychopharmacology and Biological Psychiatry, 35*, 818–830.

Price, R. B., Iosifescu, D. V., Murrough, J. W., Chang, L. C., Al Jurdi, R. K., Iqbal, S. Z., Soleimani, L., Charney, D. S., Foulkes, A. L. & Mathew, S. J. (2014). Effects of ketamine on explicit and implicit suicidal cognition: A randomized controlled trial in treatment-resistant depression. *Depression and Anxiety, 31*, 335–43.

Priya, P. K., Rajappa, M., Kattimani, S., Mohanraj, P. S. & Revathy, G. (2016). Association of neurotrophins, inflammation and stress with suicide risk in young adults. *Clinica Chimica Acta, 457*, 41–5.

Prosser, A., Helfer, B. & Leucht, S. (2016). Biological v. psychosocial treatments: A myth about pharmacotherapy v. psychotherapy. *British Journal of Psychiatry, 208*, 309–11.

Pustilnik, A., Elkana, O., Vatine, J. J., Franko, M. & Hamdan, S. (2017). Neuropsychological markers of suicidal risk in the context of medical rehabilitation. *Archives of Suicide Research, 21*, 293–306.

Rahnev, D. A., Maniscalco, B., Luber, B., Lau, H. & Lisanby, S. H. (2012). Direct injection of noise to the visual cortex decreases accuracy but increases decision confidence. *Journal of Neurophysiology*, *107*, 1556–63.

Rajkumar, R., Fam, J., Yeo, E. Y. M. & Dawe, G. S. (2015). Ketamine and suicidal ideation in depression: Jumping the gun? *Pharmacological Research*, *99*, 23–35.

Randall, J. R., Bowe, B. H., Dong, K. A., Nock, M. K. & Colman, I. (2013). Assessment of self-harm risk using implicit thoughts. *Psychological Assessment*, *25*, 714–21.

Rasmussen, S. A., O'Connor, R. C. & Brodie, D. (2008). The role of perfectionism and autobiographical memory in a sample of parasuicide patients: An exploratory study. *Crisis*, *29*, 64–72.

Raust, A., Slama, F., Flavie, M., Roy, I., Chenu, A., Koncke, D., Fouques, D., Jollant, F., Jouvent, E., Courtet, P., Leboyer, M. & Bellivier, F. (2007). Prefrontal cortex dysfunction in patients with suicidal behaviour. *Psychological Medicine*, *37*, 411–19.

Reeves, R.R. & Ladner, M. E. (2010). Antidepressant-induced suicidality: An update. *CNS Neuroscience & Therapeutics*, *16*, 227–34.

Reichl, C., Heyera, A., Brunner, R., Parzerc, P., Völker, J. M., Resch, F. & Kaess, M. (2016). Hypothalamic-pituitary-adrenal axis, childhood adversity and adolescent non-suicidal self-injury. *Psychoneuroendocrinology*, *74*, 203–11.

Reisch, T., Seifritz, E., Esposito, F., Wiest, R., Valach, L. & Michel, K. (2010). An fMRI study on mental pain and suicidal behavior. *Journal of Affective Disorders*, *126*, 321–5.

Reitz, S., Kluetsch, R., Niedtfeld, I, Korz, T., Lis, S., Paret, C., Kirsch, P. Meyer-Lindenberg, A., Treede, R. D., Baumgartner, U., Bohus, M. & Schmahl, C. (2015). Incision and stress regulation in borderline personality disorder: Neurobiological mechanisms of self-injurious behaviour. *British Journal of Psychiatry*, *207*, 165–72.

Renteria, M. E., Schmall, L., Hibar, D. P., Couvy-Duchesnel, B., Strike, L. T., Mills, N. T. et al. (2017). Subcortical brain structure and suicidal behaviour in major depressive disorder: A meta-analysis from the ENIGMA-MDD working group. *Translational Psychiatry*, *7*, 1116.

Resnick, S., Smith, R., Beard, J., Holena, D., Reilly, P., Schwab, C. W., Seamon, M. J. (2017). Firearm deaths in America: Can we learn from 462,000 lives lost? *Annals of Surgery*, *266*, 432–40.

Retterstøl, N. (1993). *Suicide: A European perspective*. London: Cambridge University Press.

Ribeiro, J. D., Franklin, K. R., Fox, K. R., Bentley, K. H., Kleiman, E. M., Chang, B. P. & Nock, M. K. (2016). Self-injurious thoughts and behaviors as risk factors for future suicide ideation, attempts, and death: A meta-analysis of longitudinal studies. *Psychological Medicine*, *46*, no. 2, 225–36.

Richard-Devantoy, S., Berlim, M. T. & Jollant, F. (2014). A meta-analysis of neuropsychological markers of vulnerability to suicidal behavior in mood disorders. *Psychological Medicine*, *44*, 1663–73.

(2015). Suicidal behaviour and memory: A systematic review and meta-analysis. *World Journal of Biological Psychiatry*, *16*, 544–66.

Richard-Devantoy, S., Ding, Y., Lepage, M., Turecki, G. & Jollant, F. (2016a). Cognitive inhibition in depression and suicidal behaviour: A neuroimaging study. *Psychological Medicine*, *46*, 933–44.

Richard-Devantoy, S., Ding, Y., Turecki, G. & Jollant, F. (2016b). Attentional bias toward suicide-relevant information: A cross-sectional study and a meta-analysis. *Journal of Affective Disorders*, *196*, 101–8.

Richard-Devantoy, S., Olié, E., Guillaume, S. & Courtet, P. (2016c). Decision-making in unipolar and bipolar suicide. *Journal of Affective Disorders*, *190*, 128–36.

Rihmer, Z. & Döhme, P. (2016). Major mood disorders and suicidal behavior. In R. C. O'Connor & J. Pirkis (Eds.), *The international handbook of suicide prevention*. Chichester: Wiley.

Rihmer, Z. & Gonda, X. (2013). Pharmacological prevention of suicide in patients with major mood disorder. *Neuroscience and Biobehavioral Reviews*, *37*, 2398–403.

Roberts, S., Keers, R., Lester, K. J., Coleman, J. R., Breen, G., Arendt, K., Blatter-Meunier, J., Cooper, P., Creswell, C., Fjermestad, K., Havik, O. E., Herren, C., Hogendoorn, S. M., Hudson, J. L., Krause, K., Lyneham, H. J., Morris, T., Nauta, M., Rapee, R. M., Rey, Y., Schneider, S., Schneider, S. C., Silverman, W. K., Thastum, M., Thirlwall, K., Waite, P., Eley, T. & Wong, C. C. Y. (2015). HPA axis-related genens and response to psychological therapies: Genetics and epigenetics. *Depression & Anxiety*, *32*, 861–70.

Robinson, O. J., Vytal, K., Cornwell, B. R. & Grillon, C. (2013). The impact of anxiety upon cognition: Perspectives from human threat of shock studies. *Frontiers in Human Neuroscience*, *7*, 203.

Rockett, I. R. H., Lilly, C. L., Jia, H., Larkin, G. L., Miller, T. R., Nelson, L. S., Nolte, K. B., Putnam, S. L., Smith, G. S. & Caine, E. D. (2016). Self-injury mortality in the United States in the early 21st century: A comparison with proximally ranked diseases. *JAMA Psychiatry*, *73*, 1072–81.

Ross, O., Skatova, A., Madlon-Kay, S. & Daw, N. D. (2016). Cognitive control predicts use of model-based reinforcement learning. *Journal of Cognitive Neuroscience*, *27*, 319–33.

Roth, T. L., Lubin, F. D., Funk, A. J. & Sweatt, J. D. (2009). Lasting epigenetic influence of early-life adversity on the BDNF gene. *Biological Psychiatry*, *65*, 760–9.

Rowland, L. M., Bustillo, J. R., Mullins, P. G., Jung, R. E., Lenroot, R., Landgraf, E., Barrow, R., Yeo, R., Lauriello, J. & Brooks, W. M. (2005). Effects of ketamine on anterior cingulate glutamate metabolism in healthy humans: A 4-T proton MRS study. *American Journal of Psychiatry*, *162*, 394–6.

Roy, A. (2012). Gene-environment interaction and suicidal behaviour. In Y. Dwivedi (Ed.), *The biological basis of suicide*. Boca Raton, FL: CRC Press.

Roy, A., Gorodetsky, E., Yuan, Q., Goldman, D. & Enoch, M. A. (2010). Interaction of FKBP5, a stress-related gene, with childhood trauma increases the risk for attempting suicide. *Neuropsychopharmacology*, *35*, 1674–83.

Roy, A., Hodgkinson, C. A., DeLuca, V., Goldman, D. & Enoch, M. A. (2012). Two HPA axis genes, CRHBP and FKBP5, interact with childhood trauma to increase the risk for suicidal behavior. *Journal of Psychiatric Research*, *46*, 72–9.

Roy, A., Hu, X. Z., Janal, M. N. & Goldman, D. (2007). Interaction between childhood trauma and serotonin transporter gene variation in suicide. *Neuropsychopharmacology*, *32*, 2046–52.

Roy, B. & Dwivedi, Y. (2017). Understanding epigenetic architecture of suicide neurobiology: A critical perspective. *Neuroscience and Biobehavioral Reviews*, *72*, 10–27.

Roy, B., Shelton, R. C. & Dwivedi, Y. (2017). DNA methylation and expression of stress related genes in PBMC of MDD patients with and without serious suicidal ideation. *Journal of Psychiatric Research*, *89*, 115–24.

Rubinstein, D. H. (1986). A stress–diathesis theory of suicide. *Suicide and Life-Threatening Behavior*, *16*, 182–97.

Rüsch, N., Spoletini, I., Wilke, M., Martinotti, G., Bria, P., Trequattrini, A., Bonaviri, G., Caltagirone, C. & Spalletta, G. (2008). Inferior frontal white matter volume and suicidality in schizophrenia. *Psychiatry Research Neuroimaging*, *164*, 206–14.

Rutherford, B. R., Wager, T. D. & Roose, S. P. (2010). Expectancy and the treatment of depression: A review of experimental methodology and effects on patient outcome. *Current Psychiatry Review*, *6*, 1–10.

Rutherford, B. R., Wall, M. M., Brown, P. J., Choo, T. H., Wager, T. D., Peterson, B. S., Chung, S., Kirsch, I. & Roose, S. P. (2017). Patient expectancy as a mediator of placebo effects in antidepressant trials. *American Journal of Psychiatry*, *174*, 135–42.

Rutherford, B. R., Wall, M. M., Glass, A. & Stewart, J. W. (2014). The role of patient expectancy in placebo and nocebo effects in antidepressant trials. *Journal of Clinical Psychiatry*, *75*, 1040–6.

Ryding, E., Ahnlide, J. A., Lindström, M. B., Rosén, I. & Träskman-Bendz, L. (2006). Regional brain serotonin and dopamine transporter binding capacity in suicide attempters relate to impulsiveness and mental energy. *Psychiatry Research Neuroimaging*, *148*, 195–203.

Sachs-Ericsson, N., Corsentino, E., Rushing, N. C. & Sheffler, J. (2013). Early childhood abuse and late-life suicidal ideation. *Aging and Mental Health*, *17*, no. 4, 489–94.

Sachs-Ericsson, N., Hames, J. L., Joiner, T. E., Corsentino, M. S., Rushing, N. C., Palmer, E., Gotlib, I. H., Selby, E. A., Zarit, S. & Steffens, D. C. (2014). Differences between suicide attempters and non-attempters in depressed older patients: Depression severity, white matter lesions, and cognitive functioning. *American Journal of Geriatric Psychiatry*, *22*, 75–85.

Sachs-Ericsson, N. J., Rushing, N. C., Stanley, I. H. & Sheffler, J. (2015). In my end is my beginning: Developmental trajectories of adverse childhood experiences to late-life suicide. *Aging & Mental Health*, *20*, 139–65.

Sackheim, H.A. (2017). Modern electroconvulsive therapy: Vastly improved yet greatly underused. *JAMA Psychiatry*, *74*, 779–80.

Sadeh, N., Wolf, E. J., Logue, M. W., Hayes, J. P., Stone, A., Griffin, L. M., Schichman, S. A. & Miller, M. W. (2016). Epigenetic variation at SKA2 predicts suicide phenotypes and internalizing psychopathology. *Depression and Anxiety*, *33*, 308–15.

Sagar, R., Tsang, A., Ustun, T. B., Vassilev, S., Viana, M. C. & Williams, D. R. (2010). Childhood adversities and adult psychopathology in the WHO World Mental Health Surveys. *British Journal of Psychiatry*, *197*, 378–85.

Salpekar, J. A., Joshi, P. T., Axelson, D. A., Reinblatt, S. P., Yenokyan, G., Sanyal, A., Walkup, J. T., Vitiello, B., Luby, J. L., Wagner, K. D., Nusrat, N. & Riddle, M. A. (2015). Depression and suicidality outcomes in the treatment of early age mania study. *Journal of the American Academy of Child and Adolescent Psychiatry*, *4*, 999–1007.

Sanacora, G., Frye, M. A., McDonald, W., Mathew, S. J., Turner, M. S., Schatzberg, A. F., Summergrad, P. & Nemeroff, C. B., for the American Psychiatric Association (APA) Council of Research Task Force on Novel Biomarkers and Treatments (2017). A consensus statement on the use of ketamine in the treatment of mood disorders. *JAMA Psychiatry*, *74*, 399–405.

Sargalska, J., Miranda, R. & Marroquin, B. (2011). Being certain about an absence of the positive: Specificity in relation to hopelessness and suicidal ideation. *International Journal of Cognitive Therapy*, *4*, 104–16.

Sauder, C. L., Derbridge, C. M. & Beauchaine, T. P. (2015). Neural responses to monetary incentives among self-injury adolescent girls. *Development and Psychopathology*, *28*, 277–91.

Schaffer, A., Isometsa, E. T., Tondo, L., Moreno, D., Turecki, G., Reis, C., Cassidy, F., Sinyor, M., Azorin, J. M., Kessing, L. V., Ha, K., Goldstein, T., Weizman, A., Beautrais, A., Chou, Y. H., Diazgranados, N., Levitt, A. J., Zarate, C. A., Rihmer, Z. & Yatham, N. (2015). International Society for Bipolar Disorders Task Force on Suicide: Meta-analyses and meta-regression of correlates of suicide attempts and suicide deaths in bipolar disorder. *Bipolar Disorder*, *17*, 1–16.

Schmaal, L., Marquand, A. F., Rhebergen, D., van Tol, M. J., Ruhe, H. G., van der Wee, N. J., Veltman, D. J. & Penninx, B.W. (2015). Predicting the naturalistic course of major depressive disorder using clinical and multimodal neuroimaging information: A multivariate pattern recognition study. *Biological Psychiatry*, *78*, 278–86.

Schmitt, L. I., Wimmer, R. D., Nakajima, M., Happ, M., Mofakham, S. & Halassa, M. M. (2017). Thalamic amplification of cortical connectivity sustains attentional control. *Nature*, *545*, 219–23.

Schneider, B., Maurer, K., Sark, D., Heiskel, H., Weber, B. & Frolich, L. (2004). Concordance of DSM-IV Axis I and II diagnoses by personal and informant's interview. *Psychiatry Research*, *127*, 121–36.

Schneider, E., El Hajj, N., Müller, F., Navarro, B. & Haaf, T. (2015). Epigenetic dysregulation in the prefrontal cortex of suicide completers. *Cytogenetic and Genome Research*, *146*, 19–27.

Schnieder, T. P., Trencevska, I., Rosoklija, G., Stankov, A., Mann, J. J., Smiley, J. & Dwork, A. J. (2014). Microglia of prefrontal white matter in suicide. *Journal of Neuropathology and Experimental Neurology*, *73*, 880–9.

Scholes, K. E., Harrison, B. J., O'Neill, B. V., Leung, S., Croft, R. J, Pipingas, A., Phan, K. L. & Nathan, P. J. (2007). Acute serotonin and dopamine depletion improves attentional control: Findings from the Stroop task. *Neuropsychopharmacology*, *32*, 1600–10.

Schotte, D. E. & Clum, G. A. (1982). Suicide ideation in a college population. *Journal of Consulting and Clinical Psychology*, *50*, 690–6.

Schulman, J. J., Cancro, R., Lowe, S., Lu, F., Walton, K. D. & Llinas, R. R. (2011). Imaging of thalamocortical dysrhythmia in neuropsychiatry. *Frontiers in Human Neuroscience*, *5*, 69.

Seguin, M., Beauchamp, G., Robert, M., Di Mambro, M. & Turecki, G. (2014). Developmental model of suicide trajectories. *British Journal of Psychiatry*, *205*, 120–6.

Seguin, M., Lesage, A., Turecki, G., Bouchard, M., Chawky, N., Tremblay, N., Daigle, F. & Guy, A. (2007). Life trajectories and burden of adversity: Mapping the developmental profiles of suicide mortality. *Psychological Medicine*, *37*, 1575–83.

Seligman, E. (1972). Learned helplessness. *Annual Review in Medicine*, *23*, 407–12.

Sequeira, A., Mamdani, F., Ernst, C., Vawter, M. P. & Turecki, G. (2009). Global brain gene expression analysis links glutamatergic and GABAergic alterations to suicide and major depression. *PLoS One*, *4*, e6585.

Serafini, G., Pompili, M., Innamorati, M., Fusar-Poli, P., Akiskal, H. S., Rihmer, Z., Lester, D., Romano, A., de Oliveira, I. R.., Strusi, L., Ferracuti, S., Girardi, P. & Tatarelli, R. (2011). Affective temperamental profiles are associated with white matter hyperintensity and suicidal risk in patients with mood disorders. *Journal of Affective Disorders*, *129*, 47–55.

Serafini, G., Pompili, M., Lindqvist, D., Dwivedi, Y. & Girardi, P. (2013). The role of neuropeptides in suicidal behavior: A systematic review. *BioMed Research International*, 687575.

Seymour, K., Jones, R. N., Cushman, G. K., Galvan, T., Puzia, M. E., Kim, K. L., Spirito, A. & Dickstein, D. P. (2016). Emotional face recognition in adolescent suicide attempters and adolescents engaging in non-suicidal self-injury. *European Child and Adolescent Psychiatry*, *25*, 247–59.

Shaffer, A., Isometsä, E. T., Tondo, L., Moreno, D., Turecki, G., Reis, C., Cassidy, F., Sinyor, M., Azorin, J. M., Kessing, L. V., Ha, K., Goldstein, T., Weizman, A., Beautrais, A., Chou, Y. H., Diazgrandos, N., Levitt, A. J., Zarate, C. A., Rihmer, Z. & Yatham, L. N. (2015). International Society for Bipolar Disorders Task Force on Suicide: Meta-analysis and meta-regression of correlates of suicide attempts and suicide deaths in bipolar disorder. *Bipolar Disorder*, 17, no. 1, 1–16.

Sharot, T. (2011). The optimism bias. *Current Biology*, *21*, R941–R945. (2012). The optimism bias. A TED talk on February 2012 [Internet]. TED conferences LLC, New York, NY. Available at www.ted.com/talks/tali_sharot_the_optimism_bias.html.

Sharot, T. & Garrett, N. (2016). Forming beliefs: Why valence matters. *Trends in Cognitive Sciences*, *20*, 25–33.

Sharot, T., Kanai, R., Marston, D., Korn, C. W., Rees, G. & Dolan, R. J. (2012). Selectively altering belief formation in the human brain. *Proceedings of the National Academy of Science*, *109*, 17058–62.

Sharot, T., Korn, C. W. & Dolan, R. J. (2011). How unrealistic optimism is maintained in the face of reality. *Nature Neuroscience, 14*, 1475–9.

Sheng, C. F. S., Stickley, A., Konishi, S. & Watanabe, C. (2016). Ambient air pollution and suicide in Tokyo, 2001–2011 *Journal of Affective Disorders, 201*, 194–202.

Shepard, D. S., Gurewich, D., Lwin, A. K., Reed, G. A. & Silverman, M. M. (2016). Suicide and suicidal attempts in the United States: Costs and policy implications. *Suicide and Life-Threatening Behavior, 46*, 352–62.

Sherman, S. M. (2016). Thalamus plays a central role in ongoing cortical functioning. *Nature Neuroscience, 19*, 533–41.

Sherman, S. M. & Guillery, R. W. (1998). On the actions that one nerve cell can have on another: Distinguishing between "drivers" and "modulators." *Proceedings of the National Academy of Sciences, 95*, 7121–6.

Shinozaki, G., Romanowicz, M., Mrazek, D. A. & Kung, S. (2013). State dependent gene-environment interaction: Serotonin transporter gene-child abuse interaction associated with suicide attempt history among depressed psychiatric inpatients. *Journal of Affective Disorders, 150*, 1200–3.

Shneidman, E. S. (1981). The psychologic autopsy. *Suicide and Life-Threatening Behavior, 11*, 5–12.

Sidley, G. L., Whitaker, K., Calam, R. M. & Wells, A. (1997). The relationship between problem-solving and autobiographical memory in parasuicide patients. *Behavioural and Cognitive Psychotherapy, 25*, 195–202.

Silverman, M. M. (2016). Challenges to defining and classifying suicide and suicidal behaviors. In R. C. O'Connor & J. Pirkis (Eds.), *The international handbook of suicide prevention*. Chichester: Wiley.

Simon, G. E. (2006). How can we know whether antidepressants increase suicide risk? *American Journal of Psychiatry, 163*, 1861–3.

Sinclair, J. M. A., Crane, C., Hawton, K. & Williams, J. M. G. (2007). The role of autobiographical memory specificity in deliberate self-harm: Correlates and consequences. *Journal of Affective Disorders, 102*, 11–18.

Snider, J. E., Hane, S. & Berman, A. L. (2006). Standardizing the psychological autopsy: Addressing the Daubert standard. *Suicide and Life-Threatening Behavior, 36*, 511–18.

Soloff, P. H., Chiappetta, L., Mason, N. S., Becker, C. & Price, J. C. (2014). Effects of serotonin-2A receptor binding and gender on personality traits and suicidal behavior in borderline personality disorder. *Psychiatry Research – Neuroimaging, 222*, 140–8.

Soloff, P. H., Price, J. C., Meltzer, C. C., Fabio, A., Frank, G. K. & Kaye, W. H. (2007). 5HT2A receptor binding is increased in borderline personality disorder. *Biological Psychiatry*, *62*, 580–7.

Soloff, P. H., Pruitt, P., Sharma, M., Radwan, J., White, R. & Diwadkar, V. A. (2012). Structural brain abnormalities and suicidal behavior in borderline personality disorder. *Journal of Psychiatric Research*, *46*, 516–25.

Sourander, A., Klomek, A. B., Niemelä, S., Haavisto, A., Gyllenberg, D., Helenius, H., Sillanmaki, L., Ristkari, T., Kumpulainen, K., Tamminen, T., Moilanen, I., Piha, J., Almqvist, F. & Gould, M. S. (2009). Childhood predictors of completed and severe suicide attempts: Findings from the Finnish 1981 Birth Cohort Study. *Archives of General Psychiatry*, *66*, 398–406.

Spence, S. A. (2009). *The actor's brain: Exploring the cognitive neuroscience of free will*. Oxford: Oxford University Press.

Spoletini, I., Piras, F., Fagioli, S., Rubino, I. A., Martinotti, G., Siracusano, A., Caltagirone, C. & Spalletta, G. (2011). Suicidal attempts and increased right amygdala volume in schizophrenia. *Schizophrenia Research*, *125*, 30–40.

Stefansson, J., Chatzittofis, A., Nordström, P., Arver, S., Asberg, M. & Jokinen, J. (2016). CSF and plasma testosterone in attempted suicide. *Psychoneuroendocrinology*, *74*, 1–6.

Stein, D. J., Chiu, W. T., Hwang, I., Kessler, R. C., Sampson, N. & Nock, M. K. (2010). Cross-national analysis of the associations between traumatic events and suicidal behavior: Findings from the WHO World Mental Health Surveys. *PLoS One*, *5*, e10574.

Stephan, K. E., Schlagenhauf, F., Huys, Q., Raman, S., Aponte, E. A., Brodersen, K. H., Rigoux, L., Moran, R. J., Daunizeau, J., Dolan, R. J., Friston, K. J. & Heinz, A. (2017). Computational neuroimaging strategies for single patient predictions. *NeuroImage*, *145*, 180–99.

Steward, J. G., Glenn, C. R., Esposito, E. C., Cha, C. B., Nock, M. K. & Auerbach, R. P. (2017). Cognitive control deficits differentiate adolescent suicide ideators from attempters. *Journal of Clinical Psychiatry*, *78*, 614–21.

Stone, A. (1971). Suicide precipitated by psychotherapy. *American Journal of Psychotherapy*, *25*, 18–28.

Stone, M., Laughren, T., Jones, M. L., Levenson, M., Holland, P. C., Hughes, A., Hammad, T. A., Temple, R. & Rochester, G. (2009). Risk of suicidality in clinical trials of antidepressants in adults: Analysis of propriety data submitted to US Food and Drug Administration. *British Medical Journal*, *339*, b2880.

Strike, L. T., Couvy-Duchesne, B., Hansell, N. K., Cuellar-Partida, G., Medland, S. E. & Wright, M. J. (2015). Genetics and brain morphology. *Neuropsychological Reviews*, *25*, 63–96.

Stuckler, D. & Basu, S. (2013). *The body economic: Why austerity kills*. New York, NY: Basic Books.

Sublette, M. E., Hibbeln, J. R., Galfalvy, H., Oquendo, M. A. & Mann, J. J. (2006). Omega-3 polyunsaturated essential fatty acid status as a predictor of future suicide risk. *American Journal of Psychiatry*, *163*, 1100–2.

Sublette, M. E., Milak, M. S., Galfalvy, H. C., Oquendo, M. A., Malone, K. M. & Mann, J. J. (2013). Regional brain glucose uptake distinguishes suicide attempters from non-attempters in major depression. *Archives of Suicide Research*, *17*, 434–47.

Suderman, M., McGowan, P. O., Sasaki, A., Huang, T. C., Hallett, M. T., Meaney, M. J., Turecki, G. & Szyf, M. (2012). Conserved epigenetic sensitivity to early life experience in the rat and human hippocampus. *Proceedings of the National Academy of Sciences of the United States of America*, *109*, 17266–72.

Sudol, K. & Mann, J. J. (2017). Biomarkers of suicide attempt behavior: Towards a biological model of risk. *Current Psychiatry Reports*, *19*, 31.

Sullivan, G. M., Oquendo, M. A., Milak, M., Miller, J. M., Burke, A., Ogden, R. T., Parsey, R. V. & Mann, J. J. (2015). Positron emission tomography quantification of serotonin 1A receptor binding in suicide attempters with major depression. *JAMA Psychiatry*, *72*, 169–78.

Sun, Y., Farzan, F., Mulsant, B. H., Rajji, T. K., Fitzgerald, P. B., Barr, M. S., Downar, J., Wong, W., Blumberger, D. M. & Daskalakis, Z. J. (2016). Indicators for remission of suicidal ideation following magnetic seizure therapy in patients with treatment-resistant depression. *JAMA Psychiatry*, *73*, 337–45.

Szanto, K., Bruine de Bruin, W., Parker, A. M., Hallquist, M. N., Vanyukov, P. M. & Dombrovski, A. Y. (2015). Decision-making competence and attempted suicide. *Journal of Clinical Psychiatry*, *76*, 1590–7.

Szymkowicz, S. M., McLaren, M. E., Suryadera, U. & Woods, A. J. (2016). Transcranial direct stimulation use in the treatment of neuropsychiatric disorders: A brief review. *Psychiatric Annals*, *46*, 642–6.

Tatarelli, R., Girardi, P. & Amore, M. (2008). Suicide in the elderly: A psychological autopsy study in a north Italy area (1994–2004). *American Journal of Geriatric Psychiatry*, *16*, 727–35.

Teicher, M. H. & Samson, J. A. (2013). Childhood maltreatment and psychopathology: A case for ecophenotypic variants as clinically and neurobiologically distinct subtypes. *American Journal of Psychiatry*, *170*, 1114–33.

(2016). Enduring neurobiological effects of childhood abuse and neglect. *Journal of Child Psychology and Psychiatry*, 57, 241–66.

Teicher, M. H., Samson, J. A., Anderson, C. M. & Ohashi, K. (2016). The effects of childhood maltreatment on brain structure, function and connectivity. *Nature Reviews Neuroscience*, *17*, 652–66.

Tiihonen, J., Haukka, J., Taylor, M., Haddad, P. M., Patel, M. X. & Korhonen P. (2011). A nationwide cohort study of oral and depot antipsychotics after first hospitalization for schizophrenia. *American Journal of Psychiatry*, *168*, 603–9.

Tiihonen, J., Lonnqvist, J. & Wahlbeck, K. (2006). Antidepressants and the risk of suicide, attempted suicide, and overall mortality in a nationwide cohort. *Archives of General Psychiatry*, *63*, 1358–67.

Tkachev, D., Mimmack, M. L., Huffaker, S. J., Ryan, M. & Bahn, S. (2007). Further evidence for altered myelin biosynthesis and glutamatergic dysfunction in schizophrenia. *International Journal of Neuropsychopharmacology*, *10*, 557–63.

Tondo, L. & Baldessarini, R. J. (2016). Suicidal behaviour in mood disorders: Response to pharmacological treatment. *Current Psychiatry Reports*, *18*, 88.

Toplak, M. E., Sorge, G. B., Benoit, A., West, R. F. & Stanovich, K. E. (2010). Decision-making and cognitive abilities: A review of associations between Iowa Gambling Task performance, executive functions and intelligence. *Clinical Psychology Review*, *30*, 562–81.

Tops, M., van der Pompe, G., Wijers, A. A., Den Boer, J. A., Meijman, T. F. & Korf, J. (2004). Free recall of pleasant words from recency positions is especially sensitive to acute administration of cortisol. *Psychoneuroendocrinology*, *29*, 327–38.

Toranzo, J. M., Calvo, M., Padilla, E., Ballinger, T., Lucia, D., Swisher, T. et al. (2011). Dopaminergic projection abnormalities in untreated schizophrenia and unaffected first degree relatives. *Social Neuroscience Abstracts*, *41*, 680.

Troister, T. & Holden, R. R. (2010). Comparing psychache, depression and hopelessness in their associations with suicidality: A test of Shneidman's theory of suicide. *Personality and Individual Differences*, *7*, 689–93.

Tsafrir, S., Chubarov, E., Shoval, G., Levi, M., Nahshoni, E., Ratmansky, M., Weizman, A. & Zalsman, G. (2014). Cognitive traits in inpatient adolescents with and without prior suicide attempts and non-suicidal self-injury. *Comprehensive Psychiatry*, *55*, 370–3.

Tsai, A. C., Lucas, M., Odereke, O. I., O'Reilly, E. J., Mirzaei, F., Kawachi, I., Ascherio, A. & Willlett, W. C. (2014). Suicide mortality in relation to dietary intake of n-3 and n-6 polyunsaturated fatty acids and fish: Equivocal findings from three large US cohort studies. *American Journal of Epidemiology*, *179*, 1458–66.

Tsai, J. F. (2015). Suicide risk: Sunshine or temperature increase? *JAMA Psychiatry*, *72*, 624–5.

Tsypes, A., Owens, M., Hajcak, G. & Brandon, E. (2017). Neural responses to gains and losses in children of suicide attempters. *Journal of Abnormal Psychology*, *126*, 237–43.

Turecki, G. (2005). Dissecting the suicide phenotype: The role of impulsive-aggressive behaviours. *Journal of Psychiatry and Neuroscience*, *30*, 398–408.

 (2014a). Epigenetics and suicidal behavior research pathways. *American Journal of Preventive Medicine*, *47*, S144–S151.

 (2014b). The molecular bases of the suicidal brain. *Nature Reviews Neuroscience*, *15*, 802–16.

 (2016). Epigenetics of suicidal behaviour. In W. P. Kashka & D. Rujescu (Eds.), *Biological aspects of suicidal behaviour*. Basel: Karger.

Turecki, G. & Brent, D. (2016). Suicide and suicidal behaviour. *Lancet*, *387*, 1227–39.

Turecki, G. & Meaney, M. J. (2016). Effects of the social environment and stress on glucocorticoid receptor gene methylation: A systematic review. *Biological Psychiatry*, *79*, 87–96.

Turecki, G., Ernst, C., Jollant, F., Labonté, B. & Mechawar, N. (2012). The neurodevelopmental origins of suicidal behavior. *Trends in Neurosciences*, *35*, 14–23.

Tyrka, A. R., Burgers, D. E., Philips, N. S., Price, L. H. & Carpenter, L. L. (2013). The neurobiological correlates of childhood adversity and implications for treatment. *Acta Psychiatrica Scandinavica*, *128*, 434–46.

Tyrka, A. R., Price, L. H., Marsit, C., Walters, O. C. & Carpenter, L. L. (2012). Childhood adversity and epigenetic modulation of the leukocyte glucocorticoid receptor: Preliminary findings in healthy adults. *PLoS One*, *7*, e30148.

US Department of Health and Human Services, Children's Bureau. (2017). *Child maltreatment 2015*. Available at www.acf.hhs.gov/sites/default/files/cb/cm2015.pdf.

Valuck, R. J., Libby, A. M. & Sills, M. R. (2004). Antidepressant treatment and risk of suicide attempt by adolescents with major depressive disorder: A propensity-adjusted retrospective cohort study. *CNS Drugs*, *18*, 1119–32.

Van Dam, N. T., Rando, K., Potenza, M. N., Tuit, K. & Sinha, R. (2014). Childhood maltreatment, altered limbic neurobiology and substance abuse relapse severity via trauma-specific reductions in limbic gray matter volume. *JAMA Psychiatry*, *71*, 917–25.

van Heeringen, K. (Ed.) (2001). *Understanding suicidal behaviour: The suicidal process approach to research, treatment and prevention.* Chichester: John Wiley & Sons.

van Heeringen, K. (2010). The story of Valerie. In M. Pompili (Ed.), *Suicide in the words of suicidologists* (pp. 215–17). New York, NY: Nova Science Publishers.

van Heeringen, K. & Mann, J. J. (2014). The neurobiology of suicide. *Lancet Psychiatry*, *1*, 63–74.

van Heeringen, K., Audenaert, K., Van Laere, K., Dumont, F., Slegers, G., Mertens, J. & Dierckx, R. A. (2003). Prefrontal 5-HT2a receptor binding index, hopelessness, and personality characteristics in attempted suicide. *Journal of Affective Disorders*, *74*, 149–58.

van Heeringen, K., Bijttebier, S. & Godfrin, K. (2011). Suicidal brains: A review of functional and structural brain studies in association with suicidal behaviour. *Neuroscience and Biobehavioural Reviews*, *35*, 688–98.

van Heeringen, K., Bijttebier, S., Desmyter, S., Vervaet, M. & Baeken, C. (2014). Is there a neuroanatomical basis of the vulnerability to suicidal behavior? A coordinate-based meta-analysis of structural and functional MRI studies. *Frontiers in Human Neuroscience*, *8*, 824.

van Heeringen, K., Godfrin, K. & Bijttebier, S. (2011). Understanding the suicidal brain: A review of neuropsychological studies of suicidal ideation and behaviour. In R. C. O'Connor, S. Platt, & J. Gordon (Eds.), *International handbook of suicide prevention: Research, policy and practice.* Hoboken, NJ: Wiley Blackwell.

van Heeringen, K., Van den Abbeele, D., Vervaet, M., Soenen, L. & Audenaert, K. (2010). The functional neuroanatomy of mental pain in depression. *Psychiatry Research*, *181*, 141–4.

van Heeringen, K., Wu, G. R., Vervaet, M., Vanderhasselt, M. A. & Baeken, C. (2017). Decreased resting state metabolic activity in frontopolar and parietal brain regions is associated with suicide plans in depressed individuals. *Journal of Psychiatric Research*, *84*, 243–48.

Van Ijzendoorn, M. H., Caspers, K., Bakermans-Kranenburg, M. J., Beach, S. R. & Philibert, R. (2010). Methylation matters: Interaction between methylation density and serotonin transporter genotype predicts unresolved loss or trauma. *Biological Psychiatry*, *68*, 405–7.

Van Orden, K. A., Witte, T. K., Cukrowicz, K. C., Braithwaite, S., Selby, E. A. & Joiner, T. E. (2010). The interpersonal theory of suicide. *Psychological Reviews*, 117, no. 2, 575–600.

Vancayseele, N., Portzky, G. & van Heeringen, K. (2016). Increase in self-injury as a method of self-harm in Ghent, Belgium: 1987–2013. *PLoS One*, *11*, e0156711.

Vang, R. J., Ryding, E., Träskman-Bendz, L. & Lindstrom, M. B. (2010). Size of basal ganglia in suicide attempters, and its association with temperament and serotonin transporter density. *Psychiatry Research*, *183*, 177–9.

Vanyukov, P. M., Szanto, K., Hallquist, M. N., Siegle, G. J., Reynolds, C. F. III, Forman, S. D., Aizenstein, H. J. & Dombrovski, A. Y. (2016). Paralimbic and lateral prefrontal encoding of reward value during intertemporal choice in attempted suicide. *Psychological Medicine*, *46*, 381–91.

Verrocchio, M. C., Carrozzino, D., Marchetti, D., Andreasson, K., Fulcheri, M. & Bech, P. (2016). Mental pain and suicide: A systematic review of the literature. *Frontiers in Psychiatry*, *7*, 108.

Vinckier, F., Gaillard, R., Palimenteri, S., Rigoux, L., Salvador, A., Fornito, A., Adapa, R., Krebs, M. O., Pessiglione, M. & Fletcher, P. C. (2016). Confidence and psychosis: A neuro-computational account of contingency learning disruption by NMDA blockade. *Molecular Psychiatry*, *21*, 946–55.

Vita, A., De Peri, L. & Sacchetti, E. (2015). Lithium in drinking water and suicide prevention: A review of the evidence. *International Clinical Psychopharmacology*, *30*, 1–5.

Voracek, M. & Loible, L. M. (2007). Genetics of suicide: A systematic review of twin studies. *Wiener Klinische Wochenschriften*, *119*, 463–475.

Voracek, M. & Sonneck, G. (2007). Surname study of suicide in Austria: Differences in regional suicide rates correspond to the genetic structure of the population. *Wiener Klinische Wochenschriften*, *119*, 355–360.

Vyssoki, B., Kapusta, N. D., Praschak-Rieder, N., Dorffner, G. & Wileit, M. (2014). Direct effect of sunshine on suicide. *JAMA Psychiatry*, *71*, 1231–7.

Wagner, G., Koch, K., Schachtzabel, C., Schultz, C. C., Sauer, H. & Schlösser, R. G. (2011). Structural brain alterations in patients with major depressive disorder and high risk for suicide: Evidence for a distinct neurobiological entity? *Neuroimage*, *54*, 1607–14.

Wagner, G., Schultz, C. C., Koch, K., Schachtzabel, C., Sauer, H. & Schlösser, R. G. (2012). Prefrontal cortical thickness in depressed patients with highrisk for suicidal behaviour. *Journal of Psychiatric Research*, *46*, 1449–55.

Walsh, N. D., Dalgleish, T., Lombardo, M. V., Dunn, V. J., Van Harmelen, A. L., Ban, M. & Goodyer, I. M. (2014). General and specific effects of early-life psychosocial adversities on adolescent grey matter volume. *NeuroImage*, *4*, 308–18.

Weaver, I. C. G., Cervoni, N., Champagne, F. A., D'Alessio, A. C., Sharma, S., Seckl, J. R., Dymov, S., Szyf, M. & Meaney, M. J. (2004). Epigenetic programming by maternal behavior. *Nature Neuroscience*, *7*, 847–54.

Weik, U., Ruhweza, J. & Deinzer, R. (2017). Reduced cortisol output during public speaking stress in ostracized women. *Frontiers in Psychology*, *8*, 60.

Weinstock, M. (2008). The long-term behavioural consequences of prenatal stress. *Neuroscience and Biobehavioral Reviews*, *32*, 1073–86.

Welk, B., McArthur, E., Ordon, M., Anderson, K. K., Hayward, J. & Dixon, S. (2017). Association of suicidality and depression with 5alpha-reductase inhibitors. *JAMA Internal Medicine*, *177*, 683–91.

Wender, P. H., Kety, S. S. & Rosenthal, D. (1986). Psychiatric disorders in the biological and adoptive families of adopted individuals with affective disorders. *Archives of General Psychiatry*, *43*, 923–9.

Wenzel, A. & Beck, A. T. (2008). A cognitive model of suicidal behavior: Theory and treatment. *Applied & Preventive Psychology*, *12*, no. 4, 189–201.

Westheide, J., Quednow, B. B., Kuhn, K. U., Hoppe, C., Cooper-Mahkorn, D., Hawellek, B., Eichler, P., Maier, W. & Wagner, M. (2008). Executive performance of depressed suicide attempters: The role of suicidal ideation. *European Archives of Psychiatry and Clinical Neuroscience*, *258*, 414–21.

Whalley, K. (2016). Breaking down ketamine's actions. *Nature Reviews Neuroscience*, *17*, 399.

Whitaker, A. H., Van Rossem, R., Feldman, J. F., Schonfeld, I. S., Pinto-Martin, J. A., Tore, C., Shaffer, D. & Paneth, N. (1997). Psychiatric outcomes in low-birth-weight children at age six years: Relation to neonatal cranial ultrasound abnormalities. *Archives of General Psychiatry*, *54*, 847–56.

Whitlock, J., Muehlenkamp, J., Eckenrode, J., Purington, A., Barrera, P., Baral-Abrams, G. & Smith, E. (2013). Non-suicidal self-injury as a gateway to suicide in adolescents and young adults. *Journal of Adolescent Health*, *52*, 486–92.

WHO (2014). *Preventing suicide: A global imperative*. Geneva: World Health Organization.

(2017). Suicide rates (per 100,000 population). Available at www.who.int/gho/mental_health/suicide_rates/en/.

Wilkinson, P., Kelvin, R., Roberts, C., Dubicka, B. & Goodyer, I. (2011). Clinical and psychosocial predictors of suicide attempts and nonsuicidal self-injury in the Adolescent Depression Antidepressants and Psychotherapy Trial (ADAPT). *American Journal of Psychiatry, 168*, 495–501.

Willeumier, K., Taylor, D. V. & Amen, D. G. (2011). Decreased cerebral blood flow in the limbic and prefrontal cortex using SPECT imaging in a cohort of completed suicides. *Translational Psychiatry, 1*, 28.

Williams, J. M. G. (1996). Depression and the specificity of autobiographical memory. In D. C. Rubin (Ed.), *Remembering our past: Studies in autobiographical memory* (pp. 244–67). Cambridge: Cambridge University Press.

(2001). *The cry of pain.* London: Penguin.

Williams, J. M. G. & Broadbent, K. (1986). Autobiographical memory in suicide attempters. *Journal of Abnormal Psychology, 95*, no. 2, 144–9.

Williams, J. M. G. & Dritschel, B. H. (1988). Emotional disturbance and the specificity of autobiographical memory. *Cognition and Emotion, 2*, 221–34.

Williams, J. M. G. & Pollock, L. (2001). Psychological aspects of the suicidal process. In K. van Heeringen (Ed.), *Understanding suicidal behaviour: The suicidal process approach to research, treatment and prevention* (pp. 76–94). Chichester: John Wiley.

Williams, J. M. G., Barnhofer, T., Crane, C. & Beck, A. T. (2005a). Problem solving deteriorates following mood challenge in formerly depressed patients with a history of suicidal ideation. *Journal of Abnormal Psychology, 114*, 421–31.

Williams, J. M. G., Barnhofer, T., Crane, C., Hermans, D., Raes, F., Watkins, E. & Dalgleish, T. (2007). Autobiographical memory specificity and emotional disorder. *Psychological Medicine, 133*, 122–48.

Williams, J. M. G., Crane, C., Barnhofer, T. & Duggan, D. (2005b). Psychology and suicidal behavior: Elaborating the entrapment model. In K. Hawton (Ed.), *Suicide and suicidal behavior: From science to practice* (pp. 71–90). Oxford: Oxford University Press.

Williams, J. M. G., Fennell, M., Barnhofer, T., Crane, R. & Silverton, S. (2015). *Mindfulness and the transformation of despair: Working with people at risk of suicide.* New York: Guilford Press.

Williams, J. M. G., van der Does, A. J. W., Barnhofer, T., Crane, C. & Zegal, Z. S. (2008). Cognitive reactivity, suicidal ideation and future fluency: Preliminary investigation of a differential activation theory of hopelessness/suicidality. *Cognitive Therapy and Research, 32,* 83–104.

Windfuhr, K., Steeg, S., Hunt, I. M. & Kapur, N. (2016). International perspectives on the epidemiology and etiology of suicide and self-harm. In R. C. O'Connor & J. Pirkis (Eds.), *The international handbook of suicide prevention.* Chichester: Wiley.

Witt, K. (2017). The use of emergency department-based psychological interventions to reduce repetition of self-harm. *Lancet Psychiatry, 4,* 428–9.

Yager, J. (2015). Addressing patients' psychic pain. *American Journal of Psychiatry, 172,* 939–43.

Yang, A. C., Tsai, S. J. & Huang, N. E. (2011). Decomposing the association of completed suicide with air pollution, weather and unemployment data at different time scales. *Journal of Affective Disorders, 129,* 275–81.

Yeh, Y. W., Ho, P. S., Chen, C. Y., Kuo, S. C., Liang, C. S., Ma, K. H., Shiue, C. Y., Huang, W. S., Cheng, C. Y., Wang, T. Y., Lu, R. B. & Huang, S. Y. (2015). Incongruent reduction of serotonin transporter associated with suicide attempts in patients with major depressive disorder: A positron emission tomography study with 4-[^{18}F]-ADAM. *International Journal of Neuropsychopharmacology, 18,* 1–9.

Yin, H., Pantazatos, S. P., Galfalvy, H., Huang, Y., Rosoklija, G. B., Dwork, A. J., Burke, A., Arango, V., Oquendo, M. A. & Mann, J. J. (2016). A pilot integrative genomics study of GABA and glutamate neurotransmitter systems in suicide, suicidal behavior, and major depressive disorder. *American Journal of Medical Genetics Part B, 171,* 414–26.

Yoshimasu, K., Kiyohara, C., Miyashita, C. and the Stress Research Group of the Japanese Society for Hygiene (2008). Suicidal risk factors and completed suicide: Meta-analyses based on psychological autopsy studies. *Environmental Health and Preventive Medicine, 13,* 243–56.

Young, K. A., Bonkale, W. L., Holcomb, L. A., Hicks, P. B. & German, D. C. (2008). Major depression, 5HTTLPR genotype, suicide and antidepressant influence on thalamic volume. *British Journal of Psychiatry, 192,* 285–9.

Young, K. A., Holcomb, L. A., Bonkale, W. L., Hicks, P. B. & German, D. C. (2007). 5HTTLPR polymorphism and enlargement of the pulvinar: Unlocking the backdoor to the limbic system. *Biological Psychiatry, 61,* 813–18.

Yovell, Y., Bar, G., Mashiah, M., Baruch, Y., Briskman, I., Asherov, J., Lotan, A., Rigbi, A. & Panksepp, J. (2016). Ultra-low-dose buprenorphine as a time-limited treatment for severe suicidal ideation:

A randomized controlled trial. *American Journal of Psychiatry*, *173*, 491–8.

Yuan, X. & Devine, D. P. (2016). The role of anxiety in vulnerability for self-injurious behaviour: Studies in a rodent model. *Behavioural Brain Research*, *311*, 201–209.

Yurgelun-Todd, D. A., Bueler, C. E., McGlade, E. C., Churchwell, J. C., Brenner, L. A. & Lopez-Larson, M. P. (2011). Neuroimaging correlates of traumatic brain injury and suicidal behavior. *Journal of Head Trauma Rehabilitation*, *26*, 276–89.

Zeng, L. L., Liu, L., Liu, Y., Shen, H., Li, Y. & Hu, D. (2012). Antidepressant treatment normalizes white matter volume in patients with major depression. *PLoS One*, 7, no. 8, e44248.

Zhang, J., Wieczorek, W., Conwell, Y., Tu, X. M., Wu, B. Y. & Xiao, S. (2010). Characteristics of young rural Chinese suicides: A psychological autopsy study. *Psychological Medicine*, *40*, 581–9.

Zhang, S., Chen, J. M., Kuang, L., Cao, J., Zhang, H., Ai, M., Wang, W., Zhang, S. D., Wang, S. Y., Liu, S. J. & Fang, W. D. (2016). Association between abnormal default mode network activity and suicidality in depressed adolescents. *BMC Psychiatry*, *16*, 337.

Zhang, Y., Catts, V. S., Sheedy, D., McCrossin, T., Krill, J. J. & Shannon Weickert, C. (2016). Cortical gray matter volume reduction in people with schizophrenia is associated with neuro-inflammation. *Translational Psychiatry*, *6*, 982.

Zou, Y., Li, H., Shi, C., Zhou, H. & Zhang, J. (2017). Efficacy of psychological-pain theory-based cognitive therapy in suicidal patients with major depressive disorder: A pilot study. *Psychiatry Research*, *249*, 23–9.

Zuckerman, M. (1999). *Vulnerability to psychopathology: A biosocial model.* Washington, DC: American Psychological Association.

Index

Abuse
  childhood, *see* Childhood abuse
  substance, 15, 20, 34, 42, 129
Acetaminophen, 192
Acquired capacity/capability, 4, 32–4, 142, 222
ACTH, 64, 66, 169, *see* Adrenocorticotropic
  hormone
Adoption, 52
Adrenocorticotropic hormone (ACTH), 56,
  64, 169
Adversity, 12, 27–8, 42, 50, 61, 67, 83,
  125–45, 163
Aggression, 11, 13, 29, 34–6, 41–2, 45, 76,
  82, 109, 112, 127, 130, 141, 189, 237
Alcohol, 15
Alcoholism, 15, 20, 34–5, 129
Altitude, 53, 215, 229–30
Amino acid, 47, 50, 60, 72, 76
Amygdala, 70, 106, 110–11, 115, 137–8, 140,
  143, 187, 202, 249, 259
Analgesic, 19, 194
Angry face, xi, 24, 36–7, 66, 86, 90, 113, 120,
  232, 249
Animal model, 40, 42–3, 61–2, 140, 144, 215,
  251
Anterior cingulate gyrus, 36, 74, 79, 105,
  108–10, 113–14, 116, 118, 121–2, 137,
  140, 157, 192, 194, 196, 212–13, 239, 254
Anterior limb of the internal capsule
  (ALIC), 105
Anterior thalamic radiation, 105, 122
Antidepressant, 21, 54, 57, 99, 182–8, 192,
  199, 203–4, 216, 225, 230, 239, 258–9,
  261, 266
Antipsychotic, 191
Anxiety, 70, 82, 173–4, 176, 185, 201–2, 209
Astroglia, 57
Attention, 18, 20, 31, 36, 45, 75–6, 85–9, 91,
  94–8, 113–14, 120–1, 123, 128, 138, 150,
  152–3, 156–9, 162–3, 194, 197, 199, 201,
  210, 214, 218, 222–3, 225, 230, 234–5,
  250, 256
Attention bias modification (ABM), 201
Autobiographic memory, 85, 89–90, 96–7
Autobiographical Memory Test, 90
Autopsy, 10, 15, 40, 44–7, 49, 127, 129
Awareness, 19, 44

Basal ganglia, 70, 78, 106, 112, 122, 229, 264
BDNF, 56, 80, 84, 121, 131, 135, 142, 169,
  174, 186, 193, 196, 202, 206, 215, 233,
  236–7, 243, 249, 254 *see* Brain-derived
  neurotrophic factor
Behavioral inhibition, 2, 153, 161, 164
Belief, 146, 148, 150, 154, 156, 160, 162, 226,
  244
Benzodiazepines, 183, 190, 223
Biomarker, 82–3, 135, 137, 168, 172, 174,
  178, 180, 196, 228, 236, 249
Bipolar disorder, 15
Black-box warning, 21, 185–6
Borderline personality disorder, 34–5, 105,
  111, 134–6, 186, 192
Brain-derived neurotrophic factor (BDNF),
  see BDNF
Brodmann area 10, 108–9
Burdensomeness, 32–4
Buspirone, 56

Capability, 4, 33, 142, 222
Carbon monoxide, 20
Cerebrospinal fluid (CSF), 30, 55, 57, 74,
  170, 172, 195, 213, 230
Certainty, 146, 148–50, 154, 159–60, 163,
  212, 236
Chaperone protein, 67, 69, 134, 174
Childhood abuse, xii, 12, 28, 34, 42, 50, 69,
  75, 120, 125–9, 131–4, 136, 139–43, 145,
  195, 211, 216, 224, 227, 229, 237, 239,
  242–3, 245, 258, 261, 263

Childhood adversity, 202
Childhood physical abuse (CPA),
    see Childhood abuse
Childhood sexual abuse (CSA),
    see Childhood abuse
Childhood trauma, xii, 28, 61, 68, 75, 82,
    131–3, 135, 138
Choice behavior, 161, 163, 197, 199
Cholesterol, 43, 64, 80–1, 83, 171, 176, 221,
    224, 230, 247
Cingulate, 36, 74, 79, 105–10, 113–14,
    116–18, 121–2, 134, 137, 140–1, 157,
    192, 194, 196–8
Circadian rhythm, 54
Climate, 53–4
Clozapine, 38, 191, 203
Cluster, 15, 17, 96, 125, 138
Cognitive
    biomarker, 169–70
    control, 96–7, 105, 116–17
    deficits, 12, 36–8, 98
    flexibility, 91, 96
    impulsivity, 13
    inhibition, 96, 118
    predisposition, 25–6
    rigidity, 29
    therapy, 136, 200–2
Cohort study, 14, 53, 81, 172–4, 176, 184,
    206
Computational, 79, 120, 131, 144, 146,
    160–3, 179, 199
Confidence, 149, 154
Contagious, 17
Continuous Performance Test, 88
Corpus callosum, 106–7, 137–8, 141
Cortex
    dorsolateral, 29, 79–80, 105–7, 110, 116,
        122, 197
    dorsomedial, 37
    frontopolar, 150, 154, 158, 163, 199
    orbitofrontal, 105–8, 110, 113, 115–16,
        118, 137–8, 156, 197
    parietal, 120, 122, 163, 199
    ventrolateral, 36, 114
    ventromedial, 29, 74, 96, 105–9, 113–15,
        150, 157, 193

Corticotropin-releasing hormone (CRH),
    64, 66, 132, 169
Cortisol, 13, 54, 56, 64–6, 82–3, 98, 140, 142,
    157, 171, 173–4, 177, 189, 206, 208, 234,
    238, 242, 246, 248, 250, 261, 265
Cry of pain, 23, 25, 30, 43, 87
Cyberball, 66, 102, 114
Cytokine, 55, 77–9, 84, 131, 170, 193, 226
Cytomegalovirus, 14

D-cycloserine, 194, 202, 241
Darwin, Charles, 87
Decision making, 12, 29, 86, 93–6, 101–2,
    108–9, 115–17, 119, 123, 159, 206, 211,
    219, 221, 230, 253, 260–1
Deep brain stimulation (DBS), 198, 203
Defeat, 31, 34, 43–4, 61, 87, 98, 148, 155,
    159–60, 164, 226, 231
Deliberate self-harm (DSH), 2
Demographic influences, 8, 41, 49, 128, 156
Depression, 15
Dexamethasone-suppression test (DST),
    56, 66, 134, 170
Diathesis, 1, 4, 11, 16, 22–4, 26–32, 34–6, 38,
    41, 43, 50, 64, 78, 93, 98, 120, 157, 170,
    172, 175, 195, 234, 254
Diet, 53, 57, 81, 84, 262
Diffusion tensor imaging (DTI), 58
Distal risk factors, 11–14, 16, 24, 35, 50, 61,
    109, 125, 207, 209
DNA, 49
DNA methylation, 50, 67–9, 80, 82–3,
    133–7, 140, 173–4, 208, 219, 228, 236,
    239, 248, 254
Dopamine, 72, 76, 112, 169, 171, 189, 225,
    229, 255–6
Dorsolateral prefrontal cortex, 79–80, 105,
    107–8, 110, 113, 116–17, 122, 138, 219
Drugs 71, 81, 136, 182–5, 190–1, 194, 202–4,
    220, 262
DSH, *see* Deliberate self-harm
DST, *see* Dexamethasone-suppression test
DTI, 58, 104–5, 112, 122, 137, 207,
    see Diffusion tensor imaging
Durkheim, Emile, 41, 224
Dysfunctional attitudes, 111–12, 243

Early-life adversity (ELA), 12, 42, 50–1, 67, 83–4, 123, 125–6, 141, 144–5, 236, 254
Eating disorder, 15
Electroconvulsive therapy (ECT), 21
Endophenotypet, 13, 33–5, 207, 216, 241
Entrapment, 33–4, 43–4, 61, 95, 226, 266
Epidemiology, 51, 53, 61, 82, 213, 217, 226, 229, 235–6, 243, 262, 267
Epigenetic, 50, 61, 63, 67–9, 71, 80, 82–4, 125, 132–3, 135–6, 140, 144–5, 157–8, 173–4, 177, 193, 204, 208, 217, 225, 228, 233, 235–6, 239, 242, 251, 253–6, 260, 262, 265
Escape, 10, 15, 31, 42–4, 95, 97, 115, 148, 208
Executive, 86, 97, 120, 190, 197, 218, 223, 234, 237, 241–2, 261, 265
Expectancy, 158, 186, 188, 197, 203–4, 247

Fatty acids, 53, 80, 169, 173, 230, 251, 262
Fenfluramine, 66, 107, 112, 171
Fetal growth, 11, 98
Financial crisis, 7
Firearm, 11, 16, 19
FKBP, 69, 132, 134, 136, 140, 175, 227, 236, 254
Fluency, 31, 90, 97, 214, 267
fMRI, 36, 59, 107, 109, 111, 113–14, 116–17, 123, 138, 156, 179, 207, 252, 263
Fractional anisotropy (FA), 58, 104, 112, 137, 239
Frontal gyrus, 122
Frontopolar, 150, 154, 158, 163, 199, 214, 231, 263
Frontothalamic, 104
Future Thinking Task, 90

GABA, 13, 72, 76, 108, 158, 189, 207, 236, 267
Gene expression, 47, 56, 67–9, 74, 140, 172–3, 176, 178, 202, 227, 257
Genome, 12, 48–50, 68, 82, 121, 132–6, 173, 206–7, 236, 256
Genome-wide association studies (GWAS), 49
Glucocorticoid, 64, 69, 133, 143, 157, 174, 236, 239, 242, 249, 262

Glucose, 57, 60, 64, 107, 171, 260
Glutamate, 13, 72, 76, 78, 83, 108, 131, 158, 193–4, 196, 227, 229, 254, 257, 261, 267
Go/No-go task, 117
Gray matter, 57, 59, 80, 103, 105, 115, 118, 121–3, 131, 137, 139–41, 155, 189, 212, 214, 223, 227, 237, 263, 268
Guns, 11, 16–17, 20
GWAS, 121, 136, 207, see Genome-wide association studies

Helplessness, 43–4, 208, 257
Heritability, 12, 47, 51–2, 61, 67, 98, 121, 209–10
Hippocampus, 29, 67, 70, 80, 106, 108–9, 117, 121, 133–4, 136–8, 140–1, 143, 193, 219, 227, 239, 249, 260
Histone modification, 67
Hopelessness, 14–16, 27, 29–32, 38, 42–4, 98, 109, 111–12, 119, 130, 136, 146, 148–9, 156, 158, 163, 171, 188, 197, 203, 214, 221, 240, 243, 247, 256, 261, 263, 267
Hormone, 29, 42, 56–7, 64, 82, 98, 135, 169, 171, 189, 195, 206, 215
HPA, 55, 65–8, 78, 83, 131, 133–4, 140, 157, 170, 174–5, 177, 208, 232, 235, 242, 253–4, see Hypothalamus-pituitary-adrenal axis
Human immunodeficiency virus, 9, 14
Hyperintensity, 103–5, 121, 224, 250
Hypnotics, 183, 190
Hypothalamus, 56, 64, 70, 208
Hypothalamus-pituitary-adrenal (HPA) axis, 56

Immunological, 14
Implicit association test (IAT) 169
Impulsivity, 11–13, 29, 34–6, 41, 82, 92, 109, 112, 116, 136, 189, 223, 240, 242
Indicated prevention, 19, 21–2
Infection, 14
Inferior frontal gyrus, 106, 110, 118, 122, 150, 162, 197
Inferior parietal lobule, 108, 150
Inflammation, 58, 64, 77–81, 83, 120, 131–2, 144, 169, 193, 217, 219–20, 229, 251, 268

Insula, 108, 110, 113–14, 122, 140, 192, 212
Interferon, 77, 206
Internal capsule, 104–5, 122, 137, 198, 203, 215, 220
Internet, 17
Interpersonal-psychological theory, 27, 32, 39, 142, 228, 264
Iowa Gambling Task (IGT), 94, 115, 159, 261

Ketamine, 60, 76, 152, 158, 162, 182, 192–4, 196, 225, 231, 245, 251, 254–5, 265
Kindling, 26, 29

Lethality, 2, 9–10, 29, 36, 74, 91, 97, 107–8, 112, 157, 223, 248
Linkage, 49
Lithium, 8, 21, 38, 53–4, 60, 71, 84, 105, 122, 172, 182, 189, 203–5, 214, 230, 238, 248
Lymphocyte, 55

Maastricht Acute Stress Test, 66
Magnetic resonance imaging (MRI), 58
Magnetic seizure therapy (MST), 197, 260
Magnetic transfer imaging (MTI), 58
Means-Ends Problem Solving (MEPS), 92
Means restriction, 19
Media, 17
Medial forebrain bundle, 122, 198, 219
Melatonin, 54
Memory, 29, 64, 79, 85–6, 89–90, 94–5, 97–9, 196–7, 212, 224, 231, 233, 237, 252–3, 258, 266
Mental pain, 1, 3, 10, 14–16, 38, 97, 109, 119, 122, 191–2, 252, 263
Methylation, 50, 67–9, 80, 82–3, 133, 135–6, 140, 157, 173–4, 177, 202, 219, 228, 233–4, 236–7, 248–9, 254, 262–3
Microarray, 49, 208
Mineralocorticoid, 64
Mood disorder, 15
Motivational–volitional model, 33–4, 41, 222, 246
MRI, see Magnetic resonance imaging
mRNA, 47, 50, 69, 71, 80, 134–5, 209, 244
Myelin, 57, 103, 121, 140, 209, 261
Myths, 1, 17, 23, 204–5

Neurogenesis, 53, 79, 131, 138, 143, 189–90
Neuroimaging, 57, 115, 213, 227–8, 233, 247, 249, 254–5, 268
Neuropeptide, 83, 257
Neuropil, 57
Neuroprotective, 53, 84, 190
Neurostimulation, 146, 156, 163, 182, 195, 198–9, 203–4
Neurotransmission, 72, 209
Neurotrophic, 53, 56, 77, 80, 135, 144, 169, 172, 189
Neurotrophin, 79–80, 131–2, 135, 251
NMDA, 76, 78–9, 83, 158, 162, 193–4, 202, 204, 245, 264
Nonsuicidal self-injury, 2–4, 7–9, 12, 22, 33, 66, 110–11, 114, 122, 213, 233, 266
NSSI, 2–4, 7, 9, 12, 110–11, 114, 122
NTRK1, 121
Nuclear magnetic resonance (NMR), 58, 60, 196, 209–10
Nucleus accumbens, 108, 110, 198

Oligodendrocytes, 57, 141
Omega-3 fatty acids, 53, 81–2, 171, 173, 260
Orbitofrontal cortex, 104–5, 108, 110, 112–13, 115–16, 118, 122, 137, 156, 197, 211, 232, 238
Oscillatory, 163, 199
Oxytocin, 82, 171, 195, 215, 229, 237

Pain
    mental, 1, 3, 10, 13–16, 22–3, 25, 30–1, 37–9, 42–3, 87, 95, 97, 109–11, 119, 122, 191, 200, 209, 222, 224, 231, 242, 252, 263–4, 266–8
    physical, 23, 33–4, 115, 121, 142, 163, 190–1, 195, 224, 248
    sensitivity, 31, 37, 192
Pain killer, 191
Paracetamol, 192
Parasite, 14, 42, 77
Parasuicide, 2, 213, 224, 231, 239–40, 252, 258
Parental neglect, 12, 126, 129
Pavlovian, 153–4, 160–1, 226, 229, 231
Pavlovian-instrumental transfer, 153, 160

Perception, 31, 44, 86–7, 115, 119, 148, 152, 195, 222, 225
Personality disorder, 15
Pessimism, 16, 29, 112, 159, 236
Pesticides, 16, 19
PET, 42, 59, 102, 107–8, 111, 209
Platelet, 56
Pollution, 55, 213, 238, 258, 267
Polyamine, 64, 70–1, 172
Population-attributable risk (PAR), 128
Postmortem, 29, 46–7, 70–1, 78, 140
Precision, 13, 149–50, 152–6, 158, 160–3, 172, 199–200, 233, 237, 244
Precuneus, 107, 111
Prediction, 148
Prefrontal cortex, 29, 69, 74, 76, 80, 96, 105, 107–10, 114–15, 117, 123, 135–7, 141, 150, 154, 157–8, 187, 193, 197, 207, 213, 238, 256, 266
Prevention, 17
Prior belief, 149–50, 152, 155, 160, 163–4, 175
Problem-solving, 12, 27, 29, 31, 34, 86, 92, 96, 98, 226, 233, 246, 250, 258, 266
Prolactin, 56, 66
Proximal risk factors, 11–12, 14, 16–17, 24, 26, 32, 50, 61, 109, 209, 253
Pruning, 143, 153, 160–1, 231
Psychache, 15
Psychological autopsy, 10, 40, 44–7, 127, 129, 218, 229, 234, 251, 258, 260, 267
Psychotherapy, 182, 194, 199–204, 216, 221, 233, 249, 251, 259
PTSD, 28
PUFA, 53, 81, 169
Pulvinar, 121, 150, 152, 156, 233, 267
Putamen, 108, 115, 122

Raphe, 72, 108, 157
Response inhibition, 38, 94, 97, 117, 199, 248
Resting state, 59
RNA, 47, 49–50, 69, 71, 80, 134–5, 176, 209

Saliva, 55, 57, 65, 173–4, 177, 238
SAT 1, 71, 172–3, 176, 180, 225, 244

Scar, 26, 112, 125, 165
Schema, 130, 147, 201, 212
Schizophrenia, 15
Schools, 21
Season, 54
Selective prevention, 19–20, 22
Self-injury mortality, 6
Sensitivity, 79, 131, 144
Sensitization, 26, 30
Serotonin (5-HT) 11, 13, 27–8, 30, 35, 54, 56, 64, 66, 72, 74, 78–9, 81, 83, 106–8, 111–12, 121, 132, 136, 141, 144, 146–7, 152–4, 156–7, 161, 169–72, 176, 183, 188–9, 193, 212–13, 217, 222, 233, 235, 238, 243, 248, 254–6, 258, 260, 263, 267
Serotonin receptor, 56, 72–5, 81, 107–8, 111, 121, 132, 152, 157, 171, 212–13, 233, 235, 243, 258, 260, 263
Serotonin transporter (5-HTT), 54, 56, 70, 72, 74, 77, 79, 83, 106, 108, 112, 121, 132, 136, 144, 156–7, 171–2, 186, 238, 243, 248, 254–5, 258, 263, 267
Sex hormone, 64, 82
Sexual abuse, 28, 35, 67, 126–7, 129–30, 140–2, 212, 221–2, 240, 249, see also Childhood sexual abuse
Shared environment, 52
SKA2, 67, 69, 173–4, 177, 180, 233, 255
Solar radiation, 54
SPECT, 59, 107–8, 110–12, 212–13, 266
Specificity, 31, 56, 58, 79, 90, 96, 109, 119, 166–7, 170, 175, 237, 256, 258, 266
Spectroscopy, 60, 76, 78, 108, 110, 121, 196
Spermidine, 71, 172, 225
Spermine, 71, 172, 225
SSRI, 183, 188
Stress, 7, 10–14, 23–44, 56–7, 63–71, 75–87, 93, 98, 110, 111–14, 120–2, 129, 132–44, 157, 169–77, 189, 202, 206, 208, 217, 220, 225, 231, 233–6, 239, 241, 244–8, 250–4, 262, 265, 267
Stress–diathesis model, 1, 23, 27, 30, 34–6, 38, 64, 78, 120, 170, 172, 175
Stress-response system, 12, 23, 56, 64, 66, 132–4, 136, 141, 144
Striatum, 104, 110, 115, 118, 137, 150

Stroop test, 88, 96
Substance use, 15
Suicidal process, 10, 17, 21, 29–30, 39, 263, 266
Sunshine, 8, 54, 240, 262, 264
Superior frontal gyrus, 36, 111, 113, 150
Surname, 52

Temporal gyrus, 107, 110, 140, 211
Thalamocortical, 107
Thalamus, 70, 79, 104, 106, 110, 112, 117–18, 120–3, 137, 141, 146, 150–2, 156, 207, 219–20, 239, 250, 267
Thwarted belongingness, 32–3
TMS, see Transcranial magnetic stimulation
Toxoplasma, 14, 42, 77–8, 249
Trail Making Test, 91
Transcranial direct current stimulation (tDCS), 163, 198–9, 210
Transcranial magnetic stimulation (TMS), 162, 196–8, 210
Trauma, 11, 27–8, 61, 68, 75, 82, 110, 129, 131–7, 158, 177, 211, 233, 236, 241, 249, 254, 259, 263, 268

Trier Social Stress Test, 66, 142
Twins, 52, 129, 264

Unemployment, 6, 27, 267
Universal prevention, 19

Valence, 90, 149, 153, 155, 158, 160, 162–3, 199, 210, 257
Value attribution, 37
Vasopressin, 227
Ventrolateral, 36, 105, 114
Ventromedial, 74, 96, 107–8, 115, 150, 154, 157, 238
Volition, 33–4, 41, 161, 210, 222, 246
Vulnerability, xi–xii, 4, 11–12, 16, 20–6, 30, 32, 36, 38, 41, 50, 55, 64, 75, 79, 86–7, 89, 93, 95–8, 100, 109, 112–13, 116, 118, 120, 122–3, 125, 133, 138, 155, 159–60, 162, 177, 180, 207, 215, 231, 253, 263, 268

Wallerian degeneration, 59
White matter, 58, 78, 102–5, 109, 112, 118, 120–2, 137, 143, 150, 155, 163, 198, 207, 215, 220, 224, 235, 237, 250, 254–7
Wisconsin Card Sorting Test, 91